I0188474

Prince Henry's A School at War

1939-1945

Graham Shutt

Fisher King Publishing

PRINCE HENRY'S - A SCHOOL AT WAR

Fisher King Publishing Ltd,
The Studio,
Arthington Lane,
Pool in Wharfedale,
LS21 1JZ,
England.

www.fisherkingpublishing.co.uk

A CIP catalogue record of this book is available from the British Library

Print ISBN 978-1-910406-70-0

'We may finally consider with interest that the school which assembled on the first day of the first term of war is a very different one from that which has now seen its close in Europe. Of our four hundred and fifty pupils, considerably fewer than a hundred have been with us from start to finish – and of the Staff, just over half. It serves to remind us that the School is more than the individuals who go to make it up. Its character is shaped by them and they in turn receive its imprint on their own. It is our hope and firm belief that the schools of this country, and among them our own Free Grammar School of Prince Henry, will never fail, whether in war or peace, to give a worthy answer and inspire to high resolve.'

John Wilde, Headmaster:
'Otliensian', Vol. XXVII, Summer Term, 1945

Softly thro' the gates of night steals dawn,
Darkness doth flee for a new day is born.

Extract from the poem 'Daybreak', by Rosemary Broady, U4A: 'Otliensian', Vol. XXVIII, Spring Term, 1946

About the Author

Graham Shutt lives in Otley, West Yorkshire. He is married with three grown up children and two grand-children, Sammy and Eloise. He was born in September 1946 in Reedley, near Burnley, Lancashire and spent his early years in the village of Crawshawbooth in the Rossendale valley.

After a secondary education at Bacup & Rawtenstall Grammar School and Nelson Grammar School he entered Liverpool University and graduated in 1968 with a B.A. Honours degree in Economics, and obtained a Cert.Ed. in 1969.

In 1979 he was awarded the degree of M.Phil. from Leeds University for a thesis on 'Wharfedale Water Mills.' He taught at Prince Henry's Grammar School for 42 years as Head of Economics and Business Studies and Acting Deputy Head. He retired in 2011. His interests include watching Burnley F.C., collecting Burnley football programmes, books, stamps and comics. He keeps reasonably fit by walking and gardening.

Preface

Forty-two years spent working at Prince Henry's gives ample time to appreciate the history and traditions of a School that is over four hundred years old. Forty years of teaching was followed by a final two years as Examinations' Officer, much of the time being spent in the room in which examination materials were stored, but which also housed those archives that had not previously been transferred to Leeds. Under the agreement negotiated on transfer, the school is allowed to borrow back the archives stored in Leeds. Thus, the first reason for writing this book was in place – access to a wealth of archive material – Governors' Minute Books, Admission Registers, the School Magazine, statistical returns, miscellaneous documents, photographs, trophies and cups no longer presented. The transfer of newspapers from the British Library at St. Pancras to Boston Spa, giving easy access to the back copies of the '*Wharfedale and Airedale Observer*,' was also a great help.

But what aspect of the history of Prince Henry's to write about? The only published book about the school, '*The Chronicles of the Free Grammar School of Prince Henry at Otley*,' by Fred Cobley, was published in 1923, and covers the history of the School up to its re-opening on 18 September 1918 in the Mechanics' Institute. So, perhaps a book to cover the development of the School since 1918?

The decision to concentrate on the period of the Second World War came about because of

1. The removal of the War Memorial from the Main Corridor in order to accommodate Art examination work. This Memorial commemorates the forty-one pupils and staff who died in the Second World War. There was a danger that the plaque would end up with other relics and would be forgotten. Thankfully, it was moved to a more prominent position in the entrance foyer.

2. Public subscriptions funded the Memorial plaque, but with the money left over, a piano was purchased by the Old Scholars. This piano eventually found its way into Lower Hall, and open access meant that it became shabby and unplayable. It was decided to dispose of it, but fortunately the brass plaque on it was saved:

   1939-1945
IN MEMORY OF THE OLD SCHOLARS
OF THIS SCHOOL WHO GAVE THEIR
LIVES IN THE SERVICE OF THEIR COUNTRY
"FORTITER"

3. Among the many trophies and cups no longer presented to students there is one dedicated to Ian Naylor. He was a very good athlete, especially in the one-mile race, in which he held the School record. The cup was presented to the School by his parents following Ian's death in 1945. He was eight years old

> when he joined Prince Henry's in 1934, and left in 1943 to join the Navy. He was killed on 7 April 1945, aged eighteen. His loss affected the School greatly because he was so young and most pupils and staff in the School would have known him. There is a danger that, like the 'Ian Naylor Cup', he would be forgotten. If such a high profile loss is not remembered, then what about the other forty people listed on the War Memorial?

But this book is not only about those 463 ex-pupils and staff who were in the Armed Forces, forty-one of whom were killed in the War, or about those who were wounded, or those who were prisoners of war in German, Italian or Japanese hands. It is also about the life of the school in the years 1939 – 1945 and the 998 pupils who were there at the time, forty-one of whom were at Prince Henry's for the length of the war. It is dedicated to everybody associated with Prince Henry's Grammar School before and during the Second World War.

Lest we forget.

CONTENTS

The outside front cover of Prince Henry's at War shows a 1953 painting of Prince Henry's Grammar School by Edith Marion Wilde (1897-1982), wife of the wartime Headmaster, John Wilde (1899-1986).

The image on the title page and outside back cover of this book shows the cover of the Summer 1945, 'Victory' edition of the school magazine, the 'Otliensian'. It was designed by Mr W.D. Carter, the Art Master.

Introduction

The Foundation of the School

The only published work on the history of Prince Henry's Grammar School is Fred Cobley's *'Chronicles of the Free Grammar School of Prince Henry at Otley'* (published 1923 by William Walker & Sons (Otley) Ltd.). Cobley had access to most of the historical documents that evidence the foundation of the school and the book is thus the source of the re-telling of the origins of the School that appears from time to time in The *'Otliensian'* and is also included in an unpublished *'Summary History'* written by Neville Bousfield, Headmaster of Prince Henry's from 1959-1984.

KEY DATES:

1 February 1602 – will of Thomas Cave

4 May 1603 – death of Thomas Cave

30 April 1607 – granting of the Royal Charter*

7 December 1610 – judgment of the Council of the North in favour of the Foundation

1611 – the Free Grammar School of Prince Henry opened its doors

1614 – permanent school buildings completed and opened

**which is within the four-year limit in the terms of the Will*

The benefactor and founder of Prince Henry's was Thomas Cave, a "chapman" of Wakefield. In his will he bequeathed £250 for the establishment of a school in Otley, with provisos that

- an equivalent sum was contributed by the local parishioners and other donors,
- the funds were invested in land to yield an annual income of 40 marks (£26 13s 4d) per annum to provide the stipends of the Master and Usher, and
- the school was founded within four years of his death.

If these conditions were not fulfilled, the legacy would go to his kinsfolk. He died on the fourth of May 1603.

Why would a resident of Wakefield leave money in his will to found a school in Otley? Cobley suggests that it was because Thomas Cave was born in the Parish of Otley. 'Cave' was a common surname locally and the Otley Parish Registers contain *'the entry of Thomas Cave's birth at Burley, which place was at that period a part of the ancient Parish of Otley.'* (*'Chronicles'* p.15).

Thomas had established himself as a 'chapman' (draper/merchant) in Wakefield and as a cloth merchant in London. In his later life he became a very wealthy man. He was one of the first Governors of the Queen Elizabeth Grammar School Wakefield, which had been founded in 1591.

Thomas Cave – Yeoman

'Was another chapman or draper from Westgate. He subsequently became one of the chief benefactors of the school by establishing the Scholarships which bear his name at Clare College, Cambridge. He also founded the grammar school at Otley.' (web-site ***'Wakefield Grammar School, Governors')***

In a 'golden age' of grammar school foundation, Thomas Cave was motivated to do for Otley what he had done for Wakefield. The parishioners and benevolent donors of Otley set out to meet the terms of Cave's will and succeeded in more than doubling the amount of the legacy. They petitioned the King for the granting of a Royal Charter, which was dated the thirtieth of April in the fifth year of the reign of James I (i.e. 1607). The conditions of the will were therefore fulfilled with only three days to go.

William Harrison, the vicar of Otley, had been sent down to London to petition the King, James I, for the Charter. Against the wishes of the Governors he had written into the Charter his own tenure of the Headship for his natural life, and so he became the School's first Headmaster.

The 'Free Grammar School of Prince Henry at Otley' was dedicated to Henry, Prince of Wales – the eldest son of James I. Henry was popular, liked sport, especially martial arts, and was fascinated by strategy and tactics. Sadly, at nineteen years of age, he died (probably of typhoid fever). His brother Charles succeeded their father to the throne. It can only be speculation as to whether the English Civil War would still have taken place if Henry had lived to become the king, but his death could have marked a significant turning point in the history of Britain.

The one aspect of the will that remained to be completed was the use of the legacy and additional money raised to purchase the land that would provide the annual income to pay the Headmaster and the Usher. Arrangements had been agreed to buy some land in Otley, but before the deal had been completed the relatives and legatees of Thomas Cave took out an action against the Governors at the Council of the North in York, arguing that the four-year deadline had not been met. The Council found in favour of the governors who argued that they had been unable to complete the transaction because Cave's executors had refused to release the funds.

However, for some reason the Governors purchased a different parcel of land by paying £380 for sixty acres and a farmstead in the Parish of Lanmouth, about six miles from Thirsk. In March 1612, the land was leased to James and Mary Green and their heirs for a thousand years at a fixed rent of 40 marks per annum, equivalent to £26 13s 4d per year. Cobley criticizes the Governors' 'error of judgment:'

'From that investment, the Governors have ever since received the yearly sum of £26 13s 4d, Lord Harewood now paying the rent charge. Whether the Governors in their day had a legal right to tie up the School property for a period so far beyond that which they could supervise is a question upon which there has been, at various times, some differences of opinion, and severe strictures have been made, both from the platform and in the Press, during recent years about the short-sighted policy of the Governors. The unfortunate fact remains that property which three centuries ago yielded £26 13s 4d. per annum, is yielding to the revenue of the Grammar School no more today, notwithstanding its greatly enhanced value in these modern times. No doubt the Governors made a great error of judgment in granting a lease for such a long term of years, and the effects of that error of judgment will continue to be felt in future years.' ('Chronicles' p.70)

From time to time the issue has been raised at Governors' meetings, but it appears that nothing will change until the lease expires in 2612!

Nevertheless, the way was now clear for the School to open, and in the year of our Lord 1611 the Free Grammar School of Prince Henry opened its doors. At first, the doors were those of the Vicarage on Kirkgate, Otley. It would not be until 1614 that permanent buildings were built and occupied.

The Closure of the School

'The Free Grammar School at Otley had done good work for some 250 years, but in the last 13 years, from 1861 to 1874, it had had to struggle for an existence owing to the lack of an adequate endowment to supplement the fees received from the small number of pupils.' (*'Chronicles'* p 126)

The *'lack of an adequate endowment'* meant that the School did not have the funds to attract a Schoolmaster, a situation made worse by the resulting decline in the number of pupils attending the school. Additional funding, to supplement the fixed rent from Lanmouth, was provided by renting out the unused part of the school for use as a County Court, but this was insufficient to meet the outgoings.

From 1861 the School had been placed under the management of a Board of Trustees in the place of the Governors, and fees from all pupils had been levied to help to pay the salaries of the Master and his assistant. This led to competition from private schools, such as Dr. Samuel Kerr's successful academy, and from the new elementary schools, particularly the National Schools established by the Church of England, and led to the closure of Prince Henry's Grammar School in 1874.

Bousfield argues that most other local grammar schools survived, and that *'perhaps for the only time in history the governors lacked the necessary energy and wisdom for success.'* However, Prince Henry's must have always educated only a relatively small number of boys; the population of Otley was insufficient to provide a large intake, and the fact that the Parish of Otley was spread over a large, rural area made it difficult for pupils to attend the school. A report from 1867 states that in the second half of the year there were only 30 pupils, 20 of whom were under 10 years of age.

Given the dates, it is tempting to draw the conclusion that the Education Act of 1870 played some part in the closure of Prince Henry's. It was the first of a series of Acts of Parliament passed between 1870 and 1893 to make elementary education compulsory in England and Wales for children aged between 5 and 12. The Bill was sponsored by the Rt. Hon. W.E. Forster, who lived in Burley-in-Wharfedale for much of his life.

The Act allowed voluntary schools – such as Prince Henry's – to continue unchanged, but set up a system of 'School Boards' to build and manage schools in areas where they were needed. The Boards were locally elected bodies that were funded from the local rates. However, parents had to pay fees unless they could not afford to do so, until a further change in the law in 1891. In 1880 a further Education Act made school attendance compulsory for children between the ages of five and ten. This was raised to 12 years of age in 1893. However, many children worked outside school hours, especially when part of the 'half-time system' where they might work in the morning and attend school in the afternoon. Truancy continued to be a major problem because parents could not afford to give up the income earned by their children.

An Otley School Board was established in 1876 and in 1880 North Parade School was built and opened as the first Board School in Otley. Although educational provision did increase in Otley after 1870, this is unlikely to have had an impact on Prince Henry's sufficient to cause its closure in 1874. However, when the school was re-opened in 1918 it became part of the national education system, funded partly by the West Riding County Council.

The re-opening of the School

The Trustees had two problems – what to do with the School building, and how best to use the limited endowment. Two views were put forward; one suggestion was that the endowment should be used to fund Scholarships tenable at local Grammar Schools such as Leeds and Ripon, the other that the endowment be allowed to accumulate until sufficient funds were available to allow the School to be re-opened. The fact that the Old Grammar School building was unoccupied and falling into disrepair led to pressure to sell the building, thus increasing the funds available for scholarships. In 1883 the building was sold to Mr Thomas Constable for £800.

A new Scheme in 1888 restored the term 'Governors' as administrators of the Trust instead of Trustees, and established four Exhibitions of £15 each, tenable for three years at any Grammar School approved by the Governors. However, a minority of Governors was prepared to fight for the alternative proposal – to invest the endowment to accumulate sufficient funds to re-open the school.

When the School closed in 1874 the Governors held funds of £145. By 1888 *'there was a sum of £922 invested in Consolidated Stock, and also on deposit in a local bank a further sum of £609.' ('Chronicles' p. 137).* This would equate to the initial £145, plus the funds from the sale of the school, plus the yearly income from the land near

Thirsk, plus the interest on the deposits. In 1895 the funds were increased with a legacy of £500 from the estate of Mr Robert Craven, of Bramhope. This encouraged the Governors to believe that the School could be re-opened within a short period of time.

On 18 October 1899 a deputation of Governors inspected rooms at the Mechanics' Institute for use as temporary premises for the School. The Directors of the Mechanics' Institute agreed generous terms and a deputation of Governors met with the Charity Commissioners to confirm the feasibility of the re-opening of the School.

Mechanics' Institute, Otley

However, the West Riding County Council then announced their intention of building a number of secondary schools in the area, a scheme that would certainly delay the objectives of the Governors. Negotiations continued but *'the passing of the Education Act of 1902 completely altered the situation, and the scheme of the Governors was laid aside to await developments' ('Chronicles' p. 137)*

From July 1903 to March 1905 nothing further was done. During these years the West Riding was busy with a large scheme to ensure adequate provision for higher education in areas where it was considered most needed. One of these areas was Wharfedale, including Otley. The question was, which was the best site for such a centre in Wharfedale?

The Otley representatives felt that they had a strong case; a Grammar School Foundation already existed; there was a capital fund of £3,364 earning an annual income of about £120. Their answer was to re-open the Grammar School, with grant assistance from the county authorities. The representatives from Guiseley favoured the building of a new Secondary School in their area taking in pupils from Guiseley, Menston, Yeadon, Rawdon and Horsforth. Eventually the County Authorities decided to build a Secondary School in the Guiseley area. The question of a Secondary School for Otley was left open for future consideration.

On 27 June 1905 Otley people realized that *'energetic and immediate action was necessary if they were to ensure for their children any educational benefits from the considerable sum which had now accrued to the Old Grammar School Foundation.'* ('*Chronicles*' pp. 139-140). A meeting of the ratepayers on 20 November 1905 resolved:

'That this meeting of ratepayers heartily endorses the action of their Urban District Council in seeking to obtain, through the Education Committee of the West Riding County Council, the establishment of a secondary school in Otley for boys and girls.' ('Chronicles' p.140)

Another Inquiry took place in Otley on 21 November 1906, when the Board of Education suggested the building of a Secondary School for girls in Otley. This was not accepted by the Otley delegates and a year later, on 12 November 1907, the following communication was received by the Governors from the Board of Education:

'I am directed to inform you that the Board of Education has now decided, as the result of the Conference that took place at Otley on the 21st of November, 1906, and after consideration of subsequent correspondence and of reports which they have received from H.M. Inspector, that a sufficient case has been shown for the establishment of a Secondary School for boys and girls in Otley. They are therefore prepared to approve the proposal of the Governors to establish such a School there, and the amendment of the existing scheme which is required to give effect to this proposal will be taken in hand without delay.'

The Governors suggested several modifications to the Scheme, which were accepted by the Education Department, and sealed in May 1909. The First World War intervened before the School could re-open, but finally in 1918 Prince Henry's Grammar School opened its doors for the second time.

The re-opened Prince Henry's Grammar School admitted its first pupils on 19 September 1918, the day after the official re-opening ceremony.

Most schools developed the 'House system' to encourage competition and to enable more students to take part in competitive sports. At Prince Henry's the Houses were named initially after their colours – Blue, Red, White and Yellow. In 1931 they were re-named Cave, Duncan, Fairfax and Fawkes respectively. White House became Fairfax and its colour was changed to green. The names of the Houses were chosen to commemorate people who had rendered notable service to the School.

Thomas CAVE left £250 in his will as a bequest to be used for the foundation of a Grammar school at Otley. Thomas A. DUNCAN was Chairman of the Governors from 1908-1925 and played a major part in the re-opening of the School after its closure through financial and staffing problems from 1874-1918. Members of the FAIRFAX family were closely involved as Governors of the new School when it was founded in 1608. Charles Fairfax, son of Thomas Fairfax of Denton, designed the School crest. The FAWKES family of Farnley Hall also took a keen interest in the School from its earliest days when Thomas Fawkes was one of the first Governors. Major Le G.G.W. Horton-Fawkes was a Governor from 1939-1963, being Chairman of the Governors from 1946-1962.

The War Years 1939-1945

To mark the end of the war in Europe the flag was hoisted in front of the School, and on 8 May and 9 May 1945 there was a holiday to celebrate VE Day. On 10 May there was a short ceremony at Morning Assembly to celebrate the Allied victory.

In his editorial in the *'Otliensian'*, the Headmaster, Mr Wilde, pointed out that:

'For five years and two terms we have been swept along in the track of the whirlwind. We have grown so accustomed to the atmosphere of war that we find it difficult to adjust ourselves to more natural conditions.' He was thankful that *'the cause of freedom has prevailed'*, and expressed pride in the part played in the *'fight for freedom by our Old Scholars. All, we make no doubt, have served faithfully, not a few have borne themselves with conspicuous distinction, and some have given all they had, and will come back no more. To the relatives of these fallen we offer our deep sympathy.'*

Referring to the 'difficulties' experienced in the School over the period of the war, Mr Wilde argued that they were a mere inconvenience compared with what others had to suffer.

'True, we have had plenty of that, and we have borne it with cheerfulness and resource. We have lived in an atmosphere of improvisation, of make do and mend, which is not conducive to education at its best. Our ingenuity has been given more scope than our sense of fitness. We have threaded a labyrinthine way along corridors made half impassable with blast walls. We have peered out through netted windows like felons behind prison bars. Our table linen has sunk far below the austere and we ourselves have learned to cultivate an apostolic disregard for wherewithal we shall be clothed. Our games fields are gently returning to nature and cover point picks up great handfuls of lush grass together with the ball. We have had the pleasure of being hosts to evacuees, at first an exceeding great army, now dwindled to a mere handful still remaining with us.'

The government had been determined to stay out of European disputes, fearing a repeat of the 1914-1918 war, but in September 1938 it found itself on the verge of just such a crisis. Hitler demanded that the Sudetenland, a German speaking part of Czechoslovakia, be annexed to Germany. France was committed by treaty to support Czechoslovakia; Britain was committed to support France.

Neither Germany nor Czechoslovakia would give way and war looked inevitable. In Britain hasty preparations were made in expectation of mass air raids, trenches were dug in parks and open land; people in designated danger areas, mainly in large towns and cities, were issued with gas masks; and the authorities prepared for the evacuation of two million people from London. Included in those to be evacuated were half a million schoolchildren, but the move was called off before the vast majority of the children went.

A last-minute meeting held in Munich between Hitler, Chamberlain, Deladier (France) and Mussolini (Italy) gave Hitler everything he wanted. The Czechs, who were not represented at the meeting, were told that if they did not accept the agreement, they would be left to fight the German army alone.

This news was greeted with wild excitement in Britain and France. Britain was inadequately prepared for war and many people were concerned about the possibility of bombs and poison gas being dropped on British cities. But, the euphoria of Munich was short-lived.

Civil defence preparations had begun some time before Munich; in February 1938 'black-out' plans were announced, banning all exterior lighting from shops, homes and motor vehicles in time of war; an air-raid warning system was already well established by the time of Munich. Households were encouraged to prepare for raids, with advice given on building trenches in the back garden, making a room into a gas-proof refuge room, or installing a shelter. A month after Munich Sir John Anderson, in charge of Air Raid Precautions (A.R.P.) promised a mass-produced shelter that people could erect for themselves in their own homes. The *'Anderson Shelter'* was to be supplied free to poorer families.

In mid-March 1939, in spite of the promises made at Munich, German troops marched into what was left of Czechoslovakia and threatened Poland. At the end of March Chamberlain guaranteed Polish independence. Preparations for war were scaled up once again. In July 1939 every household in Britain received a set of official Civil Defence pamphlets; the first was entitled 'Some Things You Should Know if War Comes'. Subsequent leaflets looked at gas masks, the black-out, evacuation, food in wartime and fire precautions. Throughout the summer preparations accelerated, as did attempts at negotiation, but when German troops marched into Poland on 1 September 1939, war was inevitable.

News of the declaration of war in Otley came on Sunday morning when many people were at church; in some places the announcement of Mr Chamberlain's broadcast news was given by the preacher from the pulpit; in others, services were shortened so that worshippers could return home to listen to the broadcast on the wireless.

The news was met with quiet soberness, the vast majority of people being whole-heartedly behind the decision. The experiences of the 1914-1918 conflict were too recent to present war as a romantic and quixotic attack on fascism, and most people had already accepted the inevitability of a war for freedom based on the failure of Germany to accede to demands made by Britain and her allies.

Preparations had been made much earlier in 1938 through plans for mass evacuation of children and mothers from areas of high risk, and the creation of a working system of air-raid prevention through the recruitment of local volunteers to act as air-raid wardens, auxiliary firemen, police constables and ambulance drivers.

Indeed the evacuation into Wharfedale on the previous Friday and Saturday, and the 'black-out' exercise on Saturday night had already prepared people in the district for the announcement of war.

On 8 September 1939 – a week after the declaration of war – the '*Wharfedale and Airedale Observer*' published an article listing the activities of the previous week:

'A feverishly active weekend, culminating in the actual declaration of war at 11 a.m. on Sunday, has found Wharfedale and Airedale people, in common with the great majority of people of the country, calm and steady.

The tremendous number of people, who, for months past, have known what they would be expected to do if, unhappily, the peace efforts put forward by the Government failed, have been given the signal to set about those tasks, and right willingly they have done so.

A Great and Willing Work

'The last days of the period of suspense were active ones, and stories of many hours of continuous duty by voluntary workers are common throughout the district. The result was, that when war was announced, Wharfedale and Airedale people could pause for a moment from their tasks, say "Well, that's that," and again bend their backs to their great and willing work to safeguard the lives and property of themselves and their neighbours.

The enormous ramifications of A.R.P. and other work that has had to be done, has had the inestimable value of giving almost everyone who is willing to take a hand something to do, and something with which to keep their minds and hands occupied in these trying days.

Evacuees Welcomed

'On Friday and Saturday evacuees flowed into many townships from the danger zones of the cities, and hundreds of voluntary workers made them welcome, registered them, found them billets, and introduced them to the people who have played their own part so magnificently by offering to care for the homeless.

These latter people, who often at considerable personal inconvenience, have voluntarily agreed to take complete strangers into their households, and, in many cases, actually into the bosom of their own families, have been doing as magnificent a work as any who might, possibly, be engaged for the moment on more spectacular tasks.

Territorials Mobilised

'The local Territorials were called up on Friday, and the remainder of the local lads who form the Otley and Ilkley Troops of the Wharfedale Battery of Artillery joined that nucleus of the Battery that had been in khaki for some days previously.

They are a grand lot of young fellows, and the spirit among them is a wonderfully happy one. By this time everyone knows everyone else, and the comradeship and friendships that were a feature of the War their fathers fought is already in evidence.

'Black-out' Preparation

'The work of painting the street corners and marking the lamp-posts and other obstructions with white paint was well advanced by the week-end, and is now complete – just in time to make the value of this work apparent in the darkness of these black-out nights.

Saturday was a harassing day. It was still touch and go, and no one knew whether it was to be peace or war, although the chances of the latter were obviously by far the heavier. Local football matches were cancelled, including Otley's very attractive first home Rugby Union game of the season against Kendal. Cancelled also was the Washburn Valley agricultural show; which should have been held at Fewston on Saturday.

Sandbags Appear

'On Friday and Saturday commenced the work of sandbagging public buildings. First to be attended to in Otley was the Council Offices, where is also the local A.R.P. report centre, which, since the grave turn of events on Friday, has been manned day and night. Also sand-bagged was the police station, the Drill Hall and the Wharfedale Rural Council offices.

Black-out regulations were fore-shadowed, and there was a big run on shops selling dark paper and blinds. There were many chinks through which light could be seen on Friday night, but experience and close supervision by the authorities soon found out the weak spots, and on Saturday there was a great improvement.

At War!

'On Sunday. September 3 at 11 a.m., Britain was at war, and, horrible as was the news to all lovers of peace, at least the suspense was over.

Everyone knew his or her job, and right manfully have those jobs been set about.

There was, obviously, immense activity at local government headquarters, as schemes that had long been planned were put into action.

The regulations for motor car lighting were tightened to a war footing, and local pedestrians, on the whole, have responded well to the appeals that they should keep to the footpath at night, and only cross roads at recognized spots, or to give every assistance to the motorist, who is driving along with lights that provide no illumination of objects in his path. Not all cyclists at once realized that in the conditions reflectors were absolutely useless and that if they depended on them they were running a grave personal risk. Rear lights for cyclists are now compulsory, and it is an excellent thing that it should be so.

Air-Raid Alarm Sounds

'On Sunday night many townships – Otley, Rawdon and Horsforth amongst them – had their first taste of "war" when the air-raid alarms sounded, but, although there was deep anxiety, there was no panic, and the A.R.P. workers were found to be alert and ready for their job.

How Otley came to get the public warning at all is somewhat of a mystery. No public alarm was given at Ilkley. Burley, Menston or Aireborough.

One result of the unpleasant experience of the public alarm at Otley was to emphasise to everyone the very real need for the fullest co-operation in observing the lighting restrictions, and now it would be difficult to find even the faintest chink of light in the town after dark has fallen. Biggest offenders early in the week were the licensed houses and fried fish shops, all of which had their special problems, but most of them quickly thought out quite ingenious schemes to overcome those difficulties.

Gas Masks Everywhere

'After Sunday gas masks are to be seen everywhere. All the children carry them wherever they go. Seldom is a shopping basket to be seen without the gas mask box conveniently placed on top of its contents, and business men have tied longer pieces of string to their boxes and go about their tasks with the box slung across their shoulders like a camera case. On Monday most of the farmers at the local auction marts had brought their masks with them.

Grim Determination

'On Monday local people started the first full day of the war keyed up with the grim determination that England as a whole is feeling, to see the thing through. In the glorious sunshine it has seemed impossible that such a terrible thing could have happened, but everywhere were reminders of the evil that Hitler has forced upon us. Cinemas were closed, social events cancelled, and voluntary workers were still carrying on with the work that must be done if Wharfedale and Airedale is to be safe for those who live here and those who have sought shelter in this lovely district from the horrors that threaten the large cities.

Gas Masks and Sunshine

'The sunshine of a dwindling summer continued to bathe the valley on Tuesday, and the sight of children and adults going about their business with the familiar gas mask container slung over their shoulders, added to the growing feeling of the fantastic un-reality of the whole situation.

Work on sand-bagging public and essential buildings, including some of the workshops, continued so long as there was daylight, helped by the fine weather.

On Tuesday night there was a further reminder of the grim days in which we are living. It was a wonderful sight as the long, straight fingers of light wove patterns against the star-studded sky, crossing and re-crossing each other's paths.'

The onset of the War can be seen in the correspondence received in Governors' Meetings, starting with *'Air Raid Precautions'* in May 1938. The Headmaster presented *'a comprehensive report upon the arrangements required to be made in connection with Air Raid Precautions'* at the January 1939 Meeting. The correspondence received at the Meeting on 4 October 1939 included:

(a) *Air Raid Precautions*

(b) *Evacuation of School Children*

(c) *Darkening of School Windows*

(d) *Check of children's respirators and respirator drill*

(e) *Protection against incendiary bombs*

(f) *Use of school premises for military purposes*

(g) *Reception of evacuated children in Secondary Schools*

(h) *Teachers and war service*

(i) *Compensation Defence Order 1939*

(j) *Fuel and Lighting Order 1939*

The first reference in the *'Otliensian'* to the impending war was a rumour that *'somewhere in the School there is an A.R.P. volunteer aged 14 years. Congratulations to this unknown patriot.'* He had volunteered his services and been registered under A.R.P. *"report centres and communications"* which was open to youths under 18 years, to carry messages by motor cycle, pedal cycle, and on foot. Several others from Forms VI and UVA joined this patriot in attending a course of evening classes in A.R.P.

'The course has included lectures of types and properties of war gasses, their detection and recognition, conditions favourable to their use, methods of dealing with attack and treatment of injuries. Following a lecture on all three types of respirator, members of the class were able to test the efficiency of their own civilian gas masks when we arranged a visit of the Home Office Gas Van to School on June 15th.' ('Otliensian,' Vol. XX1, Summer 1939)

At the Governors' Meeting held on 19 May 1939 the Headmaster announced in connection with A.R.P. work that, *'not only had many staff taken courses and some qualified as wardens, but there was at present a class for senior pupils, taken after school hours, in which instruction was given in this very important work.'*

At the same meeting the Clerk reported that there had been an application for the use of the school playing fields at weekends by the military, for searchlight practice, during the next three months. One detachment of 10 men, with lorry and searchlight, would arrive each weekend. The Emergency Committee agreed to grant the use of the fields for this purpose and the Governors agreed that no charge should be made.

The agenda for the Governors' meeting held on 14 July 1939 included evacuation proposals in event of emergency. However, much more time was spent in a discussion on school uniform, which initially concerned tenders for the supply of blazers. The continuing discussion may well illustrate the commonly held view that in spite of the possibility of, and preparation for, war, 'life goes on.'

'Mr H. Brearley (Burley) said there were other matters besides blazers that needed consideration. At most schools it was compulsory that boys should wear a regulation cap, but at Otley they seemed to please themselves. The girls went to school in the latest Paris model hats, "and all sorts of things." The girls ought to be compelled to wear a uniform hat, such as black velour in winter and a panama in summer.

Mr Phil S. Wade said that he did not think he had noticed any Paris model hats at the school.

Mr Brearley: I have. They wear them at all sorts of angles.

Mr Whiteley agreed the scholars should wear the proper hats.

The Headmaster (Mr John Wilde) said that he welcomed the views of the Governors on this matter.

He agreed that the boys did not always wear their caps, but he thought the girls were being rather maligned. Most of them did wear school hats, although in wet weather quite a lot of them wore what he understood were called "pixie hoods".

Mr Wade said the boys should certainly be required to purchase and wear a school cap. He had always thought such was the case.

The Headmaster said as a matter of fact the wearing of hats and caps was already compulsory at the school, but this appeared to have been honoured more by breach than the observation.

Mrs. Kettlewood said she thought the Governors had been slack in the past on the question of a school uniform, which should certainly be enforced, but at the same time they must see the articles could be obtained at a reasonable price.

The Headmaster said there was no compulsion on any scholar to wear a blazer. If, however, they did wear a blazer, then he felt it should be of a type that was uniform throughout the school. The other day he had been teaching a class and within six feet of him had been three different sorts of blazers.

Mr Preston: Ever since I have been on the Board, when this matter has been brought forward, it has been said 'the parents cannot afford it'.

Mr Brearley: They can all afford a cap.

Mrs. Hampshire said that she did not think that the girls actually wore differently shaped hats. It was simply the way they put them on.

Mr Brearley: they turn them up and down, and all sorts of ways.

The samples of blazers were passed round, and the lady members felt the quality of the cloth, and tried some of them on.

Mr Preston said it should be compulsory for scholars to have both a blazer and a cap.

Mr C. J. F. Atkinson: if too expensive a quality of blazer was selected they might be making it difficult for some of the parents.

A sub-committee, consisting of the lady members, along with Mr Brearley, was appointed to consider the blazers, and make a recommendation to the Governors, who at a later meeting, will consider whether blazers should be compulsory wear.'

At the end of the summer holidays (1939) members of the Staff and senior boys responded to the Headmaster's call to dig a trench near the new cricket field. In October 1939 permission was requested for the provision of a second trench in the School grounds. Rehearsals took place to prepare for possible enemy air attack. The fitting of black-out curtains meant that it was possible for evening classes to be restarted. Speaking to the Governors on 6 October 1939, Mr Wilde, talking about air-raid precautions said that they had not been asked to make any provision in the way of shelter accommodation because the school was in a reception area and therefore considered safe. Nevertheless it was felt that some arrangements should be made, and by using some of their own money and the energies of the staff, they had dug a trench. In the event of a raid, some of the scholars would go there and others would be underneath two floors. The pupils had had fire and respirator drills. The darkening of the school windows was a very big task, but a local joiner had been given the contract, and he would make a start when the materials were available.

Term started on Tuesday, 12 September 1939. The first few months became known as the 'phoney war' because very little occurred. Gas masks were issued to all British civilians at the start of World War Two. They came in cardboard boxes, with a strap for carrying them on the shoulder. There was a very real fear in Britain that Nazi German bombers would drop poison gas bombs.

At school, gas mask drills were common; the teacher would blow his whistle and the children would put on their masks and carry on working, so as to get used to wearing them. In an air raid drill, children would line up, and then walk in crocodile file to the trenches or air raid shelters. Many wartime children later admitted that they struggled to take the gas mask drill seriously and that their masks were frequently the source of games and much fun, especially because, with the mask fitted, blowing out created rude noises!

By January 1940 the view that the 'safe' reception areas such as Wharfedale were very unlikely to be subject to air raids led to a ruling by the Ministry of Home Security that it was not now necessary for school children in reception areas always to carry gas masks, and headmasters were asked to inform pupils accordingly. In discussing this ruling some Governors, especially Mr Wade, said it was a *'ridiculous suggestion'*. Mr Wilde said that from a practical point of view there was a danger in bringing masks to school that they would be knocked about or lost. It had been *'rather a nightmare'* when masks were reported lost, as the school had to be turned upside down to find them. *'Provided we are free from the responsibility we are rather pleased at school that this ruling has been given, and hope for the best in the matter of air raids'*, said Mr Wilde. The Governors decided to take no action. However, at the meeting on 12 December 1941, approval was given to a recommendation that 'strong action' should be taken to ensure that pupils always carried their gas masks.

The following editorial was published in the *'Wharfedale and Airedale Observer'* on 4 April 1941:

'Another interesting study in psychology is the dilatory response to the campaign urging people to carry their gas masks. All the school children carry them, of course, because they have to, and for a like reason, so do policemen, wardens and soldiers, but the appeal to the general public seems to have fallen on deaf ears. Why should this be so? I do not think it is entirely a matter of indifference, but rather reflects our attitude to Hitler. We do not care two hoots about him or his threats, and we are not going to put ourselves to any more inconvenience on his behalf than we can help. Foolhardy, possibly, but quite understandable. All the same, it is due to those who are trying to look after our welfare that we should take reasonable precautions. We know, or ought to know, that Hitler will stop at nothing to wreak his vengeance, and there is ample evidence that matters are not now going all his way. So we had better be sensible and carry our masks.'

This editorial was a response to concerns expressed at a meeting of Otley Urban Council on 17 February 1941 over the laxity of the public in carrying gas masks. Councillor D. H. Smallwood expressed his concern at so many people walking about the streets without gasmasks, and Councillor, Mrs. Johnson commented:

'It is a pity that people have to have this stressed upon them. It is a serious matter, and I ask people to use their commonsense. Gas masks have not been provided as ornaments for the sideboard, but to be taken about with them wherever they go, whether it is five minutes' shopping or an afternoon out of town.'

Another aspect of the War which impacted on Prince Henry's involved the evacuation of children from areas considered to be unsafe, to the safer 'reception areas.' Children were to be evacuated with their schools, and billeted with householders in these reception areas. On 1 September 1939 the order to begin the evacuation was given. Otley, the Wharfedale Rural area, and Ilkley Urban District, including Burley and Menston, were scheduled as 'safe' areas. For months work had been under way on preparing schemes to receive the evacuees, especially in the provision of billets. Mrs. Linfoot, who was in charge of the scheme, said that in some cases householders were taking as many as eight children. In the first wave of evacuation it was expected that nearly 3,000 children, mothers and other evacuees would be brought to Otley, a further 2,500 into the Wharfedale Rural District, and 4,000 to the Ilkley, Burley and Menston area.

The '*Wharfedale and Airedale Observer*' published 1 September 1939 reported on the arrival of the first evacuees:

'Today only school children from Leeds are expected, and the first of them, about 400 secondary school children were due to arrive at 10.30 this morning. At 12.50 p.m. primary school children are expected to arrive, and by the end of the day 1,237 will have been received into the town. At the time of writing it is expected the remainder, including mothers with babies, younger children and expectant mothers will arrive on Saturday.

All of them will be conveyed from Leeds to Otley in motor coaches, and at Otley they will be received at the North Parade School.

There their names will be entered on a card index showing to which homes they have been allocated, and then they will undergo a medical inspection. From the North Parade School the members of the Women's Voluntary Services will convey them to their billets.'

Many children moved, but many others did not. As the 'phoney war' dragged on and the threatened bombing failed to materialize, many returned home. The fall of France and the fear of invasion following Dunkirk led to a fresh wave of evacuation after 1940. In many cases schools would share the building with the local school – the local school in the morning, the evacuated school in the afternoon, or vice versa.

There was also a lot of 'private evacuation' where people who did not qualify for the government scheme left the danger areas, or those who did not qualify were sent to relatives in the country. In some cases, children were sent abroad; some moved from the Otley area to Canada. It was estimated that as many as two million people took part in private evacuation between June and September 1939. Anne Sowerby was in Form 2 at Prince Henry's from September 1939 until July 1940 when she was evacuated to Canada.

'We learn with pleasure that Anne Sowerby, aged ten, only daughter of Mr and Mrs. T. Sowerby of Tranmere Park, Guiseley, is settling down happily in her new home in Canada. Anne sailed by herself and is staying with some friends for the duration of the war.' ('Otliensian,' Vol. XXIII, Spring 1941)

There were evacuees who attended Prince Henry's Grammar School, including the girls from Roundhay Girls High School, but most of these were 'private' and many were from nearby cities such as Leeds and Bradford. In many cases, as with the Roundhay girls, these private evacuees returned to their own schools once it became clear that bombing attacks were unlikely.

The school was shared with Roundhay Girls' High School. Prince Henry's students attended the morning shift from 8.30 a.m. to 12.45 p.m., the Roundhay Girls attended in the afternoon. There was also Saturday morning school. In spite of these changes it was felt that *'none of the essential elements of our school life is being in any way neglected.'* In addition to the Roundhay Girls, several private evacuees were welcomed.

In his report to the Governors on 6 October 1939, the Headmaster, Mr Wilde, stated that the school was *'uncomfortably crowded'*, with 450 scholars consisting of 218 boys and 232 girls. The number of girls had actually dropped from 259, largely accounted for by the opening of Ilkley Grammar School as a co-educational school. The number of boys had made a *'tremendous jump, quite apart from any who had come to the school as private evacuees.'* It was noted that 37 pupils had been received at the school that had been private evacuees. Some of these had been attending West Riding Secondary Schools elsewhere, and others County Borough Schools, as fee-payers and as scholarship holders. The Headmaster noted that *'they had come from London, Birmingham, Hull, Sheffield and other places to live with relatives.'*

175 girls from Roundhay were evacuated to Otley and taught at Prince Henry's. However, this represented only a third of the pupils normally taught at Roundhay Girls High School. The others had chosen not to move in spite of the fact that their school was closed and they were receiving no formal education. A prize giving for Roundhay School was held in Otley on Saturday 18 November 1939. Miss Nixon, Headmistress of Roundhay Girls School pointed out that because all the staff had moved to Otley with the girls, classes were smaller than normal and more individual tuition and rapid work was possible. She thanked the people of Otley for making the girls welcome in their homes, and said *'we shall not forget Otley, its peace, the loveliness of its dale and hills, and its readiness to care for us amid the throes of danger will be a happy and abiding memory.'* She also suggested that the girls were *'learning quite a lot about cows and sheep and trees.'*

Speaking at the prize giving, Mr J. Croysdale, Chairman of Leeds Education Committee, pointed out that something would have to be done for the education of those left in the city:

'I hope that city schools will not be re-opened if it means that children who are happily evacuated are tempted to return to Leeds. I am not a censor of the parents of Leeds. The scheme was voluntary and there are different problems in different homes, but parents whose children are in comfortable homes in Otley, have done very well in giving first place to the welfare and safety of their children. There will have to be some education in Leeds very shortly, but I do hope that nothing is done to bring back these children to Leeds. It is important that we realize that Leeds is not yet as safe as we would like it to be.'

However, early misgivings about the likely impact of the war in and around Leeds were misplaced and at the start of the Spring Term (1940) the Roundhay Girls returned 'home' and morning (8.45 a.m. to 12.20 p.m.) and afternoon sessions (1.50 p.m. to 3.50 p.m.) recommenced at Prince Henry's. The Headmaster reported to the Governors on 19 January 1940 that all but two of the Roundhay girls had returned to Leeds, and many of the privately evacuated pupils had also left.

In his report given at the Upper School Speech Day held on 7 December 1942, Mr Wilde said:

'Our numbers have continued high beginning with 465 in October a year ago, and finishing at the end of last term with 445. It may interest you to know how the districts on which we chiefly draw are represented in these figures. The count was taken when our numbers totalled 435, 13 private evacuees being excluded. From Otley we had 205 pupils, from Bramhope 31, Pool 18, Burley 40, Ilkley 16. Menston 38, Yeadon and Guiseley 43. The remainder were made up in smaller numbers from Leathley, Farnley, Weston, Askwith, Rigton, Hawksworth, Arthington, Leeds, Shipley, Baildon and Bradford.'

In July 1940 the Governors were informed that in the event of a second evacuation, arrangements for sending Leeds pupils to the school would be similar to the first evacuation, and asking that the necessary preparations should be made.

There is no evidence that the students from both schools behaved less than impeccably, but the Governors wrote to the Leeds Education Committee *'stressing the necessity for a reasonable proportion of mistresses to remain in Otley during the week-ends for the purpose of supervising the girls.'* It was suggested that it was not fair that many of the mistresses should return to Leeds and leave the children either to roam the streets or to be the sole responsibility of the Otley householders. The '*Wharfedale and Airedale Observer*' published 12 July 1940 reported on the Governors' meeting as follows:

'Caring for these children, particularly for the older girls, is a big responsibility, and this is increasing, as anyone who knocks about Otley just now will appreciate, said Mr Wade. It will be intensified if the girls have no proper supervision at the week-ends.

Mr H. W. Preston agreed with Mr Wade's view. Some of the Leeds girls would be growing into young women and certainly wanted looking after. An opinion on the same lines had been expressed at the first evacuation, said Mr Preston, who added, "We were practically told to mind our own business and that we had nothing to do with the mistresses from Leeds. If we have any trouble this time can we refuse to accept their children?"

Mr Wade: "so far as I am concerned, I would be in favour of closing the school if we did not get a satisfactory promise."

Mrs. Kettlewood said Mr Wade had spoken very wisely. "Last time many of the Roundhay Girls' High School mistresses did go home, while the local teachers were working hard all their spare time."

Mr H Brearley: "Did the children go home too?"

Mr Wade: "Quite a few did, by permission of their own mistresses."

Mr Brearley: "And I know that some of the Leeds Modern Boys at Ilkley cycled home at week-ends. The principle is wrong. If you evacuate children, surely they should not be allowed to go home at week-ends."

A resolution urging that Leeds mistresses should be asked to stay in Otley at week ends was unanimously approved.'

In Spring 1940 Mr G.K. Nield became the first member of staff to join the Forces as a member of the Field Security Police. Regretfully, Mr Nield was killed in a fatal accident on January 1 1941. Later that term Mr E. Davison and Mr B.M. Denham left to join the R.A.F. as instructors. In Summer 1941, Mr G. Chapman left to join the Royal Artillery and Mr H. Evans, the R.A.F. They were joined in Spring 1943 by Mr J.H. Watson (R.A.F.), and in Summer 1943 by the Headmaster's Secretary, Mrs. H. Lewis (W.R.N.S.).

One of the problems faced by Britain during the war was the fact that most of our food was imported and, as in the First World War, German U-boats tried to starve the country into submission by sinking the ships bringing in the food. Growing as much food as possible – known as *'digging for victory'* – became a vital part of the war effort. Men, women and children would all help, growing fruit and vegetables in their gardens and on allotments.

In May 1940 an application for permission to keep poultry on part of the playing fields of the school was refused by the Governors on the proposition of Mr H. W. Preston seconded by Mrs. Kettlewood. It is not clear whether this application was seen as a means of improving food production during the war, but parts of the playing fields were soon to be converted to plots for the production of crops and vegetables grown by the pupils of the school.

'During the Summer holidays (1940) a small number of boys did farming work, and fourteen others gave up their time to assist in the production of the instruments of war in the School Workshop. G.Clarke, J.Swale, D.Lee and J.Mounsey have joined the Auxiliary Fire Service; N.Q.King and G.E. Watson are members of the Home Guard.'

In July 1940 the Governors received a letter from the County Authority recommending that the summer holidays this year should not exceed three weeks, instead of the usual six weeks, and that the governors in consultation with the Headmaster should decide dates. Mr Wilde suggested that the best plan would be to break up at the usual time, and return three weeks earlier, thus cutting down the holiday by three weeks. Mr Wade felt that teachers were extremely fortunate in getting any holidays at all, and even three weeks was more than many others were getting!

The Autumn Term, 1940, opened on 19 August , the summer holidays being shortened. Some compensation was gained with a fortnight's break at half-term. The continuation of British summer time throughout the year meant that morning school began at 9.15

a.m., 30 minutes later than usual. Because of the black-out, after school games and meetings were confined to those pupils living in Otley.

During the additional fortnight at the start of term normal school was held in the mornings and the afternoons were given over to a variety of activities; *'we were entertained in various ways by members of the School, and also by visitors who kindly came and told us something of their different experiences.' There were lectures on Juvenile Courts, A.R.P., - made more interesting by the handing round of relics of bombs collected by the lecturer – Dutch Life, Tibet, Photography, – by the Headmaster – Firearms, (N.Q.King) and Pond Life (May Slater and Myrle Boyington).*

'The boys of the Upper School enjoyed an interesting afternoon visiting the Tank Corps. The Lower School whiled away some of the time by playing cards and indoor games and attending a concert which was given by some of the scholars. Thanks to Miss Horsley they quite forgot School troubles when they had a delightful picnic in Weston Woods.'

Mr Wilde, in his report to the Governors on 4 October 1940 referred to the afternoon *'recreational-educational'* activities. These included organ recitals for both boys and girls, the school being granted the use of the organs at the Parish Church and the Congregational Church, lectures by the staff and other persons; debates, additional handicraft lessons, including one on cookery for the boys, which was *'exceedingly appreciated;'* and organised games. Mr Wilde felt that it was a *'very profitable fortnight.'*

At the same meeting two letters were read from the West Riding County Council, the first suggesting that Governors might consider the granting of a mid-term holiday up to a fortnight. The Governors decided to grant a fortnight's holiday commencing on Friday 18 October 1940. The second concerned the Education Authority's decision that conscientious objectors should not be allowed to take appointments, temporarily or permanently, of school staff who had been called up to the Forces. The question had not yet arisen at Prince Henry's, and the Governors decided to leave discussion on the matter until such time as it did arise. A third letter, from the Board of Education, stated that during a recent air raid warning a number of parents went to a certain school to take their children home. The headmaster refused to allow the children to leave and locked up the school to prevent the parents getting in; the letter pointed out that whilst it was not desirable that parents should take their children away at such times, they should not be forcibly prevented from doing so.

First Aid classes, more Air Raid drills and the installation of netting on some windows as protection against flying glass accompanied the resumption of normal school in September. In March 1942 the remaining windows were treated with anti-splinter glass.

The annual Speech Day was spread over two days in December 1940, the Upper School Prize giving being on Saturday 30 November, and the Lower School on the following Wednesday. At the Upper School Speech Day Mr Wade presided and the Chairman of Governors, Mr Atkinson, presented the prizes. Mr Wade spoke about the need to take care over spreading rumours. *'By setting your face against repeating rumours you will be doing a fine national effort. When you hear a rumour, before repeating it, go to someone in authority in the school and find out if it is correct.'*

Mr Wilde, in his report pointed out that many old scholars were now serving in the Forces and concluded as follows:

'As the months have gone by the war has cast an ever darker shadow on our work. We have not yet been called on to endure the calamities which have already overwhelmed so many schools, and what the coming months may bring is beyond our conjecture. But whatever may come we have our part to play. Our work must go on. It is not spectacular work, but it is a vital national service.

Not the least disquieting aspect of our times is the plight of education. The lamps are indeed being put out. This problem must be faced or we shall find that we have bought victory at the price of thousands of young people who will embark on life without knowing how to live. Resolved as we are to press on to victory in the war, and convinced as we are of the justice of our cause, we must none the less keep still before us the ideals for which our doors are open – the ideals of the good life, the things that are most excellent, the values on which the world of the future depends.'

At the Governors' meeting on 17 January 1940 the Chairman said that letters had been received on the question of fire-watchers for the school. It was pointed out that schools of the size of Prince Henry's were singularly liable to be hit in the event of a raid, and the Governors were asked to consider the protection of the building by providing firewatchers who would give the alarm if incendiary bombs fell on the premises. It was suggested that members of staff might be prepared to assist, and Mr Wilde pointed out that a number of staff resided within a short distance of the school and would be able to give an alarm.

On 18 March 1941, the Headmaster and Mrs Wilde began the rota of staff fire-watching, and to mark the occasion there were two alerts during the night. Incendiary bombs could cause havoc, particularly if they landed on a roof and set fire to attics and roof spaces. Staff were paid a subsistence allowance for fire-watching duties, and the school accounts contain details of the payments made from October 1941 until June 1943, a total of £137 15s 4d – about 4/- per night. In October 1943 new Fire Guard Orders came into effect, designed to make the system more efficient by concentrating resources on those areas under the greatest risk of attack from the Luftwaffe.

Introducing the Defence (Fire Guard) Regulations, 1943, Herbert Morrison, the Home Secretary, in stressing the need for a more efficient service, pointed out that:

'The risk we have to meet is greater in some places than in some others. The new Orders have been so drafted as to take account of that. There can be relaxation where the authority concerned decides that the risk is small, although such relaxation must be cancelled if and when risk increases. We shall try to strike the right balance between the risk that exists for the time being and the protection that is required to meet it. The guiding principle is that everywhere there should be an efficient organization, adequate,

but not more than adequate, to the risk in that particular place.'

He also considered the problem of the payment of fire-guards:

'No one knows the figure with complete accuracy, but there are about 5,000,000 people undertaking fire-guard duties and every night one-seventh of them, 750,000, are on duty. Of that 5,000,000 about 100,000 are under special arrangements. The ordinary person gets nothing. That is true of a good many of the domestic fire-guards. A certain number get a subsistence allowance, generally 3s. a night, or a little more during the long winter nights. Another lot are paid wages for fire-guard duties. I am not talking about full-time fire guards to whom it is a sole occupation and who do it every night but the man and woman who does 48 hours a month and is paid wages for it. Some of these people are paid up to 2s. an hour--that was the maximum.'

'In the result, we have 4,900,000 persons doing a civic duty, and about 100,000 being paid, in many cases at handsome rates. This is a cause of great discontent among those who do the work voluntarily. The State is being exploited to the tune, as far as I can guess, of £4,000,000 a year paid to a narrow aristocracy of 100,000 fire-guards. What the rest are doing is a civic duty and the sub-committee were unanimous—and not only the sub-committee but the Select Committee—that this state of affairs should be brought to an end.'

Otley, and in particular Prince Henry's, must have been considered to be low risk!

On 9 July 1941 the Governors resolved, on the proposition of Mr W. Whiteley, seconded by Colonel K. Duncan, that the Education Officer be asked to consider the question of making representations to the proper quarter for an order authorising that the purchase of clothing used by the pupils for school sports or gymnastic purposes should be obtainable free from coupons, so that the number of coupons available for a pupil's normal clothing was not curtailed. There is no evidence that this appeal proved successful.

Difficulties of pupils in obtaining sports equipment were again mentioned at the Governors' meeting held on 20 January 1943. Mr Wilde commented that the solution of '*small domestic matters*' were '*veritable triumphs' – even the finding of a lost gym shoe is a cause for rejoicing.*' The '*Wharfedale and Airedale Observer*', published 22 January 1943, reported further on the discussion:

'Mr A L Dawson said a mother had complained to him that her boy had twice been given detention for not having gym shoes. He asked if pupils were given detention if they had not proper sports equipment.

Mr Wilde said it was realized that children had difficulty in obtaining sports equipment, and no child was penalized because of lack of proper equipment. It was possible that a pupil had been given detention for not bringing equipment which he had got. He suggested that the proper way to deal with such complaints would be for the parent to communicate with him.

It was explained that children were unable to purchase "gym" shoes. To meet the difficulty, the County authority had undertaken to purchase large quantities of "gym" shoes and supply them to schools, where they would be loaned to the pupils for use during school hours.'

The paper shortage led to the decision not to publish the School Magazine for Summer 1941 and it was decided that in future only two editions per year would be produced.

At the end of the Summer Term, 1941, two air-raid shelters were built, and several blast walls were erected, creating maze-like corridors in School. *'Air raid practice has ensured that everybody will know what to do in case of an emergency.'* The blast walls were staggered, thus enabling some pupils to take the opportunity of hiding from teachers!

The two air raid shelters were at the east and west end of the school next to the chemistry laboratory and the gymnasium.

In March 1942 The Governors agreed to allow the School grounds to be used by the Home Guard, under the command of Colonel Duncan, on Sunday mornings for gun laying practice. This use was extended in May to include Wednesday evenings. There were also several occasions when the school premises were used for residential courses by such organisations as the National Association of Girls Training Corps and the local Messenger Corps.

Another important change saw the ploughing up of part of the School field for the sowing of food crops. About 1¼ acres were planted with potatoes and a good crop, estimated at between seven and eight tons, was harvested in Autumn 1941. The potatoes were used in the school canteen and lawn mowings from the school grounds were used as fertiliser. Continued progress was made in 1942 when:

'Parties of volunteers gave assistance with the cultivation of the School field throughout the summer term and the holidays. The work included the earthing up of potatoes, the thinning, side-dressing and hoeing of swedes, and the planting out of greens. Last year's LVA established a record when they dibbed out over two thousand plants in about two hours. The Arran Pilot potatoes, planted on April 13th, were lifted on August 13th, when we were again lucky with the weather. Mr Harrison very kindly lent us a spinner and tractor, with two expert drivers, and a party of pupils, staff and friends spent a strenuous day gathering several tons of potatoes. Thanks were given to the friends of the School, who used their guns with such good effect and shot the poachers.'

Many parties of boys gave help to local farmers both in term time and in the holidays.

'This summer (1942) farming is again a vital industry in the country's fight for victory, and both our boys and girls have put in much time in activities on the land. Parties of boys have given assistance to local farmers, while early potatoes have been planted on one-third of the school field, with swedes and greens on the remainder. The Upper Fourth and Lower Fifth Forms have taken it in turn to help with the cultivation of the school field, on Saturday mornings; the Upper Fifth and Sixth Forms have given their time in the holidays. Miss Seaton is in charge of this work.'

Local farmers used some pupils in Summer 1940, but Mr Wilde reported to the Governors that the response from local farmers had been very poor. It was suggested that Major Horton-Fawkes, a school Governor and Chairman of the local War Agricultural Committee should be asked to help because he was in touch with local farmers and their needs.

In June 1941, with the approval of the Education Authorities and Governors, and with the permission of parents, Mr Wilde announced that the school was ready to provide parties of pupils, under the supervision of a member of staff, to help in seasonable work on farms. The first party of scholars worked on Cragg Farm, Stainburn. The '*Wharfedale and Airedale Observer*' (1 August 1941) reported that about 90 boys from Prince Henry's had volunteered for farm work, and in that week three parties, totalling about 40 boys, had been engaged at farms at Tadcaster, Pool and Farnley. Mr Wilde announced that boys were still available for work on the farms and asked that farmers requiring such help should get in touch with him. Where a fair amount of labour was required, a party of about 20 boys would be sent under the charge of a master.

In 1942, 57 parties were sent out to help neighbouring farmers and 3,400 hours were worked. A letter was received from the War Agricultural Committee, chaired by Major Horton-Fawkes, Governor of the School, in appreciation of the work done. In term-time a rota system operated with two boys at a time from each form, accompanied by a member of staff, so that the impact on schoolwork would be minimised. Pupils were paid for their efforts, but, *'the Head Master has suggested that for work done this term time, at least, the money earned might well be pooled and devoted to some good cause.'*

Commenting on 'work on the land' in his report at the 1942 Speech Day, Mr Wilde said that:

'Most of the boys have taken part in this work at one time or another. Altogether, from April to August, we sent out 46 parties, and did 2,768¼ hours' work. The masters took turns to accompany the boys, and those of you who are used to boys will realize all that that implies. Still, this has been valuable work, and I think that the parents have done their share in packing lunches, washing clothes, and refraining from complaining when arrangements have had to be altered because of the weather or when boys have come home later than expected. It makes all the difference to me in organising this work to have such good-humoured co-operation. On our school field too, we have done very well to cultivate over an acre of land and raise a mixed crop of early potatoes, swedes and winter greens. The girls have helped well here, and once again the staff has lent a willing hand also. Foremost in this enterprise, both in planning and execution, we have greatly appreciated the zeal and efficiency of our Biology mistress, Miss Seaton.'

In Spring 1944 it was reported that:

'As in previous years the School has done its part in supplying labour to the farms of the district. Since last July we have put in just over six hundred boy hours in school time and our work appears to have given satisfaction. Parties have been out to the following farms: Cragg Farm, Huby: Mr Lupton's Farm, Leathley; Mr Thorpe's Farm, Clifton; Ashfield Farm, Weston Lane; The Nunnery Farm, Arthington; Mr Outhwaite's Farm, Arthington; and Mr Houseman's Farm, Norwood Edge. On Saturday and during the holidays it is estimated that just under three thousand boy hours have been put in on farm work. On the School ground Miss Seaton was responsible for the raising of a good flax crop last year and is this year growing rye. We have been concerned at damage done to our crop by intruders in the past, but we hope we shall not have this trouble to contend with in the coming season.'

In December 1943 a request was made to the West Riding Education Committee for the provision of chestnut fencing *'on the side of the school playing fields adjacent to the War-time Nursery building.'* In reply the Education Officer stated that the Board of Education would not release materials for this purpose. The Governors' response was *'that there was a possibility of a crop of rye grass being grown on the ground in question and that sheep would be turned on to the land eventually.'* It was also suggested that the matter would be taken up with the War Agricultural Executive Committee. The importance of agriculture won out when in July 1944 the County Architect recommended that a portion of ground be fenced off.

A Gardening Club was formed in Spring 1942. Work in the quadrangle led to the creation of a nursery for raising kale, cabbages, Brussels sprouts and other greens for planting out in the School field.

'War has been declared on a flock of greenfinches which removed the kale seedlings; all the germinating seeds have now been covered with netting and cotton. Work has also been carried out on the vegetable plot in the Shrubbery, where early potatoes planted in March are nearly ready. The produce from this plot will be sold in aid of war charities.'

An 'Experimental Plot' was later set up and the sale of vegetables from the plot enabled two guineas to be sent to the 'Wharfedale Prisoners of War Fund.'

At a meeting held on 15 May 1942 the Governors were asked to consider a request in a letter from the West Riding War Agricultural Committee that the number of rooks in the school grounds should be drastically reduced. The Headmaster (Mr J.Wilde) said the letter drew attention to the enormous damage to crops done by rooks, and said it had been reported there was a rookery in the school grounds. The Governors were asked to reduce the number of rooks. If suitable action were not taken, the War Agricultural Committee would carry out the work and charge the cost to the Governors.

Mr W. Whiteley suggested Mr R.T.A. Renton, who was a member of the War Agricultural Committee, should deal with the matter. Mr Renton pointed out that he was unable to do so because he was the one responsible for reporting the matter, and everyone with a rookery on their land had been notified in this way:

'Mr Renton went on to say that on the previous Sunday afternoon he shot two rooks as they left the fields. On examination, one of the rooks had in its crop 108 grains of corn and the other 94 grains. One of his neighbours had had to re-sow two acres of land because of the damage done by rooks, which found the line of the drill in which grain was sown and then followed the line, systematically cleaning it of grain as they went.

Mr Whiteley pointed out that shooting the rooks was not a job for anyone. His own experience was that the average cost was about 4s per rook.'

It was decided to leave the Clerk, Mr Cecil Newstead, and the Headmaster, to make the necessary arrangements.

Another area that everyone in the family could help with was salvage. The nation was kept at the task by paper drives, collecting aluminium saucepans for aircraft manufacture, iron gates and railings for munitions, and rubber, rags and bones.

In March 1941 a War Effort Club was formed to promote the war effort in School. Various activities took place, as shown below:

Wool-Week	28 April to 5 May	3lb. 8oz. of wool plus two blankets	Wool was knitted up into blankets
Waste Paper Week	16 June to 20 June	Paper sold to Garnett's Mill	15s. 11d. raised
Silver Paper Week	23 June to 27 June		Sold and raised 7s. 6d.
Bones week	30 June to 4 July	A 'special drive for the collection of bones'	No mention of success!
Clothes Week		Considerable number of useful garments	Given to the evacuees in Otley
Other activities	Play presented by U4A Money given direct to Red Cross Fund		£2 6s. 1d.

A total of £7 6s. 8d., plus more than twelve blankets, was raised, the money being given to the Garden Party Fund.

The War Effort Club benefitted from the constant and helpful encouragement of Miss Hodd.

Miss Foster undertook to provide similar encouragement for the Merchant Navy Comforts Service:

'In response to my appeal for knitted comforts for the men of the Merchant Navy, many people offered to knit socks, gloves, mittens and scarves; two nobly undertook a sweater; another gave considerable help by the use of a knitting machine. I should like to thank all these volunteers, and also the mothers and grandmothers who have joined in and given such valuable help. The two parcels which we have already sent have been much appreciated. I hope soon to send another consignment, as the need is great; the stocks at the depot have all been distributed, particularly to men sailing on the Russian route. I have plenty of wool, so please continue to knit.'

In the Summer of 1942 the School gates and railings disappeared to provide materials for the production of armaments. When they were first requisitioned an appeal was made to retain the school gates, but after discussion with government officials the main gates, railings from the gates to the boundary bordering Farnley Lane, and the railings dividing the playing fields on the west side of the school were removed. Other railings were retained.

The Ministry of Works set a national target of 500,000 tons of scrap metal from gates and railings, in order to supply ships, tanks and armaments to fight the war. It was stated that '*a large garden gate, weighing say two hundredweights, will supply enough metal to make 100 rifle barrels, or the steel parts of ten Bren guns. The railings from a street of 150 houses equal, in weight of metal, a Valentine tank.*' No substitutes for railings were permitted at the public expense and licences for alternative material, such as timber, were not granted because *'supplies of materials will not allow this 'luxury' in war-time.'*

The shorter summer holiday in 1944 was again accompanied by a longer half-term break. During this break, from October 7th to 25th, several pupils and staff attended a Harvest Camp in Long Sutton, Lincolnshire. *'The week-days were spent, after getting up at 6.15 a.m., in picking potatoes. By lunch-time we were thoroughly tired and the half-hour break seemed much too short. Our backs ached all the afternoon, but eventually "knocking off" time arrived.*

'Work continued with unabated fury, the "graves" slowly grew longer, while the days of work apparently grew shorter. Our backs slowly (ah, too slowly) lost their stiffness, but our interest in the work dwindled till we were mere stooping machines, mechanically picking potatoes.

'The black-out meant lights out at 9.45 p.m. However, there were opportunities to cycle around the area with trips to the "notorious marshes", surrounding towns, churches and museums. The evenings were whiled away with sing-songs, dancing, a treasure hunt, charades and a chess and draughts tournament.

'Unfortunately – for some! – it rained for much of the second week and the camp was abandoned earlier than expected when the rain continued into the third week. On Tuesday a few girls worked. The rest of us entrained the cycles and did all the packing and cleaning up that was possible. We had our last sing-song at night. On Wednesday we were all up at 6.15 a.m. as usual, and handed in our bedding and blankets. We were ready by 9.00. a.m., when the coach and lorries arrived to take us and our luggage to Spalding. The Headmaster, Mrs. Wilde and Miss Rycroft heroically stayed behind to clear up. At Spalding we caught a train to Doncaster, and after a long wait there we caught a slow train to Leeds. From Leeds we returned to our beloved Wharfedale with hills – real live hills!'

Eventually, just before Christmas, the Headmaster informed the pupils that each of them would receive £1 11s. 0d. for the work done during the Camp.

In spite of the weather and complaints about the hard work, another party of staff and pupils went back to Long Sutton in the following year, when *'the October weather favoured the party, and some good work was done.'*

Significant sums of money were raised throughout the war through the School Savings' Association that had existed in School since 1923. The number of members grew significantly during the war and by Summer 1940 over 250 pupils were regular savers. The Honorary Secretary of the Otley and Wharfedale Savings' Committee was Mr David Nealy, a member of the School staff. After the war his work was acknowledged by the award of the M.B.E. in the King's Birthday Honours' List.

In Autumn 1940 Mr Nealy reported that:

'For the six months ending October 31st 1940, £221 have been invested in Savings Certificates by the members of the Association. This is a considerable sum of money, but we are not satisfied that it represents the maximum effort of which the School is capable in this direction. Only a little more than half of the pupils in the School are members. We urge all pupils to save and invest their savings in Savings Certificates. The School Savings' Association exists to help you to help the country.'

Each year a theme highlighting a specific aspect of the war was used to draw attention to the National War Savings Campaign. In 1941 *'War Weapons Week'* ran from 8 to 15 February with a target total for the Otley and Wharfedale area of £75,000. Pupils were asked to design posters drawing attention to the National War Savings Campaign, of which fifteen were chosen for display at the Sales Centre. Model aeroplanes, made by members of the Aero Club were on display in the windows of Messrs W.B. Moss and Sons.

Each day Savings Certificates, National Defence Bonds and Savings Stamps were on sale. The final total for the School was £1,166 9s. 0d. – a truly magnificent achievement.

The final total for the Otley and Wharfedale area was £258,000, almost three and a half times the initial target.

In 1942 the Otley and Wharfedale effort was to raise funds for the large minesweeper, *"Speedwell"*, during *'Warship Week'*, which ran from 7 to 14 March. Again, the target of £150,000 was easily reached and the final total was £325,000. Model warships made by the pupils were displayed in School and later in the window of Messrs Hellewell. Entries for the painting competition were displayed at the Union Offices, where War Photographs were also on display.

In savings the amount raised in School was £1,609, but additional sums were forthcoming through various individual efforts – *'altogether a sum of £13 11s 4d, was realised in this way. "Sleeping Beauty" and "Cinderella" were presented by 3A and L4A respectively; 3A raised £2 16s and L4A £2 1s. Margaret Pratt, Audrey Fowler and Cathleen Richmond made Glitter-wax flowers and realised £3. Ten shillings was raised by Dorothy Raynes and Elizabeth Sharpe. John Slater, Richard Harrison, Mavis Woodhead and Allan Pearson held raffles and raised 8s 4d, £3 3s, 10s and 3s respectively.'*

The following year it was *'Wings for Victory Week'*. The School's total was £2,039. *'Form U5B raised the excellent sum of £182 2s., giving an average of just over £6 per member. Forms U4B, L4X and 3B all did well, reaching £140, £130 19s. and £140 8s. respectively. In addition the R.A.F. Benevolent Fund benefitted by £10. Form U4A contributed £3 10s. by holding a mock auction. Form U4B, using the same means and also by making a levy on detentions, raised £1 13s.; Form 3A collected £1 on outdoor amusements, while Form 3B held an exhibition of trophies of the last war, which brought in £1 8s. 8d. Donations were given from farm earnings by various members of the School.'*

THIS
CERTIFICATE OF HONOUR
IS AWARDED TO
Otley Prince Henry's Grammar School
SAVINGS GROUP
IN RECOGNITION OF SPECIAL ACHIEVEMENT DURING THE
WINGS FOR VICTORY
NATIONAL SAVINGS CAMPAIGN 1943
I EXTEND MY THANKS TO ALL CONCERNED IN THIS IMPORTANT NATIONAL SERVICE.
Archibald Sinclair
SECRETARY OF STATE FOR AIR

In 1944 it was *'Salute the Soldier Week'*, held from 13 to 20 May. *'The School Savings Committee, made up of form representatives, set the target at £1200; this sum was soon reached, then doubled, and by the end of the week £3,008 had been raised – the total being nearly £1,000 more than the "Wings for Victory" total in 1943. This is a splendid achievement, and it reflects great credit not only upon the School, but upon the Staff, especially Mrs. Tott and Mr D.Nealy.'*

This wasn't the end of the fund raising; a Garden Party held in Summer 1940 raised £75 for war charities, and a similar event in July 1941 raised £65. The distribution of the latter seeing £10 each being sent to St. Dunstan's, 'Aid to Russia', Dr Barnardo's, Otley Christmas Comforts, the Hull Air Raid Distress Fund and the Liverpool Air Raid Distress Fund – the final £5 going to the Otley Y.M.C.A.

Certificate of Honour

presented to

Prince Henry's Grammar Sch.

Savings Group

in grateful acknowledgement of

Successful Achievement in

SALUTE THE SOLDIER

NATIONAL SAVINGS CAMPAIGN 1944

I send my thanks to all concerned

in this important National Service

P. J. Grigg

SECRETARY OF STATE FOR WAR

Significant donations were also made to the Red Cross, partly through the *'Penny-a-Week'* scheme, and by the sale of poppies in School on behalf of the Earl Haig Fund.

In the Summer 1945 edition of the *'Otliensian'* an attempt was made to calculate the total raised by the School during the war. The total raised from Savings Schemes was listed as £11,796, that for the Red Cross as £391 6s. 0d., and the total raised for other charities at over £100.

The themed weeks raised the following amounts:

War Weapons Week	Warship Week	Wings for Victory Week	Salute the Soldier
£1166 9s. 0d.	£1609	£2039	£3008

No details are given of the amount raised in the *'Raise the Standard'* week in Autumn 1943, but it was noted at the time *'there has been a steady improvement in the school savings effort. In some forms the increase in membership has been remarkable, and worthy of commendation and imitation.'* Clearly, in addition to the boost from the themed weeks, saving continued as normal throughout the war.

It seems likely that the round figure of £100 listed as being raised for other charities is an under-estimate. The wartime total raised from the poppy appeal was £34 19s. 7d. and a whole range of events were held by individual forms and societies which took the aggregate total for 'other charities' to a significantly higher figure. It is likely that the total raised over the period of the war exceeded £15,000. Contributions in kind – blankets, clothing and comforts – added to the total.

After the end of the war donations continued. In 1946 £1,531 19s. 6d. was added to National Savings during the Otley and Wharfedale *'Thanksgiving Savings Week'*, the Aid to China Fund benefitted from £6 3s. 6d. raised through a collection in School and the sale of poppies raised £10, a record at the time.

In 1946 Mr Nealy, science master at P.H.G.S., was awarded the M.B.E in the Birthday Honours list for his work for the War Savings' Movement. He was secretary of the Otley and Wharfedale Savings' Committee from 1924-1946.

The table below summarises the amounts saved in Otley and Wharfedale in the various 'weeks' organised during the Second World War:

'Slogan'	Date	Target	Final Amount	Comment
War Weapons Week	8 February 1941- 15 February 1941	£75,000	£258,778 (£14 15s. 9d. per head of population)	Money raised for 'bombers and bombs for victory.'
Warship Week	7 March 1942- 14 March 1942	£150,000	£235,540 (£18 16s. 4d. per head of population)	Money raised equivalent to cost of construction and four refits of minesweeper 'Speedwell,' which was 'adopted' by Otley and Wharfedale.
Tanks for Attack	29 July 1942- 2 September 1942	£30,000	£46,543 (final total not known)	A ten-week intensive drive to increase the number of 'small' savers. A minimum of £30,000 led to the allocation of two tanks to the area.

Wings for Victory Week	15 May 1943-22 May 1943	£160,000	£366, 778	Four Lancaster bombers cost £160,000. Final figure was equivalent to 8 Lancasters.
Salute the Soldier Week	13 May 1944-20 May 1944	£175,000	£275,618	The target was to raise enough to pay for the equipment of an Artillery Unit.
Thanksgiving Week	22 September 1945 - 29 September 1945	£175,000	£200,860 (£12 2s. 2d. per head of population)	

At a meeting of the local Savings Committee held on 26 January 1945 it was announced that when the additional 'normal' savings were added to the amounts saved in these dedicated weeks, the total raised by the Otley & Wharfedale area was £2,174,093. When the savings raised in *'Thanksgiving Week'* are included, the war savings total was £2,537,532.

The end of the war saw a slow return to normality.

In May 1945 the Governors received a report that *'it will be necessary to consult the Ministry of Education before blast walls can be removed.'* The Governors resolved to *'press for the early removal of the blast walls as they are a source of danger in this School and would be very easy to remove.'* The Ministry of Education did not give their approval until July 1946, when the Governors also asked for the removal of *'the black paint from certain high windows in the school.'*

On Saturday 6 October 1945, for the first time since February 1940, the country reverted to 'normal' time and the clocks were put back an hour. Summertime in the U.K. was first introduced in May 1916 and in normal times covered the period between April and October each year, during which period the clock was put forward one hour. In 1941 another hour was added to Summertime, from the first week in May to the second week in August, resulting in what became known as 'double-summertime.'

At the Governors' meeting held on 10 July 1946 notification was received that in selecting students for University entry, preference would be given to men and women who had served with the Forces, who would form a 'priority' class. Canon Williams, Vicar of Otley, said he understood the proportion was that 90% of places would go to ex-servicemen and 10% to other entrants. Mr Wilde noted that *'Anyone must be absolutely brilliant just to have the slightest chance of getting to University.' ('Wharfedale and Airedale Observer,' 12 July 1946)*

At the Governors' Meeting held on 13 December 1946, the Headmaster raised the question of filling in the air-raid trench. It was suggested that he should apply for the help of local prisoner-of-war labour to carry out the work. It is not known if this was done. A Governing Body meeting held on 14 May 1947 reported:

'that the Ministry of Education have approved of the proposed conversion of the air raid shelter into sports and chemistry stores at an estimated cost of £60, and that specifications will be forwarded in due course.'

The School and Grounds Committee turned its attention to the restoration of the School Playing Fields, and the County Education committee approved an estimate of £126 for such improvements. It was agreed that the area under cultivation *'be ploughed, limed and levelled, the land to be fallowed next summer (1946) and sown in September with grass seed.'* The cricket square was to be levelled, though the Governors were concerned about the Architect's plan to relay the old turf, *'which seems to be much too weedy to make a quick recovery and if it is possible for him to obtain new turf in the neighbourhood before the work commences, the Governors would prefer that method.'*

The last item of correspondence received in 1945 related to 'Government Surplus Huts'; the Governors agreed to pass this to the Chairman of the Buildings and Grounds Committee for consideration.

The final return to normality came at the end of the Autumn Term, 1945, when Christmas parties, with a social for the Seniors, were revived.

The War – The Pupils

In his Editorial in the school magazine at the end of the War the Headmaster, Mr Wilde, noted that the *'difficulties'* experienced in the School had been *'a mere inconvenience compared with what others had to suffer.'* He suggested that having become used to 'the atmosphere of the war,' it would be 'difficult to adjust ourselves to more natural conditions.' In fact, taking into account the impact of the war on the building, the staff, supplies of food and other materials, and family life, pupils at Prince Henry's during the War would have had a similar educational and social experience as those who came before them or followed them. The attitude seems to have been to make the best of things, and to make things as *'normal'* as possible.

Before, during and after the Second World War, The Ministry of Education collected data from schools using the *'Preliminary Return for Secondary Grammar Schools'* form that was dated 1 October in each of the relevant years. The number of full-time pupils under instruction in Prince Henry's on 1 October in each year is shown in the following table.

Year	Boys	Girls	Total	% Boys	% Girls
1939	218	232	450	48.44	51.56
1940	219	230	449	48.78	51.22
1941	218	247	465	46.88	53.12
1942	226	229	455	49.67	50.33
1943	223	227	450	49.56	50.44
1944	227	228	455	49.89	50.11
1945	220	213	433	50.81	49.19

The figures took into account the new intake at the start of the school year, but would not include those pupils who entered or left the school following the submission of the form to the Ministry of Education. In the war years (1939-1945), the number of pupils remained reasonably constant, the annual average being 454. In the years from 1939-1944 the number of girls exceeded the number of boys, though from 1942-1944 the difference was marginal.

Statistics were also included for the Ministry on the *'Number of pupils admitted to the school for the first time'* in the relevant Autumn term, and on the *'Number of full-time pupils who left during or at the end of the school year'* (i.e. the previous school year). The admissions data showed total entry and pupils who had attended other grant-earning Secondary Schools. The leaving data showed the total number of leavers, pupils who were known to have transferred to other grant-earning Secondary Schools and those who *'have left the school on account of their parents having removed elsewhere, but are not known to have entered other grant-earning Secondary Schools.'*

Number of pupils admitted to school for first time						
	Autumn 1939	Autumn 1940	Autumn 1941	Autumn 1942	Autumn 1943	Autumn 1944
Boys	61	39	30	47	37	51
Girls	43	48	45	31	40	49
Total	104	87	75	78	77	100

The larger numbers in 1939-1940 may be accounted for by the initial impact of evacuees at the start of the school year, and the fact that many of them returned to their own schools at the end of the first term. Of the 56 evacuees identified in the Admission records, two-thirds left from the same form to which they had been admitted.

Number of pupils leaving school						
	1939-1940	1940-1941	1941-1942	1942-1943	1943-1944	1944-1945
Boys	55	47	55	43	53	41
Girls	71	50	57	50	53	55
Total	126	97	112	93	106	96

The data not given in the annual return is that showing the number of pupils who were admitted to the school each year after the September entry. This number can be calculated by subtracting the leavers from the October pupil count, adding the next year's Autumn admissions and subtracting the total from next year's pupil count.

Number of pupils admitted to school after September intake						
	1939-1940	1940-1941	1941-1942	1942-1943	1943-1944	1944-1945
Boys	17 (16)	16 (16)	16(16)	3 (4)	6 (6)	3(4)
Girls	21 (22)	22 (22)	8 (8)	8 (7)	5 (5)	4 (5)
Total	38 (38)	38 (38)	24 (24)	11 (11)	11(11)	7 (9)

The figures in brackets are taken from the Admission records and largely confirm the data sent to the Ministry.

The Admission records can therefore be relied upon to provide a complete record of the personal details of pupils who entered the School, but the leaving details are less complete, perhaps because even in those days teachers did not take willingly on board administrative tasks! However, details of admissions (*Salvete*) and leavers (*Valete*) were published in the school magazine, the *'Otliensian'*, and some of the gaps can be filled in from this source. There are certainly errors and omissions, but leaving dates can be estimated for the majority of pupils. Using this information, the number of pupils who were at Prince Henry's for some time during the War years was 998 (484 boys and 514 girls). It has been possible to trace 991 of these pupils in the various records, and, of these only 41 pupils (23 boys and 18 girls) were at School for the whole of the War, being admitted on or before September 1939 and not leaving until on or after July 1945.

Pupils at Prince Henry's Grammar School for the whole of the Second World War

Surname	Forename	Entry	Entry Form	Left	Leaving Form	Destination	Sex	Home
Akam	Margaret Shirley	12 09 1939	3A	26 07 1945	VI		F	Menston
Beardsworth	Desmond John	14 09 1937	I	26 07 1945	U5B		M	Guiseley
Benson	Constance Violet	13 09 1938	3B	26 07 1945	VI		F	Menston
Butland	Robert Arthur	11 01 1939	2	22 04 1947	L6		M	Guiseley
Carr	Audrey Eugenie	13 09 1938	3B	26 07 1945	VI	Student teacher	F	Otley
Chadwick	June Patricia	10 09 1936	I	26 07 1946	U6	Oxford University	F	Otley
Clarke	Anthony Douglas	13 09 1938	3B	26 07 1945	U6	Leeds University Medical School: WRC Major 1945	M	Burley
Denham	Dorothy Irene	27 04 1938	2	23 04 1948	U6		F	Otley
Eglen	James Ronald	12 09 1939	3X	26 07 1946	U6		M	Bram-hope
Foster	Margaret Elizabeth	13 09 1938	2	21 12 1945	L5A	Helping at home on the farm	F	Otley
Fowler	Audrey	29 09 1938	2	26 07 1946	U5A	School of Art	F	Otley
Harrison	Philip Tennant	12 09 1939	3X	26 07 1946	U6		M	Askwith
Holden	Jack	13 09 1938	3B	20 07 1945	VI		M	Pool
Holliday	Joan	11 09 1935	I	26 07 1945	VI	Training College of Housecraft	F	Otley
Kaye	David Robert Somers	13 09 1938	2	26 07 1946	U5B	Parents left the district	M	Guiseley
King	Pamela	12 09 1939	2	26 07 1946	U5A	Commercial School	F	Otley
Lee	Gordon	12 09 1939	3A	26 07 1946	U6	Recketts	M	Menston

Lee	Joseph Carleton	26 04 1939	2	17 April 1946	L5B	Father's Business	M	Yeadon
Leeming	Margaret	13 09 1938	2	25 07 1947	L6		F	Guiseley
Longbot-tom	John	10 09 1936	I	25 07 1946	U6	HM Forces	M	Guiseley
Longfield	Michael David	12 09 1939	3X	26 07 1946	U6	HM Forces	M	Otley
Mallinson	Joyce Mary	12 09 1939	3X	26 07 1946	U6	Training College - Domestic subjects	F	Bram-hope
Mckillop	Grace Jean	26 04 1939	2	26 07 1945	U5B		F	Burley
Miller	Geoffrey Edward	12 09 1939	3A	26 07 1946	U6		M	Burley
Mountain	Joan	13 09 1938	3B	27 07 1945	U5A	Clerical	F	Otley
Nicholson	Kenneth	12 09 1939	3A	24 10 1945	VI	Police Cadet	M	Otley
North	Robert Claud	12 09 1939	3B	26 01 1946	VI	Laboratory Assistant	M	Baildon
Paterson	Michael Dan	13 09 1938	3B	27 07 1945	VI	Bradford Technical College	M	Otley
Pratt	Malcolm Thomas Frederick	14 09 1937	I	25 07 1947	U6		M	Otley
Pratt	Margaret Elizabeth	12 09 1939	2	25 07 1947	U6		F	Otley
Price	Gerald Andrew	12 09 1939	2	23 07 1948	U5A		M	Menston
Raistrick	John Alan	12 09 1939	3X	26 07 1945	VI		M	Baildon
Richmond	Cathleen	14 09 1937	I	26 07 1945	U5A		F	Otley
Scott	Allan Harper	26 04 1939	II	26 07 1945	L5X	Keith Grammar School	M	Otley
Smith	Doreen	13 09 1938	3B	27 07 1945	U5B	Clerical	F	Otley
Sykes	John Mi-chael	12 09 1939	3A	26 07 1946	U6	HM Forces	M	Baildon
Tewarne	Sheila Mary	13 01 1938	Low-er 3	26 07 1945	VI	Leeds Teacher Training	F	Adel

Wall	Margaret Bedford	14 09 1937	I	26 07 1945	VI	At home	F	Otley
Watkinson	Antony Arthur	13 09 1938	2	23 07 1948	U6		M	Otley
White	Colin	12 09 1939	3B	27 07 1945	U5B	Technical School	M	Burley
Wilson	Colin Lawson	12 09 1939	3A	26 07 1945	U5B	Bank Clerk	M	Otley

Pupils at Prince Henry's during the War – analysis by entry/exit forms

Entry Form	Total	Total U5 & VI Form	% U5 & VI Form
1	56	38	67.9
2	158	67	42.4
Lower3	75	43	57.3
Upper3	155	136	87.5
3(ABCX)	421	295	70.1
Lower4	49	27	55.1
Upper 4	32	21	65.6
Lower5	25	13	52.0
Upper5	14	14	100
Sixth Form	4	4	100
Unknown	2	-	-
TOTAL	991	658	66.4

The 991 pupils at Prince Henry's during the War years are analysed in the above table by entry form and by the number and percentage of each entry form completing their education at Prince Henry's. Forms 1, 2 and Lower 3 were made up of pupils in the Preparatory Department. These were pupils who entered the school at under 11 years of age and were 'prepared' for a grammar school education when they reached the normal age of entry. In total they formed 29% of the 991 pupils at the school during the War. A few of them were 6 years of age on entry, though the majority were aged 8 and above.

By the start of the War only Forms 2 and L3 survived; Form 1 was no longer used, a sign that the very youngest pupils were no longer coming to the School. Prince Henry's was a fee-paying school and, if parents had the money, this was a way of obtaining a grammar school education by getting in early. In fact fees were higher for preparatory pupils than for those in the mainstream forms. Some of these pupils would have been taught in private schools, others would feel that their primary schools had done as much for their education as possible, and moved on to the Grammar School. Only 51% of the Preparatory Department pupils stayed at Prince Henry's until the 'normal' leaving age of 16 or beyond. On entry parents had to sign an agreement to keep their children at school until the pupils reached the age of 16 and to pay 'penalty' fees if they left before that date.

The normal route through the school was entry at 11 years of age followed by 5 years of mainstream education, leaving at 16 years of age, or staying on into the Sixth Form. Most pupils came to Prince Henry's after their primary school years, and were placed directly into the third form. They were usually streamed into one of three forms – 3A, 3B or 3C – but in some years there was also an additional form – 3X – which was for pupils considered to be better academically than their peers. Upper 3 was a logical move from Lower 3 for pupils in the Preparatory Department, but was still part of the third year, and when included with the 3ABCX pupils gives a total of 576 pupils during the War years; this represented 58.1% of the 991 pupils. 75% of these pupils completed their education by moving through to the Upper Fifth or Sixth Form.

From Form 3 pupils moved into the Lower Fourth, followed by the Upper Fourth, Lower Fifth and Upper Fifth, giving a total of five years in the School. The above table shows that it was less common for new students to enter the school, the older the student, and it was particularly unusual for new students to join the Sixth Form.

Of the 991 pupils at School during the War years, two-thirds kept to their agreement and stayed on until they reached the age of 16. 25% of the 991 pupils stayed on into the Sixth Form, though not necessarily into the Upper Sixth. The one-third who left early did so for a variety of reasons; some would move to other Secondary Schools in the area or further afield because their parents moved elsewhere, some left because they had obtained employment, others left for financial (*'reduced circumstances'*) or health reasons – their parents could no longer afford to keep them at School. Sometimes pupils left because of a *'lack of progress'*, and sometimes because the death or illness of their father required them to help out at home. The Governors had the task of agreeing to the request to leave early, with or without the payment of penalty fees, or disallowing the request. In the latter cases some parents still took their children out of School and the Governors took legal steps to obtain the unpaid fees. In most cases the Governors supported the requests for early leaving and the fees were waived.

There are examples of parents of pupils who were awarded scholarships to attend Prince Henry's who rejected the offer. In spite of the fact that the fees would have been paid for by the W.R.C.C., they were unwilling to meet any additional costs and reluctant to commit their children to remain at school until they were 16 years of age. The Governors' minutes include attempts by the Governors to change the minds of the parents, usually without success.

As the following table shows, Prince Henry's 'catchment' area was very wide, pupils coming traditionally from the old established Parish of Otley, with its many rural villages.

Home Address of Students at School during the War years, 1939-1945									
Adel	12	Burley-in-Wharfedale	81	Finchley (London)	1	Leeds	12	Rawdon	6
Arthington	6	Castley	1	Guiseley	80	Lindley	1	Shipley	1
Askwith	5	Clapham (London)	1	Hawksworth	1	Manchester	1	South Shields	3
Baildon	17	Clifton	3	Hornsea	1	Menston	80	Weston	2
Ben Rhydding	4	Cookridge	7	Horsforth	1	Middleton	6	Yeadon	6
Birstwith	5	Drighlington	1	Huby	11	North Rigton	1	Un-known	4
Blubberhous-es	2	Eccup	1	Ilkley	33	Norwood	1		
Bradford	6	Esholt	1	Keighley	1	Otley	452		
Bramhope	73	Farnley	9	Leathley	4	Pool	47	TOTAL	991

46% of the pupils at School for some period during the War years came from Otley. The vast majority of the other pupils came from the area surrounding Otley. The towns and villages along the A660, Ilkley, Ben Rhydding and Burley to the west, and Pool, Bramhope, Cookridge and Adel to the east contributed 257 pupils (26%). A significant number of pupils came from the area to the south of Otley along the A65 where Menston, Guiseley, Rawdon, Yeadon and Baildon accounted for a further 189 students (19%). This leaves 93 pupils, most of whom came in small numbers from the villages to the north of Otley.

The extensive area served by the school must have created difficulties with regard to transport to and from Otley. Local pupils could walk or cycle to School and at the time the railway served Otley, and pupils from Ilkley, Menston and Guiseley and from Arthington and Pool may have used the train service to and from Otley Station. It was more usual to use special buses and service buses. There were occasions when the Governors complained about the overcrowding on buses:

'The question of the overcrowding of buses between Adel and Otley was discussed and instructions were given.' (Governing Body meeting, 11 December 1940).

Complaints were also made about the timing of some service buses, which were said to arrive too late to get pupils to school for the normal starting time.

The small number of pupils from further afield may have been evacuees, though we know that some evacuees came to stay with people living in the local area, and therefore had local addresses. In his Editorial at the end of the War, the Headmaster, Mr Wilde noted that:

'We have had the pleasure of being hosts to evacuees, at first an exceeding great army, now dwindled to a mere handful still remaining with us.'

The *'exceeding great army'* was a reference to the girls from Roundhay School who shared the School in the first term of the 1939-1940 school year.

The Government started planning for evacuation in Summer 1938 when the Anderson Committee drew up plans to divide the country into areas classified as 'evacuation', 'neutral' or 'reception'. Priority evacuees were to be moved from major urban areas and billeted in private houses in more rural areas. Reception areas drew up lists of available housing in early 1939. The scheme was designed to save civilians, particularly children, from the risks associated with the bombing of cities by moving them to areas likely to be of less risk. *'Operation Pied-Piper'* began on 1 September 1939, and relocated over 3.5 million people. There were also official evacuations from the U.K. to other parts of the British Empire, such as Canada, and many private evacuations within and from the U.K. In the first three days of the official evacuation almost 1.5 million people were moved – over 800,000 of them being children of school age. The others included mothers and young children under 5, pregnant women, disabled persons and teachers and other helpers.

Otley and the surrounding villages of Wharfedale and Washburndale, including Ilkley, Burley and Menston, were designated as *'safe'* or *'reception'* areas, and were earmarked to receive nearly 10,000 children and expectant mothers. 3,000 were to be allocated to Otley, 2,500 to the Rural District, and some 4,000 to the Ilkley Urban Area. In a single day more than 1,200 youngsters, including the girls from Roundhay Secondary School, arrived in Otley. At the reception centre at North Parade School they were card-indexed, medically examined and given emergency rations to cover the next 48 hours, consisting of tins of corned beef, sweetened and unsweetened milk and biscuits. They were then allocated to local residents, who had agreed to take them into their homes.

School records, in particular information submitted to the West Riding on school leavers, provide some insight into the impact of evacuation on Prince Henry's. The list below contains details of 55 pupils who we can justifiably class as 'evacuees'. 22 of these students started at Prince Henry's in September 1939, 19 of whom left after one term. This list does not include the Roundhay Girls, who shared the school on a shift system during the first term of the school year 1939-40, but returned to their own school after one term. The initial movement of children away from urban centres was seen as something of a panic measure. In the first few months the impact of the war was minimal during what became known as the 'phoney war', and some parents decided that it was safe for their children to return home and go back to their own schools. Many of these schools were located in West Leeds, and it may well be the case that the children continued to live at home, but moved to Prince Henry's as private evacuees.

Evacuees – Prince Henry's Grammar School 1939-1945

Length	Surname	Forename	Entry	Left	Address	Destination
1939-1939	Ayres	Margaret Jean	L4A	L4A	Westbourne House, Otley	Returned to own school - West Leeds High Leeds
1939-1939	Baldwin	Peter Harrison	L4A	L4A	Overdale, Bramhope, Nr Leeds	Returned to own school - Leeds Grammar School
1939-1939	Ball	Pamela Doreen	2	2	543 Otley Road, Adel, Leeds 6	Returned to own school - Leeds Girls High School
1939-1939	Boshell	Barbara Jubb	U4B	U4B	62 Becketts Park Crescent, Headingley, Leeds	Returned to own school - Leeds Girls High School
1939-1939	Bradley	Robert George	2	2	8 Market Place, Otley	Returned to London - Parkside Prep, Edgeware
1939-1939	Britton	Rosemary Margaret	U5A	U5A	The Lilacs, 7 Broomfield, Adel, Leeds 6	Returned to own school - Lawnswood High School
1939-1939	Brook	Marjorie Agnes	L4B	L4B	24 Stainburn Crescent, Leeds 7	Returned to own school - Allerton Girls High School
1939-1939	Crossland	John Davies	U5A	U5A	c/o Ikin, Holly Park, Huby, Nr Leeds	Returned to own school - Roundhay School for Boys
1939-1939	Ellse	Bernard Leslie	3A	3A	31 Coniston Grove, Smith Lane, Bradford	Returned to own school - Bradford Grammar
1939-1939	Ellse	Denise Audrey	L5B	L5B	31 Coniston Grove, Smith Lane, Bradford	Returned to own school - Bradford Grammar
1939-1939	Green	Derek Marshall	U4B	U4B	c/o Mrs. Pullein, Otley Road, Pool	Returned to Leeds
1939-1939	Hinchliffe	John Michael	3B	3B	Lawnswood Arms, Adel, Leeds 6	Returned to own school - Leeds Boys Modern
1939-1939	Maury	Joanne Margaret	U4B	U4B	16 Becketts Park Drive, Headingley, Leeds	Returned to own school - Leeds Girl's High School
1939-1939	Moore	Kenneth Stanley	L4B	L4B	71 West Busk Lane, Otley	Returned to own school - East Barnet Modern
1939-1939	Newman	Aubrey	L5A	L5A	42 Spencer Place, Leeds 7	Returned to own school - Leeds

1939-1939	Newman	Leonard	L6	L6	42 Spencer Place, Leeds 7	Returned to City of Leeds School
1939-1939	Richardson	Barbara May	U5B	U5B	27 Spennithorne Drive, Leeds 6	Returned to own school - Lawnswood High School
1939-1939	Shaw	Audrey	U4B	U4B	17 Spennithorne Drive, Leeds 6	Returned to own school - Leeds Girls High School
1939-1939	West	Brian George	3B	3B	238 Nether Street, Finchley, London N.3	Returned to London - Holmwood Prep School
1939-1940	Ridgway	Marion Lois	3B	3B	Leathlea, the Crescent Menston	Private evacuee to North Wales
1939-1941	Turnbull	Mary Wilson	L5A	U5A	103 Cookridge Lane, Cookridge, Horsforth	Returned to Lawnswood High School
1939-1942	Hellewell	Ronald Arthur	2	L3	12 Newall Carr Road Otley	Private evacuee - home to parents in Bradford
1939-1942	Murgatroyd	Mary	U4C	U5B	53 Tottenham Lane, Hornsey N.8	Clerical Work
1940-1940	Hempling	Marcia	2	2	The Cottage, West Way, Tranmere Park, Guiseley	Evacuated to Canada - Private evacuation
1940-1940	Sowerby	Anne Maureen	2	2	6 Moorway, Tranmere Park, Guiseley	Evacuated to Canada - Toronto
1940-1941	Dealey	Elizabeth	3X	L4B	21 Greenhow Avenue, Leeds 4	Evacuee - Left the district - West Leeds Girls High
1940-1941	Hayhurst	Douglas	U5C	U5C	13 Newall Avenue, Otley	Evacuee - Returned to Norwich
1940-1941	Thompson	Elizabeth Beresford	L5C	L5C	12 Croft Avenue, Otley	Evacuee - Gone to N.Ireland
1940-1942	Moore	Catherine Eleanor	3X	L4B	3 Oakfield Court, Kings Avenue, Clapham	Evacuee - Returned to London
1940-1942	Wilkinson	Patricia Braham	U4C	U5B	18 Bentcliffe Avenue, Leeds 7	Evacuated? Training at a Leeds Nursery School
1940-1943	Humphreys	Vera Mary	3A	U4B	Rushey Leigh, Grange Road, Burley (21 Wildfell Road, Acocks Green, Birmingham)	Evacuee - Returned to Birmingham

1940-1945	Brown	Roger Anthony	3X	6	45 Prince Edward Road, Farton?, South Shields	Bank; Durham University 1946?
1941-1941	Berry	Joan Margaret	U4B	L5B	Hillside, Otley Road, Bramhope (63 Ormond Drive, Hampton, Middlesex)	Evacuee - Returned South
1941-1941	Edmondson	Audrey	3B	3B	9 Addison Road, Stretford, Manchester	Evacuee - Left the district
1941-1941	Firth	Henry Alexander	U4A	U4A	83, Harton Lane, South Sheilds	Evacuee - Returned to South Shields
1941-1941	Midgley	Elaine	L5A	L5A	114 Westgate, Otley (354 Olton Boulevard East, Awks Green, Birmingham)	Evacuee - Returned King Edward School
1941-1942	Revitt	Miles John	L3	3A	c/o Mrs Owston, Weston Lane, Otley (62 Park View, Wymondmore Hill, London N.21)	Privately evacuated to Otley; Latymer's School, London
1941-1943	Climie	Evelyn Jean Frances	2	L3	The Vicarage, Otley	Evacuee - Returned Home
1941-1945	Fyffe	Jean Irene Forbes	2	U4B	1 Ashfield Place, Huby	Returned south
1942-1943	Counsell	Frank George	3A	3X	National Chidren's Home, Bramhope	Evacuee - Returned to his mother in London
1942-1943	Johnson	Ann	2	2	Fairfield, Huby, near Leeds	Evacuee (Father member of armed forces) – Returned home
1942-1943	Wilkinson	Patricia Joan	2	L3	Durlston, South Mount Avenue, Baildon	Evacuee - Queen Mary's Lytham
1942-1943	Wilkinson	Richard Michael	2	2	Durlston, South Mount Avenue, Baildon	Evacuee - King Edward, Lytham
1942-1944	Brown	Ian Frederica Suddes	2	L4B	45 Prince Edward Rd, South Shields	Evacuee - Returned to Boarding School
1942-1944	Mawson	Jane Everill	L5B	U5B	3 Newall Mount, Otley	Returned?
1942-1944	Spenceley	Robert	3A		9 East View Terrace, Otley	Evacuee - Returned east
1943-1943	Dean	Barbara	L4A	L4A	3 Bedford Place, Otley	Returned to Bradford

1943-1945	Jobling	Margaret	3B	L4B	100 Albion Street, Otley	Evacuee - Returned south
1944-1944	Crowhurst	Michael Robert	3B	3B	c/o Mrs. Halliday, Orchard House, Huby	Evacuee - Returned south - Wembley Secondary School
1944-1944	Johns	Denis Robert	U5B	U5B	c/o Miss Smith, Smallbanks, Prince Henry's Road	Evacuee - Returned south
1944-1944	Jones	Barbara	L4A		Anley, Clarence Drive, Menston	Evacuee - Returned south
1944-1944	Jones	Bridget	U4A	U4A	Anley, Clarence Drive, Menston	Evacuee - Returned south
1944-1944	Mostyn	Christopher	L5A	L5A	c/o Mrs. Horton Fawkes	Evacuee - Returned south
1944-1944	Waud	Maud April Beatrice Evelyn	U4X	U4X	Rawdon Cragg, Nr Leeds	Evacuee - Returned to Boarding School
1944-1945	Coppard	Annette J	L5B	L5B	Oakdene, Tinshill Road, Cookridge	Evacuee - Returned south
1945-1948	George	Gordon Richard	3B	L5B	c/o Burley Lawn, Main Street, Burley	

From 1940 onwards it was more usual for evacuees from further afield to join the school. There are examples of pupils coming from London, Birmingham, South Shields, Manchester and Norwich. They arrived in smaller numbers as the War progressed, and again most of them stayed for only a short period. The destination entry in the leavers' data usually reads *'returned south'*. Local households volunteered to accommodate these evacuees. Examples included Evelyn Climie who lived at The Vicarage, Otley, from 1941-1943; Mrs. Horton-Fawkes looked after Christopher Mostyn, presumably at Farnley Hall; Miss Smith of Prince Henry's Road, Otley provided a home for Denis Johns.

There are also instances of pupils who were evacuated from Otley; Marcia Hempling and Anne Sowerby to Canada: Pauline Davies to the Isle of Man: Elizabeth Thompson to Northern Ireland: Marion Ridgway to North Wales. There are also more examples during the War years, than might normally be expected, of students moving from Prince Henry's to Boarding Schools.

The Admission Registers for pupils who attended Prince Henry's Grammar School for some time during the war years 1939-1945 identify a total of 983 students. Destinations are listed for 541 of these pupils. In general those pupils without a leaving destination are those who left after Summer 1946, and hence it is possible to draw up a list of destinations of these wartime pupils, classified under various headings:

Destination	No.	%	Description
Clerical Work	148	27.4	*115 of the leavers' destination were described as 'clerical'. The next most common was 'bank clerk' with 15 leavers.*
Transfer to other schools	78	14.4	*When parents left the area they would need to transfer their children to other schools, most of which were Grammar Schools that would accept scholarship holders. About 50% were transfers to local schools and may have involved pupils moving back home after evacuation. A few were boarding schools, and there is some indication of moves 'up-market', to what were considered to be 'better' schools. 6 students left to attend private schools or obtain private tuition.*
Parents left the district	60	11.1	*Many of these would be likely to transfer to other schools, though the leavers are listed simply as left the district, removed or returned home. The latter, 14 in number, may well have been evacuees. Two moved to Canada, one to Ireland.*
Colleges	60	11.1	*Most transfers to college were local – Leeds and Bradford – and half were to Commercial Colleges. 20% were to Teacher Training Colleges and 13% to Art Colleges. Only one moved to Agricultural College and one to Music College.*
Others	56	10.4	*28 'other' destinations are included. Individual examples include a rent collector, a tuner of pianos, a gardener, a haulage contractor, and a librarian. Three pupils joined the police, another 3 became telephonists and two were hairdressers. One pupil 'absconded' and one was listed as 'deceased'. Only one student is listed as having 'no occupation'.*
Factory Work	30	5.5	*18 different occupations/firms are listed, the most common being 11 in some form of engineering. Local trades and business were represented, though only in single cases – 'Aircraft factory', Crompton Parkinson, Leather worker, Walker's printing.*
'Home'	30	5.5	*These were leavers who left because of illness or problems at home. 12 were listed as 'at home', 13 as on 'home duties' and 3 working in the family business. 2 were allowed to leave because of their parents' 'reduced circumstances.'*
Universities	23	4.3	*19 of these students went to Leeds University. 2 to Oxford and 1 each to Durham and Cambridge.*
Chemical/ Lab. Assistant	14	2.6	*Some pupils were employed at Leeds University and went on to take academic qualifications.*
Military	12	2.2	*The Army, Navy and R.A.F. are represented, but generally pupils did not leave and join the forces immediately.*
Nurse/Nursing	11	2.0	
Shop Assistant	11	2.0	
Farm Work	8	1.5	*Surprisingly small for an agricultural area – though not jobs seen as attractive to 'grammar' school pupils!*

SCHOOL OFFICIALS

BOYS (1939-1940)		GIRLS (1939-1940)	
Head Prefect	Robert Whitaker	Head Prefect	Dorothy M. Stowe
Prefects	Andrew T. Firth Noel Q. King Reginald H. Marshall Harold J. Payne Geoffrey C. Pickles Geoffrey D. Watkinson George E. Weston Joseph L. Marshall	Prefects	Florence J. Hebden Jean M. Hall Moyra C. Hay Nancy Kettlewood Mary Walker Alice P. Foulston Nancy Mason Sheila M. Simmons Marjorie B. Wright
Rugby Captain	Andrew T.Firth	Hockey Captain	Marjorie B. Wright
Cricket Captain	Andrew T. Firth	Tennis Captain	Marjorie B. Wright

BOYS (1940-1941)		GIRLS (1940-1941)	
Head Prefect	Noel Q. King	Head Prefect	Sheila M. Simmons
Prefects	George E. Weston Eric H. Dixon Gerald Butterfield Eric Shackleton Geoffrey Clarke	Prefects	Myrle Boyington Betty Dufton Dorothy M. Ickringill Anna M. Slater
Rugby Captain	Gerald Butterfield	Hockey Captain	Dorothy M. Ickringill
Cricket Captain	Gerald Butterfield	Tennis Captain	Dorothy M. Ickringill

BOYS (1941-1942)		GIRLS (1941-1942)	
Head Prefect	George E. Weston	Head Prefect	Sheila M. Simmons
Prefects	Geoffrey Clarke Eric Shackleton Alec H.Fawcett Leslie Hully	Prefects	Betty Dufton Anna M. Slater Marjorie Berry Joan Fawcett Audrey Laverack Dorothy Smithson
Rugby Captain	Eric Shackleton	Hockey Captain	Anna M. Slater
Cricket Captain	Eric Shackleton	Tennis Captain	Anna M. Slater

BOYS (1942-1943)		GIRLS (1942-1943)	
Head Prefect	Eric Shackleton	Head Prefect	Joan Fawcett

Prefects	Leslie Hully Peter G Jackson Ian R. Naylor John C. Rigg William Turner Patrick H. Sunderland	Prefects	Margaret Call Kathleen Moxon Kathleen Prince Audrey Scrafton Dorothy Smithson
Rugby Captain	Eric Shackleton	Hockey Captain	Sheena Hay
Cricket Captain	Eric Shackleton	Tennis Captain	Barbara Thornton

BOYS (1943-1944)		GIRLS (1943-1944)	
Head Prefect	Leslie Hully	Head Prefect	Dorothy Smithson
Prefects	Phillip L.Day Harry Middleditch Michael D. Paterson George E. Thompson William Turner Daniel Byford	Prefects	Sylvia C. Brooke Audrey E. Carr Betty Champney C. Margaret Hoodless Kathleen Moxon Kathleen Prince
Rugby Captain	Leslie Hully	Hockey Captain	Sheena Hay
Cricket Captain	Leslie Hully	Tennis Captain	Audrey E Carr

BOYS (1944-1945)		GIRLS (1944-1945)	
Head Prefect	Michael D. Paterson	Head Prefect	Audrey E. Carr
Prefects	Anthony D Clarke Jack Holden Kenneth McCulloch David Maddock James R. Eglen	Prefects	Sylvia C. Brooke Constance V. Benson Patricia J. Chadwick Joan Holliday Sheila M. Lewarne Joyce M. Mallinson
Rugby Captain	Michael D. Paterson	Hockey Captain	Audrey E. Carr
Cricket Captain	Derek S. Hardwick	Tennis Captain	Audrey E. Carr

The Curriculum

The National Curriculum for secondary state schools in England, Wales and Northern Ireland was introduced as part of the Education Reform Act 1988 which required that all state school students be taught a basic curriculum comprising Religious Education and the National Curriculum. The requirement to provide Religious Education dates from the 1944 Education Act. Thus, over the period of the Second World War schools were not subject to a set curriculum imposed by legislation. Of course, most secondary schools provided the basic subjects which would enable their students to take external examinations, obtain employment or move on to further education.

During the first term of the War the School was shared with Roundhay Girls School, Prince Henry's pupils in the morning, including Saturday, Roundhay in the afternoon. For most pupils this meant 36 periods per week, six each day divided as follows:

Period 1	Period 2	Period 3	Break	Period 4	Period 5	Period 6
08.35-09.15	09.15-09.55	09.55-10.35	10.35-10.55	10.55-11.35	11.35-12.10	12.10-12.45

The pupils in the Preparatory Department left at 12.10 on each day and there was no Saturday morning school. This gave a total of 25 periods per week. The 25 periods were divided as follows:

Rel. Inst.	English	History	Geog.	Arith.	Natur-eSt	Art	Music	Gym	Games
1	6	2	2	6	2	2	1	2	1

There was a concentration on English and Arithmetic, with no Modern Language. The only 'science' subject was Nature Study, and there was no Domestic Science or 'Manual Instruction'.

At the start of the Spring Term, 1940, the Roundhay girls returned to their own school and morning and afternoon sessions recommenced, with a break for lunch. From the start of the 1940-1941 school year there were seven teaching periods per day and 35 periods per week. The four morning lessons were each 45 minutes long, the three afternoon lessons were 40 minutes long, the day being structured as follows:

Period 1	Period 2	Morning Break	Period 3	Period 4	Lunch Break	Period 5	Period 6	Period 7
09.05 - 09.50	09.50 - 10.35	10.35 - 10.50	10.50 - 11.35	11.35 - 12.20	12.20 - 14.00	14.00 - 14.40	14.40 - 15.20	15.20 - 16.00

The curriculum in the Preparatory Department continued to stress the basics. For the remainder of the War numbers were sufficient to provide two forms. The curriculum for 1940-1941 is shown below. In the summer months one of the games periods was given over to Swimming in the open-air pool in Wharfemeadows Park. 'Craft' consisted of

'Manual Instruction' – for the boys – and Needlework – for the girls.

	R.I.	Eng.	Hist.	Geog.	Arith.	NatSt	Art	Music	Craft	Gym	Games
2	1	11	3	2	6	2	2	2	(2)+(2)	2	2
L3*	1	8	3	2	8	2	2	2	(2)+(2)	2	2

**the additional period was for 'Prep'.*

The Preparatory Department curriculum remained more or less the same until the demise of preparatory departments in state secondary schools following the 1944 Education Act.

At eleven years of age the *'preparatory'* students were joined by pupils new to the school, to begin their five-year programme in preparation for the School Certificate. They would start in the third form and progress through the Lower Fourth, Upper Fourth and Lower Fifth to the Upper Fifth. Most students would then take the School Certificate examination before leaving school or, in a minority of cases, progressing to the Sixth Form. Numbers of pupils in a year group would determine the number of forms - a minimum of two forms and a maximum of three. Pupils were streamed according to ability into A, B or C forms. There was some movement between the streams, but most students could expect to remain in one stream throughout the five years. In some years the forms were labeled X, A and B, the X being made up of the students in the top stream.

In September 1939, Michael David Longfield and Joyce Mary Mallinson joined Prince Henry's in Form 3X. They both progressed through the main school, entered the Sixth Form and left from the Upper Sixth in Summer 1946. We can follow their school career to describe the curriculum.

In their first year in 'Main School', where there were 3 forms (3X, 3A & 3B), the curriculum was more or less the same for each form.

R.I.	English	History	Geog.	French	Maths	Nat.St/ Gen.Sc	Art	Music	Craft	Gym	Games
1	6	3	3	6	6	(2)/(2)	2	2	(2)/(2)	2	1

French was introduced at this stage. Mathematics was subdivided into Arithmetic, Algebra and Geometry (2 periods for each). Science was either 2 periods of Nature Study or 2 periods of General Experimental Science. Craft involved boys being taught 'Manual Instruction', girls Needlework.

In their second full year Michael and Joyce were introduced to Latin. It was expected that pupils from Lower 4X would be more likely to go on to University, entry to which would require School Certificate Latin.

Subject	Form L4X	Form L4A	Form L4B
Rel.Instruction	1	1	1
English	5	6	6
History	2	3	3
Geography	2	3	3
Latin	4	-	-
French	5	5	5
Mathematics	5	6	6
Chemistry	2	2	2
Physics/Biology	(2)/(2)	(2)/(2)	(2)/(2)
Art	2	2	2
Music	1	1	1
Craft (M/F)	(2)/(2)	(2)/(2)	(2)/(2)
Gym	1	1	1
Games	1*	1*	1*

**Swimming in Summer Term*

Latin was provided by reducing English, History, Geography, and Mathematics by one period each. Mathematics was again divided into Arithmetic, Algebra and Geometry. Science consisted of two periods of Chemistry and 2 periods of EITHER Biology or Physics. Girls were taught either Needlework or Housecraft.

In 1941-1942, their third full year, there were three forms – Upper 4X, Upper 4A and Upper 4B. The only change for Michael and Joyce compared with the previous year was that one additional period was allocated to Latin and one less to French. Again, the only choice in the curriculum was between Physics and Biology.

Subject	Form U4X	Form U4A	Form U4B
Rel.Instruction	1	1	1
English	5	6	6
History	2	2	2
Geography	2	2	2
Latin	5	-	-
French	4	5	5
Mathematics	5	6	6
Chemistry	2	3	3
Physics/Biology	(2)/(2)	(2)/(2)	(2)/(2)
Art	2	2	2
Music	1	2	2

Craft (M/F)	(2)/(2)	(2)/(2)	(2)/(2)
Gym	1	1	1
Games	1	1	1

U4A and U4B had the same curriculum as in the previous year except that Chemistry and Music were each given an additional period, re-allocated from History and Geography. There had been a significant change in the curriculum in the Lower Fourths where L4A were now given a choice between Latin and German as the second language.

In the school year 1942-1943 Michael and Joyce were in Form Lower 5X, made up of 33 students, the same as in U4X in the previous year. Form Lower 5A had 32 pupils, Form Lower 5B had 25 pupils. The main change for pupils in L5X was that they could drop Latin, the five periods freed up being allocated to Chemistry (3), Music (1) and Gym (1). It is likely that the pupils who continued with Latin were those who aspired to go to University. For all three forms, more time was allocated to Physics/Biology. For Forms L5A and L5B additional periods in Physics/Biology and Craft were allocated by reducing the time spent on English and Music.

Subject	Form L5X	Form L5A	Form L5B
Rel.Instruction	1	1	1
English	5	5	5
History	2	2	2
Geography	2	2	2
Latin	5*	-	-
French	5	5	5
Mathematics	6	6	6
Chemistry	3*	3	3
Physics/Biology	(3/(3)	(3)/(3)	(3)/(3)
Art	2	2	2
Music	1*	1	1
Craft (M/F)	(2)/(2)	(3)/(3)	(3)/(3)
Gym	1+1*	1	1
Games	1	1	1

**choice was Latin OR Chemistry(3)+Music(1)+Gym(1)*

The fifth year in *'Main School'* culminated in students sitting the School Certificate. For students in Upper 5X this meant a concentration on the 'academic' subjects at the expense of the practical and aesthetic, and hence the absence of Art, Music and Craft subjects. Students who did not take Latin took Chemistry for 4 periods, plus an additional period of French.

Subject	Form U5X	Form U5A	Form U5B
Rel.Instruction	1	1	1
English	6	6	6
History	3	3x	3x
Geography	3	3	3
Latin	5*	-	-
French	5+1*	5+1x	5+1x
Mathematics	6	6	6
Chemistry	4*	4x	4x
Physics/Biology	(4/(4)	(4)/(4)	(4)/(4)
Art	-	4x	4x
Music	-	-	-
Craft (M/F)	-	(4)/(4)x	(4)/(4)x
Gym	1	1	1
Games	1	1	1

**Choice was Latin or Chemistry(4) + additional period of French*

x Choices were Chemistry(4) or History(3) + additional period of French AND Art(4) or Craft(4)

For pupils in U5A and U5B there were other choices to be made which provided a more practical curriculum for some. Students could opt for EITHER Chemistry OR History, students selecting History also having an additional period of French. They could also choose between Art and the relevant Craft subject.

In summary the curriculum in the first five years at Prince Henry's was largely academic, Arts based and provided little choice for students. English, Mathematics, French and Geography were the only subjects that were taken by all students. Students in the top forms could take two languages – French and Latin OR French and German. All students would take at least one Science subject – Physics OR Biology, and some would also take Chemistry; but it was not possible to take three sciences. A large majority of students took History, but it was possible in Upper 5A and Upper 5B to drop History in favour of Chemistry. As students moved up the school the proportion of *'practical'* and '*aesthetic*' subjects in the curriculum fell dramatically for most, but increased substantially for others. Religious Instruction was taught to all students and all pupils were provided with time in the gym and in 'field games', including swimming in the summer months.

The School Certificate was established in 1918 by the Secondary Schools Examinations Council (S.S.E.C.). It was usually taken at age 16 and performance in each subject was graded as Fail – Pass – Credit – Distinction. A certificate was awarded to students who gained at least six passes, including English and Mathematics. Credits in at least five subjects, including English, mathematics, science or a language gave students a 'matriculation exemption'. The School Certificate was abolished in 1951 following the introduction of G.C.E. O-Levels.

Students who passed the School Certificate would normally stay on into the Sixth Form to take the Higher School Certificate at age 18.

Results: School Certificate

	1939	1940	1941	1942	1943	1944	1945
Entry	48	56	61	68	56	71	53
Pass	35	40	48	50	36	60	46
% Pass	72.9	71.4	78.7	73.5	64.3	84.5	86.8

We know from their School Certificate examination results that both Michael Longfield and Joyce Mallinson remained in the 'X' form throughout their five years of secondary school education, and that they both obtained their Certificate which was awarded for 6 passes including English and Mathematics. Neither of them took Latin; both took Chemistry; Michael took Physics and Joyce took Biology. Full results for Upper 5X are listed below:

JOINT MATRICULATION BOARD SCHOOL CERTIFICATE, 1944 (Upper 5X)

I. Birkett, J. Eglen, E. D. R. Fisher, R. A. Fisher, G. W. Harrison, G. Hinchliffe, M. D. Longfield, D. J. Moss, M. T. F. Pratt, F. L. Quinn, D. A. Simmons, Audrey S. Bickle, Doreen Court, Gertrude Cragg, Barbara Davey, Dorothy T. Denham, Freda M. Goodbourn, Molly Harrison, Cecily Houseman, Joyce Mallinson, Mary MacLennan, Olive Patrick, Margaret N. Tate, Margaret E. Wall

These 24 students were in the top stream and therefore among the best in the year group, but only 11 of them went into the Sixth Form. Out of a year group of 86 students in 1943-44, 26 entered the Lower Sixth at the start of the school year 1944-45. This represented 30% of the year group but was higher than the average in earlier years. The following table shows numbers in the Lower Sixth and Upper Sixth at the start of each school year during the War.

	Lower Sixth			Upper Sixth			Total		
	M	F	T	M	F	T	M	F	T
1939-1940	7	7	14	6	3	9	13	10	23
1940-1941	10	7	17	3	0	3	13	7	20
1941-1942	9	8	17	3	3	6	12	11	23
1942-1943	9	10	19	4	2	6	13	12	25
1943-1944	10	6	16	6	4	10	16	10	26
1944-1945	14	12	26	6	4	10	20	16	35

Numbers in the Lower Sixth were small, but there was also a significant drop out over the year, leading to much smaller numbers in the Upper Sixth. The following table compares Sixth Form numbers with the numbers in the Upper Fifths in the relevant intake years. The Upper Sixth percentage was actually smaller than that indicated because in each year group there would be a few students who stayed on for a third year in the Sixth Form.

Year Upper Fifth students		Lower Sixth students		% of Lower Sixth students from Upper Fifth Intake		Upper Sixth Students		% of Upper Sixth students from Upper Fifth intake	
1938-39	58	1939-40	14	1939-40	24.1	1940-41	3	1940-41	5.2
1939-40	74	1940-41	17	1940-41	23.0	1941-42	6	1941-42	8.1
1940-41	71	1941-42	17	1941-42	23.9	1942-43	6	1942-43	8.5
1941-42	79	1942-43	19	1942-43	24.1	1943-44	10	1943-44	12.7
1942-43	62	1943-44	16	1943-44	25.8	1944-45	10	1944-45	16.1
1943-44	86	1944-45	26	1944-45	30.2	1945-46	15	1945-46	17.4

These small numbers made it difficult to provide a broad curriculum in the Sixth Form, and larger teaching groups below the Sixth Form would subsidize the teaching resources used in the Sixth Form. In the school year 1944-1945, 90 teaching periods were devoted to the curriculum for the 36 students in the Sixth form. Religious Instruction, taught by Mr Wilde, the Headmaster, and Gym/Games were taught to all students. Most students took 3 subjects to Higher School Certificate level, plus a subject offered at Subsidiary Level. Two Subsidiary subjects would be taken if only two Higher subjects were followed. In the Lower Sixth, Michael Longfield took Higher Geography, Chemistry and Physics, plus Subsidiary Mathematics; Joyce Mallinson took Higher Geography and Biology, plus Subsidiary Chemistry and Domestic Science.

Subjects provided at Higher Certificate level were English, History, French, Geography, Mathematics, Chemistry, Physics and Biology. Usually Upper Sixth and Lower Sixth were taught together, but where numbers were sufficient – English, French, and Mathematics – they were taught as separate groups. Subsidiary subjects provided in 1944-45 included German, Latin, History, Geography, Chemistry, Biology, Mathematics, Mechanical Instruction, Domestic Science and Art. Where possible students were taught in the same group as '*Higher*' students. Some students took the opportunity to broaden their curriculum by taking Subsidiary practical or aesthetic subjects such as Art or Mechanical Instruction.

The number of students who ended up taking the Higher School Certificate was small and the number who obtained the Full Certificate was smaller still. The table below shows entry and passes during the years 1939-1945:

	1939	1940	1941	1942	1943	1944	1945
Entry	9	7	3	6	5	9	8
Pass	8	6	2	4	4	5	6
% Pass	88.9	85.7	66.7	66.7	80.0	55.6	75.0

Michael Longfield and Joyce Mallinson left Prince Henry's in July 1946. Michael passed his Higher School Certificate, Joyce did not – though she did pass her Subsidiary Domestic Science course, captained the school Hockey and Tennis teams, and was the winner of the Mainprize Cup as Girls' Champion in the 1946 Athletics Sports Day competition. Michael's leaving destination was 'H.M. Forces', Joyce went to Training College to study 'domestic subjects.'

Classrooms were segregated, boys on the left and girls on the right. Indeed, everything was segregated; boys and girls came in via different entrances, they had separate playgrounds and had separate sittings for school dinners. Staff would organise classes alphabetically so boys with surnames beginning with S to Z had a reasonable chance of sitting next to girls with surnames A to E, but everyone else would be sitting next to someone of the same sex. Even the special buses were split – boys upstairs and girls down.

Girls were usually addressed by their first name, boys by their surname. Lessons were formal, but some of the staff were less rigid than others and displayed a sense of humour, which enabled an easier atmosphere to prevail. Some subjects were, of course, taught to single sex groups – Physical Education, Domestic subjects and Mechanical Instruction. The 'rules' were relaxed in the Sixth Form where numbers in classes were smaller and boys and girls were taught together to create economic groups.

There were at the time 10 non-specialist classrooms, each of which was designed to house up to 30 pupils. The only specialist classroom was Room 2, which was the Geography room, though Rooms 1 and 3 were reserved for the Preparatory Department. If you were lucky enough to use one of these 10 rooms as a form room you could keep your books in your own desk, and your non-specialist lessons would be based in the form room and you would sit at your own desk. There were more forms than non-specialist rooms and so some forms were based in the various specialist areas for registration and were allocated a locker along one of the corridors in which to keep their books.

Forms with no proper classroom took their lessons in those rooms vacated by their 'owners', who at the time might be taking woodwork, domestic science, science, art or physical education. The bell would signal the end of the lesson and there would be a mass movement between rooms. The younger pupils – especially those in the Preparatory department – and the School Certificate forms, were usually form-room based; that left the third and fourth form pupils as peripatetic. There was a small sixth form teaching room, but on the whole the Sixth Form too would move from room to room, especially because they would be more likely to take 'specialist' subjects. Sixth formers had 'free' periods, supposedly for private study, and took these in the Library, which became in effect a sixth form common room!

Traditional manners were observed. Boys were expected to stand aside and let the girls enter and leave classrooms first. Pupils were expected to give up their seats on service buses to adults. The school uniform identified the Prince Henry's pupils and made it easier to enforce such behavior patterns outside the school. Caps had to be worn, even on school buses and detentions were awarded if the rule was flouted. Any boy being unmannerly to a girl, or misbehaving inappropriately, even outside school, could expect to be reprimanded when he returned to school on the following day.

The Staff 1939-1945

Teaching Staff, Prince Henry's Grammar School, 1954-1955

Mr Barker, German; Mr Gingell, Boys PhyEd.; Mr Harper, Maths.; Mr Smith, Boys Hft.; Mr Bell, Art; Mr Tranah, Music

Mr Denham, Physics; Mr Nealy, Chemistry; Mrs. Wheeler, Dom. Sub.; Miss Greenwood, Maths/Sci.; Miss McMath, History; Miss Bartle, Biology; Miss Wallace, Secretary; Mr Faulkner, French

Miss King, English; Miss Mason, Latin/French; Miss Horsley, Maths/ Phy.; Miss Holloway, Maths.Senior Mistress; Mr Wilde, Headmaster; Mr Pratt, History Senior Master; Mr Leech, English; Mr Padgett, French; Mr Watson, Geography

(missing from the photograph – Miss Storrs: Girls' Physical Education)

Although the above photograph was taken during the school year 1954-55 there are people and features that would be recognized by pupils in attendance at Prince Henry's at the start of the school year 1939-40, the first term after the start of the Second World War.

Staff – excluding HM	Male Full-time	Female Full-time	Male Visiting	Female Visiting	Total
1 Oct 1939	10	10	2	0	22
1 Oct 1940	10	10	2	1	23
1 Oct 1941	9	12	1	0	22
1 Oct 1942	8	13	1	0	22

1 Oct 1943	7	14	1	0	22
1 Oct 1944	8	14	0	0	22
1954-1955	13	9	0	0	22

The total number of staff remained more or less constant over the period of the War and had changed little by 1954-55. The majority of the teaching staff wore gowns, a sign that they were graduates. The exceptions were the staff that taught Art, Boys' Handicrafts, Domestic Subjects and Physical Education; these staff would have had Diplomas rather than degrees. It was normal to take photographs outside the main entrance to the school buildings.

The two significant differences over the period were the fall in the number of male staff and the decline in the number of 'visiting staff'. During the War five male members of staff temporarily left the school to join the armed forces:

- ✓ May 1940: Mr Nield was temporarily replaced by Mr Chapman, who in turn left to join the forces in October 1941 and was replaced by Miss Rycroft. Mr Nield died on 1 January 1941, the first fatality of the War. Miss Rycroft's post was made permanent from September 1943.

- ✓ Spring 1941: Mr Davison, who taught Mathematics, joined the R.A.F. as an Instructor; he was replaced by Mr Bruce. Mr Davison returned to P.H.G.S. in November 1945.

- ✓ February 1941: Mr Denham joined the R.A.F.V.R. as an Education Officer in Navigation; Miss Horsley took over his teaching of Physics, her role in charge of the Preparatory Department being taken over by Mrs. Tott. Mr Denham returned to P.H.G.S. in September 1945.

- ✓ 1941: Mr Evans joined the R.A.F. as an Instructor. Mr Pratt took over his role as teacher of Boys' Physical Exercises. Mr Evans returned to P.H.G.S. on 10 July 1946. He was 'shared' with King James' School, Knaresborough, - two days per week at Knaresborough and three at Prince Henry's. Shortly after his return the post was made full-time, and, Mr Evans having resigned, the position was filled by Mr Waite.

- ✓ Spring 1943: Mr Watson, Geography teacher, joined the R.A.F. as an Instructor. He was replaced by Miss Clark. He returned to P.H.G.S. in the middle of February 1945.

Ex-pupils had their 'favourites' among the staff, but most agree that the education they received from '*those ladies and elderly gentlemen*' was first class and stood them in good stead for later life.

'Visiting' staff were shared with other schools and taught at each of the schools for an agreed portion of the week. In some cases they were members of a 'pool' of staff employed by the West Riding County Council. The most common subjects offered were Music, Domestic Subjects and Boys'/Girls' Physical Exercise; these were subjects that were not taught for a sufficient proportion of the week to merit a full-time, permanent member of staff. By the end of the War these part-time teachers had largely been replaced by full-time staff. The first full-time teacher of Music at Prince Henry's was Frederick Fowler, appointed in June 1944. He replaced Mr Gledhill.

As noted above, the return of Mr Evans after the War prompted the Governors to consider *'that a full time appointment at this School is justified'*, and gave the necessary six months notice to terminate the agreement for the joint appointment with Knaresborough. Mr Evans resigned before the new appointment was made, and Mr K.E. Waite became the school's first full time teacher of Boys' Physical Education.

Boys were taught woodwork-metalwork-engineering: girls were taught needlework and domestic subjects. On the boys' side, Mr Lewis had been appointed as a part-time Assistant Master teaching Woodwork, Metalwork and Engineering in November 1927. The post was made full-time from 1 September 1930. The creation of a full-time post in Domestic Subjects came later, possibly because of the need to employ separate specialists in Needlework and Domestic Subjects. Miss Kershaw was appointed to Prince Henry's on 1 March 1940, to take charge of the teaching of Domestic Subjects.

The reason for the consistency in the number of teaching staff was, of course, the fact that over the period the number of pupils each year remained reasonably similar. In 17 of the 22 years listed in the following table, the number of pupils was between 430 and 470. Only in the years 1958-1960 did the numbers rise beyond 470; though there was then a significant rise in numbers, the total going beyond 500 for the first time in 1960. In most of the years shown the number of girls exceeded the number of boys. The period from 1945-1950 was one in which boys outnumbered girls, but this coincided with the decision to make Ilkley Grammar School co-educational, rather than boys only.

Year	Boys	Girls	Total	% Boys	% Girls		Year	Boys	Girls	Total	% Boys	% Girls
1939	218	232	450	48.44	51.56		1950	222	212	434	51.15	48.85
1940	219	230	449	48.78	51.22		1951	206	217	423	48.70	51.30
1941	218	247	465	46.88	53.12		1952	212	225	437	48.51	51.49
1942	226	229	455	49.67	60.33		1953	215	231	446	48.21	51.79
1943	223	227	450	49.56	50.44		1954	221	240	461	47.94	52.06
1944	227	228	455	49.89	50.11		1955	223	233	456	48.90	51.10
1945	220	213	433	50.81	49.19		1956	228	237	465	49.03	50.97
1946	219	215	434	50.46	49.54		1957	226	233	459	49.24	50.76
1947	212	205	417	50.84	49.16		1958	236	241	477	49.48	50.52
1948	222	216	438	50.68	49.32		1959	244	254	498	49.00	51.00
1949	230	219	449	51.22	48.78		1960	254	270	524	48.47	51.53

Pupils at the school at the start of the War would recognize eight staff on the 1954-55 photograph - Messrs. Wilde (1937-1959), Denham (1920-1960), Leech (1935-1971), Nealy (1921-1964), Padgett (1919-1957), Pratt (1918-1959), Watson (1930-1968), and Miss Horsley (1927-1963). These members of staff were at Prince Henry's for the majority of their working life, in some cases this was the only school at which they taught. Their aggregate teaching life at Prince Henry's was 294 years.

Form S73, a statistical return to the West Riding Education Department dated 1 October 1939, lists the following staff:

Name	Position	Subjects Taught	Teaching hrs. per week	Free Periods Per week
John Wilde	Head Master	French: Religious Instruction	5hr 35min	-
Winifred M. Handford	Senior Mistress	Mathematics, Religious Instruction	19hr 5min	6
Marjorie Bowden	Form Mistress	French, German	20hr 35min	4
Margaret Brockbank	Form Mistress	Latin, English, French	19hr 55min	5
Norah Foster	Form Mistress	English	20hr 25min	4
Miranda Harling	Form Mistress	Domestic Subjects	19hr 45min	5
Martha L. Hodd	Form Mistress	History	19hr 55min	5
Marjorie A Horsley	Form Mistress	Junior School:- English, Arithmetic, Geography, Nature Study, Music. Upper School:- Gen. Sci.	19hr 15min	6
Mrs. Russell Jones (nee Miss G. Whitehead)	Form Mistress	Gymnastics, Games, English	18hr 45min	7
Joan L. Maltby	Form Mistress	Art	19hr 50min	5
Catherine D. Seaton	Form Mistress	Biology, Nature Study	19hr 45min	5
Eric Davison	Form Master	Mathematics, Games	19hr 55min	5
Basil M. Denham	Form Master	Physics, Games	20hr 25min	4
Alfred J. Leech	Form Master	English	20hr 40min	4
William A. Lewis	Form Master	Woodwork, Metalwork	19hr 45min	5
David Nealy	Form Master	Chemistry	20hr 35min	4
George A. Nield	Form Master	French, English, Music, Games	20hr 30min	4
Wilfred W. Padgett	Form Master	French	20hr 35min	4
Richard Pratt	Form Master	History, Geography, Religious Instruction	20hr 30min	4
William S. Shaw	Form Master	Mathematics	20hr 35min	4
John H. Watson	Form Master	Geography	20hr 30min	4

Haydn Evans	Part Time	Gymnastics, Games	9hr 10min	-
Harry Gledhill	Part Time	Music	9hr 10min	-
Grace I. Halmshaw	Part Time	Domestic Subjects	4hr 35min	-

Mr G.W. Tinkler (Mathematics) was a temporary replacement for Mr Shaw.

The teaching staff at the start of the first term after the War was made up of:

Name	Position	Subjects Taught	Teaching hrs. per week	Free Periods Per week
John Wilde*	Head Master	French: Religious Instruction	8hr 0min	-
Winifred M. Hand-ford*	Senior Mistress	Mathematics, Religious Instruction, Needlework	16hr 40min	10
Richard Pratt*	Senior Master	History, Geography, Religious Instruction, Gymnastics, Games	18hr 40min	7
Marjorie Bowden*	Form Mistress	French, German	20hr 0min	5
Marjorie Brennand	Assistant Mis-tress	History, Geography, Science	19hr 20min	6
Freda Bushell	Form Mistress	Mathematics	19hr 20min	6
Nancy Dixon	Form Mistress	Gymnastics, Games, English	19hr 20min	6
Martha L. Hodd*	Assistant Mis-tress	History, Religious Instruction	18hr 40min	7
Marjorie A. Horsley*	Form Mistress	Mathematics, Physics	19hr 20min	6
Kathleen Kershaw	Form Mistress	Domestic Subjects	19hr 20min	6
Kathleen M. Knowles	Form Mistress	English	20hr 0min	5
Margaret Rycroft	Form Mistress	English, French	19hr 20min	6
Catherine D. Seaton*	Form Mistress	Biology, Nature Study	20hr 40min	4
Margaret Smith (nee Brockbank)*	Form Mistress	French, Latin	20hr 0min	5
W. Dyke Carter	Form Master	Art	20hr 40min	4
Basil M. Denham*	Form Master	Physics, Chemistry, Science, Games	20hr 0min	5
Fred Fowler	Form Master	Music, Nature Study, Mathematics	19hr 20min	6
Alfred J. Leech*	Form Master	English	20hr 0min	5
William A. Lewis*	Form Master	Handicraft	20hr 40min	4
David Nealy*	Assistant Master	Chemistry	20hr 0min	5
Wilfred W. Padgett*	Form Master	French	20hr 0min	5

William S. Shaw*	Assistant Master	Mathematics	20hr 0min	5
John H. Watson*	Form Master	Geography	20hr 0min	5

**at Prince Henry's over the duration of the War, including service in armed forces.*

Nicknames – an aside!

Nicknames for teaching staff are not as common as they used to be. They may result from some characteristic of a particular teacher, either physical or behavioural, but often their origin is difficult to explain. Pupils are generally not naïve enough to believe that teachers do not know about their particular nickname, and in some cases staff regard the award of a nickname as a backhanded compliment, showing that paradoxically they have earned some respect from their students. Nicknames remain from one generation of pupils to the next, but it was never sensible to refer to a teacher's nickname in his or her hearing. Nicknames of some of the above staff were:

'Johnnie' Wilde: 'Pecker' Pratt (because of his nose!): 'Ma' Bushell: 'Hoppy' Denham:

'Griz' Horsley (Grizelda): 'Slug' Leech: 'Lulu' Lewis: 'Jazz' Nealy: 'Pop' Padgett:

'Daddy' Watson, and in later years – 'Slinger' Faulkner; 'Granny' Mason: 'Lex' Barker

'Chick' Waite and 'Basher' Smith.

Although each member of the teaching staff had a main subject, they taught other subjects as well, particularly during the War; for example Mr Wilde taught Religious Education, French and some Geography. The major staffing of each subject from 1939-1946 is summarised below:

English	Mr Leech taught English from September 1935 until December 1970. Miss Foster taught English from September 1924 until May 1943, when she applied for leave of absence for one year to care for her parents. She was replaced by Miss Dennis from September 1943 until the end of the Summer Term, 1944, and then by Miss Knowles. Miss Foster did not return and resigned at the end of the Summer Term 1945. Miss Knowles continued to cover for Miss Foster until she left in Summer 1946. Miss Rycroft taught English and French as replacement for Mr Chapman. (see Modern Languages). She left at the end of the Summer Term 1947.

Mathematics	Miss Handford taught Mathematics for the duration of the War, and also taught some Physics following Mr Denham's transfer to the R.A.F. Mr Shaw was also at P.H.G.S. for the duration of the War apart from September 1939 to early October 1939 when he was absent through illness and replaced by Mr Tinkler. Mr Davison joined the Forces in Spring 1941 and was replaced until November 1944 by Mr Bruce. Mrs. Bushell replaced Mr Bruce/Davison from April 1945. She left in November 1945 on the return of Mr Davison. Mrs. Leech, who also taught junior English and History, covered the gap from December 1944 to March 1945.
Modern Languages	Mr Padgett (French) and Miss Bowden (French/German) were at school for the whole of the War. Mr Nield (French & English) left in April 1940 to join HM Forces and was replaced by Mr Chapman (French/German), who in turn was replaced by Miss Rycroft in October 1941 when he too joined the Forces. Mr Nield died on 1 January 1941.
Latin	Miss Brockbank (later Mrs. Smith) came to P.H.G.S. to teach Latin in January 1939. She was absent with illness from September 1941 until 30 June 1942 when she was replaced by Miss Vero. Miss Brockbank returned at the start of the Autumn Term 1942, and eventually left in December 1945, being replaced by Miss Alice Mason.
Biology	Miss Seaton taught Biology from September 1927 until the end of the Summer Term 1946.
Chemistry	Taught by Mr Nealy for the whole of the War.
Physics	Mr Denham taught Physics from September 1920 until he joined the Forces in February 1941. Miss Horsley took over most of the teaching of Physics, together with Miss Handford, until Mr Denham returned in September 1945. Miss Horsley's running of the Preparatory Department was taken over by Mrs. Tott.
Geography	Mr Watson taught Geography until March 1943 when he joined the R.A.F. and was replaced by Miss Clark. Mr Watson in turn replaced her when he returned in February 1945.
History	Miss Hodd was appointed in September 1936 as Senior History Mistress and Librarian, she was at P.H.G.S. for the duration of the War. Mr Pratt taught History until he took over Boys' Physical Education from Mr Evans when Mr Evans joined the R.A.F. Miss Button (Geography, Junior English, History and Scripture) taught History from September 1941, but left at the end of the Summer Term 1942 and was replaced by Miss Brennand from September 1942. Miss Brennand remained at school for the remainder of the War.
Art	Miss Maltby taught Art from January 1939 until February 1942 when she was replaced by Miss Southwell. She left at the end of December 1944 and was replaced by Mr Carter.

Music	Mr Gledhill was 'visiting' Music master from July 1937 until April 1944 when the post became full-time and was taken by Mr Fowler, who remained at Prince Henry's until Easter 1947.
Boys' Handicrafts	Mr Lewis taught Boys Handicraft subjects from November 1927 until his retirement in December 1947.
Domestic Subjects	Miss Harling left in October 1939 and was replaced by Miss Morris until February 1940 when Miss Kershaw in turn replaced her. Miss Kershaw, who was also involved with the management of school dinners, left at Easter 1946. Part-time 'shared' staff were employed to teach Needlework and Dressmaking; Miss Halmshaw from April 1939 until July 1940, and Miss Wrigley from September 1940 until July 1941. Both these ladies also worked jointly with Keighley Girls' Grammar School.
Physical Education (Boys)	Mr Evans was 'shared' with Knaresborough Grammar School until he joined the R.A.F. in 1941. Mr Pratt took Boys' Physical Education and Games until Mr Evans returned at the end of the Summer Term, 1946. The post remained a shared one, but the Governors decided to make it full-time, though Mr Evans did not take the job, which went to Mr Waite.
Physical Education (Girls)	Miss Whitehead taught Girls' Physical Education and English until October 1939, when Mrs. Storey took over until December 1939, pending the arrival of Miss Dixon, who was at school until the end of the Summer Term 1946. Mrs. Storey was part of the pool of West Riding staff covering Physical Education, and also did general form work in the lower school.
Preparatory Department	Miss Horsley managed the Preparatory Department from September 1927 until April 1941. She covered for Mr Denham, who joined the R.A.F., and taught Physics until Mr Denham returned in September 1945. The running of the Preparatory Department was allocated to Mrs. Tott from 23 April 1941 until 31 August 1945. The 1944 Education Act abolished Preparatory Departments in state secondary schools.

MISS MARJORIE BOWDEN

Miss Bowden was born on 1 August 1905 and was educated at Eccles Secondary School (1915-1924), and the Victoria University of Manchester (1924-1928), from where she was awarded a B.A. Honours degree in French (Class II Division II) in 1927. She obtained a Teachers' Diploma from Manchester University in 1928 and took up her first teaching post at Prince Henry's in September of that year. She was appointed as a probationary Assistant Mistress to teach French; the job was made *'definitive'* from September 1929.

Her main contribution outside the classroom was her organisation and support for swimming, and life saving. The open-air pool in Wharfemeadows Park was not ideal as a venue, but year after year many pupils were rewarded for their persistence with Royal Life Saving Society Awards at a range of levels. In 1936 she presented a cup for the

Boys' Swimming Championship. She also participated in many trips and visits, especially the Easter, Belgium expeditions.

Miss Bowden resigned at the end of the Summer Term 1949, and was replaced by Mrs. Womersley. She moved to the Lake District and opened a guesthouse near Ambleside.

MISS MARJORIE BRENNAND

Miss Brennand was born on 25 March 1909. Her father, Edwin Brennand (1883-1965) was a farmer; her mother Henrietta Brennand (née Holmes) was born in Grassington in 1883. In 1911 the family was living at Linton Falls, Linton, near Skipton. She was educated at Skipton Girls' High School (1920-1928) and the University of Leeds (1928-1932). She was awarded a B.A. Class II Honours degree in History in 1931 and a Diploma in Education in 1932.

She taught at Castle Donnington Modern School (1932-1938) and Barnsley Central School (1938-1942) before being appointed to Prince Henry's in a temporary, full-time post in September 1942 as replacement for Miss Button, teaching History and English. She left at the end of the Summer Term, 1946 to take up an appointment at Brougham Street Modern School, Skipton. She returned to Prince Henry's in November 1947 as a replacement for Miss Bower who had been appointed in September 1947 but had been unable to continue in the post because of illness.

Miss Brennand contributed much to out-of-school activities; she gave lectures to School Societies and took pupils out on excursions. She gave much time to the creation of costumes for school dramatic productions. She was also responsible for the Fiction Library. She left at the end of the Summer Term 1955 to become Senior Mistress, Upper Wharfedale Secondary School at Grassington. She died at Raikeswood Hospital, Skipton on 30 December 1958.

MISS MARGARET BROCKBANK (MRS. T SMITH)

Miss Brockbank was born on 26 March 1914 and was educated at Prince Henry's Grammar School, Otley (1925-1932) and at Leeds University (1932-1936). In 1911, her father, Fred Brockbank was listed in the Census as an Elementary School Teacher. He married Jane Ann Smith in 1910 and they were living at 53, Leeds Rd., Otley. Whilst still at School, in 1931, Margaret was awarded the French Travelling Scholarship. She was Secretary and Treasurer of the Literary and Historical Society, played hockey and tennis and was a Prefect.

She graduated in 1935 with a B.A. Double Honours degree in Latin and French (Class II). As part of her University course she spent the year 1933-1934 at the University of Bordeaux. From 1935-36 she trained as a teacher, also at Leeds University, and was awarded a Teaching Diploma in 1936.

She was employed as a temporary Assistant Mistress at Prince Henry's, - the first ex-pupil to join the Staff - following the death of Mr Robinson, from January 1937 to August 1937. She taught at New Mills County Secondary School, Derbyshire from January 1938 to December 1938, before returning to Prince Henry's as Assistant Latin Mistress in January 1939.

She was absent because of illness during 1941-1942, her place being taken temporarily by Miss M. Vero, but returned at the start of the Autumn Term 1942. She married Tom Smith in Otley in 1944, but did not leave until 31 December 1945 to set up home, her husband having been released from H.M. Forces.

ALBERT EZRA BRUCE

Mr Bruce was born on 3 September 1891 and educated at Heckmondwike Grammar School (1903-1909) and Manchester University (1909-1913), where he was awarded a B.Sc. Honours degree in Mathematics and subsidiary Physics in 1913. From 1915-1919 he served in the Army as a Signaller in the Duke of Wellington's Regiment. In the 1901 Census he was living at Nettleton Road, Mirfield, Dewsbury with his father, Ezra (1868-1909), his mother Sarah (1867-1931) and 6 brothers and sisters. His father was a Woollen Blanket Manufacturer who had married Sarah Mitchell in 1887 in Dewsbury. By 1911, Sarah was widowed and was living with her family in Marsh, Huddersfield. Two more daughters had been born, making a total of nine children. Albert is listed as a Scholar; most of his brothers and sisters were working and must have helped to support Albert in his education. Albert married Doris Langfield at Lindley St. Stephen Parish Church on 31 March 1923. They had one daughter, Betty (1924-1964).

He had a wide range of teaching jobs, including senior mathematics master at Whitcliffe Mount, Cleckheaton (1921-1934) and Hornsea Grammar School (1934-1940). He was appointed to Prince Henry's in March 1941 as a temporary replacement for Mr Davison, who had joined the R.A.F.

In November 1944 he left to take up a teaching appointment at Adwick-le-Street Grammar School and the Governors agreed to release him early from his contract. Mrs. R. Leech replaced him on a temporary basis. He returned from 6 January 1954 to 2 March 1954 to cover for Miss Horsley who was absent through illness. He died in 1978, age 87, his death being registered in Ipswich, Suffolk.

MRS. FREDA BUSHELL

Miss Freda Wilson was born in Colne, Lancashire, on 23 March 1910. Her father Walter Wilson was a power loom overlooker and in 1911 the family lived at 4 Gill St., Colne. Freda was educated at Colne Grammar School, Lancashire (1920-1928) and Durham University (1928-1932) from where she was awarded a B.A. Pass degree in Mathematics, with subsidiary Geography and English, in 1931, and a Diploma in the Theory and Practice of Teaching in 1932. She married Herbert H. Bushell in Colne in 1939.

Before coming to Prince Henry's in April 1945 she had jobs at Lowestoft Central School (1933-1935), Beckenham County High School for Girls (September 1935 to December

1935), Stourbridge County High School for Girls (January 1936 – December 1939), and Keighley Boys Grammar School (September 1940 – April 1945).

The post at Prince Henry's was a temporary one to teach Mathematics as cover for Mr Davison who was on War Service, whose post had been covered firstly by Mr Bruce and later by Mrs. Leech. She left at the end of November, 1945, to take up a post at the County High School, Oldbury, but returned in May 1946 for another temporary appointment, again replacing Mr Davison who had become Headmaster of Easingwold Grammar School. The post was made permanent from 1 April 1949.

Mrs. Bushell remained at Prince Henry's until December 31 1951. She re-married Percival J Morgan in Nelson in 1951. Freda Morgan died in 1985, her death being registered in Blackpool and Fylde.

MISS VIOLET MAUD BUTTON

Miss Button was born on 7 October 1918 and educated at Kirby Secondary School, Middlesbrough (1930-1937) and Leeds University (1937-1941). She was awarded a B.A. Class II Honours degree in 1940 and a Diploma in Education in 1941. She joined the staff at Prince Henry's in a temporary full-time capacity in September 1941 to teach Geography and some Junior History, English and Scripture.

She left at the end of the Summer Term 1942 to take up the post of Senior Geography Mistress in the Middlesbrough High School for Girls. Her place was taken by Miss Marjorie Brennand.

WALTER DYKE CARTER

Walter Dyke Carter was born on 21 January 1894 in Horwich, near Bolton, Lancashire. His father, Henry Carter (1857-1942), married Lydia Wainwright in 1880, the marriage being registered in Leicester. In the 1901 Census the family was living at 14 Church St., Horwich, and Henry was listed as a Grocer and Draper. Walter was the seventh of ten children, eight sons and two daughters. By 1911 the family had moved to Gorton Cottage, Lee Lane, Horwich and Henry was described as a House Furnisher.

Walter was educated at Rivington & Blackrod Grammar School (1907-1910), Bolton Municipal School of Art (1910-1912), Manchester Municipal School of Art (1912 – 1914/1915) and the Royal College of Art, South Kensington (1915-1916) & (1919-1923), where his time was interrupted because of his service in the First World War. He was awarded a full Associateship of the Royal College of Art in 1921 (A.R.C.A.) and a Board of Education Pedagogy Certificate in 1923.

His first teaching post was at Sheerness Technical Institute (1923-1925). He then spent 15 years at the Gravesend School of Arts and Crafts (1925-1940) and short periods at Bury High School and Lancaster Royal Grammar School, before taking over as Head of Art at Prince Henry's in February 1945.

One of his first tasks was to design the cover for the Victory edition of the School

Magazine. His letter of application for the post at Prince Henry's promised that *'we shall run our own Art or Sketch Club in the School.'* True to his word the Sketch Club was set up and met regularly each week after school.

Mr Carter left Prince Henry's at the end of the Summer Term, 1954, and was replaced by Mr Bell. He died on 7 September 1963.

GEORGE CHAPMAN

Mr Chapman was born on 17 July 1906 and educated at Manchester Grammar School (1918-1923) and Manchester University (1923-1926). He was awarded a B.A. in French and German in 1926. He was a student at Berlin University (October 1927 to May 1928) and at the Lycee de Bayonne, France (October 1935 to July 1936). He was awarded the Diplome d'Etudes Francais (Higher) in July 1936. He had a number of jobs from 1929, when he spent a year at Chesterfield Grammar School to 1937-1940 when he worked part-time at two schools in Bury.

He came to Prince Henry's, to teach French and German in May 1940, as a temporary replacement for Mr Nield who had joined H.M. Forces. His application for the appointment at Prince Henry's noted that *'In all my posts I have given active help with the games and am very good at association football, cricket and swimming.'*

In October 1941 he joined His Majesty's Forces and was replaced by Miss M. Rycroft. He died in 1979, his death being registered in Trafford.

MISS NELLIE CLARK

Miss Clark was born on 15 December 1920 and educated at Barrow Girls' Grammar School (1932-1939) and Manchester University (1939-1943). She was awarded a B.A. Class Iii Honours degree in Geography in 1942 and a Diploma in Education in 1943.

At Barrow she was, for four years, a member of the 1st XI Hockey team. At Manchester University she was Secretary and later President of the Geographical Society, Secretary of the Education Society and played hockey for the 'A' team.

Her first teaching post was at Prince Henry's as a replacement for Mr Watson who joined the R.A.F. in March 1943. She left in December 1944 and obtained a teaching post in Manchester.

ERIC DAVISON

Eric Davison was born on 8 August 1906 in Yeadon and was educated at Yeadon & Guiseley Secondary School (1919-1925) and Leeds University (1925-1929). He was awarded a First Class Honours B.Sc. degree in Mathematics in 1928 and a Diploma in Education in 1929. His first teaching post was at Prince Henry's where he was appointed as a probationary teacher of Mathematics and Physics starting in September 1929. The post was made *'definitive'* in September 1930.

At Secondary School he had been Head Prefect, Captain of the Cricket XI and Vice-Captain of the Football XI. At University he was Cricket Secretary and Vice-Captain, and Treasurer of the Education Society. He also played cricket for Guiseley C.C.

In Summer 1933 Mr Davison received a gift of a cut-glass electric lamp to celebrate his marriage to Miss Kathleen Burke of Yeadon. They were married at St. Andrew's Church, Yeadon on 24 April 1933.

At the start of the Summer Term 1936 a Boxing Club was founded and throughout its life was supported by Mr Davison and Mr Evans.

In Spring 1941 Mr Davison and Mr Denham accepted commissions with the R.A.F. as Instructors and left within a few weeks of each other, halfway through the term. Mr Davison was replaced by Mr A.E. Bruce.

Mr Davison returned to Prince Henry's in November 1945. At the end of the Summer Term, 1946, he resigned to take up the position as Headmaster of Easingwold Grammar School. In 1951 he became Headmaster at Alcester Grammar School, Warwickshire, where he remained until his retirement in 1970. Eric Davison died in January 1983, his death being registered in Stratford on Avon.

BASIL MARMADUKE DENHAM

Basil Denham was born on 6 September 1895 in Wolverhampton, where his father Henry Denham was a Cashier in a Chemical Works. By the time of the 1911 Census the family had moved to Spencer Place, Leeds where his father was a Commercial Traveller for a polish manufacturer. Basil was educated at City of Leeds Central High School (1908-1914) and Leeds University (1914-1915 & 1919-1920), where his time was disrupted by the First World War. His war service, 1916-1919, was spent in Northern France as an Air Mechanic I and Observer Cadet. (Service No. 211869)

He had been awarded an Intermediate B.Sc. in Physics, Mathematics and Geology from Leeds University in 1915, and on his return attained his full B.Sc. in Physics in 1920, and the Board of Education Teachers' Certificate in the same year. He was awarded a M.Sc. of Leeds University in 1926 and a Biology Teachers' Diploma in 1935. He was appointed as a probationary teacher to Prince Henry's in September 1920 to teach Physics and Mathematics, and the position was made '*definitive*' in September 1921.

He married in 1927 and received gifts subscribed for by staff and pupils. From 1930-1935 he did some part-time work in the Electrical Engineering Department of the Leeds College of Technology.

He was a founding member of the Natural Science Society and helped in the production of dramatic performances, especially with regard to stage lighting.

On 28 February 1941 Mr Denham joined the R.A.F.V.R. as an Education Officer – Instructor in Navigation and was commissioned as a Flight Lieutenant. During his absence Miss Horsley temporarily took over the teaching of Physics throughout the

School. Mr Denham returned to Prince Henry's in September 1945.

In 1959 Mr Denham was elected to a seat on Otley Urban District Council. He retired from Prince Henry's at the end of the Summer Term, 1960, and was replaced as Head of Physics by Mr D. W. Frost. He noted in his retirement letter that he would be available for supply if *'unexpected staffing difficulties arise'*, and in 1964 he returned briefly during the absence of Mr Frost.

To mark the occasion of Mr Denham's retirement, separate presentations were made to him on behalf of the Headmaster and the Staff, and on behalf of the members of the School. Mr Denham died in 1972.

MISS IRIS JOAN DENNIS

Miss Dennis was born on 19 June 1919 in Leicestershire, and educated at Wyggeston Grammar School for Girls (1928-1937), De Montfort Secretarial College (1937-1938) and University College, Leicester (1939-1943), where she was President of the Debating Society. She was awarded a B.A. First Class Honours degree in English, with subsidiary French, in 1942.

She came to Prince Henry's in September 1943 as temporary cover for Miss Foster. She left at the end of the Summer Term, 1944 to join the staff at Bingley Technical College. Also in 1944 she married Maurice O. Kenny, the marriage being registered in Leicester. She died in 1988, her death being registered in Hull, Yorkshire.

MISS NANCY DIXON

Miss Dixon was born on 15 March 1913 and was educated at Wakefield Girls' High School (1919-1931) and the Anstey Physical Training College (1931-1934) from where she was awarded an Anstey College Diploma in 1934. She worked at Carlisle and County High School in the Summer Term, 1935 and at Alderman Wood Secondary School, Consett (1935-1939), before coming to Prince Henry's in January 1940 to take charge of Girls' Physical Training and Games, and to also teach some Junior English.

She left at the end of the Summer Term in 1946, to marry Cyril Crowther, and was replaced for one term by Miss Addy until the arrival of Miss Fawcett. She died in 2004, her death being registered in Leeds.

HAYDN EVANS

Mr Evans was born on 3 May 1913 and was educated at Port Talbot County School (1926-1932) and the Svend Holtze college of Physical Education, Denmark (1932-1933) from where he was awarded a Diploma in Physical Education in 1933.

His first teaching post was at the County School, Kingsbury, London (September 1933 – October 1934). He was appointed as a part-time Assistant Master, starting on 20 October 1934, in charge of boys' Physical Exercises. The appointment was held under the West Riding County Authority, which means that he was part of a pool of P.E. staff that was employed at several schools during the week. He succeeded Mr J. P. Walker.

He organised the School Athletics Sports and school games. He also joined with Mr Davison in the formation of a School Boxing Club. At the end of the Summer Term 1936, he was presented with a gift from the School on the occasion of his marriage. In 1941 he joined the R.A.F. as an Instructor.

Additional pupil numbers led the Governors to ask that he be made full-time on his return.

The County Authority replied that when Mr Evans arrived back on 10 July 1946, his time should be allocated as 2 days a week at Knaresborough, King James' Grammar School and 3 days a week at Prince Henry's. The Governors responded by giving six months notice to terminate the Agreement for this Joint Appointment in order to create a full-time position. Before this could come about Mr Evans resigned and was replaced by Mr K.E. Waite who was appointed to the post of full-time Physical Training and Games Master to commence as soon as possible. Haydn Evans died, age 71, in 1985.

MISS NORAH FOSTER

Miss Foster was born on 26 November 1901 in Bingley, Yorkshire. In the 1911 Census she was living at 3 Chestnut St., Crossflats, Bingley with her father, Willie Foster, listed as an Insurance Agent, and her mother Julia.

Norah was educated at Bingley Girls' Grammar School (1912-1920), where she was Head Girl, and Manchester University (1920-1924). She was awarded a Class II B.A. Honours degree in English in 1923 and a Manchester University Education Department Teachers' Diploma in 1924. She had two short-term temporary jobs at Ossett Grammar School (English: 4 May - 22 May 1925) and Selby Girls' High School (History and English: 1 June – 31 July 1925), before being appointed to Prince Henry's as a temporary English Mistress in January 1925. She left in March 1925, but was re-appointed in September 1925 as a full-time English Mistress.

She organised the Arts Society and gave up much of her leisure time in helping to produce many of the dramatic productions put on in School.

In May 1943 she applied for leave of absence without salary for one year to look after her ailing parents. She was temporarily replaced by Miss I. J. Dennis, who was at Prince Henry's for the whole of the 1943-1944 school year. Miss Foster was unable to return and applied for further leave of absence in April 1944, which was granted without salary for the remainder of the War. The Governors agreed to advertise for a replacement for Miss Dennis, and appointed Miss K. M. Knowles. The crisis at home continued, and Miss Foster resigned at the end of the Summer Term 1945. Norah Foster died in 1975, her death being registered in Bradford.

FRED FOWLER

Mr Fowler was born on 10 February 1906 in Skipton. His father, George Edward Fowler

(1873-1950) was listed in the 1911 Census as a Drawer in a Cotton Mill. George married Ada Parsons in Skipton in 1903. By 1911 the family, including Fred and his brother George (born 1909) were living at 18 Union St., Skipton. In 1933 Fred married Elizabeth Anderson (1908-1997) at Christ Church, Skipton. They had two children, John (born 1935) and Robert (born 1939).

Fred was educated at Skipton Boys' Grammar School (1916-1924) and the City of Leeds Training College (1925-1927). He was awarded a Board of Education Teachers' Certificate in 1927. He also held a Diploma of the Licentiate Trinity College of Music, London (Music Teaching). From 1927-1931 he undertook permanent supply teaching at a number of Leeds' schools, but was the permanent full-time Music Master at Silsden Modern School from 1931-1944.

He became the first full-time Music Master at Prince Henry's when he took over from part-time staff in June 1944. His letter of application drew attention to the fact that the School Choir at Silsden had won the Wharfedale Music Festival, and that his choir had broadcast on B.B.C. Children's Hour. He suggested that *'the music at Silsden Modern School has achieved a certain degree of renown throughout the country and, if I am successful in this application, it would be my desire to make the subject as successful and enjoyable a part of School-life as I could.'*

At the end of the Spring Term 1947, Mr Fowler left for a temporary post as Lecturer in Music at the Stanley Emergency Training College, Wakefield, just opened by the West Riding Education Authority. He was replaced temporarily from 14 April 1947 by Mr L.A. Walsh, who left in June 1947 for a post at Bradford Grammar School. Mrs. Pratt filled in for the rest of the Summer Term, before a further temporary appointment was made in September 1947 when Mr C.R. Faulkner was appointed, and in the continued absence of Mr Fowler, Mr Faulkner continued in that post, because, although it had been expected that Mr Fowler would return to Prince Henry's, he moved on to Harrogate Training College and eventually accepted another permanent appointment elsewhere. Mr Faulkner took the opportunity to move into the Modern Languages Department when a vacancy arose, and Mr Trannah became Head of Music from 1 September 1951. Fred Fowler died in Doncaster in 1983.

HARRY GLEDHILL

Harry Gledhill was born on 4 November 1901 and educated at Woodhouse School (1904-1913) and Huddersfield Technical College. He was a Licentiate of Trinity College of Music and an Associate of the Royal College of Organists. In July 1937 he was appointed as visiting Music Master at Prince Henry's, having held similar part-time posts at Almondbury Grammar School, Elland Grammar School and Huddersfield College Secondary School for Boys. In 1931 he was also appointed as teacher of vocal music at Dewsbury Technical College.

His testimonial from the Headmaster of Almondbury Grammar School noted that Mr Gledhill produced a Gilbert and Sullivan opera for a week each year and that the Vice

Chancellor of Leeds University on attending a Speech Day at the school said *'the singing of the boys amazed me; it was perfect. I have never heard such singing since I came to Yorkshire and I have visited practically every school in the County.'*

He left Prince Henry's in April 1944 to take up a full-time appointment at King James' Grammar School, Almondbury, and was replaced by Mr F. Fowler – the first full-time appointment of a teacher of Music.

MISS GRACE JOAN HALMSHAW

Miss Halmshaw was born on 3 June 1916 in Dewsbury, and educated at Wheelwright Girls' Grammar School, Dewsbury (1932-1935) and the Gloucestershire Training College of Domestic Science (1935-1938) from where she was awarded a Diploma in Combined Domestic Subjects in 1938. She taught at Keighley Girls' Grammar School from September 1938 and came to Prince Henry's in April 1939 after Mrs. Potts had left. Her principal subjects were Needlework and Dressmaking and the post was part-time, and it is likely that she continued to also work part time at Keighley. She continued to work part-time at Prince Henry's until July 1940. In 1961 she married Stephen C. Andrew, the marriage being registered in Saddleworth. She died in 1996, her death being registered in Ryedale, Yorkshire.

MISS WINIFRED MARION HANDFORD

Miss Handford was born in Bath, Somerset, on 24 September 1888. Her father, Thomas, was a Pharmaceutical Chemist and by 1901 the family had moved to Harrogate. In the 1911 Census, Winifred is listed as a *'Student – Mathematical'*. She was educated at Bradford Girls' Grammar School and Girton College, Cambridge (1909-1911). She was awarded the Cambridge Mathematical Tripos Part I (Class II) in 1909 and Part II (Class II) in 1911. She attended the Cambridge Training College (1911-1912) and was awarded a Teacher's Diploma in 1913. Her first teaching appointment was at Swansea Girls' High School (1912-1913), her second at Leamington Girls' Secondary School (1913-1921). She was appointed Senior Mistress at Prince Henry's in September 1921, teaching mainly mathematics.

In her early days at Prince Henry's Miss Handford took responsibility for the costumes worn in school productions. For many years she lived on Bradford Road, Otley. She retired at the end of the Summer Term 1946, after twenty-five years as Senior Mistress. She was presented with a silver tea set by the Old Otliensians' Association, for which over 200 of her former pupils subscribed. Her successor as Senior Mistress was Miss J. E. Holloway, also a mathematician. Soon after she retired she became ill, and died in Templestowe Nursing Home, Harrogate, on 10 May 1949.

In 1950 the Old Otliensians' Association approved a scheme to present the School with a clock to be placed in the School Library in memory of Miss Handford. The clock was formally presented to the School at the Annual General Meeting of the Old Scholars in September 1950.

MISS MIRANDA HARLING

Miss Harling was born on 8 March 1911 and educated at Accrington Grammar School (1923-1929) and the College of Domestic Economy, Manchester (1929-1932). She was awarded a Certificate in Domestic Subjects in 1931 and a third-year Needlework and Dressmaking Certificate in 1932. Her first teaching post was at Prince Henry's as a probationary full-time Domestic Science Mistress starting in September 1932. The post was made *'definitive'* in September 1933.

She produced the costumes for several of the school dramatic performances, and musical concerts. She left in October 1939 to be married to John E. Parker in Manchester, and was replaced by Miss Morris. Miranda Parker died, age 82, in 1993.

MISS MARTHA LETTICE HODD

Miss Hodd was born on 28 October 1908. Her father, Francis Arnold Hodd (1874-1942) was listed in the 1911 Census as a *'Clergyman, Established Church'*. His wife Elizabeth (1875-1953) (née Elizabeth Reinhold Conrad) was born in Germany. In 1911 the family was living at Woodlee, Bradford Road, Bingley. Both Francis and Elizabeth are buried at St Oswald's Church, Leathley.

Martha was educated at Bingley Grammar School (1914-1927) and St Hilda's College, Oxford University (1927-1930) from where she was awarded a B.A. Honours degree (Class II) in Modern History in 1930. In 1931-32 she attended the Oxford University Teachers' Training Department and was awarded a Diploma in Education in 1931.

Her first teaching post was at Bingley Girls' Grammar School (1931-1934); from there she moved to Bury Girls' Grammar School (1934-1936) before coming to Prince Henry's in September as Senior History Mistress and Librarian. She also taught Junior English. She replaced Miss Sykes. Miss Hodd was the daughter of the Vicar of Menston, who was also the Rural Dean of Otley. A testimonial from Mr Wilde in 1951 notes that *'Miss Hodd was also responsible for some time for the organisation of Religious Instruction in this school and she is singularly well fitted for this.'*

She took a full part in out of school activities, including a visit to the Nansen Pioneer Camp at Long Mynd, Shropshire, in 1939. She left at the end of the Summer Term in 1947, moving to Truro Girls' High School. Miss Hodd died, after a long illness, on 18 May 1961, aged 52. At her own request, her remains were buried in Leathley churchyard, set in the Yorkshire countryside she had loved from childhood.

MISS MARJORIE ANNIE HORSLEY

Miss Marjorie Horsley was born in Halifax on 29 January 1903. In the 1911 Census the family was living on Leicester Terrace, Manor Drive, Halifax. Marjorie was the youngest of four children and her father was employed as Secretary and Manager of a Coal Society. She was educated at Halifax Girls' Secondary School (1914-1921), and at Edge Hill Training College, Liverpool University (1921-1925). She was awarded a B.Sc. Pass degree in Mathematics and Physics in 1924 and a Teachers Diploma in 1925.

Her first teaching appointment was as Assistant Mistress at St Augustine's Girls School, Halifax. (Jan. 1926 – Aug. 1927). In September 1927 she was appointed as a probationary Junior Form Mistress in charge of the Preparatory Department at Prince Henry's; the post was made *'definitive'* from September 1928. She replaced her elder sister, Hilda Jane Horsley, when the elder Miss Horsley retired on her marriage to Richard Pratt.

Miss Horsley also agreed to take over from her sister as Treasurer of the School Savings' Association, a role she continued until 1944.

She organised and helped with a range of out-of-school activities over her time at Prince Henry's:- the Dancing Club, School Concerts, trips to Belgium and the Costa Brava. During the Easter 1939 trip to Belgium she became ill and was replaced for one term by Miss M.H. Thompson M.A. (New Zealand).

Miss Horsley showed her versatility when she took over the teaching of Physics throughout the School when Mr Denham joined the R.A.F. in 1941. Although she was a graduate of Physics and Mathematics, she had been out of touch with the subjects, especially at higher levels. In fact, her results were good and she had no difficulty with discipline when teaching the senior forms.

Her work with the junior forms in the Preparatory Department was taken over by Mrs. L. Tott. The 1944 Education Act effectively ended the provision of a Preparatory Department at Prince Henry's and on the return of Mr Denham, Miss Horsley continued to share in the teaching of physics and later became a full-time teacher of mathematics. She retired from teaching at the end of the Autumn Term, 1963, and was replaced by Mr Stansfield. On retirement she presented a cup for the boys' Tennis Champion. The Old Scholars elected her as one of their Vice-Presidents and she was President of the Old Scholars' Hockey Club. She died in 1987.

MISS KATHLEEN KERSHAW

Miss Kershaw was born on 5 September 1915 and educated at Bradford Girls' Grammar School (1926-1933) and at the National Society's Training College for teachers of Domestic Subjects (1933-1936). She was awarded a London University Teachers' Certificate for Domestic Subjects in 1936. Her first teaching post was at Eastwood Senior Council School, Keighley (August 1936 to February 1940). She was appointed to Prince Henry's on 1 March 1940, to take charge of the teaching of Domestic Subjects.

She left at Easter 1946 to take up a lectureship at the Yorkshire College of Housecraft, Leeds.

Domestic Science teachers were, at this time, expected to take on some responsibility for the provision, administration and organisation of school dinners within the school, and there was a reference in tributes to her that she had performed this role well.

MISS KATHLEEN MARY KNOWLES

Miss Knowles was born on 18 January 1921 and educated at Chatsworth Private School, Boroughbridge (1926-1930), King James' Grammar School, Knaresborough, (1930-1938) and Leeds University (1938-1942). She was awarded a B.A. Class II Honours degree in English in 1941 and a Leeds University Diploma in Education in 1942. Her first teaching post was at Lancaster Girls' Grammar School (1942-1944). She came to Prince Henry's in September 1944 as an Assistant Mistress to teach English, as temporary cover during the continued absence of Miss Foster. The post was made permanent from 1 September 1945 following the resignation of Miss Foster. She was absent because of illness in the Summer Term 1946 and was replaced by Miss Seddon from September 1946.

ALFRED JACK LEECH

Jack Leech was born on 16 May 1909 in Sussex. In the 1911 Census his father, Frank Harold Leech (1881-1946) was listed as a Building Inspector. Frank married Beatrice Farrants Gill (1879-1954) in 1908, and in 1911 the family was living at West Dene, Woodleigh Road, Worthing, Sussex.

He was educated at The County High School for Boys, Worthing (1924-1927), and at Kings College, University of London (1927-1932). He was awarded a B.A. Class II Honours degree in English in 1932. Whilst studying in London he worked at the Alpha Preparatory School, Harrow (Sept. 1927 – March 1931). His first full-time teaching post was at Ackworth School, Yorkshire (Jan. 1933 – July 1935). He was appointed to Prince Henry's as an Assistant Master to teach English in September 1935. He replaced Mr Davenport. Mr Leech continued his studies on a part-time basis, and obtained a Teachers' Diploma of the University of Oxford in 1938 and a M.Ed. from Leeds University in 1941.

In 1935 he married Frances M. Cowley, the marriage being registered in Greenwich. Mrs. Leech also did some part-time teaching at Prince Henry's.

His chief interest out of school was in dramatics, but he had captained the hockey, rugby and cricket teams at Worthing and was Games Master and a House Master at the Alpha Preparatory School in Harrow.

He took over the editing of the School magazine from Mr Nealy in 1935. The first issue for which he was responsible was Vol. XVIII, Lent 1936 and he continued to edit the magazine until he retired in 1970. Each year, Mr Leech appointed an Editorial Committee to assist him, and although he maintained editorial control, the Committee was given an increasing amount of freedom to produce the magazine. In most years after 1939, the Editorial was written by a student.

Mr Leech's other major contribution to out of school life was the production of plays and other dramatic performances; his name appears constantly in the credits from the 1930s to the 1950s with a changing list of co-producers as those who left were replaced

– Miss Foster, Miss Hodd, Miss Brennand, Mr Womersley – and an even larger list of 'helpers' for costumes, make-up and staging.

Although he didn't found the Literary, Historical and Debating Society, he effectively kept a fatherly eye on it through the student Committee. Its title was eventually changed to the Senior Arts Society, but its aims and objectives remained the same. Over the years debates, speakers – staff and students -, events based on popular radio and television programmes, play readings and visits were regular features of the meetings. The Society must have played a significant part in promoting the confidence and maturity of students, especially in interviews for University places. Occasionally, Mr Leech himself took an active role.

From 7 September 1959, Mr Leech was appointed Second Master of the School, in place of Mr Pratt. Mr Leech retired at the end of the Autumn Term, 1970, after thirty-five years at Prince Henry's. The Governors presented him with two volumes of the Shorter English Dictionary on Historical Principles, signed on the flyleaf by all members of the Governing Body. The Old Otliensians presented him with a dictionary of plants, a pair of binoculars and a cheque. He died in 1980.

MRS. FRANCES MARY RUTH LEECH

Mrs. Leech, (née Frances Mary Ruth Cowley), the wife of Mr A. J. Leech, was born on 8 October 1904 in Northamptonshire, and was educated at the County Secondary School, Wolverton, Berks. (1916-1923), Whitelands College, Chelsea (1923-1924) and Kings College, London (1926-1932). She was awarded a Board of Education Teachers' Certificate in 1925, a Diploma in English Literature and Language from London University in 1926 and a B.A. Honours degree in English in 1932.

Her first teaching post was at Red Coat Girls' School, London (1927-1933), followed by a post at St Thomas Collett Senior Girls' School (1933-1935). She married Alfred Jack Leech in 1935, the marriage being registered in Greenwich. She undertook various periods of part-time work at Prince Henry's, starting in November 1944 when she took a temporary position teaching English, together with junior history and mathematics. This post was as a replacement for the appointment of Mr A. E. Bruce to Adwick-le-Street Grammar School. Mr Bruce had, in turn, been the replacement for Mr Davison who had joined the R.A.F. She left in March 1945.

Her second major stint started on 8 January 1958 when Mrs. Leech returned to teach English for two terms, following the resignation of Miss King, who went to teach in Malta. Her replacement, Miss Daly, did not start at Prince Henry's until September 1958. Mrs. Leech was given a Scale I Graded post allowance of £75 on the grounds that she was carrying out the same duties for which the allowance would have been paid if the permanent post had been filled

A further vacancy in the English department occurred in the Summer Term 1959, following the back-word given by Miss Galvin, and once again Mrs. Leech temporarily filled the gap. The re-appointment of Miss King to her previous job meant that Mrs.

Leech was no longer required. Mrs. Leech died in 1995, her death being registered in Canterbury, Kent.

WILLIAM ALEXANDER LEWIS

William Lewis was born on 7 July 1880 in Hunslet, and was educated at Cockburn High School, Leeds (1887-1897), and Leeds Cockburn Technical School (1897-1900). From 1895-1918 he worked in the engineering industry. He was an Assistant Master at Gravesend Junior Technical School (September 1918-November 1927), and whilst there he enhanced his qualifications by attending Summer Schools at Folkestone (1919) and Scarborough (1921-1922). In June 1919 he was proposed and seconded for membership of the U.K. Mechanical Engineering Society.

On 17 April 1911 he married Minnie Redshaw (1883-1961), the marriage being registered in Holbeck. Their daughter, Hilda, was born in 1912. In November 1927 he was appointed to Prince Henry's as a part-time Assistant Master teaching Woodwork, Metalwork and Engineering. The post was made full-time from 1 September 1930.

His major contribution to the outside life of the School came in his assistance with the dramatic productions and the construction and extension of the stage. Each time a production is reviewed in the *'Otliensian'*, Mr Lewis is thanked for giving up *'many hours of his leisure time'* making and erecting scenery and making improvements to the stage. He gave up his Saturday mornings by running the Model Aero Club that was formed just before the outbreak of war and continued throughout the war.

In 1945 the Governors were asked whether they wished to recommend that Mr Lewis be retained after he had reached the age of 65 on 7 July 1945 *'during the present shortage of teachers'*. The Governors agreed to make such a recommendation. Mr Lewis was willing to continue for a further year beyond 30 June 1946, and this was approved by the Ministry of Education. The County Authority suggested that Mr Lewis submit his resignation to take effect from 31 August 1947, but that he be invited to accept a temporary post to commence at the beginning of the Autumn Term, 1947, pending the appointment of a replacement.

Mr Lewis retired in December 1947, after 20 years at Prince Henry's. He was replaced by Mr Ray Smith. Mr Lewis died on 19 April 1956, his death being registered in Scarborough.

MISS JOAN LILLIAN MALTBY

Miss Maltby was born on 6 February 1917 and educated at Lady Manners Secondary School, Bakewell (1928-1934) and the Sheffield College of Arts and Crafts (1934-1938). She was awarded the Board of Education Art Teachers' Diploma in 1938. From September 1938 – November 1938 she did some part-time teaching at Sheffield College of Arts and Crafts before being appointed as a full-time Art teacher at Prince Henry's in January 1939, where she was in charge of Art throughout the School. She replaced Miss Whatley. After 3 years at Prince Henry's Miss Maltby resigned in February 1942 to take up another teaching appointment and was replaced by Miss J Southwell.

MISS MARY MORRIS

Miss Morris was born on 4 September 1924 and was educated at The Bolton School, Bolton (1922-1936) and the Manchester, Municipal College of Domestic Economy (1936-1939). She was awarded a Diploma in combined Domestic Subjects in 1939. Her first teaching post was at Prince Henrys as a temporary Assistant Mistress teaching Domestic Subjects. She was appointed from 1 November 1939 and left on 1 February 1940. She covered the work of Miss Harling until the arrival of Miss Kershaw as full-time Domestic Subjects teacher.

DAVID NEALY

Mr. D. Nealy

David Nealy was born on 1 February 1900 in Broughton, Cumberland where his father, Tom, was a coalminer and mine contractor. By 1911 the family had moved to Linefoot Farm, Dearham, nr. Maryport and Tom was listed in the Census returns as a farmer. Tom Nealy (1865-1917) married Rachel Stephenson (1870-1934) in 1899, the marriage being registered in Cockermouth.

David was educated at Workington County Secondary School (1913-1917) and the University of Liverpool (1917-1921). He was awarded a B.Sc., First Class Honours degree in Chemistry in 1920 and a Diploma in Education in 1921. His first teaching post was at the Liverpool Collegiate School in the Summer Term of 1921 before he moved to Prince Henry's to teach Chemistry as a probationary teacher in September 1921. The post was made *'definitive'* from September 1922.

When Mr Hutchinson resigned as Editor of the School Magazine in 1930, Mr Nealy took over as Editor until the arrival of Mr Leech. In 1936 he obtained a M.Sc. in Agricultural Chemistry, also from Liverpool University. In 1961 he was elected as a Fellow of the Royal Institute of Chemistry. On 29 October 1938, David Nealy married Mrs. Adeline M. Robinson at Hawkshead.

In 1922 the Prince Henry's Grammar School Savings Association, under the Chairmanship of the Headmaster, was formed. All members of the School were asked to support the Association, and Mr Nealy became Hon. Secretary. He later became the Honorary Secretary of the Otley and Wharfedale Savings Committee and organised in particular the raising of funds throughout the Second World War. By Summer 1940 over 250 pupils were regular savers, and the number of members in the School grew significantly during the war.

Each year a theme highlighting a specific aspect of the war was used to draw attention to the National War Savings Campaign. In 1941 it was '*War Weapons Week*,' in 1942 '*Warship Week*', in 1943, '*Wings for Victory Week*,' and in 1944, '*Salute the Soldier Week*.'

In the Summer 1945 edition of the '*Otliensian*' an attempt was made to calculate the total raised by the School during the war. The total raised from Savings Schemes was listed as £11,796. After the end of the war donations continued. In 1946 £1,531 19s 6d was added to National Savings during the Otley and Wharfedale 'Thanksgiving Savings Week'. As a result of his efforts Mr Nealy was awarded the M.B.E. in 1946.

Mr Nealy retired on 31 December 1964 after nearly 43 years at Prince Henry's. He was replaced as Head of Science by Mr T. B. Buncall, who was also to remain at the school for many years.

David Nealy died in 1999 – not quite making a century, but he does hold the record for the longest serving teacher at Prince Henry's. His death was registered in Bury, Lancashire.

GEORGE KENNETH NIELD

George Kenneth Nield was born on 21 March 1911 and educated at the Municipal High School Oldham, and Victoria University, Manchester. He was awarded a B.A. Class II Honours degree in French in 1933 and a Board of Education Teachers' Certificate in 1934. His first teaching post was at Ashton-under-Lyne Secondary School (1933-1934) where he taught French and Junior/Middle English and Latin. After a brief stay at the Oldham Municipal High School, he became an Assistant Master at Prince Henry's in March 1935, to teach French and English. He replaced Mr Richardson, temporarily, but the post was made permanent from September 1935. His application letter pointed out that he was musical, being a member of the Oldham Secondary School orchestra and being qualified to teach singing.

He was a member of staff on the trip to Belgium at Easter 1936 and showed his musical talent by conducting the school Orchestra at the Christmas Concert, 1938.

In April 1940 Mr Nield volunteered for service in the Field Security Wing of the Corps of Military Police, and was replaced temporarily by Mr Chapman. Sadly, Mr Nield became the first casualty of the War from Prince Henry's on 1 January 1941. Following his death, his mother presented his collection of gramophone records to the School.

WILFRED WOOD PADGETT

The number of staff at Prince Henry's was enhanced in Autumn 1919 because of an increase in the number of scholars to 204 pupils; one of the new staff was Mr W. W. Padgett. He was born on 18 May 1892 in Baildon where his father, Thomas William Padgett (1858-1923), was a Clerk working for the West Riding County Council, Thomas married Sarah Jane Ellen Waterhouse (1858-1927) in 1887.

Wilfred attended Ilkley Grammar School (1904-1910) before going to Leeds University

(1910-1913). He was awarded a B.A. in French in 1913, being described by Professor Barbier as *'the best student of his year in French'*. He was awarded a Board of Education Certificate in 1913 and a French Teachers' Diploma in 1914. His first teaching post was at Calverley Council School, which he joined in 1913, but his career was interrupted by the First World War. In 1911 the family was living on Queen's Terrace, Otley.

His military service (1915-1919) was largely spent in France. He was attached to the Intelligence Staff at the Le Havre Base, and remained there until he was demobilized on 20 January 1919. In his job application he stated:

'This gave me an exceptional opportunity of pursuing my study of the French language, of French ways and customs, for not only was I authorised to choose my own apartments and restaurants, obviously an important privilege to a student of French, but also throughout much of my period of residence in Le Havre, I was working in constant collaboration with French Officials.'

He was clearly an excellent and well-respected linguist, and he regularly improved his qualifications over his time at Prince Henry's. He was awarded the Certificate of the International Phonetic Association (1920), the Diploma for Teachers of German (1921) and a M.A. in French from Leeds University (1924). In 1921 he was elected to the Council of the Modern Languages Association, and for twenty-one years was Honorary Treasurer of the Yorkshire Branch of the Modern Languages Association.

He led his first trip abroad in 1922 when:

'At Easter Mr Padgett and Mr Pratt propose to take a party of boys selected from Fifth Forms to the Continent, to visit in particular Brussels, the Battlefields of Flanders, the Valley of the Oise, Paris, Rouen, Havre and London on return.'

Regular trips were made before and after the War to Belgium, where from a base at Blankenberghe, visits were made into surrounding areas. In 1928 arrangements were made for three boys to visit France to improve their knowledge of France. These visits became eventually the 'French Travelling Scholarship', though the funding involved some self-help on the part of Mr Padgett himself through events such as the *'French Social.'*

In 1926 Mr Padgett married Miss Dorothy Rudram, an old scholar of the school. Mr Padgett had long links with the Old Scholar's Association. It was Mr Padgett who proposed that Mr Wilde be elected President in 1937. During the Second World War he kept, and regularly updated, a list of Old Scholars serving in His Majesty's Forces. He retired in 1957, after 38 years at Prince Henry's. Mr Padgett died in hospital in 1963, aged 70. He left a widow, a son, Hugh Michael, and a daughter, Kathleen Hilary – both of whom went to Prince Henry's. The funeral was at Otley Station Road Methodist Church followed by a cremation at Lawnswood.

RICHARD PRATT

Richard Pratt was born in Ilkley on 26 December 1894. His father Thomas (1869-1926) was born near Kirby Steven, Westmoreland in 1869 and in the 1911 Census was employed as a coal driver. His mother, Margaret (née Dent) (1869-1926) was born in Marske, Yorkshire. In 1911 Richard had one brother, Thomas Edmund, then aged 9, and lived with his parents at 6 East Parade, Ilkley He attended Ilkley National School and Ilkley Grammar School (1906-1913). He spent the year 1913-1914 as a student teacher at Ilkley National School before going to Leeds University (1914-1917), where he was awarded a B.A. Honours Class II degree in History and a Board of Education Teachers' Certificate. His first teaching post was at Leeds Central High School (1917-1918), but he must have been easily tempted to apply for a job at the shortly to be re-opened Prince Henry's Grammar School, Otley. It was nearer to his home and he must have known, and probably been taught by, Mr Walter Robinson, Second Master at Ilkley Grammar School, and the first Headmaster of the re-opened Prince Henry's.

The school re-opened in the Mechanics' Institute in September 1918 with the Headmaster, three full-time staff and two 'visiting staff'. Mr Pratt was, therefore, in at the start of the 'new' school and was to remain there until his retirement in July 1959 – 41 unbroken years of service. His main subject was history, but he also taught geography, physical education and physical sciences. His starting salary was £150 per annum.

The death of the headmaster, Mr Robinson, in December, 1936 led to the Governors appointing Mr Pratt as acting headmaster of the school, pending the appointment and arrival of a new headmaster. In spite of his length of service and his period as Acting Headmaster, Mr Pratt was not appointed as Senior Master until 1939.

He involved himself in all aspects of school life – visits, Christmas parties, Sports Days, Garden Parties, Harvest Camps, and trips to the continent with his friend and colleague, Mr Padgett. He took a keen interest in school sport and was clearly a talented sportsman, coaching soccer, rugby, cricket and hockey. When the School re-opened in 1918 the main boys' game was Association Football. A student debate in Autumn 1920 resulted in a small majority being in favour of a change to Rugby, which came in 1921. According to Mr Pratt. the reasons for the change were said to be the fact that the school had a duty to find recruits for the Otley R.U.F.C. teams and that *'most of us feel that Rugby is the more manly game, and demands the more manly qualities which it is our desire to inculcate.'*

During the Second World War several members of staff joined His Majesty's Forces, among them Mr Evans, the Physical Education teacher. True to his sporting interest and expertise Mr Pratt took over and became responsible for the boys' physical training until the return of Mr Evans. He continued to coach the First XV for many years and participated – usually successfully - in Staff v School matches in Rugby, Cricket and Hockey.

Mrs. Pratt had joined the staff in January 1919 when, as Miss Hilda Horsley, she taught in the Preparatory Department of the School. She married Richard Pratt in 1927 and retired from full-time teaching. She helped out occasionally on a part-time basis and took a keen interest and participation in dramatic and musical presentations in School. They had two children, Malcolm and Margaret – both pupils at Prince Henry's.

Mr Pratt worked with all three of the first Headmasters of Prince Henry's. In 1936 the School was shocked by the untimely death of the then Headmaster, Mr Robinson. As Senior Master, Mr Pratt took over for a term before the appointment of Mr John Wilde. He continued as Senior Master for the whole of the time that Mr Wilde was Headmaster and oversaw the arrival of Mr Bousfield and the first two years of his time at the School. Mr Pratt retired in July 1959.

For many years Mr Pratt was the Treasurer of the Old Otliensians' Association and he maintained a close interest in the performances of both the Rugby section and the Hockey section. At the Associations' Christmas Dance in December 1959 he was presented with gifts, which included a fireside chair, a cocktail cabinet and a silver cigarette box. Richard Pratt died in January 1968. His obituary in the 'Wharfedale' described him as:

'probably one of the best known and certainly one of the most popular teachers ever to serve on the staff at Prince Henry's.'

MISS MARGARET RYCROFT

Miss Rycroft was born on 21 September 1918 in Nelson, Lancashire, and educated at Nelson Secondary School (1930-1936) and Manchester University (1936-1939). She was awarded a First Class B.A. Honours degree in English in 1939 and did her teacher training year at Oxford University (1939-1940), being awarded her Teaching Diploma in 1940. Her first teaching post was as a temporary Assistant Mistress taking English and French at Sowerby Bridge Secondary School (1940-1941) before she was appointed to teach English and some French at Prince Henry's in October 1941. She was a temporary replacement for Mr Chapman who had joined the R.A.F. The post was made permanent from 1 September 1943. She left at the end of the Summer Term, 1947.

MISS CATHERINE DORCAS SEATON

Miss Seaton was born on 5 June 1904. In 1911 she was living at 90 Timpson Road, Landport, Portsmouth with her father William (born 1876) and her mother Lily Elizabeth (born 1877). Her father is listed in the 1911 Census as a Shipwright.

Catherine was educated at Portsmouth Girls Secondary School (1916-1921), Portsmouth Municipal College (1923-1925), and University College, London (1923-1925). She was awarded a B.Sc. Class II Honours degree in Botany in 1925. She spent 1925-1926 at the London Day Training College and obtained a Teachers' Diploma in 1926.

At school she had been Captain of the 1st XI Hockey team and also played in the 1st

Netball team, a sign of her ongoing interest and enthusiasm in school sport. Her first teaching post was at Wanstead County High School (Summer Term 1927), before being appointed to Prince Henry's in 1927 as a probationary Assistant Mistress to teach Botany. The post was made *'definitive'* from 1 September 1928. Later she was placed in charge of the Biology Department.

She found the time to lead the Otley Parish Church Guides group, but still contributed fully to the life of the school inside and outside the classroom. She managed the School Netball Team and set up and ran a Dancing Club, which held annual dances for its members. During the Second World War she was in charge of cultivating the School grounds to aid the war effort, and took pupils to Harvest Camps.

She left Prince Henry's at the end of the Summer Term 1946. Catherine Dorcas Seaton died on 12 October 2000, aged 96 years. She was a resident at the Belmont Castle Retirement Home, Portsdown Hill, Bedhampton, Hampshire.

WILLIAM SENIOR SHAW

William Senior Shaw was born on 16 June 1892 and attended Ashton-under-Lyne Municipal Secondary School (1904-1909) before moving on to the Victoria University of Manchester (1910-1914). He was awarded a B.Sc. in 1913 and a M.Sc. and a Secondary School Teachers' Diploma in 1914. His first teaching post was at Mirfield Grammar School in September and October 1914.

He enlisted as a private in the 5th Battalion Duke of Wellington's (West Riding Regiment) in October 1914, was commissioned in March 1915 and made up to Captain in May 1916. By this time his address was 4, Farnley Lane, Otley. He was severely wounded in France in May 1917 and was put on *'permanent home service'*. He was then employed under the Ministry of National Service as a Statistical Officer in the Bolton area, but from 1 January 1919 was *'free from further military service.'* (Letter of application)

After the First World War he was appointed as an assistant teacher of mathematics, at a starting salary of £200 per annum, at Prince Henry's, where he stayed until his retirement in Summer 1952 – 33 years in total. His leaving was not without some drama because of a growing problem of deafness that afflicted him. His post was advertised and Miss Hannah Greenwood was appointed, but was unable to start until January 1953. It was therefore necessary to obtain a temporary teacher for one term, Mr Riley filling the gap. *'Captain'* Shaw died in 1974, 22 years after his retirement.

MRS. HELEN STOREY

Mrs. Storey was born on 18 May 1913 and educated at the Park School, Preston (1925-1931) and Homerton Training College, Cambridge (1931-1933) from where she was awarded a Teachers' Certificate in 1933. She was employed as part of the pool of P.E. staff in the Leeds Education Authority and helped at Prince Henry's with gymnastics and games before Miss Dixon came in January 1940. She also did some general form work in lower school. Mrs. Storey was at Prince Henry's from 23 October 1939 until 22

December 1939.

GEORGE WALFORD TINKLER

Mr Tinkler was born on 21 January 1916 and educated at Harrogate Grammar School (1928-1935) and Leeds University (1935-1939), from where he was awarded a B.Sc. degree in 1938 and a Diploma in Education in 1939. He came to Prince Henry's in September 1939 to a temporary mathematics post as cover for Mr Shaw. He left in early October 1939.

MRS. IRENE TOTT

Mrs. Tott was born on 10 May 1909 in Hunslet. In the 1911 Census her father, George Bolton (born 1880) is listed as an Iron Turner. George, his wife Kathleen Ethel (born 1885) and Irene were living at 66, Longroyd Avenue, Dewsbury. On 3 August 1939, Irene married Bernard Owen Frank Tott at St Edmund's Church, Roundhay, Leeds. Their daughter, Alison, was born in 1949.

Irene was educated at Cockburn High School, Leeds (1921-1927) and Leeds University (1927-1931). She was awarded a B.A. Pass degree in 1930 and a Board of Education Diploma in 1931, with a Commendation for Practical Teaching. She spent a term at Bentley Lane Elementary School, Leeds in 1931 before moving to Kirby Secondary School, Middlesbrough from December 1931 to August 1933. From September 1933 to August 1939 she was employed in the Preparatory department of Kirby Secondary School. She resigned from teaching when she was married in 1939, but suggested in her application to Prince Henry's that because her husband was in the R.A.F. she would like the opportunity of doing more teaching.

She was appointed at Prince Henry's on 23 April 1941 as a temporary replacement for Mr Denham, who had joined H.M. Forces. Miss Horsley took over Mr Denham's Physics timetable and Mrs. Tott replaced Miss Horsley in charge of the Junior School. In 1944 Mrs. Tott took over from Miss Horsley as the Secretary of the School Savings group.

Mrs. Tott left Prince Henry's on 31 August 1945, pending the return of Mr Denham, to take up a teaching appointment at Lawnswood Modern School. She died on 22 April 2001 at Stoke Mandeville Hospital, Buckinghamshire.

MISS MARGARET VERO

Miss Vero was born on 1 August 1916 and educated at Harrogate Grammar School (1927-1931), Brighouse Girls' Secondary School (1931-1935) and Reading University (1935–1939). She was awarded a B.A. Class III Honours degree in Latin and English Literature in 1938 and a Board of Education Teaching Certificate in the same year. She was a full-time Assistant Mistress at the Leeds, City School of Commerce (1939-1941), where she taught English, Latin and Scripture before being appointed to Prince Henry's in September 1941 as a temporary Assistant Mistress teaching Latin and some junior French during the absence through illness of Miss Brockbank. She left on 30 June 1942.

JOHN HENRY WATSON

John Watson was born in York on 5 October 1907. In 1911 his father, Frederick James Watson (1862-1912) was listed in the Census as a Railway Clerk. Frederick married Mary Jane Waite in York in 1890. In 1911 the family were living at 43, East Mount Road, York and John was the youngest of five children.

John was educated at Scarcroft Elementary School, York (1912-1920), Nunthorpe School, York (1920-1926) and Leeds University (1926-1930). He was awarded a B.A. Class II Honours degree in Geography in 1929 and a Leeds University Diploma in Education in 1930. His first, and only, teaching post was at Prince Henry's where he was appointed as a probationer to teach Geography in September 1930. The job was made '*definitive*' on 1 September 1931.

Shortly after his arrival, Mr Watson was involved in two events - an accident and marriage! He was the only uninjured passenger in a '*terrible bus accident*' on the York-Tadcaster road. At the beginning of the Autumn Term, 1931, he was the recipient of wedding presents from the Staff and School.

During the Second World War four members of staff were commissioned in the R.A.F. as Instructors in the Educational Service.

We are all extremely sorry to have to bid goodbye, for the time being, to Mr J.H.Watson, who joined the R.A.F. during last term to take up the duties of an instructor. In his place we welcome Miss N.Clark B.A. (Hons. Geography), of Manchester University ('Otliensian' Vol. XV, Summer 1943)

He returned to Prince Henry's in February 1945, after his resignation from the R.A.F. Education Service. Mr Watson retired at the end of the Summer Term 1968, after spending 38 years in what was his only teaching appointment. Mr McClintock took over as Head of the Geography Department, and Mr Watson was replaced by Mr Buckby. An appreciation published in the *'Otliensian'* included the following:

Mr Watson's work in the classroom has always been characterised by an enthusiasm for his subject, a deep interest in many matters not necessarily related to it, a friendly approach to his pupils, and a thorough and painstaking preparation. His skill with the duplicating machine has long been the envy of many a colleague. So was the fantastic accuracy of his blackboard map-drawing to the writer, until the secret of the sketched outlines on the board in Room 2 was revealed!

Outside the classroom, there are at least two areas where Mr Watson's influence has been very considerable. For many years he had full responsibility for the organisation of the School Library, and brought to this task the same thoroughness and care as he brought to his teaching. As a result, pupils were encouraged to make use of all that the Library had to offer – and Mr Watson usually found it necessary to devote most of his lunch-hour to their encouragement! But it is perhaps in the work of Careers advice that he will more particularly be remembered. For some years now, more recently with the assistance of Mr McClintock, he has spent much of his time in giving advice to individuals, in obtaining information on their behalf, in the arrangement of interviews and visits by Youth Employment representatives, and in the organisation of Careers Conventions, greatly appreciated both by school leavers and by their parents. Again, most of this work has been done in spare time, and done gladly.

The reference to Mr Watson's ability in drawing maps on blackboards was summed up in the following comment from an Old Scholar:

'There was Mr Watson, who could draw, on the board, a map of "anywhere" in the twinkling of an eye, thereby earning my undying respect until I found out he had the outlines already scratched on the board and simply followed these almost invisible lines.'

During the last week of last term, the Staff entertained Mr Watson at a social gathering and presented him with a picture, a copy of the Oxford Dictionary of Quotations and a record token. The School bade him farewell at a meeting in the Library and gave him a suitcase and an album of records. On 18 October 1968 the Old Otliensians completed the trio of presentations with a photographic enlarger and cheque at a gathering of Old Scholars at the Royal White Horse Hotel, Otley. John Watson died in York in 1988.

MISS GRETHE WHITEHEAD

Miss Grethe Whitehead was born on 24 June 1914 and was educated at Leeds Girls' High School (1920-1936) and Leeds University (1932-1936) from where she was awarded a B.A. Classics degree (Pass) in 1935 and an Education Diploma and Board of Education Certificate in 1936. Her Physical Training course at Leeds University included anatomy, physiology, hygiene, practical gymnastics and games. She did 1½ days per week at Prince Henry's as part of her teaching practice. During this period she gave a talk to the Natural Science Society on "*Travels in the Realm of Sport*" – an account of her experiences, especially at Budapest.

Her first post was at Penistone Grammar School (September 1936-March 1937) as teacher of Girls' Physical Training and English Mistress. She was appointed to a similar post at Prince Henry's from April 1937, as a replacement for Miss Coltman.

Her sporting achievements included:

Athletics	School Sports Champion 1930-1931-1932 Leeds University colours 1933-1934-1935-1936 Leeds University Athletics Captain 1935-1936 British Universities Individual Champion 1934-1935-1936, winning High Jump (1934 & 1936), Long Jump (1935), Hurdles (1934, 1935 & 1936 World University Games, Budapest 1935 – winner 80 metres Hurdles Member of British Olympic Team, 1936, Berlin, 80 metres Hurdles.
Swimming	Leeds University Swimmin Team 1932-1933-1934 Chosen to represent British Universities.

Lacrosse	Leeds University Team 1933-1934-1935-1936

Miss Whitehead left in October 1939, after her marriage on 2 October 1939 at Adel Church to Selwyn Russell Jones, art master at Macclesfield Grammar School. She presented to the School a cup to be held by the Girls' Junior Sports Champion. In September 1939 she was manageress of the women's team at the International University Games in Monte Carlo, when the team were sent home by the British Consol after the international situation became acute and the games abandoned. She died in April 2000.

JOHN WILDE

John Wilde was born in Liverpool on 6 March 1899. His father, Alfred James Wilde (1865-1955) was born in Canterbury, Kent in 1865; his mother Sarah E.Wilde (née Sarah Eleanor Bigland, 1866-1932) was born in Kendal, Westmoreland, where they were married in 1892. John's elder sister, Agnes, was born in Liverpool in 1897. In 1901 the family lived in Gertrude Road, Walton-on-the-Hill, Liverpool and Alfred was a Sanitary Inspector employed by Liverpool Corporation. By 1911 the Wilde's had moved to Clapham Road, Anfield, Liverpool, Alfred still being employed as a Sanitary Inspector.

John attended the Liverpool Institute (1912-1917) before entering Liverpool University (1917-1920). He was awarded a First Class Honours degree in French in 1921 after spending a year at the University of Strasbourg as a Reader in English. He obtained a M.A. in French in 1924, also from Liverpool University and later in his career was awarded a B.Sc. (Economics) Class 2ii from London University.

His teaching career started at Holt Secondary School, Liverpool, as Modern Languages Master (1921-1926). He then spent 1926-1928 at Taunton School, where he was an Assistant House Master. From 1928-1930 he was Senior French Master at Heaton Secondary School, Newcastle and then returned to Holt Secondary School as Senior Modern Languages Master (1930-1937). He obtained a London University Teacher's Diploma in 1932.

In 1929 he married Edith Marion Chesters (1897-1982) in Nantwich, Cheshire. On several occasions she provided teaching cover for absent staff. She was also a fine artist.

At a meeting of the Staffing sub-committee held on 25 February 1937 the Clerk reported that 209 applications had been received for the position of headmaster, following the death of Mr Walter Robinson. Eventually six people were selected for interview. A further meeting on 22 March 1937 resolved that:

'After an eliminating vote it was unanimously resolved that Mr John Wilde of 156 Brodie Avenue, Liverpool be and he is hereby appointed Headmaster of this School, subject to the usual agreement of service being entered into.'

Mr Wilde assumed the role of Headmaster on 1 June 1937. Later that term he was elected president of the Old Otliensians' Association

John Wilde spent 22 years as headmaster of Prince Henry's, six of these years being during the Second World War. Before the end of the War, the consequences of the passing of the 1944 Education Act had to be negotiated, in particular the loss of the Preparatory Department and the end of school fees. He announced his intention to retire at the end of the Spring Term 1959, at the meeting of the Governing Body held on 8 October 1958.

The last few weeks of the Spring Term provided several opportunities for presentations to be made to Mr and Mrs. Wilde. The Governors started the run at their meeting on 11 March 1959, when

'The Chairman welcomed past and present Governors who had accepted his invitation to attend the meeting for the presentation to Mr Wilde. He referred to the services given to the School and the Town by Mr and Mrs. Wilde over the past 22 years, and expressed the regrets of the Governors that Mr Wilde is leaving the School and the gratitude of the Governors for all that he and Mrs. Wilde have done during the time of his Headmastership.

'Mrs. D I Wilkinson JP, as Chairman of the Council, and Mr R Renwick, on behalf of the past Governors, also expressed their thanks and good wishes to Mr and Mrs. Wilde for the future.

'On behalf of the Governors, past and present, Miss Hunter presented Mr and Mrs. Wilde with a clock which is to be inscribed, and wished them God speed, good health and happiness in the years to come. Mr Wilde, acknowledging with thanks the gift, said how much he had appreciated that this had been made a joint presentation, and he expressed his grateful thanks to all for many kindnesses and said that the clock would remind him of a Body of Governors and Chairman so good in every respect that no Headmaster could have hoped for a better.

'Mr Wilde was asked to have an appropriate photograph taken of himself and placed in the School Library, the cost to be met from private school funds.'

Past and present members of the Staff presented farewell gifts at a dinner on 20 March. The Old Scholars held their presentation on the evening of 25 March, when Mr and Mrs. Wilde were presented with a canteen of cutlery.

The School pupils held their presentation at the final assembly of the Spring term, when the Head Girl, Angela Dennis presented a slide projector to Mr Wilde and a silver-plated coffee percolator to Mrs. Wilde. At an earlier ceremony the School Prefects had pleasure in making Mr Wilde an honorary Prefect and in presenting him with a Prefect's tie. As a parting gift, Mr Wilde presented to the school an attractive light oak display cabinet.

John Wilde died, aged 87, in January 1986 in Birkenhead.

MRS. EDITH WILDE (née Chesters)

John Wilde married Edith Marion Chesters in Nantwich, Cheshire, in 1929. She was born in Nantwich in 1897. She was employed temporarily on several occasions, including filling in as an interim emergency measure in the Autumn Term, 1946, because Miss Bartle was unable to commence duty until 1 January 1947. She was a fine artist. She died in Birkenhead in 1982, predeceasing her husband by 4 years.

MISS MURIEL CHRISTINE WRIGLEY

Miss Wrigley was born on 4 March 1914 and was educated at Selhurst Grammar School (1924-1926), Milton Mount College (1926-1932) and Battersea Polytechnic Training College (1932-1935), where she was awarded a City and Guilds Dressmaking Certificate in 1938. She taught at Christchurch Senior Girls School (1935-1937), Fairlop Upper Girls School, Ilford (1937-1939) and Folkstone Technical Institute for Girls (1939-1940). She started work part-time at Prince Henry's in September 1940, specializing in Needlework. She replaced Miss Halmshaw and it is likely that she also worked for some of the week at Keighley Girls' Grammar because the Governors of Prince Henry's paid money to the Governors of Keighley Girls' Grammar School for the teaching done by Miss Wrigley at Otley. The final amount paid was in July 1941, and this may have been when Miss Wrigley left Prince Henry's.

The Buildings

Following the granting of the Royal Charter, the school opened in the vicarage on Kirkgate. The Archbishop of York granted a site for a new building and a one-storey building was erected in 1614 in what is now Manor Square. An upper storey was added in 1790. Further improvements were made, but because of its limited endowment and small numbers of pupils the school was closed in 1874. The premises in Manor Square were sold in 1883 for £800 to Mr Thomas Constable.

Various attempts were made to re-open the school, but it did not re-open until 1918, and then only in temporary premises at the Mechanics' Institute.

The Governors agreed to purchase land for a new school on Farnley Lane from Major F.H. Fawkes of Farnley Hall, but many years would pass until the new school was built.

The Old Grammar School, Manor Square

Plans were drawn up, alterations made and further extensions requested, but progress was slow. Each time agreement was reached the Governors put forward the view that the buildings were not big enough to accommodate an increasing number of pupils, and that new extensions were needed. The new building, but not the latest extensions, was occupied after the Easter holidays in 1925.

By the end of the Summer Term, 1927, it was announced that:

'The end of Summer Term 1927, sees us fully established in our new premises. Gone are the inconveniences due to the use of Laboratories in the Mechanics' Institute, and the

loss of time in getting there. Now, Laboratories for Chemistry and Physics, Library Room, Art Room, Dining Hall and Gymnasium are all completely equipped and in daily use.' ('Otliensian' Vol. IX, Summer 1927)

Plans could now be made for the opening ceremony, which was held on 25 July 1927.

Seventeen years had elapsed between the production of the first set of plans for the building of the new School on Farnley Lane, and the opening of the School. There had been significant amendments to the original plans, though many of these occurred because increasing pupil numbers meant that the existing plans were unable to provide suitable accommodation and specialist rooms to meet their needs. As the number of pupils increased, so more staff and more rooms were needed. The new build started in Summer 1923 and took 4 years to complete. The Governors were constantly complaining about the lack of progress and it was only after the employment of a full-time Clerk of Works that the build speeded up. The alterations and amendments to the plans would not be conducive to progressing the build. It is also likely that the cost of building the new School would have had to be considered carefully, and this too may have held up the work. The tenders for the extensions were significantly larger than those for the pre-extended school, and economies in construction do seem to have had an impact on the quality of the build as witnessed by the need for modifications and repairs in the years following the opening.

The larger number of pupils also meant that there was an urgent need for increased playing fields. A committee was appointed to make preliminary negotiations for the purchase of land on the West side of the present field. At the Governing Body meeting held on 5 October 1932 it was announced that 4.9 acres of land had been purchased for £1500 with a £1000 mortgage at 4½%. The County committee and the Board of Education had made it clear that the funding of the additional playing fields should come from the Endowment, and over the next few years fund raising activities were held to pay off the debt. The mortgage was paid off on 30 June 1937. The land was held initially by a group of Governors who acted as Trustees. A Governing Body meeting held on 19 January 1938 approved the transfer of the additional playing fields to the School.

On 11 February 1935 at a meeting of the School and Grounds committee a letter was read from Mr C.E. Johnson, Land Agent to Major Fawkes, stating that Major Fawkes was prepared to make a gift to the School of a plot of land 3,022 square yards in area, situated to the north of the New Playing Fields, as an addition to the Playing Fields.

On 11 February 1935 the School and Grounds Committee discussed the need for yet more additional classrooms and a Science Lecture Room, and agreed to formulate a report to be sent to the County Council. At the same time they asked that the need for additional sanitary accommodation should again be addressed. No progress was made and following a meeting of the Governors on 16 March 1938:

'The Schools and Buildings Committee were asked to consider in connection with the proposed extensions the provision of a small biology laboratory which can be used as a lecture room and a room for the use of the Headmaster's secretary.'

Some internal changes were made, but the intervention of the War effectively put an end to any short-term hopes of more extensions to the School. Alterations to the buildings and grounds were made to make the site more secure – construction of blast walls, digging of trenches, darkening of windows, anti-splinter netting, air-raid shelters – and to make the land more productive by using the playing fields to grow crops.

So, what would a new pupil arriving at Prince Henry's in September 1939 have seen? In fact, he or she would see much the same as a new pupil arriving in 1929 or 1949. The building was set back from Farnley Lane and the site had two entrances – the boys used the left-hand path, the right-hand path was used by the girls. The right-hand path ran alongside the Headmaster's house on the south-east corner of the site. The left-hand path ran between grass tennis courts, four to the right and a single one to the left.

The main building was symmetrical in shape with a formal entrance set in the centre. Pupils did not use this entrance; girls would enter from the far right, boys from the far left. Above the main entrance was an imposing clock tower, which had been added to the original plans by the Governors. To either side of the building were toilet blocks, again to the left for the boys and to the right for the girls.

The front part of the school was linked to a parallel rear section by two wings, incorporating additional rooms set along glass-covered corridors, and by a central link at the rear of the Assembly Hall. Both the front and back parts of the school were two storeys high, though only partly so with regard to the front section. Between the two wings and the Assembly Hall were two quadrangles, which were usually out of bounds to pupils.

We can take a tour of the school with Margaret Shirley Akam, who was admitted on 12 September 1939. She lived in Menston, so probably came that first day by train or bus. She would have walked from the train station or bus station, across the bridge and on to Farnley Lane, and would have entered her new school through the girls' (east) entrance. She would have left her outside coat in the girls' cloakroom to her right. In order to visit the classrooms in numerical order we will assume that she turns immediately right and climbs the stairs to the first floor. She is faced with a long corridor on the left of which are a series of classrooms each designed to accommodate up to 30 pupils and therefore each containing 30 desks. Room 1 is normally used for younger pupils in the Preparatory Department; Room 2 is the Geography room.

The Geography Room

Halfway along this corridor is a door that leads to the Male Staff Common Room, and also contains the access to the Clock Tower. Three more classrooms – Rooms 3, also used by the Preparatory department, 4 and 5, complete the corridor.

When she reaches the end of this corridor Margaret turns right, goes down the stairs and is faced with a similar corridor, immediately below the one she has just explored. The boys' cloakroom is to her rear and is opposite Room 11, which is on the right, followed by Room 10 and Room 9. In the middle of the corridor are the School Office and the Headmaster's Study, which lie either side of the main entrance. Continuing along the corridor she would see Rooms 8, 7 and 6. She may have noticed that Rooms 11 and 6 are single-storey, hence the first floor is shorter than the ground floor.

In the middle of the corridor, on the left, is the Assembly Hall, on either side of which are two quadrangles. The Assembly Hall is an imposing room with a stage at the far end with a proper proscenium and curtains.

The Assembly Hall

Margaret now turns left along one of the two link corridors. Both corridors have glass roofs and are lined on one side with oak lockers. To the right on the corridor on the girls' side of the school is a Biology laboratory and at the end of the corridor are a Chemistry laboratory and a Physics laboratory. Turning left and climbing the stairs leads to another corridor with rooms to the right. First is the Domestic Science Room, adjacent to the Kitchen.

Above the gym is a large dining room with 14 tables, each with 13 places. One table was reserved for the staff. Beyond this is the Art room.

The Dining Hall

Margaret returns to the ground floor. To her left is the gym, flanked by changing rooms, to her right the woodwork workshop and the metalwork workshop.

This brings her to the corresponding link corridor on the boys' side, again with oak lockers to the left and a Stationery Store and Library to the right.

Behind and to the left of the school were the playing fields. The area to the left was the cricket field, which was also used as the athletics area.

The Gymnasium

To the rear of the gym there were two rugby pitches and two hockey pitches that ran parallel to the main school buildings. The bottom rugby pitch was used mainly for P.E.

lessons and rugby practice. There was then an artificially leveled hockey pitch, followed by a reserve hockey pitch, which doubled as a second cricket pitch in summer, and finally the top rugby pitch, which was used for inter-school matches and little else.

At a meeting of the Governors on 17 May 1939 the Clerk recalled that he had been instructed to apply for the early provision of a science lecture room, two classrooms and additional storage accommodation. At a previous meeting the Headmaster had *'sounded a warning note'* by pointing out that the dining room, hall, library, and occasionally the gymnasium, were used as classrooms. Almost from the re-opening of the School the Governors had argued that the school was over-crowded and that additional space was required. However, by the time that Margaret started at Prince Henry's there was to be no extension to the existing buildings, apart from some 'temporary' classrooms, until 1968 when the school became Comprehensive.

In 1939 there were two reasons for this lack of expansion, the obvious one being the outbreak of the war in September. The other reason was that Ilkley Grammar School had decided to admit girls, also from September 1939. This proposal was referred to at a Governors' meeting held on 20 January 1939 when a letter was received from the West Riding Committee noting that they were:

'disposed to approve the Ilkley Governors' proposal, but think it desirable, before going into details, to let the Governors of the Otley Grammar School know what they have in mind, and give them an opportunity of submitting any observations.'

At that time there were 55 girls from Ilkley attending Prince Henry's, and there was concern over the loss of finance that would arise from their transfer. However, the Governors felt that this was an issue for parents and that *'we have confidence that the financial effect on the Otley School will be looked after by the County Committee.'*

The matter was again discussed at the Governors' meeting held on 19 May 1939, when the Chairman, Mr Atkinson felt that, *'we should not try to prevent Ilkley girls from going to school in their own town, merely on the ground that it would reduce our numbers, but until the school is open to them, I do not think there is very much we can do.'*

Mr Wade noted:

'We have got our school perfected, so far as one can perfect a school. We have our classes and staff arranged, and before we can give an opinion, we must consider, not only the children, but the expense incurred, and also our staff. Any big withdrawal might be a serious matter in this respect. I do not want to do anything that might discourage the new school at Ilkley, which I think is the right idea, and I do not think we should pass any resolution at this stage. I move consideration of the matter be deferred for the time being.'

However, the Clerk, in giving the official reply to the request for additional accommodation noted that the reply pointed out that the future demand for accommodation for girls at the school was likely to be less than in previous years in consequence of the admission of girls to Ilkley from September, and that it was extremely unlikely that the County Committee would be able to undertake for a considerable time anything in the way of a major scheme of extensions.

Mr Atkinson, in summing up, stated that, *'This virtually turns down the request for extensions, and for the present it means that our accommodation for girls is quite inadequate.'*

The Governing Body

The Royal Charter, dated 30 April 1607 lists the names of the first Governors of the Free Grammar School of Prince Henry at Otley:

'there be and shall be for ever within the said Parish of Otley or dwelling within two miles thereof, seven honest men of the most wise discretion and religious persons, who shall be called Governors of the said possessions and revenues of the Free Grammar School of Prince Henry at Otley. And therefore to that end We have assigned, nominated, chosen and appointed by these presents our Well-loved ***Sir Thomas Fairfax*** *of Denton in the said Parish of Otley, Knight;* ***Sir Guy Palmer*** *of Lindley in the said Parish and County, Knight;* ***Sir Robert Dyneley*** *of Bramhope in the said Parish and County;* ***Thomas Fawkes*** *of Farnley in the said Parish and County, Esquire;* ***Christopher Cave*** *of Carlton in the Parish of Guiseley in the said County, yeoman;* ***Christopher Cave*** *of Otley aforesaid, yeoman; and* ***Jeffrey Pickard*** *of Menston in the said Parish of Otley and County of York, Gentleman; inhabitants of the said Parish of Otley or within two miles thereof, to be the first and present Governors of the goods, possessions and revenues of the Free Grammar School of Prince Henry at Otley; and that they for ever hereafter shall be one body corporate and politic of itself in deeds, and known by the name of the Governors of the goods, possessions and revenues of the Free Grammar School of Prince Henry at Otley, and these by the name of Governors we do incorporate and make one body corporate and politic by that name for ever to endure.'*

In the following years various amendments were made to the *'Scheme'* by which the school was governed, and the lowest point was reached when, after the School was closed because of a lack of funds and pupils, the Governors were replaced by 'Trustees'.

The possible re-opening of the School was never abandoned by the majority of the Governors. When the school closed in 1874 the funds in the control of the Governors amounted to £145. In 1888, when the new Scheme came into operation there was a sum of £1531, and in 1895 the funds were further enhanced following a legacy of £500 from the estate of Mr Robert Craven, of Bramhope. These funds encouraged the Governors to hope that the School would be re-opened in the near future. A new Scheme was introduced in 1909, though the School did not re-open in temporary premises until 1918.

The 1909 Scheme provided a governing body of fifteen persons, as follows:

Twelve Representative Governors:

6 (of whom at least two shall be women) appointed by the Otley Urban District Council: 3 (of whom at least one shall be a woman) appointed by the Wharfedale Rural District: 2 by the West Riding County Council: 1 by the Council of the University of Leeds.

Three Co-optative Governors:

to be appointed by resolution of the Governors

As soon as conveniently may be, the Governors shall provide suitable School Buildings, and in the meantime make temporary arrangements for carrying on the School.

The constitution remained the same until 1937 when the West Riding County Council sent a letter to the Governing Body about a proposed change. Representation to be:

Otley Urban District Council	6 (6)	Leeds University	1 (1)
Wharfedale Rural District Council	1 (3)	Co-opted	3 (3)
West Riding County Council	2 (2)	Ilkley Urban District Council	2 (0)
		TOTAL	15 (15)

'It was resolved on the proposition of Mr Preston seconded by Mr Yates that we agree to the suggested re-arrangements except that the Wharfedale Rural District Council shall have two representatives (one of whom shall be a woman) and the Ilkley Urban District Council one representative.' (Governing Body minutes 19 May 1937)

The Clerk of the County Council's reply was tabled at the Governing body meeting held on 14 July 1937, at which the Governors resolved to accept the proposal that the number of Governors be increased to 17; the Ilkley Urban District Council to have three representatives and the Wharfedale Rural District Council two representatives.

Although there is no reference to the change in the Governors' minutes, the number of Governors was increased to 18, with the Wharfedale Rural District Council retaining their 3 representatives. The structure of the Governing Body at the start and end of the War is shown below:

Governor – start of War	Changes during the War		Governor – end of War
Mr F. T. Hunter, Chairman: (W.R.C.C.)	Resigned as Chair May 1940	Died December 1940	Colonel Kenneth Duncan: (W.R.C.C.)
Alderman H. J., Bambridge: (W.R.C.C.)			Alderman H. J. Bambridge: (W.R.C.C.)
Professor Barbier: (Leeds University)			Professor Barbier: (Leeds University)
Mr C. J. F. Atkinson, Vice Chairman: (Otley U.D.C.)	Chair on resignation of Hunter May 1940	Died October 1943	Mr G. E. Wilkinson: (Otley U.D.C.)
Mrs. E. Kettlewood: (Otley U.D.C.)		Replaced May 1942 by Mrs. M. Johnson	Mrs. M. Johnson: (Otley U.D.C.)
Mr P. Wade: (Otley U.D.C.)	Vice Chair on resignation of Hunter, May 1940	Died Oct 1944, replaced by Mr Cecil Newstead	Mr Cecil Newstead: (Otley U.D.C.)

Miss D. C. Hunter: (Otley U.D.C.)			Miss D. C. Hunter: (Otley U.D.C.)
G. Lambert: (Otley U.D.C.)			G. Lambert: (Otley U.D.C.)
K. Milligan: (Otley U.D.C.)	The first old scholar to become a Gov-ernor.		K. Milligan: (Otley U.D.C.)
Mr H. Brearley: (Ilkley U.D.C.)	Died February 1945	Replaced by C. L. Briggs, May 1945	Mr C. L. Briggs: (Ilkley U.D.C.)
Mr J. E. Dykes: (Ilkley U.D.C.)			Mr J. E. Dykes: (Ilkley U.D.C.)
Mrs. F. S. Hampshire: (Ilkley U.D.C.)	Resigned January 1942	Replaced May 1942 by Allan L. Dawson	Allan L. Dawson: (Ilkley U.D.C.)
Mrs. M. Martin: (Wharfedale R.D.C.)			Mrs. M. Martin: (Wharfedale R.D.C.)
Mr W. Whiteley: (Wharfedale R.D.C.)	Elected vice chair on illness of Wade, May 1943	Elected Chair on death of Atkinson, October 1943	Mr W. Whiteley, Chairman: (Wharfedale R.D.C.)
Mr E. Yates: (Wharfedale R.D.C.)	Died July 1939	Replaced by County Councillor R. T. A. Renton, March 1941	County Councilor R. T. A. Renton: (Wharfedale R.D.C.)
Major Le G. G. W. Horton Fawkes: (Co-optative Governor)	Vice Chair on death of Atkinson		Major Le G. G. W. Horton Fawkes, Vice Chairman: (Co-optative Governor)
Mr H. W. Preston: (Co-optative Governor)	Died November 1942	Replaced by Rev. W. Johnstone	Rev. W. Johnstone: (Co-optative Governor)
Rev. T. J. Williams: (Co-optative Governor)	Vicar of Otley		Rev. T. J. Williams: (Co-optative Governor)

There were about 6 Governing body meetings each year during the War. Most of the work was done by committees – Finance & General Purposes, School & Grounds, Staffing, and a Ladies Committee. Provision was also made for an '*Emergency Committee*,' made up of the Chairman, Vice-Chairman, Headmaster and Clerk:

'to deal with any matter of emergency arising in connection with the present national situation, with full power to act.'

There is no evidence in the minutes that this Committee met. Indeed, there is little in the minutes to suggest that business did not continue as normal during the War years. The only change of note was that from January 1940 until March 1946 meetings were held in the afternoon in the Local Public Assistance Board Room, located on Boroughgate, rather than in the evening at the School.

Meetings were serviced by a Clerk; the position was held for many years by Mr Cecil

Newstead, but on his resignation in 1943 he was replaced by Mr Anderson. From December 1944 Mr Newstead became a Governor, replacing the late Mr Wade.

The day-to-day organisation and management of a school is the responsibility of the Head teacher. At this time the powers of the Governors were wide-ranging and significant – finance, annual estimates, accounts, tenders, staffing, occasional holidays, admission of pupils – but over time the local authority became much more involved in these issues. The Governors' minutes contain many examples of situations in which the Governors clearly feel that the local authority is too involved in the affairs of an '*Endowed*' School. This was inevitable because the local authority provided the capital and finance to enable the School to re-open and progress. There are also examples where the Governors feel that the local authority is slow to act, especially when spending by the L.E.A. is seen as insufficient, deadlines are not met or requested projects rejected. The 1944 Education Act impacted further on the management of the School, – loss of the Preparatory Department, ending of fees – on the structure of the school through potential changes in the type of school and on the role of the local authority.

Governors were expected to give up their time to attend meetings and support the School. Representative governors had to have some regard for the authorities that had appointed them. In some cases attendance at meetings was poor and, Governors were '*dismissed*' because the rules set out in the Scheme had been broken; there are examples of these Governors being re-selected by the appointing body for a further term of office! However, many Governors were local people with an interest in the School and the community. Without their enthusiasm and dogged determination Prince Henry's would not have re-opened in 1918 and may not have survived and grown. Local solicitors, industrialists, bankers and landowners used their influence and expertise to lay the foundations for a successful future for the School. Many of these people also contributed financially through prizes and scholarships. Christopher John Newstead and Thomas Arthur Duncan deserve special mention in their drive to make sure that the School re-opened in 1918.

The most important role is that of Chairman of the Governing Body. Establishing a positive, working relationship with the Headmaster was vital in the success of the School. Over the period of the Second World War there were three Chairs:

- ✓ Mr Frederic Thomas Hunter: 1925-1940
- ✓ Mr Charles Joshua Fearnside Atkinson: 1940-1943
- ✓ Mr William Whiteley: 1943-1946

Frederic Thomas Hunter (1858-1940)
Chairman of Governors 1925-1940

Frederic Hunter was born in 1857 in Bradford, but both his parents, Thomas and Anna were born in Scotland. The 1861 Census lists Thomas as a stuff merchant, living in Manningham, Bradford, but by 1871 he had retired from business and moved with his family to Weston Lane, Otley. By 1881 the family had moved to Newall Lodge, Otley, the home of Frederic and his family for the rest of their lives. In 1887, Frederic married Lucy Agnes Conyers (1866-1939). The couple had three daughters, Winifred H. Hunter, born in 1888, Dorothy C. Hunter, born in 1892 and Anna H. Hunter, born in 1896. The 1881 Census lists Frederic as a solicitor.

Mr Hunter was one of the original pre-1909 Governors and was appointed Vice-Chairman of the Provisional Governing body in November 1908. On the post-1909 Governing Body he was a representative of the West Riding County Council and remained so until, his death in 1940. In 1925, following the death of Thomas Arthur Duncan he was elected Chairman of the Governing Body.

Mrs. Hunter died in 1939 and Mr Hunter resigned as Chair of Governors in May 1940, though remained a Governor.

'The Clerk was instructed to record upon the minutes an expression of the deep gratitude of the Governors for all the valuable services rendered to the school for so many years by Mr Hunter and for the deep and kindly interest which he has taken at all times in the welfare and success of the school. The fact that Mr Hunter is to remain a member of the Governing Body was noted with pleasure and the hope was expressed that the Governing Body may have the privilege of Mr Hunter's co-operation and help for many years to come.

With these expressions the Headmaster on behalf of the members of the Staff and the officers of the School desired to be associated.'

On his death, Mr Hunter was replaced as a West Riding County Council representative by Colonel Kenneth Duncan, son of the late Mr Thomas Arthur Duncan. Mr C.J.F. Atkinson was elected Chairman and Mr P.S. Wade, Vice Chairman.

The death of Mr Hunter was announced at the meeting of the Governing Body held on 11 December 1940.

'At the outset of the meeting Mr C. J. F. Atkinson as Chairman referred in sympathetic terms to the death of Mr F. T. Hunter a Member of the Governing Body and for many

years Chairman thereof.

Mr Atkinson referred to the valuable services rendered by Mr Hunter at all times to the school, the town of Otley and Wharfedale and spoke in appreciative terms of the many services rendered so willingly by Mr Hunter to the school and of the great loss which his death meant to the school. Mr Wilde on behalf of himself and the members of staff and Major Le G. G. Horton Fawkes by letter, associated themselves with the expressions. The members stood in silence as a tribute to the memory of Mr Hunter.'

The following tribute appeared in the *'Otliensian'* (Vol. XXIII, Autumn 1940):

'The School learned with deep regret of the death of Mr F.T.Hunter on the 12th October.

Mr Hunter was among the foremost of those whose vision brought about the reopening of our School and he was a member of the Governing Body formed for that purpose. He was later Chairman of the Governors for fifteen years and had only retired from that position at the end of last year. His good work in the town was well known to all and the School had particular reason to value his generosity and kindliness. Besides giving the Chairman's prizes each year, Mr Hunter lost no opportunity in befriending us with his help and advice, coming among us often and showing in countless ways the regard which he always had for education in the town of Otley. We offer our sympathy to Miss Hunter, also one of our Governors, and to her two sisters.'

On 21 December 1949:

'The School received a beautifully carved oak reading desk in memory of Mr F. T. Hunter, a member of the Governing Body from 1904 to 1940 and Chairman for the last fifteen years of that time. The desk is the gift of Mr Hunter's three daughters. Miss D. Hunter, herself a Governor, and Mrs. Sutcliffe were present on the platform, as were also the Chairman and the Vice-Chairman, Mr K. Milligan.' (*'Otliensian'* Vol. XXXII, Spring 1950)

His daughter Miss Dorothy Hunter was a Governor from 1934 until her death in 1971.

Charles Joshua Fearnside Atkinson (1868-1943)
Chairman of Governors 1940-1943

C.J.F. Atkinson was born in Castley to Isaac and Eliza Atkinson. Isaac was a farmer and grazier, with 120 acres of land and the family later lived in Arthington. Isaac died in 1897 and Eliza and the rest of the family moved to Rosebank Villas in Burley-in-Wharfedale. The 1891 Census lists Charles as a solicitor, and his mother was said to be living *'on her own means.'* Charles married Jane Elizabeth Dower in 1899. The couple had three children, one of whom died in infancy. The 1911 Census lists Charles, Jane Elizabeth and their two children living at 'Birchgarth' in Burley-in-Wharfedale. He became a partner in the local firm of Atkinson, Dacre & Slack, who until recently (2013)

were based at 40 Boroughgate, Otley.

He was appointed to the Governing Body as a representative of Otley U.D.C. in 1913, replacing Rev. Pattinson who had resigned. He was therefore much involved with the re-opening of the School in 1918. At the Annual Speech Day in 1921 Mr Atkinson, *'noting that the girls had no cup for their sports, was pleased to present one for competition next year.'*

'A handsome silver cup, which Mr C. J. F. Atkinson promised last Speech Day for the Girls' House Championship at Prince Henry's Grammar School, has now arrived, and was on view at the last meeting of the Governing Body. Hitherto the School has possessed only one cup, this having been presented by Mr E. C. Woodman for the Boys' House Championship. The Headmaster (Mr W. Robinson) intimated that still another cup had been promised. This was by Mrs. W. G. Milligan, and would be presented each year to the boy gaining most points at the annual sports.'

(*'Otliensian' Vol. IV, Summer Term 1922*)

In 1934 Mr Atkinson presented the School with some trees:

These have been planted, and will undoubtedly improve the appearance of the newly acquired grounds. We heartily thank Mr Atkinson for his gift and for his unfailing interest at all times in the welfare of the School. (*'Otliensian' Vol. XVI, Lent 1934*)

Also in 1934 his experiences as a local solicitor were published in his book *'Recollections from a Yorkshire Dale'* (published by Heath Cranton Ltd, London 1934). In his introduction he noted that *'I come from a long race of farmers and I am still one of them at heart.'* The Foreword was written by Judge Woodcock, who had presented the prizes at the 1931 Speech Day, probably attracted through the influence of his friendship with Mr Atkinson.

On the death of Mr E.C. Woodman, Mr Atkinson was elected Vice-Chairman of the Governing Body, and in 1939, on the death of Mr F.T. Hunter, he became Chairman. His reign as Chairman was brief, for he died in 1943. His leadership in managing the School through the first four years of the Second World War cannot be under-estimated.

IN MEMORIAM – MR C.J.F. ATKINSON, M.B.E., LL.B.

'The School learned with profound regret on re-assembling in September of the grievous

loss which we had suffered in the death of our former Chairman Mr C.J.F. Atkinson, M.B.E., LL.B. We were well aware that Mr. Atkinson had been a most distinguished figure in the field of education and a very good friend to this School. He was one of those who helped powerfully in its revival twenty-five years ago and he watched over its interests to the end of his life. He was often among us at the School and we were always glad to see him. He took morning assembly on the last day before the summer holidays. The trees around our playing fields and in front of the School were his gift, and we now have them in some way as a memorial to him. We extend our very sincere sympathy to Mrs. Atkinson whom also we have been very glad to welcome among us on many occasions.' (*'Otliensian' Vol. XXVI, Spring 1944*)

He was succeeded as Chairman by Mr William Whiteley, who in turn was succeeded as Vice-Chairman by Major Le G.G.W. Horton-Fawkes.

William Whiteley (1896-1967)
Chairman of Governors 1943-1946

William Whiteley was born in Pool-in-Wharfedale in 1896, the son of William Lumb Whiteley. The Whiteley family came originally from Halifax, where William Whiteley had a paper mill at Barkisland in 1866. He subsequently moved to Horsforth and then to Syreholme, near Appletreewick, in 1875. In 1886 his three sons – Benjamin, Samuel and William Lumb Whiteley (1863-1937) – set up on their own mill at Pool-in-Wharfedale, where the firm specialized in pressboards for the textile industry.

Benjamin died in 1902 and in 1906 William bought out Samuel and became the sole proprietor. He was joined after the First World War by his sons Holmes and William junior and the business expanded, largely through the increased demand for boards for use in electrical insulation. *'Elephantide'* insulating board was its most successful product and by 1936 the mill at Pool had become the largest pressboard factory in the world. It became a private company in 1920.

In the 1930s William Lumb Whiteley handed over the responsibility for the business to his two sons. By the end of the Second World War, the fourth generation of the Whiteley family had entered the business; Holmes was joined by his two sons, David and John, and William by his son Charles William (born 1923). In 1946 the firm became a Public company.

However, in the late 1960s diminishing world markets and fierce foreign competition led to a gradual decline in demand for the company's products. In 1981 the receivers were called in by the Company's bankers. The firm was purchased by the Swiss, Weidemann Company and the Whiteley family lost control of the company.

The following extract is taken from '***A HISTORY OF POOL PAPER MILLS by Alastair Laurence: (published 1986, Smith Settle, Otley):***

'William Whiteley junior (born 1896) was certainly the 'business-man' of the family. He had great ambition, he was very outgoing and assertive, and it would be true to say that he was the main driving force behind the great expansion during the 1920s and 30s. William Whiteley was prepared to travel the world to win orders for Pool – for instance, in 1931 the Canadian market was opened up after his business trip there. By the mid 1930s the Company could name customers in the USSR, Argentina, Australia, Canada, Denmark, Sweden, France, Belgium and Poland. In recognition of his services to the industry, William Whiteley was awarded the OBE. (1965 New Years Honours List)'

In 1922 William Whiteley married Helena Little.

William Lumb Whiteley became a Governor of Prince Henry's in 1933 as a representative of the Wharfedale Rural District Council. After his death in 1937 he was replaced as a Governor by his son William. In May 1943 William Whiteley was elected Vice-Chairman of the Governing Body and was also Chair of the influential Finance and General Purposes Committee. In October 1943 he was elected Chairman of the Governing Body, following the death of Mr Atkinson. At the same meeting Major Le G. G. W. Horton-Fawkes was elected vice Chairman.

In May 1946 Mr Whiteley was replaced as Chairman by Major Fawkes.

'In accepting the office, Major Horton-Fawkes paid tribute to the work done by Councillor W. Whiteley as Chairman for the past three years, which have been difficult times. Members also expressed their thanks and appreciation to Councillor W. Whiteley, and it was 'RESOLVED: That the Governors place on record in the minutes their high appreciation of the services given by Councillor W. Whiteley in the past three years during his tenure of office as Chairman of the Board, and tender him their best wishes.'

At the same meeting:

'The Chairman referred to the recent gift by Mr Whiteley of a Chair for platform furniture and the previous suggestion that there should be a public appeal for the sum of £150 for a set of chairs and a refectory table in memory of past benefactors of the School. It was agreed that a public appeal be made in the press for the sum of £150 to complete the platform furniture, the appeal to be over the names of the Chairman and Vice-Chairman of the Governors, and that the next step be then left to the Chairman, Vice-Chairman and Mr Whiteley.'

Previously Mr Whiteley had presented to the School a memorial listing the names of the Headmasters of Prince Henry's from its foundation:

'That the Governors place on record their gratitude to the Chairman, Councillor Wm. Whiteley for his generosity in presenting the tablet as a memorial containing the names of Headmasters of the School from the time of its inception in this township of Otley, and extend to him their sincere thanks.' (Governing Body minutes, 12 December 1945)

Mr Whiteley ceased being a Governor of Prince Henry's, but became the Chairman of North Parade Secondary School Governing Body. He played an important role in the establishment of the Comprehensive School, pointing out that *'his Governors were most concerned about the Secondary School during the interim period.' (Joint Governing Bodies meeting, 22 March 1967)*. He was elected as Vice Chairman of the interim Governing Body of the new organisation. Unfortunately, on 11 September 1967, before the coming together of the two schools, Mr Whiteley died. He was buried at St Wilfred's Church in Pool-in-Wharfedale.

'The Chairman paid tribute to the long and valuable service Mr W. Whiteley had rendered to education. The Committee then stood in silence' (Prince Henry's Grammar School Governors, 4 October 1967)

The *'Otliensian' Vol. L, Spring 1968*, contained the following tribute:

'In William Whiteley we mourn a servant to education, a character and a benefactor. Almost an institution in local government and on the bench, he served education in Wharfedale for very many years. He was Chairman of Prince Henry's Governors in the forties and often spoke of his responsibility for putting the 1944 Act into effect. Later he became Chairman of the Secondary School Governors and it was appropriate that when our two schools merged he should become Vice-Chairman of the new governing body.

He was frequently very generous to Prince Henry's (not his own school, though it might have been but for a period of closure before 1918). Of his several gifts to the School, two are seen everyday by all our pupils – the handsome table and chairs which grace the Hall platform, and the Board of Headmasters (a Kilburn product from the 'Mouse' craftsman) in the main corridor outside.

Prince Henry's has cause to be deeply grateful for William Whiteley's life and generosity. Our sympathy goes out to his widow whose grace and charm we remember so vividly from the Spring Fair of 1966.'

The War – Old Scholars

At the Annual General Meeting of the Old Scholars' Association on 23 November 1939 it was decided that a record be kept of Old Scholars serving with His Majesty's Forces during the war. The first list was published in the Summer 1940 issue of the *'Otliensian'* The second list, published in Autumn 1940 also contained details of promotions, amendments and corrections. The lists were compiled by Mr Padgett.

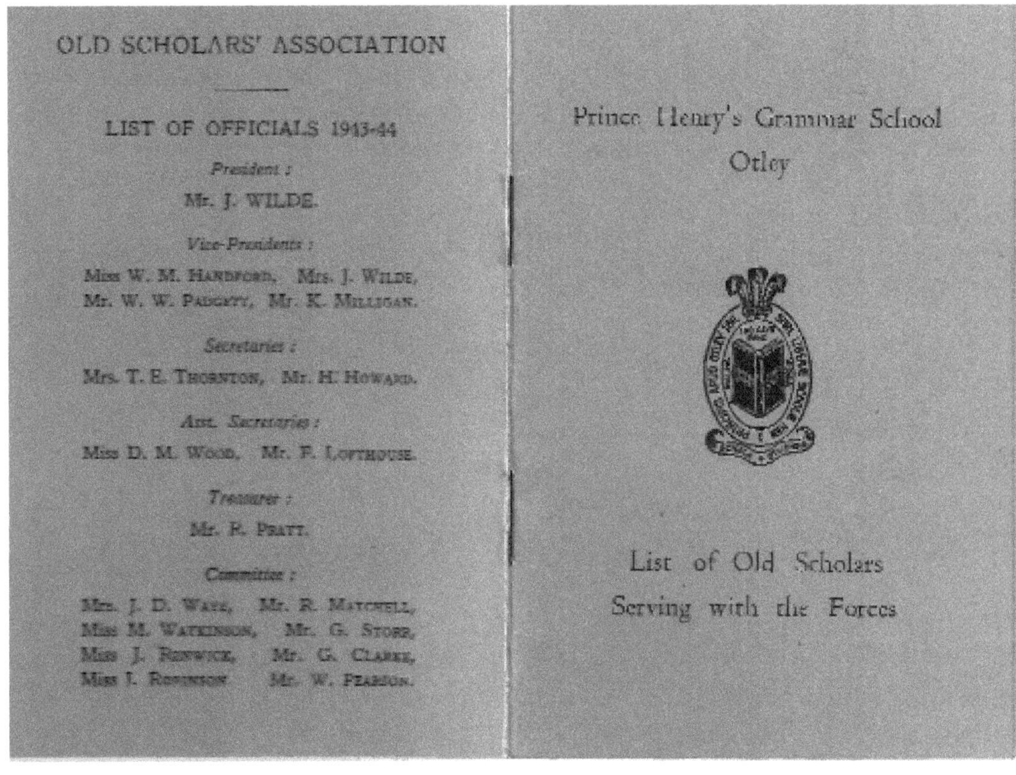

OLD SCHOLARS' ASSOCIATION

LIST OF OFFICIALS 1943-44

President :

Mr. J. WILDE.

Vice-Presidents :

Miss W. M. Handford, Mrs. J. Wilde,
Mr. W. W. Padgett, Mr. K. Milligan.

Secretaries :

Mrs. T. E. Thornton, Mr. H. Howard.

Asst. Secretaries :

Miss D. M. Wood, Mr. F. Lofthouse.

Treasurer :

Mr. R. Pratt.

Committee :

Mrs. J. D. Wade, Mr. R. Mitchell,
Miss M. Watkinson, Mr. G. Storr,
Miss J. Renwick, Mr. G. Clarke,
Miss I. Robinson Mr. W. Pearson.

Prince Henry's Grammar School
Otley

List of Old Scholars
Serving with the Forces

In 1944 it was announced that a list of all Old Scholars known to be in the Forces would be published in booklet form and sent to the family of every Old Scholar whose name was on the list.

'An examination of the list, which contains more than 400 names, reveals that Old Scholars today are to be found in almost every branch of the Services. The Army, as might be expected, has claimed the greatest number of Old Boys, whose tasks are varied as (we imagine) are the scenes of their labours. How instructive a map of the wanderings of our Old Scholars would be! More than 100 Old Boys have joined the R.A.F., while well over 30 have answered the call of the sea. There are more than 60 Old Scholars in the Women's Services. About two-fifths of these are in the A.T.S., and both the W.A.A.F and W.R.N.S. are well represented.

'As we read to the end of the list we grieve to note that eighteen Old Boys are known or

are presumed to have lost their lives. Five others are missing, four are Prisoners of War in German hands and five are in Japanese hands. We deeply lament these casualties.'

Sadly, by the end of the War a total of 40 old scholars and one member of staff had lost their lives.

The foreword, dated July 1944, by Mr Wilde, the Headmaster reads:

'To all Old Scholars now serving with H.M. Forces this little publication is addressed with the warmest greetings and sincerest good wishes of the Old Scholars' Association and the School.

We are proud that the School is fitly and fully represented in all the theatres of war. Not a few of our Old Scholars have already reached high rank in the Services and some have been decorated for their gallantry in action. These details, as far as we know them, appear in the following lists, and we extend our congratulations to all concerned. We are sure that all our serving members are bringing credit upon themselves and honour to us in whatever station they may be. We publish also a list of casualties, and we offer our sincere sympathy to their relatives.

We apologise for any omissions or inaccuracies in these pages. We can only depend on the information we receive, and we shall be grateful to any Old Scholars who can help us to keep our records up to date.

We are always delighted to hear from our Old Scholars or to see them at the School, and we hope that it will not be long before they are back among us in a world at peace.'

JOHN WILDE WINIFRED M. HANDFORD WILFRED W. PADGETT

The booklet contains the names, rank and service details of 403 Old Scholars, including fatal casualties, missing, prisoners of war and those discharged. Additional lists were included in later editions of the *'Otliensian'* following the publication of the booklet in summer 1944, and there were certainly some omissions. The information below shows the names, rank and service details for the 464 Old Scholars whose details are included in the school magazine. It is unlikely that this list is complete, but it does provide evidence of the minimum number of Old Scholars who served in the Forces during the Second World War. The 'final rank' and 'final regiment' details are based on lists published in the school magazine showing 'promotions, amendments and corrections,' and a few records have been amended using articles published in the '*Wharfedale and Airedale Observer*.'

Surname	Forename	Final Rank	Final Regiment
Ackroyd	Maurice	Corporal	Royal Artillery
Adamson	Geoffrey Arthur	Leading Aircraftman	Royal Air Force
Aldersley	Mabel Annie	Aircraftwoman Class 2	Women's Auxiliary Air Force
Allison	Frank William	Lance Bombardier	Royal Artillery
Allison	John Thomas	Corporal	Royal Air Force
Allsop	Harold Gordon Leach	Group Captain	Royal Air Force
Almond	Harold	Lance Bombardier	Royal Artillery
Anderson	Eric Reginald	Flying Officer	Royal Air Force
Armitage	Alan Howard	Corporal	Royal Air Force
Armitage	Albert Edward	Aircraftman Class 2	Royal Air Force
Armitage	Philip Hugh	Apprentice Surveyor	Royal Engineers (Military Survey)
Armitstead	John Richard	Private	General Service Corps
Atkinson	Eric	Sapper	Royal Engineers
Atkinson	Reginald Walker	Lieutenant Colonel	Royal Corps of Signals
Aveyard	Leslie	Corporal	Royal Corps of Signals
Ayrton	Harry	Lieutenant-Colonel	Royal Army Ordnance Corps
Bairstow	Arnold	Corporal	Royal Electrical and Mechanical Engineers
Bairstow	Hannah	Sergeant	Women's Auxiliary Air Force
Baldwin	Herbert William Simms	Pilot Officer	Royal Air Force
Balls	Dennis Hugh	Aircraftman Class 2	Royal Air Force
Barber	Norman Charles Drake	Signaller	Royal Corps of Signals
Barber*	Peter William	Sergeant	Royal Air Force
Barford	Michael Fred	Aircraftman Class 2	Royal Air Force
Barker	Anthony Yewdall	Lance Bombardier	Royal Artillery
Barker	Colin Cecil	Lieutenant	East Yorks
Barker	Frederick Terry	Leading Aircraftman	Royal Air Force
Barker	Hazel Nora	-	Women's Land Army

Barker	Robert Peter Geoffrey	Sergeant	Royal Northumberland Fusiliers
Barker	Sheila Margaret	Private	Auxiliary Territorial Service
Barker	William Holroyd	Leading Aircraftman	Royal Air Force
Barrett	John Raymond	Trooper	Royal Armoured Corps
Barrett	Norman	Driver	Royal Engineers
Bateson	Mark Leslie	Lieutenant Commander	Royal Armoured Corps
Beanland	Roger	Ordinary Seaman	Royal Navy
Beevers	Margaret Lesley	Corporal	British Red Cross
Bell	Bernard	Private	General Service Corps
Bell	Harold	Lieutenant	Royal Armoured Corps
Bell	John Thornton	Major	Royal Engineers
Bell*	Ronald	Sergeant Wireless Operator	Royal Air Force
Bellerby	Dorothy	Wren	Women's Royal Naval Service
Bellerby	Fred Addison	Corporal	Royal Army Ordnance Corps
Benson	Denis	Marine	Royal Marines
Bentley*	Harry Norman	Staff Sergeant	Royal Electrical and Mechanical Engineers
Birkett	Harold Ernest	Sergeant	Royal Air Force
Bishop	Edward Eric	Corporal	Royal Army Medical Corps
Biss	Ronald Dolby	Captain	Durham Light Infantry/ Royal Artillery
Bisson	Louis Raymond	Sergeant	Royal Air Force
Blakey	Isabel	Leading Wren/Petty Officer	Women's Royal Naval Service
Blakey	Joseph	Petty Officer	Royal Navy
Bodiley	Arthur Phineas	Major	Royal Corps of Signals
Bolton	George Harry	Aircraftman Class 1	Royal Army Ordnance Corps
Booth	Gordon Henry	Signalman	Royal Corps of Signals
Bottomley	Granville	Corporal	Royal Air Force
Boyce	Kenneth	Private	L.N.L.
Boyes	Joan Kathleen	Wren	Women's Royal Naval Service

Bradford	Paul	Sick Berth Attendant	Royal Navy
Bradley	Norman	Chief Petty Officer	Royal Navy
Braithwaite	George Lovell	Bombardier	Royal Artillery
Braithwaite	Robert Alfred	Private	???
Bramley	Stanley Frederick	Aircraftman Class 2	Royal Air Force
Brearley	Derek George	Sub-Lieutenant	R.N.V.R. – Fleet Air Arm
Brearley	Harold Stuart	Midshipman	R.N.V.R. – Fleet Air Arm
Broadbelt	Woodrow Wilson	Leading Aircraftman	Royal Air Force
Brown	Derek Arthur	Ordinary Seaman	Royal Navy
Brown	Ewart	Trooper	Royal Tank Regiment
Brown	Freda	Sergeant	Auxiliary Territorial Service
Brown	Harold	Lance Corporal	Royal Corps of Signals
Brown	Harry A	Staff Sergeant	Royal Electrical and Mechanical Engineers
Brownfoot	Maurice Andrew	Petty Officer	Royal Navy
Brunskill	Gilbert Smeaton	Chief Petty Officer	Royal Navy
Bunting*	James Arthur	Flight Sergeant	Royal Air Force
Burns	Ronald	Lance Corporal	Royal Air Force
Butler	Elsie Marguerite	Private	Auxiliary Territorial Service
Butterfield	Gerald	Lieutenant	Royal Engineers
Butterworth	Joan	Corporal	Women's Auxiliary Air Force
Buttery	Phyllis	Sergeant	Auxiliary Territorial Service
Byford	Daniel	Aircraftman Class 2	Royal Air Force
Carrick	Edgar	Leading Aircraftman	Royal Air Force
Cavill	William	Corporal	Royal Air Force
Caygill	Margaret	Nursing Sister - Flying Officer	Royal Air Force
Chaffer	Thomas Arthur	Sergeant	Royal Air Force
Chapman	Eric	Gunner	Royal Artillery
Chapman (Staff)	George	Captain	Intelligence Corps
Chapman	Joan Doreen	Wren	Women's Royal Naval Service
Cheetham	Herbert Arthur	Flight-Lieutenant	Royal Air Force
Child	Douglas	L/Sergeant	Royal Artillery
Child	William	Gunner	Royal Artillery

Clapham*	John Stanley	Sergeant	Royal Air Force
Clark	William	Leading Aircraftman	Royal Air Force
Clarke	Anthony Peter	Lieutenant	Royal Armoured Corps
Clarke	Geoffrey	Ordinary Telegraphist	Royal Navy
Clarkson	Gordon Alfred	Sergeant	Royal Army Ordnance Corps
Clayton	Edward Gordon	Private	Royal Army Ordnance Corps
Close	Ian Bransby	Signalman	Royal Corps of Signals
Cockerham	Jack	Sergeant Navigator	Royal Air Force
Collier	Vincent	Staff Sergeant	Royal Army Ordnance Corps
Collinson	Mark	Lance Bombardier	Royal Artillery
Cooper	Ernest	Craftsman	Royal Electrical & Mechanical Engineers
Cooper	Henry Christopher	Captain	Royal Artillery
Cooper	James Stanley	Second Lieutenant	West Yorks
Crawshaw	John Maurice	Lance Bombardier	Royal Artillery
Crawshaw	Robert	Second Lieutenant	R.S.C.
Cribb	Peter Henry	Group Captain	Royal Air Force
Cribb (nee Walter)	Patricia Grace	Aircraftwoman Class 1	Women's Auxiliary Air Force
Crosland*	Jack	Warrant Officer/Pilot	Royal Air Fore Volunteer Reserve
Cross	William Brian Norman	Midshipman	Royal Navy
Crossley	Jack	Sergeant	Coldstream Guards
Crossley	Robert Michael	Private	West Yorks
Crothers	Pamela Kathleen	Aircraftwoman Class 2	Women's Auxiliary Air Force
Dale	William Birdsall	Craftsman	Royal Electrical and Mechanical Engineers
Davison (Staff)	Eric	Flight Lieutenant	Royal Air Force Volunteer Reserve
Dawson	Cyril	Sergeant Pilot	Royal Air Force

Dawson	Elisabeth Patricia Leslie	Aircraftwoman Class 2	Women's Auxiliary Air Force
Dawson	George Walker	Sergeant	Royal Artillery
Day	John Spencer	Staff Sergeant	Royal Army Medical Corps
Dean	Esther Margaret	Corporal	Auxiliary Territorial Service
Denham (Staff)	Basil M	Flight Lieutenant	Royal Air Force Volunteer Reserve
Denison	Joan Mary	-	Women's Land Army
Dibb	Leslie	Pilot Officer	Royal Air Force
Dickinson	Geoffrey William	Aircraftman Class 2	Royal Air Force
Dixon	Eric Hubert	Aircraftman Class 2	Royal Air Force
Dobson	James	Lance Corporal	Royal Army Ordnance Corps
Dodgshon*	Geoffrey	Captain	Manchester Regiment
Dodgshon	Harry	Trooper	Royal Tank Regiment
Dodgshon	Maurice	Leading Aircraftman	Royal Air Force
Downs	John Howard	Rifleman	Rifle Brigade
Duffissey	Alban Robert	Boy	Royal Artillery
Dunwell*	Henry Howes	Flight Sergeant	Royal Air Force
England	Douglas	Corporal	Royal Artillery
England	Neville	Leading Aircraftman	Royal Air Force
Evans (Staff)	Haydn	Pilot Officer	Royal Air Force
Exley	Michael Arthur	Gunner	Royal Artillery
Fairbanks*	Gordon Maguire	Third Officer	Merchant Navy
Fairburn	Richard	Chief Petty Officer	Royal Navy
Farnell	Joseph Gordon	Chief Petty Officer	Royal Navy
Fawcett	Edward Michael	Sergeant	Royal Army Medical Corps
Firth	Andrew Trevor	Captain	Royal Artillery
Firth	John Douglas	Bombardier	Royal Artillery
Foggin	Kenneth	Private	Royal Welsh Fusiliers
Fortune	Noel	Leading Aircraftman	Royal Air Force Volunteer Reserve
Foster	Samuel Ronald	Lance Corporal	3rd H.C.T. Regt.
Foulds	Dudley	Trooper	Commandoes
Foulston	Angela Shirley	Wren	Women's Royal Naval Service
Foulston	Patricia Alice	Sergeant	Auxiliary Territorial Service

Francis	Eleanor Mary	Sergeant	Auxiliary Territorial Service
Furness	Derek Heaton	Warrant Officer	Royal Air Force
Gardner	Margaret Nancy	Private	Auxiliary Territorial Service
Garnett	Mary	Nursing Member	British Red Cross
Garside	Roy	Leading Writer	Royal Navy
Garth	Anthony	Pilot Officer	Royal Air Force
Geenty	Henry	Flying Officer	Royal Air Force
Gill	John	Leading Seaman Apprentice	Royal Navy
Gledhill	Edward Alan	Private	Royal Armoured Corps
Glover	Eric Benjamin	Lieutenant	Royal Artillery
Goldsborough	Leslie	Gunner	Royal Artillery
Granger	Edward Vere	Corporal	Royal Corps of Signals
Granville	Arthur Derrick	Private	Royal Army Ordnance Corps
Grass	Maurice	Trooper	Royal Armoured Corps
Graville	Norman Hanson	Gunner	Royal Artillery
Greaves	Harold	Aircraftman Class 2	Royal Air Force
Greenwood	Joshua Colin	Aircraftman Class 2	Royal Air Force
Greenwood	Joyce Mildred	Aircraftwoman	Women's Auxiliary Air Force
Greetham	Frederick Harry	Trooper	Yorkshire Hussars
Gunniss	Frank Raymond	Corporal	Intelligence Corps
Haigh	Phillip Carleton	Sergeant	Royal Air Force
Hainsworth	Harold	Lance Bombardier	Royal Artillery
Hall	Jean Margaret	Leading Aircraftwoman	Women's Auxiliary Air Force
Haller	Thomas William	Leading Aircraftman	Royal Air Force
Halliwell	Douglas Harold	Flight-Lieutenant	Royal Air Force. Voluntary Reserve
Halliwell*	Kenneth Stephen	Sergeant Pilot	Royal Air Force. Voluntary Reserve
Hammond	George	Petty Officer	Royal Navy
Hargreaves	Geoffrey	Captain	West Yorks/ Lincolnshire Regiment
Harrison	Arthur	Corporal	Royal Army Medical Corps
Harrison*	Charles Leslie	Sergeant Pilot	Royal Air Force

Harrison	Herbert	Driver	Royal Corps of Signals
Harrison	John Ronald	Sergeant	Royal Electrical and Mechanical Engineers
Harrison	Lisle Christine	Wren	Women's Royal Naval Service
Hartley	Joan Marguerite	Third Officer	Women's Royal Naval Service
Hartley	Philip David	Signalman	Royal Corps of Signals
Hayhurst	Douglas	Leading Aircraftman	Royal Air Force
Hellewell*	Margery	Civilian	-
Hensby	William Royal Morris	Second Lieutenant	Pioneer Corps
Hessey	Robert S	Warrant Officer	Royal Air Force
Hildreth	Thomas Gordon	Sergeant	Royal Army Ordnance Corps
Hindle	Charles Norman	Corporal	Royal Corps of Signals
Hixon	Jack	Leading Aircraftman	Royal Air Force
Hobson	George	Sergeant	Royal Air Force
Hobson	Joan	Wren	Women's Royal Naval Service
Holden	Jack	Pilot Officer	Royal Navy
Holgate	Frances Olive	Private	Auxiliary Territorial Service
Holliday	Margaret Allan	-	Women's Land Army
Holmes	Ethel Mary	Private	Auxiliary Territorial Service
Holmes*	George Malcolm	Ordinary Seaman	Royal Navy
Holmes	Reginald Morton	Lieutenant	Royal Artillery
Holroyd	John Victor	-	-
Hooker	Dennis Ralph	Aircraftman Class 2	Royal Air Force
Horner	Kenneth William	Major	Royal Marines
Houlgate	Frederick Victor	Flying Officer	Royal Air Force
Howard	Stanley	Lance Bombardier	Royal Artillery
Hudson	Eric	Aircraftman Class 2	Royal Air Force
Hudson	John	-	Merchant Navy
Hudson	John Peter	Sapper	Royal Engineers
Hully	Leslie	Aircraftman Class 2	Royal Air Force
Ickringill	Dorothy May	Wren	Women's Royal Naval Service

Ickringill	John Rycroft	Private	General Service Corps
Illingworth	Rowena Townsend	-	Voluntary Aid Detachment (Nurse
Imeson*	Robert Stanton	Sergeant	Royal Air Force
Ineson	Jack	Lieutenant	R.N.F.
Ingelson	Frederick Joseph	Aircraftman Class 2	Royal Air Force
Irwin	Sidney Albert Victor	Sergeant	Royal Corps of Signals
Jackson	Hubert A.	Leading Aircraftman	Royal Air Force
Jackson	Kenneth	Aircraftman Class 2	Royal Air Force
Jackson	Philip Henry	Aircraftman Class 2	Royal Air Force
Jennings	Peter	Aircraftman Class 2	Royal Air Force
Jones	Barbara	Corporal	Women's Auxiliary Air Force
Jowett	Arthur Raymond	Driver	Royal Artillery
Jowett	Thomas Leslie	Corporal	Royal Air Force
Judson	Sybil	Sergeant	Auxiliary Territorial Service
Kay	Douglas Arnold	Corporal	Royal Army Ordnance Corps
Kay*	Ronald	-	Merchant Navy
Kay	William Herbert	Private	General Service Corps
Kerby	Charles Watkinson	Staff Sergeant	Royal Engineers
Kerby	Herbert	B.S.M.	Royal Artillery
Kershaw	John Bertram	Aircraftman Class 2	Royal Air Force
Kettlewood	Jack	Trooper	Royal Tank Regiment
Kidson	H.	Signalman	Royal Corps of Signals
King	June Mary	-	Women's Land Army
King	Noel Quinton	Lieutenant	Royal Army Service Corps
Knapton	Peter Mallorie	Aircraftman Class 2	Royal Air Force
Knowles	Brian Woodward	Leading Aircraftman	Royal Air Force
Labram	Stephen George	Sergeant	H.A.C.
Lake	Wilfred Oliver	Aircraftman Class 2	Royal Air Force
Land	Dorothy Elizabeth	Nurse	C.N.R.
Land	Jack Hewitt	First Radio Officer (A)	Merchant Navy

Langham	Frank William	L/Sergeant	Royal Army Ordnance Corps
Langham	John Edward	Signalman	Royal Corps of Signals
Langton	Leslie	Signalman	Royal Corps of Signals
Laud	Albert Gordon	Private	Royal Army Pay Corps
Lawrie	Edward Parker Milligan	Driver	Royal Army Ordnance Corps
Lawson	James	Corporal	R.A.F. Regt.
Leach	George Charles	Ordinary Seaman	Royal Navy
Leach	Joan	Wren	Women's Royal Naval Service
Leach	Rowland Beresford	Sick Berth Attendant	Royal Navy
Lee	Brian	Second radio Officer	Merchant Navy
Lee	Denis	Lieutenant	Royal Engineers
Lewis	Catherine May	Private	Auxiliary Territorial Service
Lewis	Frank Holgate	Lance Corporal	Royal Engineers
Lewis	Hilda	Regulating Petty Officer	Women's Royal Naval Service
Lewis	Margaret Emily	Private	Auxiliary Territorial Service
Liddle	Edwin Alison	Leading Aircraftman	Royal Air Force
Light	Charles Vernon	Lieutenant Colonel	Royal Army Medical Corps
Lilley*	Bernard Dallah	Pilot Officer	Royal Air Force Volunteer Reserve
Lockwood	Brian Charles Melvin	Private	???
Longfield	John Raymond	Corporal	Kings Own Yorkshire Light Infantry
Lucas	Geoffrey Rhodes	Leading Aircraftman	Royal Air Force
Lund	John Evans	Ordinary Seaman	Royal Navy
Lupton*	Mark	Sergeant-Observer	Royal Air Force
MacDonald	John Colin Campbell	Sergeant	Royal Army Medical Corps
Mackintosh	Frank	Flight Lieutenant	Royal Air Force
Mainprize	William Leonard	Flying Officer	Royal Air Force
Mallinson	Harold	Captain	Royal Artillery
Marshall	Jean	Warrant Officer	Auxiliary Territorial Service

Marshall	Joseph Lincoln	Private	West Yorks
Marshall	Reginald Harold	Driver	Royal Army Ordnance Corps
Mason*	James Edward	Signaller	Royal Artillery
Mason	Nancy	Private	Auxiliary Territorial Service
Massey	Stanley	Aircraftman Class 2	Royal Air Force
McDonnell	Dennis	Guardsman	Irish Guards
Mensforth	Margaret	Corporal	Women's Auxiliary Air Force
Metcalf	Thomas Howard	Aircraftman Class 2	Royal Air Force
Metcalfe	Harold Arthur	Private	General Service Corps
Midgley	Frank	Trooper	Royal Armoured Corps
Midgley	Fred	Sergeant	Royal Air Force
Midgley	Thomas Henry	Sergeant	C.M.P.
Miller*	Arthur	Private	Royal Army Pay Corps
Miller	Eric Eaton	Corporal	Duke of Wellington's
Miller	Norman Armitage	Lance Corporal	Lothian & Border Yeomanry
Moon	Fred	Regimental Sergeant Major	Royal Army Ordnance Corps
Moon	William Clifford	Leading Seaman Apprentice	Merchant Navy
Moore	Anthony Wilmot	Captain	Royal Engineers
Moore	Brian Hardy	Corporal	Royal Corps of Signals
More	Thomas James	Ordinary Seaman	Royal Navy
Morris	Christopher Henry	-	Merchant Navy
Morris	Leonard John	Ordinary Seaman	Royal Navy
Morton*	Anthony Alan	Lieutenant	1st Wilts (India Command)
Moss	Philip Howard	Company Sergeant Major	Green Howards
Moss	Richard Noel	Flight-Lieutenant	Royal Air Force
Moulds	John Peter	Signalman	Royal Corps of Signals
Mounsey	John Sydney	Sergeant A.G.	Royal Air Force
Mountain	Edith Mary	-	Women's Land Army
Mountain	Ronald	Lance Corporal	Royal Army Pay Corps

Moxon	Hilda	Wren	Women's Royal Naval Service
Mudd	Charles Derek	Sergeant	Royal Armoured Corps
Mudd	John	Sergeant Pilot	Royal Air Force
Mulligan	Dorothea Mary	Wren	Women's Royal Naval Service
Myers	Barbara	Nursing Member	British Red Cross
Myers	John	Private	Pioneer Corps
Naylor	Dennis Oliver	Aircraftman Class 2	Royal Air Force
Naylor*	Ian Rochester	Midshipman	Royal Navy
Neal	Norman	Craftsman	Royal Electrical and Mechanical Engineers
Nettleton	Fred Spencer	Trooper	Royal Armoured Corps
Newbould	Irene	Aircraftwoman Class 2	Women's Auxiliary Air Force
Newell*	Harold	Flying Officer	Royal Air Force
Newhouse	Frank	Private	Parachute Regt
Newstead	Henry John	Staff Sergeant	Royal Army Ordnance Corps
Newton	Dorothy	Corporal	Auxiliary Territorial Service
Nicholls	Clarence Arthur	Sergeant	Royal Air Force
Nicholson	James Hugh	Pilot Officer	Royal Air Force
Nicholson*	Norman	Sergeant Observer	Royal Air Force
Nicholson	Rosamund	Private	Auxiliary Territorial Service
Nield* (Staff)	George K	Lance Corporal	Intelligence Corps
Nottage	James Alfred Bernard	Gunner	Royal Artillery
Nuttall	Donald	Leading Aircraftman	Royal Air Force
Offermans	John Victor	Private	Belgian Army
Oliver	John Arthur	Flying Officer	Royal Air Force
Outtersides	Derek Gladstone	Leading Aircraftman	Royal Air Force
Overend*	Harry	Flying Officer	Royal Air Force
Oxley	Dennis Robinson	Private	West Yorks
Palmer	Basil Foster	Corporal	Royal Air Force
Paton	Leslie	Aircraftman Class 2	Royal Air Force
Paul*	Eric George	Sergeant	Royal Air Force
Payne	Harold James	Flying Officer	Royal Air Force

Payne	John Arthur	Petty Officer	Fleet Air Arm
Payne	Kenneth Jack	Flight Lieutenant	Royal Air Force
Pearson	George William	Ordinary Seaman	Royal Navy
Petty	Charles Francis Carr	Aircraftman Class 2	Royal Air Force
Petty	Dennis	Ordinary Seaman	Royal Navy
Phillips	Norman	Staff Sergeant	Royal Electrical and Mechanical Engineers
Pickard	Charles Stanley	Private	Royal Army Medical Corps
Pickard*	Harry	Petty Officer	Royal Navy
Pickles*	Geoffrey Claude	Sub-Lieutenant (A)	Fleet Air Arm
Pratt	Christopher B	Private	Kings Own Yorkshire Light Infantry
Price	Peter Charles John	N.A.2	Royal Armoured Corps
Pullan	Betty	Lance Corporal	Auxiliary Territorial Service
Pullan*	Harold	Flying Officer	Royal Air Force
Pullan	John Roderick	N.A.A. (E)	Fleet Air Arm
Pullein	Dorothy Betty	Private	Auxiliary Territorial Service
Randle	Charles	N.A.2	Fleet Air Arm
Rathmell*	Thomas	Ordinary Seaman	Royal Navy
Raymond	Geoffrey Foss	Flight Lieutenant	Royal Air Force
Rhodes	Harold	Ordinary Seaman	Royal Navy
Rhodes	Herbert Nicoll	Craftsman	Royal Electrical and Mechanical Engineers
Rhodes	Jack	Private	Kings Own Yorkshire Light Infantry
Rhodes	Kenneth Wishart	Lieutenant	Royal Armoured Corps
Rhodes	Norman Walter	Captain	Royal Corps of Signals
Richardson	S Y	Flight Lieutenant	Royal Air Force
Ridealgh	Henry Reginald	Aircraftman Class 2	Royal Air Force
Rigg	Herbert	Staff Sergeant	Royal Electrical and Mechanical Engineers
Rigg	John Craven	Aircraftman Class 2	Royal Air Force
Roberts	Harold Edward	Private	Royal Army Ordnance Corps
Robertshaw	John	Flight Lieutenant	Royal Air Force

Robertshaw	Thomas R	Signalman	Royal Corps of Signals
Robinson	Edgar Howarth	Driver	Royal Army Service Corps
Robinson	Edward Warburton	Staff Sergeant	Royal Army Service Corps
Robinson	Harold	Private	Royal Armoured Corps
Robinson	John R	Driver	Royal Engineers
Robinson	John Reynard	L/Sergeant	Royal Artillery
Robinson	Norman Bairstow	Aircraftman Class 2	Royal Air Force Volunteer Reserve
Robinson	Peter	Flight Sergeant - Navigator	Royal Air Force
Robinson	Philip Brefitt	L/Sergeant	Royal Artillery
Robinson	William Keith	Bombardier	Royal Artillery
Sands	William Morley	Private	Gordon Highlanders
Saunders*	George William	Gunner	Royal Artillery
Schofield	Charles Frederick	Leading Aircraftman	Fleet Air Arm
Scott	Thomas Fenton	Sergeant	Royal Army Medical Corps
Senior	Lucy	Corporal	Auxiliary Territorial Service
Shackleton	Donald Briggs	Leading Aircraftman	Royal Air Force
Shackleton	Eric	Lieutenant	Indian Army
Shapcott	Nancy	-	Women's Land Army
Sharman	Alice	Staff Sergeant	Auxiliary Territorial Service
Shaw	Ronald	Private	Royal Army Ordnance Corps
Simpson	Florence Grace	Lance Corporal	Auxiliary Territorial Service
Skaife	Harold	Captain	Royal Engineers
Slater	Vera	Company Sergeant Major	Auxiliary Territorial Service
Smith	Angela Mary	Wren	Women's Royal Naval Service
Smith	Emily Margaret	-	Women's Land Army
Smith	Frederick Arthur	Major	Royal Corps of Signals
Smith*	Jack Lawrence	Sapper	Royal Engineers
Smith*	John Ramsden	Leading Aircraftman	Royal Air Force
Smith	Michael	Aircraftman Class 2	Royal Air Force
Smith	Ronald Henry	Captain	Green Howards
Smith	Sylvia Bowes	-	Women's Land Army

Smithies	Arnold	Leading Aircraftman	Royal Air Force
Stephenson	Geoffrey	Lance Corporal	Royal Corps of Signals
Stewart	Gilbert Thomas	Private	General Service Corps
Storr	Geoffrey William	Aircraftman Class 2	Royal Air Force
Stott	Dorothy	Private	Auxiliary Territorial Service
Sully*	Alfred Peter	Sergeant-Observer	Royal Air Force
Sully	Jean Emma	-	Women's Land Army
Sunderland	Frederick Arthur	Lieutenant	Royal Engineers
Sunderland	Patrick H	Officer Cadet	Royal Engineers
Sutcliffe	Marion	Wren	Women's Royal Naval Service
Swale	Jack	Ordinary Seaman	Royal Navy
Swales	Edith Margaret	Aircraftwoman Class 2	Women's Auxiliary Air Force
Tee	Kathleen Mary	Major	Auxiliary Territorial Service
Tempest	Donald James	Private	Duke of Wellington's
Tenniswood	Harold	A.M.2	Royal Naval Volunteer Reserve
Thomas	Cyril	Private	Royal Army Pay Corps
Thomlinson	Frederick George	Lieutenant-Colonel	Kings Own Yorkshire Light Infantry
Thompson*	Geoffrey Elliott	Sergeant	Royal Air Force
Thompson	Harold Charles	Lieutenant	Green Howards
Thorn	Francis William	Lieutenant	Indian Army Pioneers
Thorne	Brian Roche	Ordinary Seaman	Royal Navy
Thornton	Edwin Thomas	Staff Sergeant	Intelligence Corps
Thornton	Eric	Petty Officer	Royal Navy
Todd	Doris E	Private	Auxiliary Territorial Service
Tootill	Derek Lewes	Apprentice Surveyor	Royal Engineers (Military Survey)
Towers	Fred	Corporal	Royal Artillery
Towers	Joseph	Sapper	Royal Engineers
Traylen	Anthony Robert Kilby	Aircraftman Class 2	Royal Air Force
Tuckett	John	Sub-Lieutenant	Royal Navy Rerserve
Turner	Dorothy	Leading Aircraftwoman	Women's Auxiliary Air Force

Underwood	Edgar Arthur	Lance Corporal	Royal Army Medical Corps
Waddington*	Gordon Edmund	Flight Sergeant	Royal Air Force
Waddington	John Charlesworth	Corporal	Royal Air Force
Wales	Gwendoline Ivy	Leading Aircraftwoman	Women's Auxiliary Air Force
Wales	John Derek	Signaller	Royal Navy
Walker	Alan Dearlove	Sergeant	Northamptonshire Reg.
Walker	Arthur	Private	Royal Army Ordnance Corps
Walker	Peter	Flight Lieutenant	Royal Air Force
Wall	Eileen Mary	Lance Corporal	Auxiliary Territorial Service
Walter	David Anthony	Cadet	Merchant Navy
Walter*	John Francis Stansfield	Sergeant	Royal Electrical and Mechanical Engineers
Warburton	Dorothy	Private	Auxiliary Territorial Service
Warburton	John Ronald	Officer Cadet	Merchant Navy
Ward	Kenneth Gordon	Ordinary Seaman	Royal Navy
Wardman	Ernest	Leading Aircraftman	Royal Air Force Volunteer Reserve
Warrington	Jack	Lance Corporal	Royal Corps of Signals
Wate	Charles Derek	Ordinary Seaman	Royal Navy
Watkins	Ronald Geoffrey	Lance Corporal	Royal Electrical and Mechanical Engineers
Watkinson	Doris Mary	Petty Officer	Women's Royal Naval Service
Watkinson	Geoffrey Denton	Flying Officer	Royal Air Force
Watmough	Myra Joyce	Wren	Women's Royal Naval Service
Watson (Staff)	John H	Flight Lieutenant	Royal Air Force
Watson	Maurice Dennis	Warrant Officer	Royal Air Force
Watson	Peter	Private	West Yorks
Watson*	William Thomas	Lieutenant	Durham Light Infantry
Waye	James Douglas	Captain	Royal Artillery
Wear*	Eric Frederick	Aircraftman Class 2	Royal Air Force
Wells	Albert Edward Yates	Signaller	Royal Navy

Weston	George Edward	Lieutenant	Royal Corps of Signals
Whitaker	Robert	Sergeant	Corps of Military Police
Whitaker*	Stanley	Pilot Officer	Royal Air Force
White	Alec	Private	General Service Corps
White	Marjorie Gertrude	Corporal	Women's Auxiliary Air Force
Whiteley	Douglas Allison	Corporal	Royal Army Ordnance Corps
Whitley	Kenneth Hale	Sergeant	Royal Air Force
Wildon	John	Leading Aircraftman	Royal Air Force
Wilkinson	Audrey	Aircraftwoman Class 2	Women's Auxiliary Air Force
Wilkinson	Claude Athelstan	Lieutenant	Durham Light Infantry
Wilkinson	Kenneth	Sergeant	Highland Light Infantry
Wilkinson	Patricia Braham	Nurse	British Red Cross
Wilkinson	Thomas Raymond	Sergeant Pilot	Royal Air Force
Wilson	Raymond	Leading Aircraftman	Royal Air Force
Winterburn*	Norman Percy	Sergeant	Royal Air Force
Wolf	Thomas	Private	Pioneer Corps
Wolfe	Oswald L A	Aircraftman Class 2	Royal Air Force
Wolfenden	Joseph Richard	Pilot Officer	Fleet Air Arm
Wolfenden	Raymond	J.P.E.M.	Royal Navy
Wood	Barbara Mary	Aircraftwoman Class 1	Women's Auxiliary Air Force
Wood	Ernest George	Aircraftman Class 2	Royal Air Force
Woods	John Reginald	Trooper	Royal Armoured Corps
Yeadon	Edwin Riley	Aircraftman Class 2	Royal Air Force
Young	William Henry	Signalman	Royal Corps of Signals

**DIED IN SERVICE - COMMEMORATED ON MEMORIAL PLAQUE*

Of the 464 people listed above, 384 (83%) were male and 80 (17%) female. There were students in the forces from every intake from 1918-19, when the School re-opened, until 1942-43. Over this period, almost 2 out of every 5 male students (39.4%) joined the Forces; the female percentage was 6.5%. Two thirds of the male students from intake years 1928-1935 (66.2%) were members of His Majesty's Forces (12.2% of females over the same period). The largest percentage of male students from a single year intake was 78% in 1928-1929, with 32 of the 41 students in the forces. In thirteen of the twenty one intake years from 1918-1938 over 50% of males were in the Forces, and in seven of those years over 60% joined up.

	Air Force	Army	Navy (Royal and Merchant)	Others (including W.L.A and Nursing)
Total	160	214	74	16
Percentage	34.5%	46.1%	15.9%	3.5%

If the line in the introduction to the publication of the forces booklet - *How instructive a map of the wanderings of our Old Scholars would be!* – was investigated further, it would show that old scholars and staff of Prince Henry's Grammar School were represented in every service, in most theatres of war, in most countries and at many of the most important events. Indeed, the history of the war could be traced through the '*wanderings*' of the Otliensians. Evidence shows that old scholars from Prince Henry's were involved in the following events:

Membership of the local Territorial Army Battalion: Membership of the Home Guard, Auxiliary Fire Service, A.T.S., Women's Land Army, A.T.C.: The action against the German invasion of Norway: the British Expeditionary Force: the evacuation from Dunkirk and other Channel ports, including naval assistance: the Battle of Britain: anti-aircraft defences during the 'blitz': the defeat of Italy in North Africa: the 'long-range' desert group: the defence of, and evacuation from Crete: the Allied invasion of Iraq and Syria: the capitulation of Singapore: the Siege of Malta: fighting the Japanese in Burma: Bomber Command and the 'thousand bomber' raids: Fighter Command – spitfire pilots: the battle for Tobruk: the Battle of the Atlantic – torpedoed by U-boats: Arctic convoys to and from Russia – sunk by mines: the Battle of El Alamein: the Chindits in Burma: battles in Tunisia and Libya which effectively ended the axis occupation in Africa: the invasion of Sicily and Italy: the battles for Anzio and Monte Cassino: the battle of Kohima: D-Day – the British Liberation Army: the battle for Normandy: Arnhem – Operation 'Market Garden': the crossing of the Rhine and the advance into Germany: M.T.B. attacks on E-boats in the North Sea: attacks on the battleship 'Tirpitz': the war in the Pacific – submarine depth-charged by the Japanese: aid given to U.S.A. in Pacific – support of attack on Okinawa: prisoners of war in Italy and Germany – repatriation via 'long marches': prisoners of war in Japan – building of Burma-Siam railway – death from malnutrition.

In the later stages of the War, when many countries had been liberated but retained an allied military presence, members of the forces wrote to local newspapers about sight-seeing trips taken in places such as Egypt, the Holy Land, Rome and India. Soldiers in particular could be away from home for over four years; R.A.F. recruits trained under the 'Empire Training Scheme' in Canada and South Africa; naval personnel visited places they could never have dreamed of before the war – India, Australia, Canada, Japan and the Pacific Islands. The War certainly broadened their horizons and made it more difficult for them to settle back into their old lives when they were eventually demobilised.

A trawl through the *'Wharfedale and Airedale Observer'* over the War years gives some idea of the countries visited by some of the old scholars of Prince Henry's:

Norway, Greece, Crete, Italy, Sicily, Malta, France, Belgium, Netherlands, Germany, Austria, Iceland, Ireland, Algeria, Libya, Tunisia, Egypt, Sudan, Syria, Transjordan, Palestine, Iraq, India, Ceylon, Burma, Singapore, Japan, Falkland Isles, Azores, Canada, United States of America, Rhodesia, South Africa, Australia, Madagascar, Nigeria, Russia.

THE OLD SCHOLARS' WAR MEMORIAL

Shortly before Christmas 1947 an Appeal was launched to provide a War Memorial, in the form of a memorial tablet, to be placed in the School Library. The total amount raised was £351 16s. 10d. and it was agreed that surplus funds would be used to buy furniture for the Hall. The ceremony of unveiling and dedication took place on 17 May 1949.

The Editorial, written by Mr Leech, in the Summer 1949 edition of the *'Otliensian'* included the following:

'The memorial Tablet, bearing forty-one names, is, in the simplicity of its design and by virtue of its quality, worthy of those whom it commemorates. It is appropriate that the Tablet should be placed in the Library, whose shelves contain the wisdom both of the past and the present, for the life-blood of knowledge is the freedom which all Britons who died in the War fought to defend.

'Our Old Scholars have, indeed, left more than a memorial; they have left a great charge to us all, to all who pass through this School – that, so help us God, the Faith and the Freedom for which they died shall not pass away ever. This duty is laid on each one of us, however difficult it may be to achieve, however remote it may seem from the routine of school life. Had Britain been defeated in 1940, our School would certainly be very different from what it is today. We do not know exactly what the impact of a Nazi-

controlled educational system would have been on Prince Henry's Grammar School, but it is certain that we should no longer be able to cherish openly much that we hold dear.'

The Chairman of the Governors, Major Le G.G.W. Horton-Fawkes, opened the unveiling and dedication ceremony, which was held in the Library. After a short speech he handed over to the Chairman of the Old Scholars' Association, Mr C. Derek Mudd. He spoke as follows:

'Before I unveil this tablet, may I, on behalf of the Old Scholars of Prince Henry's Grammar School, address a few remarks, in particular to the relatives of the scholars whose names are now engraved on the plaque and to the representatives of the present generation of scholars.

'An occasion of this kind is not enhanced by lengthy speeches. Nevertheless, I feel that some mention must be made of the scholars in memory of whom this tablet has been erected.

'They have all, without exception, set before us the example of 'Fortiter'. Many of them had had experience of 'the larger world' before they were called upon to make the supreme sacrifice – others had barely left the sheltered precincts of this School. Indeed, 'stern life's flag' was unfurled for them in a bitter world.

'Memories are short, and the years 1939-45 are, for many, years to be forgotten, but those of you here tonight who are parents, brothers and sisters and near relatives of these Old Scholars, do not need to be reminded of their sacrifice. For you, tablets and memorials can be but the tribute of those who, too, have known and remember your loved ones.

'To those of us who were their contemporaries, their names recall happy friendships, victories on the sports field and in the scholastic sphere, and experiences of school life shared in the adventurous spirit of adolescence . One thinks of the schoolboy ambitions and aspirations which were discussed in this very room – of the idealism which was propounded in the School debating Society. It was striving for these very ideals that toll was taken of their youthful lives.

'It would be wrong for me to single out any individual names from the list, but the presence of the name of one woman reminds us that the girls of Prince Henry's were later among the women of England who, too, were called upon to endure misery and privations in the cause of Freedom – and throughout these years there remained the quiet and yet determined spirit of 'Fortiter'.

'To you, who frequent this Library in the course of your present studies, the presence of this memorial tablet will be a reminder in perhaps a less personal way. To you, these names will be – just names; but you cannot but feel proud to be associated with the School which now, in this somewhat inadequate way, pays tribute to former Otliensians – to Otliensians who helped to create the traditions and reputation which the School now enjoys.

'On the walls throughout this building are to be found photographed records of prowess in the field of sport and honours boards recording success in the world of scholarship. It is my hope that this memorial will take its pride of place and be revered and honoured by all who, in future years, are granted the privilege and responsibility of scholarship here – that it may 'stand in the Comitium plain for all folk to see' – and may their names live for evermore and honour be paid to them by an emulation of their true interpretation of 'Fortiter'.'

The Chairman of the Old Scholars' Association then unveiled the Memorial Tablet, after which the Roll of Honour was read by the Headmaster. Finally, the ceremony of dedication was conducted by the Vicar of Otley, Canon T J Williams.

The list of names of Old Scholars who died in the Second World War, 1939-1945. NOTE – one name is missing – that of Harold Newell.

The money remaining in the Fund after the purchase of the War Memorial was used to purchase a Bechstein grand piano that was formally presented to the School on 29 May 1952.

'On Thursday May 29th, in the presence of a large number of parents, friends and past scholars, a Bechstein grand piano was formally presented to the School in completion of the Old Scholars' War Memorial scheme.' The *'Otliensian,' (Vol. XXXIV, Summer 1952)* reported the event as follows:

'The Chairman of the Governors, Major Le G. G. W. Horton-Fawkes, O.B.E., presided and referred to the tablet in the Library, unveiled in May 1949, in memory of the Old

Scholars who fell in the Second World War. Major Horton-Fawkes recalled that in 1949 he had said, "We are met not in a spirit of mourning but in a spirit of pride and thankfulness." He remarked that there were now two emblems in the School by which the fallen Old Scholars would be remembered, the memorial tablet and the piano, a very fitting combination for:

Music when soft voices die, Vibrates in the memory.'

'Mr D. Waye, Chairman of the Old Scholars' Association, said that he was certain that the Fallen would have wished the School to receive some benefit from the memorial and he felt that the idea of having it in two parts had been an inspiration of the Memorial Committee. Mr Waye thanked all who had contributed to the memorial fund and then unlocked the piano. He read out the inscription as follows:

1939 – 1945
IN MEMORY OF THE OLD SCHOLARS
OF THIS SCHOOL WHO GAVE THEIR
LIVES IN THE SERVICE OF THEIR COUNTRY
"FORTITER"

'There followed a concert arranged by Mr Trannah and greatly appreciated by the large audience.

'At the conclusion of the concert the Headmaster, who associated himself with the opening remarks of the Chairman and Mr Waye, said that it had been a memorable occasion, He mentioned that he had received many letters from Old Scholars and friends approving of the way in which the fund had been used. The Headmaster expressed his great pleasure at the thought of having the grand piano for constant use in the School, saying that it would be an inspiration at morning assembly. He invited those present to examine the piano and visit the Library where the memorial tablet could be seen, and also the School's Charter. The Charter had at last been restored and suitably framed through the generosity of the Vice-Chairman of the Governors, to whom the School was deeply indebted. The Headmaster also thanked all who had contributed to the success of the evening.'

The Memorial tablet was moved from the Library into the Main Corridor of the newly extended school in 1969, and was later re-erected in a prime location in the Foyer/Reception area after the building of the new Science Block. Sadly, the Bechstein piano, after much use in assemblies and musical concerts, was declared irreparable and was removed in 2010.

The School Song, 'Fortiter' was sung at each Speech Day and would have been sung at the dedication of the Memorial tablet. The words were written by Mr J. Hutchinson, and the music by Mr J.A. Earnshaw, both masters at Prince Henry's.

CHORUS (Sung after each verse)

What though the task be hard to do,
With courage we will see it through,
What though the race be hard to run,
With courage we will see it done.
For 'Fortiter' shall urge us on,
Until the glorious goal be won.

Prince founded school whose honoured age
Touches a far historic page,
Once more thy spirit deeply known,
Moves us, whose hearts are richly sown.
To sing of fields of work and play,
Where we can ever win the day,
If 'Fortiter' runs through our world,
To make us one inspired whole.

In days of stress, in days of strain,
In work of hand, in work of brain,
In School-year full of duty's call,
Thy 'Fortiter' inspire us all.
To ever strive towards the Light,
To seek the cause of Truth and Right,
So that each life may be through thee
A great consummate Victory.

And when we join that larger world,
Where stern life's flag shall be unfurled,
Thy spirit burning in us still,
Shall make us toil with gladsome will;
And in that game we must play there,
We cannot err, we cannot err –
For 'Fortiter' shall be our shield
'Gainst which all doubt and fear must yield.

'The spirit and life of our School has been expressed in the words and music of our School Song, "Fortiter". Mr Hutchinson has composed the words, and Mr Earnshaw has set them to splendid music. A reputed firm in London are printing our song, which will be sold at 6d per copy, and we wish every pupil to assist our efforts in making this important addition to our School.' ('Otliensian,' Vol III No 1 Autumn 1920)

The school magazine, The *'Otliensian'* continued to be published during the war, though the shortage of paper meant that the number of issues was reduced from three to two per annum. It continued to provide a picture of school-life, and most pupils looked forward to its publication. There was an expectation that the majority of pupils – or parents! – would buy and keep the magazine and it is clear from talking to ex-pupils that they often kept their copies. During the war the *'Otliensian'* also contained details of ex-pupils serving in H.M. Forces and these, together with the section on 'News of Old Scholars' reinforced the togetherness and comradeship so important in such critical times.

The first issue in Summer 1919 set out the aims and objectives for the new publication:

(a) To provide a contemporary record and history of events and progress:

(b) To present it as a termly publication:

(c) To appeal to every boy and girl to support the Magazine, as an important school institution, in every way possible, in particular because:

(d) It must be self-supporting, so we hope that every family represented in the School will purchase a copy each term, so that we need not be hindered by any financial worry, and:

(e) That the older boys and girls will, before very long, begin to offer contributions for publication, so that it may become a real school magazine, and that the scholars will realise that it is their affair as much as ours.

The final issue – No. 138 – was published in Summer 1985. By then one annual A4 issue was printed within the school, as opposed to three A5 issues per annum printed by an outside company: advertisements helped to provide the funds to finance the printing of the magazine, which was distributed free to all pupils: a large proportion of the magazine showcased pupils' work: there was a correspondingly smaller proportion devoted to results and other archive material: although editorial control was maintained by the head and staff, the students were much more involved.

Mr Bousfield, writing in the Summer 1983 (Volume 65) issue noted that '*one of our achievements as a Comprehensive School may well be the maintenance of this Otliensian magazine.*' Only two more issues were published – the final one containing a tribute to Mr Bousfield on his retirement.

The War Dead – The Ultimate Sacrifice

Forty old scholars and one member of staff of Prince Henry's Grammar School died in the Second World War. One was female and a civilian; forty were male and members of the armed forces. The youngest person to die was 18 years of age (Ian Rochester Naylor), and the oldest was 37 years of age (Margery Jennings). The average age of those who died was 24.7 years. The breakdown by age was:

20 and below	21 – 25	26 -30	31- 35
6	20	11	4

The breakdown by service is shown below:

Air Force	23	Royal Air Force (R.A.F.) Royal Air Force Volunteer Reserve (R.A.F.V.R.)	3 20
Army	10	Royal Electrical & Mechanical Engineers (R.E.M.E.) Royal Artillery Royal Engineers Royal Army Pay Corps Royal Berkshire Regiment West Yorkshire Regiment Intelligence Corps. (Field Security Police)	2 3 1 1 1 1 1
Royal Navy	5	Royal Navy Royal Naval Volunteer Reserve	3 2
Merchant Navy	2		2
Civilian	1	Nurse – Medical Auxiliary Service	1

Of the 160 old scholars who joined the Air Force, representing 34.3% of the total in the services, 23 died. This is equivalent to a death rate for old scholars in the Air Force of 14.5%. Corresponding figures for the Army were 4.7%, and for the Navy 9.5%.

The Royal Air Force Volunteer Reserve was formed in July 1936 to provide individuals to supplement the Auxiliary Air Force, which had been formed in 1925. The A.A.F. was organised on a Squadron basis, with local recruitment similar to the Territorial Army Regiments. The object was to provide a reserve of aircrew for use in the event of war. Recruits were confined to men between the ages of 18 and 25 who had been accepted for part-time training as pilots, observers and wireless operators. By September 1939, the R.A.F.V.R. was made up of 6,646 pilots, 1,625 observers and 1,946 wireless operators.

When war broke out in 1939 the Air Ministry employed the R.A.F.V.R. as the principal means for aircrew entry to serve with the R.A.F. By the end of 1941 over half of Bomber Command aircrew were members of the R.A.F.V.R., and eventually probably more than 95% of the R.A.F. aircrew in the Command were serving members of the R.A.F.V.R.

The catchment area for Prince Henry's was larger than it is today because of the lack of competing Grammar Schools in the immediate area. The school could not compete with the more established Grammar Schools in Leeds and Bradford, but attracted students from Guiseley, Menston and Ilkley as well as from Pool, Bramhope, Arthington and the nearby villages of North Yorkshire. Ilkley Grammar School was less competitive in terms of entry because at the time it was boys only.

Fees were charged for the pupils attending the school, but increasingly the Governors, local businesses and individuals provided scholarships and the West Riding County Council paid the fees of those pupils who were assessed as sufficiently able to benefit from a Grammar School education. Many of the old scholars who died in the War had received West Riding Minor Scholarships on entry to Prince Henry's. On receipt of these scholarships, parents had to agree to keep their children at school for a minimum number of years. In some cases the students left school before this agreed date, and were said to have 'broken their agreement'. This would usually be because parents argued that, in spite of the scholarship, they could no longer afford to keep their child in school or because the pupil had found a job. In some cases this was allowed by the Governors because of the financial problems experienced by parents; in other cases the parents would be expected to pay back the fees received. The relatively small number of pupils who stayed on into the Sixth Form was a reflection of the lack of finance and the need to supplement the family income through employment.

For several years Prince Henry's ran a 'Preparatory' department and it was not unusual for pupils to enter the school at an early age. Charles Leslie Harrison was 7 years old when he was admitted in September 1925: Ian Rochester Naylor was 8 when he was admitted in September 1934 and remained at the school until November 1943. Some of these pupils would have passed the entrance examination and would qualify for a scholarship when they became 11 years old, until then parents would be expected to pay the relevant school fees. The provision of preparatory departments in state schools ended with the 1944 Education Act.

Prince Henry's was a relatively small, rural Grammar School with an annual intake over the 1920s that averaged about 60 pupils. When the school re-opened in 1918 it started with 125 pupils (74 boys and 51 girls). The following table shows how numbers grew over time:

1918	1919	1920	1921	1922	1923	1924	1925	1926	1927
125	202	260	298	269	242	271	249	262	314

1928	1929	1930	1931	1932	1933	1934	1935	1936	1937
342	354	389	423	437	432	428	439	433	429

1938	1939	1940	1941	1942	1943	1944	1945	1946	1947
440	450	449	465	466	450	455	433	434	417

The trend shows an overall increase in pupil numbers, but there are years when the number of leavers exceeded the number of new entrants. Of the 40 old scholars who died in the War, 29 entered the school in the period 1928/1929 to 1935/1936. Eight of these pupils were in the 1928-1929 intake, and four of these were in the same class. Also in this class was Jack Ineson, who was a Japanese prisoner of war, and J.D. Firth. (see 'Wounded')

SALVETE! SEPTEMBER 1928

Upper VA	***Watson William Thomas***
Upper IVA	***Paul Eric G.***
Upper IVC	Myers Betty
Upper IIIA	Fairburn R., Hensby W. R. M., Hymas D., Johnson A. S.,Jowett T. L., Mann J., Midgley T. H., ***Pickard H.***, Rhodes N. W., Shaw R., Smith R. H., Clements Nora, Heathcote Edna M., Holden Sadie, Michel Nora, Palmer Joan Eileen, Pearson Irene, Roundhill Doris, Simpson Margaret, Stevens Mary Ellen, Stubbs Jessie, Todd Verona Allen, Townsend Jean, Williamson Marion K., Bradley N.
Upper IIIB	Broadbelt W. W., ***Clapham J. S.***, Clarkson G. A., Dodgshon H., Firth J. D., Goldsborough H., Hindle Charles N., Ineson J.**, *Kay Ronald, Mason J. E.*,** Payne K. J., Towers J., ***Wear E. F.***, Wilkinson C. A., Bairstow A.
Upper IIIC	Carr Mary M., Cowburn Kathleen G., Dixon Kathleen, Fozard Marjorie, Hainsworth Doreen M., Holmes Amy G., Kendrew Mary L., Morrett Margaret K., Ratcliffe Constance M., Rayner Amy, Rignall Rosamund, Roper Olive G., Sykes Molly, Watkinson Beatrice M., Whitaker Marjorie
Lower III	Armitage A. H., Poskitt Margaret
Form II	***Dodgshon Geoffrey***, Tillotson Dennis H.
Form I	Booth G. H., Brown Harry, Reece Roderick George, Holliday Margaret A., Lawson Edith J., Wainwright Edith M., Watkinson Margaret D., Boothroyd Clarice Edwina.

Of the 34 boys in the 1928 intake, 30 served in H.M. Forces, and are included in the list in the previous chapter.

In each of three other intake years, three pupils who later died in the War were in the same class. The small size of the school and the fact that a large majority of the students came from Otley meant that most pupils would know each other well. Many of them went to primary school in Otley and would have grown up together. They played together in Rugby and Cricket teams; they competed in the annual Athletic Sports, sometimes vying for the overall championship. They took part in the more academic extra-curricular activities; they acted in school plays, gave lectures to the Natural Sciences Society and to the Literary, Historical and Debating society. They took a full part in the life of the School.

Many students – not only the ones who gave their lives in the War – were clearly very proud of their school. They stayed in touch by writing letters to the Headmaster, and some of these were published in the school magazine; they paid visits to the School and spoke in assemblies about their experiences. They joined the 'Old Otliensians' and continued to play Rugby and Cricket, took part in plays and attended social events. Their on-going careers and lives were followed closely in the *"News of Old Scholars"* section of the magazine, which included appointments, examination successes, engagements, marriages, births and deaths.

Name	War Memorial	Birth/ Death	Age	Service/Unit	Rank	Service Number	Burial place
Barber Peter William	Otley Memorial Garden	17-07-20 - 02-09-40	20	Royal Air Force 37 Squadron	Sergeant	647990	Runnymede Memorial
Bell Ronald	Otley Memorial Garden	08-11-20 - 24-05-43	22	R.A.F.V.R. 75 Squadron	Sergeant – Wireless Operator/ Air Gunner	1077692	Beesd General Cemetery, Netherlands
Bentley Harry Norman	Otley Memorial Garden	31-07-18 -16-01-45	26	Royal Electrical & Mechanical Engineers	Staff Sergeant	925890	Ancona War Cemetery, Italy
Bunting James Arthur	Otley Memorial Garden	30-01-20 -16-01-42	21	Royal Air Force 408 Squadron (Royal Canadian Air Force)	Flight Sergeant - Observer	580639	Otley (Newall with Clifton & Lindley) Cemetery
Clapham John Stanley	Burley-in-Wharfedale	28-02-17 -02-06-42	25	R.A.F.V.R. 10 Squadron	Flight Sergeant	935675	Runnymede Memorial
Crosland Jack	Otley Memorial Garden	30-05-22 - 29-10-45	24	R.A.F.V.R.	Warrant Officer – Pilot	1332341	Kiel War Cemetery, Germany
Dodgshon Geoffrey	Otley Memorial Garden + Otley Methodist Church	30-10-19 -11-10-44	24	Royal Artillery 9th Battalion, Manchester Regiment	Captain	262489	Assisi War Cemetery, Italy
Dunwell Henry Howes	Otley Memorial Garden + Woodhouse Grove School	09-10-22 -14-06-43	20	R.A.F.V.R.	Sergeant – Pilot	1622615	Harare (Pioneer) Cemetery, Bulawayo, Zimbabwe
Fairbanks Gordon Maguire		12-06-13 -26-01-42	28	Merchant Navy S.S. Refast	Third Officer		Tower Hill Memorial

Halliwell Kenneth Stephen	Monton Unitarian Church, Salford	04-09-22 -31-03-45	22	R.A.F.V.R. 5RFU (Refresher Flying Unit)	Sergeant – Pilot	1026402	Salerno War Cemetery, Italy
Harrison Charles Leslie	Otley Memorial Garden	16-11-17 -10-07-41	23	R.A.F.V.R. 72 Squadron	Sergeant	936721	Runnymede Memorial
Holmes George Malcolm	Pool-in-Wharfedale + Pool Village Hall	31-03-13 -01-11-42	29	Royal Navy S.S. Mendoza	Able Seaman	C/JX 248115	Chatham Naval Memorial
Imeson Robert Stanton	Otley Memorial Garden	25-04-20 -02-12-43	23	R.A.F.V.R. 103 Squadron	Sergeant – Flight Engineer	1480164	Berlin (1939-1945) War Cemetery
Jennings Margery (nee Hellewell)	Otley Memorial Garden + Otley Methodist Church	20-11-18 -12-05-45	37	Nurse, Medical Auxiliary Service	Civilian		Loebok Lingau, Sumatra
Kay Ronald	Otley Memorial Garden + St Luke's, West Hartlepool	14-03-17 -27-02-41	24	Merchant Navy S.S. Stanwold	Donkeyman		Stranton Cemetery, Hartlepool
Lilley Bernard Dallah		30-11-22 -03-01-45	22	R.A.F.V.R. 272 Squadron	Flying Officer	154285	Malta Memorial, Valetta
Lupton Mark	Owston, All Saints' Church	19-06-08 -23-01-43	34	R.A.F.V.R. 410 Squadron (Royal Canadian Air Force)	Sergeant	1456999	Runnymede Memorial
Mason James Edward	Burley-in-Wharfedale	10-05-17 -27-12-43	26	Royal Artillery 122 Field Regiment	Gunner	963864	Kanchanaburi War Cemetery, Thailand
Miller Arthur	Burley-in-Wharfedale	11-01-13 -01-06-43	38	Royal Army Pay Corps	Private	7671995	Burley-in-Wharfedale (St. Mary) Cemetery

Morton Anthony Alan	Otley Memorial Garden	06-01-18 -19-04-44	26	Royal Berkshire Regiment: Secondary Regiment 1st Batallion Wiltshire Regiment	Lieut.	293001	Rangoon Memorial, Myanmar
Naylor Ian Rochester	Guiseley	11-05-26 -07-04-45	18	Royal Navy Volunteer Reserve: H.M.M.T.B. 494	Mid-shipman	D/JX 287428	Portsmouth Naval Memorial
Newell Harold	Otley Memorial Garden	11-09-12 -27-04-44	31	R.A.F.V.R.	Flying Officer	143589	Leeds Crematorium – Lawnswood
Nicholson Norman	Otley Memorial Garden	24-03-24 -29-05-44	23	R.A.F.V.R. 1657 H.C.U.	Sergeant - Navigator	1624728	Otley (Newall with Clifton & Lindley) Cemetery
Nield George Kenneth	Otley Memorial Garden	21-03-11 -04-01-41	29	Intelligence Corps (Field Security Police)	Lance Corporal	7687379	Oldham (Hollinwood) Cemetery
Overend Harry	Burley-in-Wharfedale	26-08-21 -19-11-44	23	R.A.F.V.R. 613 Squadron	Flying Officer (Pilot)	146439	Burley-in-Wharfedale (St. Mary) Cemetery
Paul George Eric	Otley Memorial Garden	16-10-15 -21-09-41	25	R.A.F.V.R. 103 Squadron	Sergeant – Wireless Operator/ Air Gunner	1112339	Otley (Newall with Clifton & Lindley) Cemetery
Pickard Harry	Guiseley	22-08-16 -22-11-44	28	Royal Navy H.M. Submarine Stratagem	Petty Officer	P/JX 137672	Portsmouth Naval Memorial
Pickles Geoffrey Claude	Otley Memorial Garden	26-06-24 -16-04-45	20	Royal Naval Volunteer Reserve: 837 Squadron	Sub-Lieut. (A) H.M.S. Glory		Cambeltown Cemetery, Argyllshire, Scotland
Pullan Harold	Otley Memorial Garden	28-08-21 -16-05-44	22	R.A.F.V.R.	Flying Officer (Pilot)	152542	Ramleh War Cemetery, Israel
Rathmell Thomas	Menston St John's	21-09-22 -06-07-42	19	Royal Navy H.M.S. Niger	Able Seaman	D/JX 287428	Plymouth Naval Memorial

Saunders George William	Otley Memorial Garden	12-05-20 -05-07-44	24	Royal Artillery 70th Field Regiment	Gunner	922251	Caserta War Cemetery, Italy
Smith Jack Lawrence	Otley Memorial Garden	23-10-18 -09-11-45	27	Royal Engineers	Sapper		Otley (Newall with Clifton & Lindley) Cemetery
Smith John Ramsden	Guiseley	14-06-13 -19-02-43	29	R.A.F.V.R.	Sergeant – Navigator	1459381	Aireborough (Guiseley) Cemetery
Sully Alfred Peter	Otley Memorial Garden	12-06-20 -30-08-40	20	Royal Air Force 107 Squadron	Sergeant – Observer	581542	Bergen-Op-Zoom War Cemetery, Netherlands
Thompson Geoffrey Elliott	Guiseley	19-01-20 -08-11-43	23	R.A.F.V.R.	Aircraft-man 2ND Class	1356432	Ambon War Cemetery, Indonesia
Waddington Gordon Edmund	King James School, Knares-borough	08-06-22 -15-11-43	21	R.A.F.V.R. 183 Squadron	Flight Sergeant	1379975	Runnymede Memorial
Walter: John Francis Stansfield	Menston, St John's	25-04-22 -06-08-45	23	Royal Electrical & Mechanical Engineers	Sergeant	7634808	Labuan War Cemetery, Borneo
Watson: William Thomas		16-04-12 -23-04-44	32	West Yorkshire Regiment (Prince of Wales Own) & Durham Light Infantry	Lieut.	200775	Rangoon Memorial, Myanmar
Wear: Eric Frederick	Burley-in-Wharfedale	23-10-17 -24-04-42	24	R.A.F.V.R. 148 Squadron	Sergeant - Observer	999231	Catania War Cemetery: Sicily
Whitaker: Stanley	Otley Memorial Garden	17-09-14 -23-10-44	30	R.A.F.V.R. 625 Squadron	Flying Officer	168796	Runnymede Memorial
Winterburn Norman Percy	Otley Memorial Garden	08-05-22 -20-09-43	21	R.A.F.V.R. 156 Squadron	Sergeant - Wireless Operator/ Air Gunner	1439760	Otley (Newall with Clifton & Lindley) Cemetery

Peter William Barber (1920-1940)

Royal Air Force (37 Squadron)
Sergeant - Service Number: 647990
Died 2 September 1940 (Age 20) - Runnymede Memorial (Panel 11)

Peter William Barber (born 17 July 1920) was the son of F. Barber, tobacco manufacturer of Kirkgate Otley. He attended North Parade Elementary School and was admitted to the Preparatory Department at Prince Henry's on 11 September 1929. On admission he was 9 years of age and was placed in Form II. He spent 7 years at Prince Henry's and left on 29 July 1936 from Form Lower 5A.

At school he was prominent as an athlete, as his Sports Day record shows:

<table>
<tr><td>1930</td><td>100 yards (Under 10) – First place</td><td>Egg & Spoon Race (Forms 1 & 2) – Fourth place</td><td></td><td></td></tr>
<tr><td>1932</td><td>100 yards (Under 12) – First place</td><td>High Jump (Under 14) – First place</td><td>Long Jump (Under 14) – Fourth place</td><td>Junior Individual Championship – Second place</td></tr>
<tr><td>1933</td><td>High Jump (Under 14) – Joint First Place</td><td>Long Jump (Under 14) – Second place</td><td>Junior Individual Championship – Third</td><td></td></tr>
<tr><td rowspan="2">1934</td><td>100 yards (Under 14) – First place</td><td>220 yards (Under 14) – Second place</td><td>High Jump (Under 14)- First place</td><td>Long Jump (Under 14) -Second place</td></tr>
<tr><td>Novelty Obstacle Race – First Place</td><td>Junior Individual Championship – First</td><td></td><td></td></tr>
</table>

On Sports' Day 1934 A.P. Sully won the 220 yards (Under 14) and the Long Jump (Under 14) and came second in the High Jump (Under 14) and the Novelty Obstacle Race, pushing Barber all the way in the Junior Championship. It was Sully who eventually went on to become Senior Individual Champion in both 1935 and 1936. Both Sully and Barber joined the R.A.F. at the outbreak of war and, sadly, both died within days of each other in 1940.

Barber played both Rugby and cricket for School, but he distinguished himself as a swimmer. He became one of the best swimmers in the district and gave every promise of becoming diving champion of Yorkshire, having already competed and been placed in the championship whilst still a junior. In 1935 he gave a lecture on swimming and diving to the members of the *Literary, Historical and Debating Society*, skills '*in which the lecturer has frequently demonstrated his proficiency.*'

In July 1940 the Headmaster received a letter from Sergeant Barber in which he revealed his pride in being a member of the R.A.F and in his athletic achievements. Parts of the letter were printed in the School Magazine and are included below:

Peter Barber

'Up to a couple of months ago my work in the Service was of no real importance; now that I am an experienced member of an operational crew I am proud to say that my work is both interesting and important and at times most uncomfortable, especially when Jerry starts a show.

'I understand that some of the chaps I went to school with are at present serving in the R.A.F.; unfortunately, I have not had the pleasure of meeting them apart from the boy I joined up with, Ken Whitley. I was at the wireless school with him, also at the armaments school. After leaving there he went to France, from where I understand he returned safely. At the wireless school Ken and myself had the honour of being included in the rugger side.

'I am writing this letter in the crew room, standing by, pending a coastal patrol. The room is absolutely packed out with airmen all chatting about their experiences. A pilot has just burst forth into song the subject of which, needless to say, is that much discussed person, Hitler.'

37 Squadron was reformed in 1937 as a heavy bomber squadron equipped with the Harrow bomber. In May 1939 it was re-equipped with the more modern Vickers Wellington I. The squadron went into action seven hours after the British ultimatum to Germany expired, flying a sweep over Heligoland Bight. Because of heavy losses Bomber Command abandoned this sort of daylight raid, and the squadron became a night bomber unit.

On the evening of 1 September 1940 a total of seventy-one aircraft took part in night raids on Germany and Italy. Wellington N2992 of 37 Squadron, Feltwell, target Hannover, flew into the North Sea on its return. The only survivor was Pilot Officer M.S. Burberry who was rescued two days later by *H.M.S. Niger*. Pilot Officer G.H. Jackson, Pilot Officer H. Philippe, Sergeant C.J. Hooper, Sergeant T.C.M. Browne (R.N.Z.A.F.) and Sergeant P.W. Barber were all presumed drowned. In his report on the incident Burberry indicated that he may have fallen asleep, but his Station Commander thought that an incorrect altimeter setting was the more likely cause of the tragedy.

Rank	Service	Forename	Surname	Age	Service No.	Grave/Memorial
Pilot Officer		M.S.	Burberry			Survived
Pilot Officer	Royal Air Force	George Hauteville	Jackson	24	40831	Bergen-op-Zoom Canadian War Cemetery

Pilot Officer	R.A.F. Volunteer Reserve	Henri	Philippe	29	78663	Runnymede Memorial Panel 9
Sergeant	R.A.F. Volunteer Reserve	Cyril John	Hooper	21	755311	Runnymede Memorial Panel 15
Sergeant	Royal New Zealand Air Force	Thomas Chamberlain Molyneux	Browne	19	40201	Runnymede Memorial Panel 27
Sergeant	Royal Air Force	Peter William	Barber	20	647990	Runnymede Memorial Panel 11

(RAF Bomber Command Losses Vol. 1 1939-1940 by W R Chorley)

The Runnymede Memorial

The Runnymede Memorial lies overlooking the River Thames on Cooper's Hill at Englefield Green between Windsor and Egham on the A308, 4 miles from Windsor. The Air Forces Memorial at Runnymede commemorates by name over 20,000 airmen who were lost in the Second World War during operations from bases in the United Kingdom and North and Western Europe, and who have no known graves. They served in Bomber, Fighter, Coastal, Transport, Flying Training and Maintenance Commands, and came from all parts of the Commonwealth. Some were from countries in continental Europe which had been overrun but whose airmen continued to fight in the ranks of the Royal Air Force. (*Commonwealth War Graves Commission*)

In Westminster Abbey there is a chapel dedicated to the memory of the men of the Royal Air Force killed in the Battle of Britain. The Chapel was unveiled by King George VI on 10 July 1947. The principal part of this memorial – the stained-glass window – specially commemorates the men who flew with Fighter Command. North of the Chapel, a Roll of Honour containing the names of 1,497 pilots and aircrew killed during the battle rests on a wrought-iron lectern. Included in the list are the names of two Otliensians – Sergeant Peter William Barber and Sergeant Alfred Peter Sully.

By a cruel twist of fate Peter Barber was not the first old scholar to die in the War; his friend Alfred Peter Sully, died three days earlier on 30 August 1940.

Ronald Bell (1920-1943)

Royal Air Force Volunteer Reserve (75 Squadron)
Sergeant: Wireless Operator/Air Gunner - Service Number: 10776792
Died 24 May 1943 (Age 22) - Beesd General Cemetery (Coll. Grave 1-2)
Son of Bernard and Hilda Bell of Otley, Yorkshire; husband of Margueritte Bell, of Otley.

Flight Sergeant Ronald Bell, Royal Air Force Volunteer Reserve (born 8 November 1920) was at school from September 1932 – Form Upper 3B - until February 1935 – Form Upper 4A. He attended Otley, North Parade School from 1926-1932. At that time he

R. Bell.

lived on Croft Avenue, Otley, with his parents, his father was a motor engineer. *'At school he was of a quiet and happy disposition and took part in all activities.'* He played the part of a soldier in the production of *'Alice through the Looking Glass'* in 1934 and came third in the Obstacle Race (12-14) on Sports day in 1934. On leaving he became a window dresser and salesman at the Otley branch of Freeman, Hardy and Willis. When he left school, he *'broke his agreement and paid the penalty,'* an indication that his parents could no longer afford to keep him at school in what were difficult economic times.

He volunteered for the R.A.F. in January 1941 and trained as a Wireless Operator/Air Gunner. He was attached to a New Zealand bomber squadron in this country, and in April 1943 he and his five colleagues visited Otley and stayed with Sergeant Bell's parents for most of their leave.

On 25 April 1942 he married Marguerite Cairns, (born 1 May 1924). He was reported missing on what was only his second operational flight over the Continent in May 1943. On 25 November 1943 his wife gave birth to a daughter. Sandra M. Bell, sister to a son, Tony.

On 23 May 1943 at 23.15 Short Stirling Bomber BK783 of 75 Squadron left R.A.F. Newmarket as part of a formation of 826 bombers on a raid over Dortmund in Germany. The formation was made up of 343 Lancasters, 199 Halifaxes, 151 Wellingtons, 120 Stirlings and 13 Mosquitos.

At 02.14 BK783 was shot down by a German night-fighter and crashed into a ditch at Beesd, 21 km S.S.E. of Utrecht. Six of the crew were killed; the injured rear-gunner survived and was taken as a prisoner of war by the Germans. 38 aircraft (4.6% of the force) were lost – 8 Lancasters, 18 Halifaxes, 6 Stirlings and 6 Wellingtons. Despite these losses the mission was a success. The Pathfinders marked the target accurately in clear weather conditions, and major damage was caused to the city of Dortmund, including the large Hoesch AG steelworks, which ceased production.

The six members of BK783 who died were buried in the local, Beesd Cemetery in three graves that stand side by side. The Cemetery is situated in the town of Beesd in the Gelderland district of the Netherlands. The crew members were:

Name	Nationality	Service	Rank	Age
Frederick John Leigh Joblin (417063)	New Zealand	Royal New Zealand Air Force	Sergeant (Bomb Aimer)	25

George Watson Turnbull (421342)	New Zealand	Royal New Zealand Air Force	Sergeant (Navigator)	24
Stanley John Wayman (1391814)	United Kingdom	Royal Air Force Volunteer Reserve	Sergeant (Flight Engineer)	21
Derrick George Amos Storey (1809725)	United Kingdom	Royal Air Force Volunteer Reserve	Sergeant (Air Gunner)	19
Stephen Muir Tietjens (415640)	New Zealand	Royal New Zealand Air Force	Sergeant (Pilot)	26
Ronald Bell (1077692)	United Kingdom	Royal Air Force Volunteer Reserve	Sergeant (Wireless Operator/ Rear Gunner)	22
Leslie. R. Vale	United Kingdom	Royal Air Force Volunteer Reserve	Sergeant – Rear Gunner (P.O.W.)	N/A

(R.A.F. Bomber Command Losses, Vol. 4 1943 by W.R. Chorley)

No 75 Squadron (R.A.F.) reformed in 1937 as a bomber squadron, equipped with a variety of aircraft. In April 1940, the New Zealand Flight was re-designated No 75 (New Zealand) Squadron because it had been set up and paid for by the people of New Zealand. For the rest of the war it operated with Bomber Command. From October 1942 to August 1943 the Squadron operated the Short Stirling I aircraft, and from February 1943 to April 1944, the Short Stirling III. From March 1944 to October 1945 the aircraft operated were the Avro Lancaster Mark I and the Lancaster Mark III.

At the end of the War many of these 'sponsored' squadrons were disbanded, but because 75 Squadron had a heavy New Zealand contingent it was turned over to the Royal New Zealand Air Force.

Harry Norman Bentley (1918-1945)

Royal Electrical & Mechanical Engineers
Staff Sergeant - Service Number: 925890
Died 16 January 1945 (Age 26) - Ancona War Cemetery, Italy (Grave IV.F.14)
Son of Harry Norman Bentley and Mary Ellen Bentley (née Hargreaves), of Otley, Yorkshire.

Staff Sergeant Harry Norman Bentley, R.E.M.E. (born 31 July 1918) lived in Silver Mill Hill, Otley. His father, also named Harry Norman Bentley, was a Printers' Engineer, who married Mary Ellen Hargreaves in Otley in 1916. Harry attended Otley National Elementary School and was admitted to Prince Henry's in September 1929 (Form Upper

H. N. Bentley

3B), following the granting of a W.R.C.C. *'Special Place Award'* tenable for five years. He left in July 1934 (Upper 5B), and became a mechanic with Dawson, Payne and Elliott Ltd., Printers' Engineers, Otley.

In the call-up for recruits before the outbreak of war, he joined the local Artillery Battery and went with it to France. In 1940 he was evacuated from Cherbourg. In 1942 he transferred to R.E.M.E. when the Corps was formed and soon rose to the rank of Staff Sergeant. He went to North Africa in 1943, and took part in the Italian campaign, being one of the first to land at Anzio. The news of his death from tropical fever on 16 January 1945 in a British General Hospital with the C.M.F. (Central Mediterranean Force) in Italy, was a great shock to all who knew him.

At School he took part in all activities. He was a strong, vigorous forward in the School Rugby XV, and soon after leaving School he became a regular member of the Otley Rugby Union team. On Sports Day in 1932 he took second place in the High Jump, but his future lay with Rugby rather than athletics, and even then he started slowly. His team comment in 1933 indicated that he was *'rather slow and fails to get down to loose scrums.'* The following year he was described as *'a strong, robust forward, working hard in the set scrums and very much at home in loose rushes. Has scored one or two tries by keen backing up. He should learn to open out the game with a pass after breaking clear.'* He was awarded his school colours in 1934.

He had a brief but successful drama career, playing the part of Duke Frederick in *'As You Like It'* in 1933; *'at the wrestling, he was an efficient master of ceremonies. To Orlando he spoke with the right tone of admiration mingled with regret; he did re-enter "with his eyes full of anger", and later gave a right stern dismissal to Oliver. Considering that Bentley took over the part at the eleventh hour, his acting was highly satisfactory.'* In 1934 he played one of Mr Hardcastle's servants in *'She Stoops to Conquer'*.

Academically, he didn't win form prizes, but he passed his School Certificate in 1934 and was awarded the Royal Life Saving Bronze Medal in the same year.

Ancona War Cemetery

On 3 September 1943 the Allies invaded the Italian mainland, the invasion coinciding with an armistice made with the Italians who then re-entered the war on the Allied side. Following the fall of Rome to the Allies in June 1944, the German retreat was ordered and successive stands were made on a series of defensive positions known as the Trasimene, Arezzo, Arno and Gothic Lines. The cemetery at Ancona reflects the Allied progress up the Adriatic coast in August and September 1944. The cemetery site was chosen in September and graves were brought from a wide area round about, extending from Pescara, 80 kilometres farther south, to Pesaro, over 48 kilometres north of Ancona. They include those of casualties from the first attacks on the eastern sector of the German defensive Gothic Line, near Fano and Pesaro, at the end of August and early in September. Ancona itself had been taken by the Poles on 18 July 1944 and, being little touched by the war, served as the main port for supplies for the attack on the Gothic Line and for the final break through the following spring at Argenta. Ancona War Cemetery contains 1,109 Commonwealth burials of the Second World War, 964 have been identified. (*Commonwealth War Graves Commission*)

James Arthur Bunting (1920-1942)

Royal Air Force (408, Royal Canadian Air Force, Squadron)
Flight Sergeant/Observer-Service Number 580639
Died 16 January 1942 (Age21) - Otley, Newall-with-Clifton and Lindley, Cemetery (Section 1 Grave 211)
Son of Mr and Mrs. J.C. Bunting, Otley, Yorkshire

Flight Sergeant James Arthur Bunting, R.A.F., (born 30 January 1920) was at school from September 1931 (Form Upper 3A) until November 1935 (Upper 5B). He attended Otley National Elementary School from 1929-1931 and was given a W.R.C.C. *'Special Place Award'* in 1931 tenable for school life. The W.R.C.C. allowed him to leave early and therefore break this agreement owing to his parents' financial position. On leaving school he became a Motor Engineer at Borough Garage, Otley. He lived in North Street, Otley and his father, John C. Bunting, was a dyer. John married Phyllis M. Cartwright in 1919.

In 1935 James played cricket for the school 1st XI as a batsman. In 4 innings he scored 38 runs for an average of 9.50, with a highest score of 22 against Ilkley Grammar School. Before leaving school he obtained his School Certificate.

He joined the R.A.F. in February 1939 and was promoted Sergeant after six months. He began his operational flying with 49 Squadron in December 1939, as a wireless operator. His first operation was on 21 December 1939. While with 49 Squadron he completed an amazing 41 Hampden operations as navigator and bomb aimer. He was posted to 14 O.T.U. Cottesmore, but returned to operational flights with 408 Squadron (Royal Canadian Air Force), and it was with this Squadron that he was killed in action.

He was stationed at R.A.F. Balderton and was killed when his Hampden aircraft (AE393 EQ-G) crashed on Wassett Fell, near West Burton, Bishopdale, 13 miles south-west of Catterick, on return from operations over Hamburg. 96 aircraft took part in the mission; 3 Wellingtons and 1 Hampden were lost and eight further aircraft crashed in England. He had volunteered to fill a vacant position in an aircrew when he met his death on the return journey. At school he was said to have '*had a likeable personality, and his many friends pay tribute to his enthusiasm and readiness to give a helping hand to anyone.*'

Rank	Service	Forename	Surname	Age	Service No.	Grave/Memorial
Pilot- Acting Squadron Leader	Royal Canadian Air Force	Wilfred Jasper	Burnett		40076	Injured but survived
Flight Sergeant – Observer	R.A.F.	James Arthur	Bunting	21	580639	Otley (Newall-with-Clifton and LIndley) Cemetery
Sergeant – Wireless operator/ Air Gunner	R.A.F.V.R	John Robinson	Appleby	26	995056	Stockton on Tees Cemetery, County Durham
Sergeant – Air Gunner	R.A.F.	Maurice	Jones	21	619483	Tibshelf Churchyard, Derbyshire

(R.A.F. Bomber Command Losses Vol. 3, 1942 by W.R.Chorley.)

'The crew became lost whilst flying in low cloud on their return to Yorkshire and over-flew the Vale of York. The pilot reported the altimeter had read at 5,000 ft. prior to impact. Two of the crew were thrown out of the aircraft into snow and were killed, two others were trapped in the cockpit area and were rescued by a number of farmers who were alerted to the crash and made their way up to the site through deep snow. Sadly one of these airmen died soon after being rescued but the pilot survived and was initially treated for his injuries at a nearby farm before being taken to hospital. An investigation concluded that the altimeter was probably reading incorrectly at the time of the crash.'
(**www.yorkshire-aircraft.co.uk**) see also below '*Hell on High Ground 2*' by David Earl.)

The following article was published in the '*Yorkshire Evening Post*' on 19 January 1942:

'Mr and Mrs. J.C. Bunting, North Street, Otley, have been notified of the death of their only son, Flight Sergeant James Arthur Bunting (21). He joined the R.A.F. in February, 1939, and was promoted Sergeant six months later. Then he went to Canada, and when he returned, took up duties as an instructor. He recommenced flying duties four months ago. He had volunteered to take up a vacant position when he was killed. He was assistant scout master in the 2nd Otley troop and a King's Scout, and was one of the two Scouts chosen to represent the Wharfedale Association at the Coronation of the King in London.'

At his funeral in Otley, Boy Scouts of the 2nd Otley Troop formed a guard of honour and carried his coffin.

Otley (Newall-with-Clifton and Lindley) Cemetery is on the Pool Road out of Otley to the east. There are 54 identified casualties buried there, including four Old Scholars of Prince Henry's who died in the Second World War.

The following extract is from ***'HELL ON HIGH GROUND VOLUME 2; WORLD WAR II AIR CRASH SITES'*** **by David W. Earl, (*published by Airlife Publishing Limited -1999*)**

'Goose' Down on Dalefoot – Hampden AE393

On 15 January 1942, Hampden AE393, coded EQ-G for George, took off from RAF Balderton, Nottinghamshire for an Operational sortie to Hamburg, Germany's second largest city. The aircraft was based with 408 R.C.A.F. (Goose) Squadron. On that particular night, leaving base at 1715 hours, AE393 was piloted by S/Ldr. W.J.Burnett D.F.C., R.C.A.F. Other members of the crew that fateful night were the navigator F/Sgt. J. A. Bunting, the wireless operator, Sgt. J. R. Appleby and the air gunner, Sgt. M. Jones.

Returning from Hamburg, heavy snow showers were encountered by many of the aircraft and visibility was extremely poor. It was almost inevitable that some of the aircraft would become engulfed in this blizzard, and thus lose their bearings. S/Ldr. Burnett's aircraft would be one of these. Having flown too far north, due to inadequate radio bearings, AE393 had now been in the air for almost ten hours. It entered an area of high ground above the Yorkshire Dales, ending up over Bishopdale near West Burton, where at 0300 hours it struck a section of hillside known as Howgill Scar, around three quarters of a mile south-east of 'Dalefoot Farm.' There was no fire, but a menacing thud as the twin-engined bomber crumpled into a pile of twisted wreckage on the snow-covered fell.

Returning home in the early hours of the morning on Friday 16 January were two local girls, Letty Spence and her sister from 'West Lane House', just off the B6160 (Skipton to West Burton road). They had been to a party in the village that night and heard the bomber fly over. Seconds later a dull thud was heard and the aircraft's engine fell silent – AE393 had crashed.

Shortly after hearing the crash, they rushed home to rouse their father, Mr Eric Spence, who in turn woke his son. The pair ran up the hill across the road, to 'Dalefoot Farm', home of Tom Dinsdale. The party of three then set off up the fell in search of the downed aircraft. When they reached the top of the ridge, now marked by the end of Dalefoot Plantation, a strong smell of petrol filled the air. As there had been no fire on impact, it was obvious the fuel tanks had ruptured, which in turn would lead the trio to the scene of the crash.

At the site hundreds of propaganda leaflets were strewn across the hillside. It was noticed that two of the crew had been flung from the wrecked Hampden and had been killed as a result. The two airmen were the wireless operator, Sgt. J. R. Appleby, and the air gunner, Sgt. M. Jones. Amidst the tangled wreckage, however, were the pilot and the navigator, both still alive , but very badly injured. Because of the position the two airmen lay inside the crumpled cockpit, rescue attempts were severely hampered and it was decided that more help was needed. So, leaving Eric Spence and son at the site, Tom Dinsdale set off back down the moor to get help from the village. First he called on the local doctor, Dr. Ord from West Burton, then a team of servicemen with a stretcher were summoned, and Tom and crew once again set off up the steep hillside to the scene of the crash.

It had been over an hour now since the bomber was discovered and unfortunately, by the time the group got there, the navigator, F/Sgt. Bunting, had succumbed to his injuries. At this point Tom must have felt cheated. If only that airman could have hung on another half hour, they may have got him out. Struggling with the tangled wreckage, they finally released the pilot. Placing him on the stretcher they began to make the icy descent, temperatures were now below freezing and the snow on the moor was treacherous under foot. Somehow they made it down to 'Dalefoot Farm', where blankets and a warm fire were a welcome sight to the Squadron Leader. Here they laid him down and the doctor tended his wounds. Then, a short while later, the military arrived at the farm to take him to the hospital at Catterick Camp, where after spending several months recuperating, he made a remarkable recovery. Despite being left with a scar on the side of his face, he was extremely lucky to be alive.

From the outcome of the investigation on this aircraft, it would appear that r/t failure and unsuitable loop bearings, along with the bad weather, played a large part in the downfall of G-George. However, an unusual remark on the form 1180 accident card, states that the last thing the pilot remembers is flying above cloud at 5,000 feet. This is strange, for Howgill Scar only touches a height of around 1,350 feet. However, surviving a crash such as this, it is understandable his memory was a little hazy.

John Stanley Clapham (1917-1942)

Royal Air Force Volunteer Reserve (10 Squadron) - Flight Sergeant-Service Number: 935675 - Died 2 June 1942 (Age 25) - Runnymede Memorial (Panel 73) - Son of Leonard and Alice Clapham, of Burley-in-Wharfedale, Yorkshire

Flt./Sgt. Clapham.

Flight Sergeant John Stanley Clapham (born 28 February 1917) was the younger son of Mr and Mrs. Leonard Clapham, Lawn Avenue, Burley-in-Wharfedale. His father was an Asylum Attendant who married Alice Robinson in 1914. John was at school from September 1928 (Form Upper 3B) until July 1933 (Upper 5B) having received a W.R.C.C. 'Special Place Award', tenable for 4 years and 2 terms. He had previously attended Burley National School. On leaving School he took up an appointment with Messrs Dacre Son and Hartley, an Otley firm of auctioneers and valuers.

He was good at school work and prominent in School games, especially cricket. His promise as a slow-medium right arm bowler of accurate length was fulfilled after leaving school when he quickly became one of the best-known bowlers in local club cricket. On being called up for National Service he volunteered for flying duties with the R.A.F.

He won a form prize in 1929 – 'honourable mention' Form Upper 3B – and obtained his School Certificate in 1933. He played a little bit of Rugby; a match report against Ashville College notes that the school:

'*were unfortunate to lose the services of Clapham, who had been playing well up to the time of his injury.*' But his passion and skill lay mainly in cricket

In Summer 1931 his cricket criticism said that he '*can play quite a good forcing game, but lacks confidence in match play. His main fault is striking across the ball*. In three innings he scored only 6 runs, but in bowling he took 3 wickets at an average of 7.3, and it was in bowling that he was to excel. In 1933 he topped the bowling averages with 21 wickets at an average of 3.38 and was awarded a Cricket Prize. '*The success of the 1st XI has been mainly due to excellent bowling by Clapham, Mason and Bolton, the bowling of Clapham in particular being very outstanding*.' His name appears regularly in match reports:

- ***May 13th Pannal Ash College (away):*** *Clapham bowled unchanged throughout the innings and had the remarkable analysis of 7 wickets for 16 runs.*
- ***May 20th Roundhay Secondary School (home);*** *The bowling of Clapham once again proved too good for the Roundhay batsmen and they were dismissed for 38 runs. Clapham followed up his previous week's success by capturing 6 wickets for 18 runs.*

- ***June 17th Old Scholars (home):*** *Clapham at one period had taken 5 wickets for 2 runs, and his final analysis turned out as follows – 6.1 overs, 2 maidens, 6 wickets, 8 runs.*

His batting remained a weakness - 14 runs in 4 innings, but in a match for the Old Otliensians against Otley Mills C. C. in 1936 he managed to score 90 runs! The '*Wharfedale and Airedale Observer*', published 5 June 1942, described him as:

'...one of the most outstanding cricketers in Wharfedale. As a medium-paced bowler he captured many wickets for the Burley club, and also had a season with Baildon Green in the Bradford League. A pleasant disposition and his ability made him a popular figure wherever he played. He was also a well-known Association football player in the local league.'

He joined up on the Tuesday following the declaration of war and became an air gunner. In early 1941 he was shot down in the English Channel whilst on reconnaissance and was rescued by a R.A.F. launch. A few weeks before the fatal crash, his plane crashed on landing, and he and other members of the crew escaped just before it burst into flames.

No. 10 Squadron was reformed in January 1928 as a heavy bomber unit, moving to Dishforth in 1937. In 1941 they changed to flying Handley Page Halifax BI's and from August 1942 to the Halifax BII.

Clapham was reported missing following the 1,000-bomber raid against Essen in early June 1942. In an *'In Memoriam'*, he was described as being *'of quiet, but happy disposition, he was popular with the Staff and with his fellows and his loss is a blow to all who knew him.'* The second raid carried out by the *'Thousand Force'* targeted Essen; the first had targeted Cologne. 956 aircraft were dispatched, but crews found great difficulty in finding the target because of low cloud and ground haze. Bombing was very scattered. 31 bombers were lost, including 8 Halifaxes. 'Bomber' Harris had originally planned to send 1000 planes on one or two bombing raids coinciding with each full moon, though he later abandoned the idea.

Clapham was part of the crew of Halifax II W1143 EY-F that took off from Leeming. The plane crashed in the Haringvllet off Hellevoetsluis (Zuid Holland), 25 km southwest of Rotterdam. The plane was part of 78 Squadron but had been borrowed by 10 Squadron for the mission.

Rank	Service	Forename	Surname	Age	Service No.	Grave/Memorial
Pilot Officer	R.N.Z.A.F.	Henry Garfield	Clothier	26	404442	Crooswijk General Cemetery
Sergeant		W R	Forbes			Prisoner of War
Flying Officer	R.N.Z.A.F.	John Raymond Francis	Ganderton	27	403599	Runnymede Memorial

Flight Sergeant	R.A.F.V.R.	John Stanley	Clapham	25	935675	Runnymede Memorial
Sergeant	R.A.F.V.R.	James	Simpson	29	1310209	Runnymede Memorial
Sergeant	R.C.A.F.	Albert Ovide	Mireau	??	R/87341	Runnymede Memorial
Flight Sergeant	R.A.F.V.R.	Terence Albert George	Morris	22	915537	Runnymede Memorial

(RAF Bomber Command Losses of the Second World War 1942 – W R Chorley – page 111)

Jack Crosland (1922-1945)

Royal Air Force Volunteer Reserve
Warrant Officer (Pilot) - Service Number: 1332341
Died 29 October 1945 (Age 24) - Kiel War Cemetery (Grave 6.E.15)
Son of James Arthur Crosland and Lillian Maud Crosland (née D'Arcy);
husband of Teresa May Crosland, of Worcester Park, Surrey.

J. Crosland

Warrant Officer Jack Crosland, Royal Air Force Volunteer Reserve, (born 30 May 1922) lived on Valley View, Otley. His father, James Arthur Crosland (born, Leeds 1889; died, London 1950), was listed in the 1911 Census as a 'tea traveller'. (P.H.G.S. admission form lists him as a 'salesman'). He must have moved around the country because Jack's birth was registered in Basford, Nottinghamshire, and the family later moved from Otley to London. In 1915 James married Lillian Mary D'Arcy (1895-1978) at Bramley, Leeds. Jack attended Otley, North Parade Elementary School from 1925-1934 and Prince Henry's from September 1934 (Form Upper 3A) to July 1936 (Upper 4C), when his parents went to live in London. He received a W.R.C.C. *'Special Place Award'* in September 1934, tenable for his total school career. Although he was only at Prince Henry's for two years he participated in a school play (1935) and Sports Day (1936). He played the part of 'Haroun-al-Rached – the Caliph' in the play *'Twice as Much'* and, in the Under-14 events on Sports Day came 4th in the 220 yards and the Long Jump and 3rd in the High Jump.

'He had a happy, friendly nature, and news of his death was received with great regret. After five years service as a fighter pilot in various war zones, he was killed in a flying accident at Sylt, on October 29th, 1945. He leaves a widow and a son.' He married Teresa M. Witchell in 1942 and the birth of their son, Michael J. Crosland, was registered at West Ham, Essex in 1944.

Sylt is an island in northern Germany, part of the Nordfriesland district, Schleswig-Holstein. It is part of the North Frisian Islands, and is the northernmost island of Germany. It is known for its tourist resorts, as well as for its 40km. long sandy beach.

His death was reported in an article in the '*Wharfedale and Airedale Observer*' on 9 November 1945, as follows:

'Mr and Mrs. J. A. Crosland, of 40 Warren Road, Leyton, E.10, London and formerly of 55 Valley View, Leeds Road, Otley, have been officially notified that their only son, warrant Officer Jack Crosland, R.A.F.V.R., after five years service as a pilot has been killed in a flying accident whilst on duty over Germany, on October 29, 1945.

'Warrant Officer Crosland, who was 23 years of age, attended Otley North Parade School, under Mr Tom Johnson, and later Prince Henry's Grammar School under the late Mr Walter Robinson. He was also a member of the Otley Parish Church troop of scouts during the time of Canon Lowe, the Rev Howarth and the Rev. C. King. He moved to London in August 1936.

'He entered the Civil Service and was posted to the Scottish Home Office. He served with the First Aid Section of Civil Defence as stretcher-bearer during the first London blitz in 1940, until he joined the R.A.F.V.R. in January 1941. He spent 11 months in U.S.A., where he received his initial training as fighter-pilot, and was presented with his silver wings and diploma by the Chief of the U.S. Air Force.

'After service in various war zones at home and abroad, he was posted to No 602 Squadron which, under the command of Squadron Leader Sutherland, played a prominent part in the strafing of the V2 rocket sites during the second London blitz. He leaves a widow and a baby son, Michael John, who was twelve months old on Tuesday.

Kiel War Cemetery

Kiel is a city in the north of German, approximately 100 km north of Hamburg. The cemetery contains 983 Commonwealth burials of the Second World War, 96 of them unidentified. Most of those buried here were airmen lost in bombing raids over Northern Europe, whose graves were brought in from cemeteries throughout northwest Germany. *(Commonwealth War Graves Commission)*

Geoffrey Dodgshon (1919-1944)

Royal Artillery, Manchester Regiment (9th Battalion)
Captain - Service Number: 262489
Died 11 October 1944 (Age 24) - Assisi War Cemetery (Grave II.H,3)
Son of Thomas William and Annie Maria Dodgshon (née Hardisty), of Otley, Yorkshire.

Captain Geoffrey Dodgshon, Royal Artillery (born 30 October 1919) was at School from September 1928 (Form II) to November 1935 (Form Upper 5A). He previously attended North Parade Elementary School in Otley. He lived on Newall Mount, Otley and his father, Thomas William Dodgshon (1888-1958), was a Corn Merchant in the town.

Thomas married Annie Maria Hardisty (1888-1928) in 1908.

G. Dodgshon

Geoffrey was described as *'one of the most popular boys at School, with a most happy, cheery disposition.'* He took part in the Annual Sports in 1929, coming second in the 100 yards (Under 10) and fourth in the Egg and Spoon Race (Forms I and II). He also played Rugby for the school. Only once did he receive a form prize – coming third in Form II, but he did succeed in passing his School Certificate in 1935. He was a keen Rugby player at school, and later played regularly with the Otliensians. He left to assist his father in the family business.

He joined the Royal Corps of Signals in January 1940 and spent two years with the forces of occupation in Iceland, where he was promoted to the rank of Sergeant. He was accepted at O.C.T.U. in August 1942 and took a commission as Second Lieutenant with the Manchester Regiment. He moved overseas shortly after his marriage in April 1942, to Miss Constance Mary Brown, eventually ending up in Italy via North Africa and Sicily. He had only recently been promoted to Captain when he was killed in action in Italy.

The following extracts are taken from ***'VOLUNTARY INFANTRY OF ASHTON-UNDER-LYNE 1859-1971' by Robert Bonner (published by Fleur de Lys Publishers, 2005).*** They represent a summary of pp.88-97.

On 12th December 1943 the 9th Battalion left from Bootle, via Algeria, for Sicily, and landed at Syracuse on 8th January 1944. They began training and preparing for a move to the battlefields of Italy, but were delayed because much of their equipment and the rear party were held up in North Africa. Most of the equipment arrived in Syracuse by 3rd February, but the balance of the battalion did not get there until 14th February. An advance party left Sicily for the mainland on 1st April and reached Vasto on the Adriatic coast, south of Pescaro, on 6th April. The remainder of the Battalion arrived at Scerni on April 10th and 11th and the Ninth were told that they would be required to take over a sector of the front line in Italy on 12th April.

In August the machine guns and mortars of the battalion were used to good effect to support the Allied assault on the Gothic Line. The attack commenced on 25th August 1944.

On 10th September an observation position on the Gemmano Ridge manned by 13 Platoon was hit by shellfire and Lieutenant Nelson, Lance Sergeant Roughly and Private Howcroft were all killed. Lieutenant Dodgshon took over and assisted 6th Lincolns by engaging suspected German mortar positions.

The whole Gemmano ridge was now under continual enemy heavy mortar and shellfire.

The fighting continued backward and forward and it was not until 14th September, following attacks to the right and the left, that the ridge was isolated and the enemy withdrew. The heavy fighting continued and the 9th machine gunners persisted in their support of the regiments involved in the advance.

On 10th October 6th York and Lancaster Regiment entered Longiano in the evening but almost immediately there were counter-attacks and shelling. Lieutenant Geoffrey Dodgshon commanding 13 Platoon was killed by shellfire in Longiano and the same shell seriously wounded Private Smith.

Shortly after, following two months of continuous fighting the battalion came out of the line with the rest of the Division. Their break was short-lived and on 31st October, orders were received to relieve 10th Indian Division. The Ninth stayed in the line until 11th December. Over the period from the end of August to December 9th, 26 soldiers from the Battalion had been killed in action, the highest number of the campaign.

The entire Allied advance was halted in December by the need to rest the troops, ending an advance of more than eighty miles, fighting all the way and crossing eighteen rivers. The Ninth moved to a rest area at Monte Rubbiano, south of Ancona on the Adriatic coast where it spent Christmas 1944.

The Ninth later moved to Greece and then back to Italy, where on 3rd May 1945 they heard that all enemy forces in Italy had surrendered unconditionally to the Allies. The War in Europe ended on 8th May with the unconditional surrender of the Germans. The Ninth continued their move up the east coast of Italy and north into Austria. Demobilisation began in October 1945 and was completed by January 1946.

He was buried in the Assisi Cemetery. His loss was noted in a small article published in the *'Yorkshire Post and Leeds Intelligencer'* on 24 October 1944:

Captain Geoffrey Dodgshon (24) youngest son of Mr. and Mrs. T.W. Dodgshon of Dale Garth, Weston Lane, Otley, has been killed in action in Italy.

Assisi War Cemetery

On 3 September 1943 the Allies invaded the Italian mainland, the invasion coinciding with an armistice made with the Italians, who then re-entered the war on the Allied side. Progress through southern Italy was rapid despite stiff resistance, but the advance was checked for some months at the German winter defensive position known as the Gustav line. The line eventually fell in May 1944 and as the Germans withdrew, Rome was taken by the Allies on 3 June. Many of the burials in the Assisi War Cemetery date from June and July 1944 when the Germans were making their first attempts to stop the Allied advance north of Rome in this region. The site for the cemetery was selected in September 1944 and burials were brought in from the surrounding battlefields. Assisi War cemetery contains 945 Commonwealth burials from the Second World War. *(Commonwealth War Graves Commission)*

Henry Howes Dunwell (1922-1943)

Royal Air Force Volunteer Reserve-Sergeant Pilot - Service Number: 1622615
Died 14 June 1943 (Age 20) - Harare (Pioneer) Cemetery, Bulawayo, Zimbabwe
(European War Graves Plot, Grave 100)
Son of Arthur and Lily Dunwell, of Otley, West Yorkshire.

Flt.-Sgt. Dunwell

Flight Sergeant Henry Howes Dunwell, Royal Air Force Volunteer Reserve (born 9 October 1922) was a pupil at Prince Henry's from September 1930 (Form I) until December 1934 (Upper 4C), when he transferred to Woodhouse Grove School, Apperley Bridge, as a boarder. He had previously been at Westgate Elementary School. He lived on Station Road, Otley and his father, Arthur Dunwell (1888-1960), was a farmer. Arthur married Lily Howes in 1915.

When he first started at Prince Henry's he was only 7 years of age. At this time the School was fee paying and there were a significant number of pupils who were under 11 years of age. In his first year he was placed third in his form; in his second year he came second. He had the potential to become a good athlete; in 1932 he was first in the 100 yards (Under 10), second in the 100 yards (Under 12), and second in the Egg & Spoon Race (Forms I & II).

When he left Woodhouse Grove he was articled to Mr B. E. Brayshaw, an Otley firm of accountants. He retained his links with Prince Henry's by playing for the Old Scholars' teams at the beginning of the war. He volunteered for the R.A.F. in January 1942, and was called up in July, going to Southern Rhodesia a month later for training.

He was killed on 14 June 1943 in a flying accident in Rhodesia, now Zimbabwe, when he was acting as an instructor, and was buried in the Harare (Pioneer) Cemetery in Bulawayo. There are 261 identified casualties, including 224 Commonwealth burials from the Second World War. His name is also inscribed on the gravestone identifying the Dunwell family plot in Otley Cemetery.

After his death his parents received several letters from Henry's colleagues in Southern Rhodesia. *'One of the best pilots ever passed out in South Africa'*, commented one colleague who had been with him throughout his training. Another letter stated:

'Henry was an excellent and keen flier. He gained his 'wings' and was recommended for a commission at the time of his death. He was killed in a trainer aircraft, which was being piloted by the pupil when it crashed. He is buried at Salisbury.'

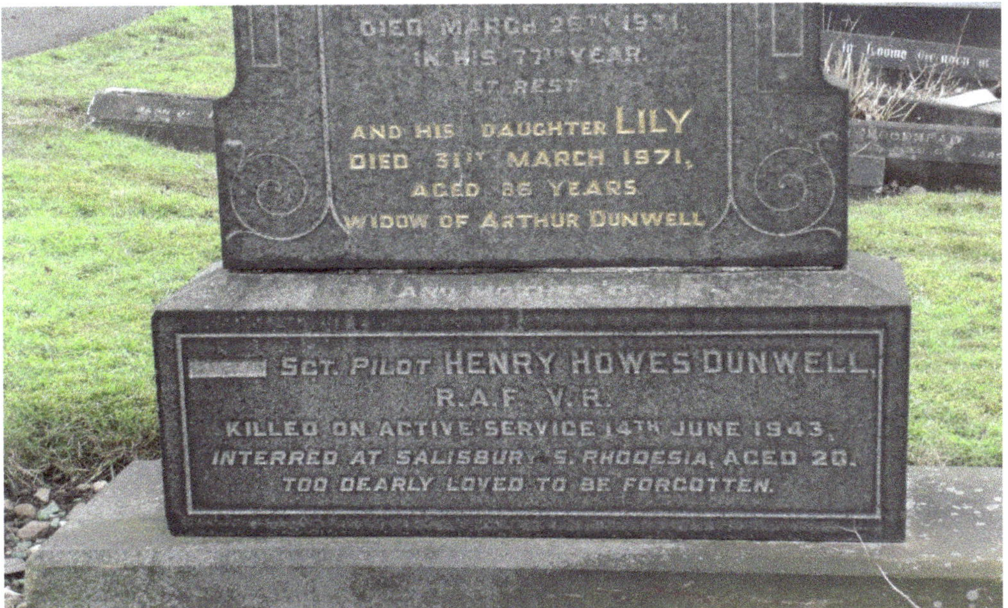

Gordon Maguire Fairbanks (1913-1942)

Merchant Navy (S.S. Refast) - Third Officer - Died 26 January 1942 (Age 28) - Tower Hill Memorial (Panel 86) - Son of Richard and Norah Christine Fairbanks; husband of Lilian Fairbanks, of Austhorpe, Halton, Leeds, Yorkshire.

Third Officer Gordon Maguire Fairbanks, Merchant Navy, (born 12 June 1913 – birth registered in Selby) lived at 3 Springfield Mount Leeds. His father, Richard William Fairbanks (1870-1951), was described as a retired civil servant, though his occupation when Gordon's two brothers later came to Prince Henry's was listed as *'Ex-Sergeant, Cape Mounted Rifles'*. Richard married Nora Christine Walford (1883-1949), in Leeds in 1912.

Gordon had previously attended Mrs. Blacker's Private School, Pool-in-Wharfedale. He joined Prince Henry's in September 1923 (Form Lower 3A) and left in July 1927 (Upper 5C) to become a fitter. A note on his admission form indicates that he *'left owing to the difficulties of travelling from Leeds and his parents' financial position.'* In his early days at school Fairbanks showed some signs of athletic ability, winning the 100 yards (Under 12) at Sports Day in 1925, and coming second in both the 100 yards (Under 14) and 220 yards (Under 14) in 1927.

A note in the Summer 1929 edition of the *'Otliensian'* mentioned that Gordon Fairbanks *'Has joined his ship the 'Rockpool' which sailed for Italy at Easter.'*

In 1940 he married Lilian Clark.

The *S.S. Refast* was originally called *Gulflight* when it was completed in August 1914 for Gulf Oil Co, New York. On 1 May 1915, the neutral tanker was torpedoed and badly damaged by U-30 in the approaches to the English Channel. She was the first American ship to be torpedoed in the First World War. In 1938 she was sold to Britain and renamed *Refast.*

On 3 January 1942 the *Refast* left London as part of Convoy ON-56 en route for Baton Rouge via Loch Ewe. At 18.58 on 26 January 1942, the *Refast* was torpedoed by *U-582* south of St John's, Newfoundland. The ship sank by the stern at 19.15 hours after being hit by two more torpedoes at 19.07 and 19.08. Ten crew members were lost, including Gordon Fairbanks. The master, 27 crew members and 4 gunners were picked up by the British steam merchant *Mariposa* and landed at Halifax, Nova Scotia, the following day.

U-582 was sunk by an American Catalina aircraft on 5 October 1942 south west of Iceland; the captain and his entire crew of 46 men died.

The ten men lost in the sinking of the *Refast* are commemorated on a plaque (Panel 86) on the Tower Hill Memorial.

George Chadwick	Donkeyman	Age 33
Donald Lewis Davie	Cabin Boy	Age 18
William Elliott	Fireman	Age 30
Gordon Maguire Fairbanks	Third Officer	Age 28
Sidney John Mann	Able Seaman	Age 30
James Henry Mead	Fireman	Age 28
John Patrick Moran	Donkeyman	Age 56
Ronald Mould	Ordinary Seaman	Age 18
Cecil John Newcombe	First Radio Officer	Age 32
Robert Corbett Boyle	Chief Steward	Age 25

The Memorial stands on the south side of the garden of Trinity Square, London, close to the Tower of London. It commemorates men and women of the Merchant Navy and Fishing Fleets who died in both World Wars who have no known grave. In the Second World War 4,786 merchant ships were lost, with a total of 32,000 lives. The First World War section of the Tower Hill Memorial commemorates almost 12,000 Mercantile Marine casualties who have no grave but the sea. The Memorial was designed by Sir Edwin Lutyens with sculpture by Sir William Reid-Dick. It was unveiled by Queen Mary on 12 December 1928. The Second World War extension, designed by Sir Edward Maufe, with sculpture by Charles Wheeler, commemorates almost 24,000 names. The number of identified casualties commemorated is 35,800. (*Commonwealth War Graves Commission*)

Probate on his estate was granted to his wife, Lilian, on 27 May 1942. Their address was given as 1 Beechwood Avenue, Burley, Leeds, and he left effects of £154 5s 5d.

Kenneth Stephen Halliwell (1922-1945)

Royal Air Force Volunteer Reserve (5R.F.U.) - Sergeant, Pilot- Service Number: 1026402 - Died 31 March 1945 (Age 22) - Salerno War Cemetery (Grave VI.F.26) - Son of Harold and Florence May Halliwell, of Shipley, Yorkshire.

K. S. Halliwell

Sergeant Pilot Kenneth Stephen Halliwell, R.A.F.V.R. (born 4 September 1922) joined Prince Henry's in November 1935 (Form Lower 4A) when his family came to reside at Hawthorn Villas, Bingley Road, Menston. He had previously been at Wyke County School, Bradford, Carr Lane Council School, Wyke, and from September 1932 - October 1935 at Carlton Secondary School, Bradford. His father, Harold Halliwell, was a salesman. Harold married Florence Mary Stephens in Salford in 1919. Kenneth was given a W.R.C.C. Special Place Award in November 1935. He left the school in July 1938 (Form Lower 5B) to take up employment as an articled clerk with Messrs. Rawlinson, Smith and Mitchell, chartered accountants, Bradford.

He joined the R.A.F.V.R. in 1940, and had been overseas since November 1943. He was awarded his 'wings' in South Africa in 1944. His brother, Douglas H. Halliwell, also educated at Prince Henry's, was also in the R.A.F.V.R. He volunteered in May 1940 and trained as a wireless operator – air gunner. He was promoted Pilot Officer in 1943.

'5RFU' – No.5 Refresher Flying Unit: the Desert Air Force Training Flight became 5RFU in July 1944. It was based at Perugia, Gaudo and other locations in Italy. It is probable that Kenneth was a spitfire pilot.

Salerno War Cemetery

Commonwealth and American forces landed near Salerno on 8/9 September 1943 and there was fierce fighting for some days in the bridgehead that they established. The site for the cemetery was chosen in November 1943 and it contains many burials resulting from the landings and fighting that followed, but graves were also later brought in from a wide area of southwestern Italy. Salerno War Cemetery contains 1,846 Commonwealth burials of the Second World War, 107 of them unidentified. (*Commonwealth War Graves Commission*)

Kenneth Stephen Halliwell is listed on the World War II war memorial at Monton Unitarian Church, Salford.

Charles Leslie Harrison (1917-1941)

Royal Air Force Volunteer Reserve (72 Squadron) - Sergeant Pilot- Service Number: 936721 - Died 10 July 1941 (Age 23) - Runnymede Memorial (Panel 44) - Son of Wilkes and Edith Harrison, of Otley, Yorkshire.

Sergeant Charles Leslie Harrison, R.A.F.V.R., (born 16 November 1917) lived on Grosvenor Terrace, Otley; his father, Wilkes Harrison (1891-1954), was a Printers' Engineer, who married Edith Longstaffe in 1913. He entered Prince Henry's in September 1925 (Form Upper I), when he was only 7 years of age, and left in December 1933 (Upper 5B) to take up employment as an Insurance Clerk.

His claim to fame in acting/singing came in 1926 when he played the part of Little Boy Blue opposite Barbara Lewis as Little Bo-Peep in the School Concert, and in 1930 when he was the Knave of Hearts in a presentation by the Junior School of five episodes from '*Alice in Wonderland*.'

He was awarded the third form prize in Form I in 1926 and 'honourable mention' in both 1927 (Form II) and 1928 (Lower III). His tea cosy was '*commented upon favourably by everybody*' in the Art Exhibition of 1927. He was elected as a Committee member of the Natural Science Society in 1932 and attained his School Certificate in 1933.

1926	*Egg & Spoon Race (Forms 1 & II) – Third place*	
1927	*80 yards (Under 10) – Joint Second place*	*Egg & Spoon Race (Forms I & II) – First Place*
1929	*100 yards (Under 10) – Fourth Place*	
1931	*100 yards (Under 14) – Third Place*	*220 yards (Under 14) – Third Place*
1932	*High Jump (Open) – Joint Fourth Place*	
1933	*High Jump (Open) – Third Place*	

He was a member of the First XV Rugby team from 1932, being awarded his Rugby colours in 1934. His player profile in 1933 notes that he '*has improved. Keeps up with the ball, and is showing more spirit.*' His athletics record on Sports Days confirms that he was a pupil who threw himself into school activities and was always willing to try.

Prince Henry's Grammar School Rugby XV 1932-1933

T.E.Thornton F. Lofthouse
Mr Pratt S. Greenwood C.Hobday N. Miller G. Hobson L. Harrison
S. Labram C. Cooper J. Goodall W.H. Kay J.E. Mason E.A. Underwood S. Whittaker
A.R. Jowett H. Dodgshon

When he was reported missing, '*The Otliensian*' commented that while at School '*his bright, happy nature made everybody his friend.*'

Before the war he was a member of the Bradford Flying Club and the Bradford Model Yacht and Power Boat Club. In 1932, at the age of 14, he won the principal trophy of the Boat Club's handicap race for the Sydney Carter Cup at Larkfield Dam, Rawdon.

He volunteered for the R.A.F. at the outbreak of war, and was awarded his 'wings' within six months of his call-up, and a month later was flying a Spitfire with the famous 72nd Basutoland Squadron. In the early days of the war Leslie, like other fighter pilots, was on duty 24 hours a day – eight hours flying, eight hours at readiness and eight hours available. He was posted missing from the Biggin Hill Fighter Squadron on 10 July 1941.

72 Squadron was formed at Netheravon on 2 July 1917 and after undertaking operations in the Middle East and Turkey in the First World War, was disbanded in September 1919. It was reformed on 22 February 1937, flying Gladiators, until April 1939 when it changed to Spitfires.

Air defence and convoy protection duties followed the outbreak of War until the unit moved to support the evacuation at Dunkirk in June 1940. During the Battle of Britain, No 72 spent the early days at Acklington as part of No 13 Group, before moving south during September to aid the main defence force. It was during this phase that Charles Harrison was lost. In September 1942, the Squadron moved to North Africa to support the Tunisian campaign, and then to Malta, in support of the Allied Eighth Army as it advanced through Scilly and Southern France until the German surrender, when it moved to Austria where it was disbanded in December 1946.

The 72 Squadron Diary for 10 July 1941 contains the following entry:

'11 aircraft took part in No. 11 Group Wing sweep (from Biggin Hill) to Hardelot – Fruges – St Omer. When between Fruges and St Omer squadron was attacked by ME. 109s (two groups of six each).

They were also attacked whilst returning via Gravelines. F/O Godlewski, Sgt Casey and Sgt Harrison did not return. Seven aircraft landed safely at Coltishall at 1320hrs and 1 aircraft crash landed there at the same time; the pilot Sgt Rosser, was uninjured.'

(Royal Air Force Fighter Command Losses of the Second World War: Vol. 1 – Operational Losses: Aircraft and Crews 1939-1941 by Normal L. R. Franks.)

Sergeant Harrison was flying Supermarine Spitfire Mark V, No. P8604, and because his body was never found he is commemorated on the Runnymede Memorial, which lies overlooking the River Thames on Cooper's Hill at Englefield Green between Windsor and Egham on the A308, 4 miles from Windsor. The Air Forces Memorial at Runnymede commemorates by name over 20,000 airmen who were lost in the Second World War during operations from bases in the United Kingdom and North and Western Europe, and who have no known graves. They served in Bomber, Fighter, Coastal, Transport, Flying Training and Maintenance Commands, and came from all parts of the Commonwealth. Some were from countries in continental Europe which had been overrun but whose airmen continued to fight in the ranks of the Royal Air Force. (*Commonwealth War Graves Commission*)

In 2003, whilst walking on a beach near La Panne in Belgium, Franz Degel and his daughter found a silver bracelet inscribed '*Harrison C.L. 936721 RAFVR.*' This discovery led to an appeal for any relatives of Sergeant Harrison to contact the Aircrew Association. Sgt. Harrison's cousin, Frank Longstaffe, who still lived in Otley, replied to the request and the bracelet was mounted and framed and presented to the family. A replica was presented to the still existing 72 Squadron, based at R.A.F. Linton-on-Ouse. The following newspaper article, written by Lesley Tate, was published in the '*Wharfedale and Airedale Observer*', 2 October 2003:

War Bracelet found in Belgium

A wartime Spitfire pilot believed to have been shot down over Belgium in the 1940s is to be remembered thanks to his identity bracelet. More than 60 years after Otley born Sergeant Leslie Harrison vanished without trace, his silver bracelet has been swept up on a beach in Belgium. The bracelet, inscribed with Sgt. Harrison's name and identity number was handed over to the Aircrew Association, and following an appeal in The Wharfedale, his closest living relative has come forward.

Sgt. Harrison's cousin, Frank Longstaffe of Newall Avenue, said he was amazed when he read the appeal in The Wharfedale. Sgt. Harrison's two other remaining relatives, cousins Eileen Wilby, lives in Otley and Margaret Longstaffe lives in Burley-in-Wharfedale.

"It came as a bit of a shock to me when I read it in the paper, it was such a long time ago and although we haven't forgotten him, we don't really think of him."
Sgt. Harrison was only 21 when he went missing. His body has never been found. It was believed that Sgt Harrison was shot down in 1941 somewhere over Belgium while on a fighter sweep with his Gravesend based 72 Squadron. But further research by his Squadron has revealed the possibility that he survived the 1941 crash, was transferred to another squadron only to be shot down a few months later.

Mr Longstaffe said "I can remember a squadron leader coming to see my auntie to say he was missing, but this is the only thing they've ever found of him."

Sgt Harrison was a part time pilot employed at Yeadon Aerodrome before the war and in 1939 joined up and started flying the elite Spitfires. He was the son of Wilks and Edith Harrison of Otley and is believed to be the only Spitfire pilot in Otley. For many years his photograph took pride of place in the window of a Westgate photographers. Now more than 60 years later Sgt Harrison's bracelet has been swept up on a beach in Belgium at Neuport between Dunkirk and Ostend.

"His bracelet must have been in the sea for 60 years," said Mr Longstaffe.

It was handed over to the Aircrew Association which set about trying to trace Sgt. Harrison's closest surviving relative. Mr Longstaffe has now been in touch with the association and is waiting to find out when the bracelet will be returned. He plans to return the bracelet to Sgt. Harrison's squadron, the 72 Squadron.

"The secretary of the 72 Squadron has said he is going to send me the diary of what happened, it's all beginning to unfold," said Mr Longstaffe.

His name, one of the first 288, appears on the Memorial in the Pilots' Memorial Chapel, St George's Chapel of Remembrance at Biggin Hill in Kent. It was dedicated on the Battle of Britain Anniversary in 1943, and was the first memorial of the war. The Chapel was rebuilt in 1951 after the original was destroyed by fire in 1946, and the memorial now has the names of 454 allied aircrew, who were based at Biggin Hill and died in operational flights. A *'Lamp of Remembrance'* is kept alight as a symbol of perpetual remembrance, and the name of each pilot is mentioned in the prayers at St George's Chapel on the anniversary of the day he failed to return from operations.

George Malcolm Holmes (1913-1942)

Royal Navy (S.S.Mendoza) - Able Seaman-Service Number: C/JX 248115 - Died 1 November 1942 (Age 29) - Chatham Naval Memorial (Panel 54, Column 2) - Son of George and Margaret Ann Holmes, husband of Vida Jane Holmes of Guildford, Surrey.

George Malcolm Holmes, Royal Navy, (date of birth 31 March 1913, birth registered in Hunslet) started at Prince Henry's in September 1924 (Lower 3A) after 2 years at Leeds Modern School. He lived at Woodgarth, Pool-in-Wharfedale; his father, George, was an architect, who married Margaret Annie Morton in Leeds in 1910. George junior left school in March 1929 (Form Lower 5A). In 1927 he was placed first in his class and received a prize. He played 1st XV Rugby, being awarded his colours in 1929. In 1940 he married Vida Jane Hailstone in Birmingham.

S.S. Mendoza

The *S.S. Mendoza* was a Ministry of War Transport liner of 8,234 tons. In October 1942, captained by Captain B.T.Batho, this ex-Vichy French ship captured by a British armed merchant cruiser and now sailing under the Blue Funnel flag, was sailing from Mombasa when she was torpedoed and sunk by the German submarine U-178 about 130 kilometres from its destination, Durban, South Africa.

The ship had been forced to sail without an armoured escort and was carrying 153 crew and some 250 passengers, when she was hit, taking the lives of 28 of her crew and 122 service personnel. The Captain gave the order to abandon ship and ten of the twelve lifeboats were launched successfully, the other two being damaged beyond repair.

'Before everybody could leave the vessel, a second torpedo struck the port side, causing a secondary explosion. With no other options open to them the remaining men had to jump for their lives, even though some of them were severely burned. The survivors were picked up by the lifeboats and a short while later an aircraft appeared and signalled that assistance was on its way. However, no rescue had arrived by dusk and the Captain ordered the lifeboats to attempt to reach land of their own accord.'

'Shortly after daybreak the American ship S.S. Alava was able to pick up some of the survivors. Unfortunately before Captain Batho could board the vessel, he slipped, fell into the water, his body crushed between the ship and the lifeboat. The U-178 was scuttled on August 25, 1944 at Bordeaux, France.'

Chatham Naval Memorial

Chatham Naval Memorial commemorates 8,517 sailors of the First World War and 10,098 of the Second World War, each of whom have no known graves, the majority of deaths having occurred at sea. The three manning ports in Great Britain – Chatham, Plymouth and Portsmouth – each have an identical memorial that also provides a leading mark for shipping.

The Chatham Memorial was unveiled on 26 April 1924, and the site was extended after the Second World War to provide space to commemorate the naval dead without graves from that war. *(Commonwealth War Graves Commission)*

Robert Stanton Imeson (1920-1943)

Royal Air Force Volunteer Reserve(103 Squadron) - Sergeant-Flight Engineer - Service Number 1480164 - Died 2 December 1943 (Age 23) - Berlin 1939-1945 War Cemetery (Coll. Grave 5.D. 14-20) - Adopted son of Joshua M. Imeson and Ethel Imeson, Otley, Yorkshire

Flight Engineer Robert Stanton Imeson, R.A.F.V.R. (born 25 April 1920) lived on Bank Parade, Otley and entered Prince Henry's in September 1931 (Form Upper 3B) on a County Minor Scholarship tenable for school life. He had previously attended Otley North Parade Elementary School from 1923-1931. His adoptive father, Joshua M. Imeson (1885-1966) was a turner. He married Ethel Court in Wharfedale in 1920 and shortly after they adopted Robert junior. Robert Stanton *'broke his agreement with the W.R.C.C. and paid the penalty'* – he left in April 1935 (Lower 5A) to become a mechanic. In his first year at School he won second prize in his form. The 'In Memoriam' comment in *'The Otliensian'* says that he *'took a keen interest in games and was a playing member of the Old Scholar's Rugby Club.'*

R. S. Imeson.

He was a keen swimmer, and former secretary of Otley Swimming Club. He won a silver cup for boxing in the R.A.F. and was also a gymnast, being a member of a Woodhouse club. In June 1938 he went to the rescue of a boy who was in imminent danger of drowning in the River Wharfe at Otley weir, and was later awarded an honorary testimonial of the Royal Humane Society.

Before joining the R.A.F. he was Labour Officer at Crompton Parkinson Ltd, Guiseley, prior to which he was on the office staff at Ledgard's Garage, Otley.

He volunteered for the R.A.F. in July 1941 and was made a Sergeant in 1942. At first he was a flight mechanic on the ground staff, but later trained for flying duties. He took part in some of the 1,000 bomber raids over Berlin, the Ruhr and the north west German cities.

He was on his last raid before completing a tour of operational duty when he was at first reported missing, presumed killed, after a flight over Germany, but was eventually reported killed in action. He was originally buried with his six comrades at Philadelphia, near Storkov, about 28 miles southeast of Berlin.

103 Squadron, based at Newton and Elsham Woods, came to 1 Group in July 1940 after returning from operations in France with the Advanced Air Striking Force and served continuously with 1 Group until the end of the war, carrying out intensive operations during that long period and often suffering heavy casualties. They carried out the most bombing raids in 1 Group, suffered most losses in 1 Group and suffered the highest percentage losses in 1 Group Lancaster squadrons.

On 2 December 1943 458 aircraft, including 425 Lancasters, targeted Berlin. There were no major diversions and the bombers took an absolutely direct route across the North Sea and Holland and then on to Berlin.

The Germans identified Berlin as the target 19 minutes before Zero Hour and many fighters were waiting there. Incorrectly forecast winds scattered the bomber stream, particularly on the return flight and German fighters scored further victories here. A total of 40 bombers, including 37 Lancasters, were lost, representing 8.7% of the force.

Inaccurate wind forecasts caused great difficulties for the Pathfinders in establishing their positions and as a result the attack was scattered over a wide area of southern Berlin and the countryside south of the city; this may explain why Imeson's Lancaster crashed south east of Berlin.

The full crew of Lancaster JB 401 were:

Name	Nationality	Service	Rank	Age
Francis Thomas Hopps (133250)	United Kingdom	Royal Air Force Volunteer Reserve	Flight Lieutenant	28
Robert Stanton Imeson (1480164)	United Kingdom	Royal Air Force Volunteer Reserve	Sergeant	23
Frederick John Roberts (J/18831)	Canada	Royal Canadian Airforce	Pilot Officer	NA
Walter Leonard Sargent (1321977)	United Kingdom	Royal Air Force Volunteer Reserve	Sergeant	23
Roy Thomas (1334293)	United Kingdom	Royal Air Force Volunteer Reserve	Sergeant	22
Jack Bays Daniel (1473420)	United Kingdom	Royal Air Force Volunteer Reserve	Sergeant	20
Roland Edward Black (R/123878)	Canada	Royal Canadian Airforce	Sergeant - Warrant Officer Class 2	20

(*R.A.F. Bomber Command Losses Vol. 4 1943 by W.R. Chorley.*)

Berlin 1939-1945 War Cemetery

The site of the Berlin 1939-45 War Cemetery was selected in 1945, soon after hostilities ceased. Graves were brought to the cemetery from the Berlin area and from eastern German. The great majority of those buried here, approximately 80% of the total, were airmen who were lost in the air raids over Berlin and the towns in eastern Germany.

The remainder were men who died as prisoners of war, some of them in the forced march in to Germany from camps in Poland, in advance of the advancing Russians. The cemetery contains 3,595 Commonwealth burials of the Second World War, 397 of them unidentified. (*Commonwealth War Graves Commission*)

Margery Jennings (née Hellewell) (1908-1945)

Nurse, Medical Auxiliary Service - Died 12 May 1945 (Age 37) - Daughter of the late Arthur Coates Hellewell and Florence Beaumont Hellewell of 2, Kirkgate, Otley, Yorkshire: wife of Capt. Cyril Oswald Jennings, Royal Engineers.
Died at Lubbock Linggau

Margery Hellewell (born 20 November 1908) was in the first intake of the re-opened Prince Henry's Grammar School on 19 September 1918 (Class IIA). Her admission number was '18' and her brother, William Clifford Hellewell, joined the school at the same time. Her father, Arthur Coates Hellewell (1876-1934), who was also a Governor of the School, was a Grocer, with a shop on Kirkgate. In 1898 he married Florence Beaumont Eastburn. According to the 1911 Census they were living at 8 Fern Bank, Otley, and had 5 children – Arthur Sydney (born 1899), Herbert Arnold (born 1902), Charles Wilson (born 1907), William Clifford (born 1907), and Margery (born 1908). Arthur, as a well-known local businessman, played an important part in the re-opening of Prince Henry's in 1918 and, not surprisingly, sent his two youngest children to the school. He was to go on to become Chairman of Otley Urban District Council. Margery had previously attended Otley, North Parade Elementary School. She left Prince Henry's in July 1924 (Upper 5B) to go into her father's business.

In Summer 1919 both Margery and William presented books to the school library, which at the time was stocked mainly by donations from students. William was a leading light in sport in the School, but Margery played her part by competing in Sports Days. She came third in the 100 yards (Under 12) and second in the High Jump (Under 12) in 1920, and became something of a High Jump specialist in future years, coming first in both 1921 (Under 13) and 1922 (Under 14). In 1924 in the 'Open' competition she finished fourth.

Academically she was awarded the third place prize in her form in 1919, the School Scripture prize in 1921, an 'honourable mention' in her form in 1923, and the School Music prize in 1924. She took main parts in two School plays; in *'Twelfth Night'* in 1923:

'Margery Hellewell, as Viola, gave a delightfully natural interpretation of the modest heroine, who, though disguised in male attire, and acting a bold part, could not wholly suppress her gentleness and shrinking delicacy of feeling.'

And in *'A Midsummer Night's Dream'* in 1924:

'Hermia (Margery Hellewell) acted the part of a despairing daughter under the yoke of an unreasonable father very sympathetically. She was equally happy in her personification of a yielding lover, and a rather selfishly hopeful friend.'

On Wednesday 2 July 1930 she married Cyril Oswald Jennings at the Otley Wesleyan Church. After spending some time in South Africa, the couple went to Malaya where Mr Jennings became Government Buildings Inspector in Kuala Lumpur in 1935. After the start of the war, he joined the Royal Engineers.

Margery Jennings was serving with the Medical Auxiliary service in Malaya in 1942 and was taken prisoner by the Japanese on Bangka Island, off Sumatra, in mid-February of that year. She was interned in various camps and died in one at Loebok Lingau (Sumatra) on 12 May 1945. Her husband, Captain C. O. Jennings, was a prisoner of war at Palembang, following his escape from Singapore and his subsequent capture on Java, but never managed to meet with his wife during their imprisonment in separate camps.

The following article, published in the *'Yorkshire Post and Leeds Intelligencer,'* 5 November 1943, was the first indication her relatives had that she was a prisoner of war:

News of Otley Woman After Two Years

'After a silence of nearly two years news has been received through the Red Cross that Mrs. Margery Jennings, of Otley, is interned in Sumatra, She is a daughter of the late Mr. A.C. Hellewell, a former chairman of Otley Urban Council. Her husband, Capt. Cyril O. Jennings, was reported to be a prisoner of war six months ago.'

In January 1944, Margery's brother, Arthur Sydney Hellewell received a postcard from his sister which had been written on 13 March 1943. Reported in the *'Wharfedale and Airedale Observer'* of 7 January 1944, it read:

'Inform all concerned, both well here. Separated. Prayers justified. God keep you. United love. Both cheerful. Conducting choral society, singing, playing. Formed Young Women's Club'

In September 1945 a telegram was received from Captain Jennings stating that his wife had died, and that he was returning home at once.

On 19 November 1945, a memorial service was held for her at Otley, Trinity Methodist Church, as reported in the *'Yorkshire Post & Leeds Intelligencer'*:

Tribute to Otley Heroine

'Many Otley people attended a memorial service at Trinity Methodist Church today for Mrs. Margery Jennings, who died in a Japanese internment camp at Muntok, Banga Island, on May 12 this year, News of her death has been confirmed by her husband, Captain C.O. Jennings, Royal Engineers, who was also interned and has recently arrived in England after repatriation. They were living in Malaya at the time of the Japanese invasion and were interned in separate camps.

'Mrs. Jennings was a daughter of the late Mr. A.C. Hellewell, a former chairman of Otley Urban Council, and she had been closely associated with the Otley Methodist Church. Her husband was present at the memorial service.

'The Rev. G.K. Grice, superintendent minister, who devoted his sermon to a tribute to Mrs Jennings, said that in Singapore she was associated with an American Mission. Her husband had spoken to a number of women who survived the internment camp and all

of them testified that she was a joy and inspiration to those about her by her continued sympathy, thoughtfulness and help.

'Among her effects was found a book of verses which she composed during her internment, and these recorded the experiences through which she was passing. They revealed not only her hopes and fears, desires and yearnings, and the wretchedness and misery of the internment camp, but also her abounding faith in the Grace of God.

"She was a remarkable woman" said the minister: "a Christian worthy of the name; indeed a heroine deserving of the highest esteem."

'Mr Grice read one of the poems from the pulpit. It gave a graphic description of the miseries of life in the camp at Muntok. Among her other possessions was a poignant diary written in the margin of a Bible.'

On Sunday 24 November 1946, also at Trinity Methodist Church, Otley, a tablet to Margery Jennings' memory was dedicated. The '*Wharfedale and Airedale Observer'* reported on the dedication in its issue of 29 November 1946:

'On Sunday morning last, at the Trinity Methodist Church, Otley, a tablet to the memory of Margery Jennings, who died in a Japanese internment camp, was dedicated by the Rev. G. Kellett Grice. Mr Grice referred to the impressive memorial service held in November 1945, and spoke of the inspiration the memory of the witness and service of one who had received her early training in the Sunday School and Church life at Trinity. Mr Grice referred to Mrs. Jennings as one who turned her imprisonment into an opportunity of Christian witness and service, and of the testimony of fellow prisoners who had survived to the influence of her life upon them.

The tablet, which is of burnished brass and mounted on mahogany has been placed on the wall at the head of the pew used by members of the Hellewell family, by Capt. C. O. Jennings.

It reads:

'Margery Jennings, M.A.S., dearly loved wife of Capt. C. O. Jennings, R.E., and daughter of Mr and Mrs. A. C. Hellewell, Otley, who died on May 12 1945, in a Japanese internment Camp at Lubbock, Linggau, Sumatra."

'Through faith in Christ she lived nobly and died bravely."

There was a large congregation at the service including members of the Hellewell family, and the hymns included "In heavenly love abiding," "Be Thou my vision O Lord of my life" (favourities of Margery Jennings) and "For all the saints."

More details about her Bible Diary were published in the *'Yorkshire Post'* on 23 November 1945:

Otley Woman's War Suffering Told in Bible Diary
Unknown Heroine of Internment Camp

Today I have been reading through fragments of a poignant diary written on the margins and blank pages of an old Bible, during her years of internment, by Mrs. Margery Jennings (Margery Hellewell), an Otley woman who died in a Japanese internment camp at Muntok, Banka Island, on May 12 this year.

On the leaves of this frayed and tattered Bible, which was her father's gift to her mother, are described, in simple language, the trials, tribulations and sufferings of a Christian woman. It is the story of the depths of misery and heights of spiritual comfort the writer experienced during the long years of internment.

It is impossible not to be moved by these entries relating to the unbelievable things that a woman, known to many in Otley and Wharfedale, faced up to and finally overcame in death. She must have been one of the unknown heroines of the war.

Sick at Heart

One of the entries reads: "Wrote poem 'Solace for Grief' today. Kept out of the way as much as possible .... Feeling terribly limp and disappointed .... sad and sick at heart ....physically very weak so, plus mental spiritual strain, am a wreck today. How can I hope to advise and help others when I am so weak and helpless against (--------) myself?"

That entry was made on April 3 1944. I was unable to read the missing word.

In the early months of this year Mrs. Jennings went into hospital and her entries there were written in a fine hand on scraps of paper which were found in the back of the Bible. They tell of her illness: of 'many deaths day by day.' She sold her fountain pen and watch for money to buy extra food and was 'trusting to God and living day by day."

In March, 1945, she wrote: "Food not very plentiful except rice, and turning against even rice now, as cannot make it interesting with etceteras."

Made Her Will

"Wrote out my list of bequests in case I died while interned by Nippon --- made Mrs. (-------) my executor --- left majority of things and money to Pip (a woman friend in camp). Hope it will never be needed ---- have no feeling or premonition---- am just taking precaution of getting my few things to the right people if I do not come through."

"Wish I could think less of food. My nights are filled with restless longing for home food, particularly meat. System craves it."

And then, towards the end, is this entry: ---- "Hope to hear from loved ones soon. Oh! To be free and see you again, to get good food and have a normal life, if only one room and a few bits and pieces of furniture."

One thing is obvious. Her love of music was one of the things she turned to, whenever possible, for consolation and inspiration. An entry records that one of the many poems she wrote – "Friendship"--- written in Palembang Hospital in August, 1942, was "set to music by Margaret Dryburgh and sung in camp for first time at a variety show on July 31 1943."

The poem here, with which I end this very inadequate, but very sincere, account of Margery Jennings's poignant diary was written by her on March 20 1943.

Music

I thank God for music,
Which to my soul brings
Release and strange beauty,
As sweetly it sings
Of joy and deep sorrow,
Of love and of life;
Of strength and great blessing,
Of peace after strife

An entry in the '*Otliensian*' in *Vol. XXXII, Spring 1950*, noted that:

'It has been learned that friends of the late Mrs. Margery Jennings (nee Hellewell) have given a pulpit to Wesley Church, Singapore, and this has been dedicated to her memory. Margery died in 1945, at the age of 37, in a Japanese internment camp. After being taken prisoner by the Japanese she wrote the diary of her sufferings and those of her fellow-prisoners in the margin of her Bible.'

The diary was presented by her family to the Imperial War Museum in 1982, as noted in the following article by Michael Clarke, published in the '*Yorkshire Post*' on 6 February 1982:

Heroine who defied Japanese

An extraordinary diary of a woman's life in Japanese prisoner-of-war camps went into the archives of the Imperial War Museum, London, yesterday.

The diary, written in the margins, blank spaces and scraps of paper in a family Bible, was kept by Mrs. Margery Jennings, daughter of an Otley grocer, now regarded as an unknown heroine of the Second World War.

Until now, the diary, prized as a family heirloom, has been kept by her sister-in-law, Mrs. Linnie Hellewell in a drawer at her home in Elm Terrace, Otley. The Museum, which has described the diary as 'a most moving and remarkable document', has also received a small book of poems written by Mrs Jennings while she was interned.

Mrs. Jennings, who went to Otley Grammar School, was a well-built, dark haired, out-going girl who played the piano. She went to Malaya with her husband, Cyril Jennings, when he became Government Building Inspector in Kuala Lumpur in 1935. After the start of the war, he joined the Royal Engineers.

The couple were separated after the Japanese invasion of 1942 and were imprisoned in different camps. ...... Jennings's diary tells of the everyday drudgery, the appalling conditions, the illnesses, and how, at one point, she was in charge of 150 women.

She writes of how they ate mostly rice, vegetables, duck eggs and all suffered terrible malnutrition. Her only pleasures were the clubs she helped to run, her moonlight walks with friends and her piano playing and poetry writing.

The start of the diary tells of her escape from Singapore by boat and how she was captured at Muntok, Banka Island. On February 20, she entered, "Glad I brought my quotes. Very bad night, children dying. Food still rice but more palatable."

On May 9 she was asked to conduct the church service next day and wrote: "I hope I shall do justice to the occasion. Preparing thoughts and prayer. Walked and talked and felt extremely tired, getting more listless every day."

The camp was shared with Dutch prisoners and they appeared to be on good terms. On May 26, Mrs. Jennings wrote; "Terrifically hot day. Walked a little with Mrs. Beeston and Mrs. Maddon. Rations poor. Dutch kindly changed ten dollars for five guilders per person. Wrote poem 'Lyndyke'.

July 2 was her wedding anniversary and her inner feelings creep into the general formality of the secret account. "Twelfth wedding anniversary. My thoughts are with you Mickey (her husband's nickname) on Memory Lane. Missing you unutterably sweetie." November 20 was her birthday. She wrote "Thirty four years of age. Given lovely flowers, jam and hanky. Tiffin at No 7. Very enjoyable."

On August 3 there was news of her husband. "Memorable day. News of Mick. How I rejoice to have news even though his present circumstances are obscure."

All the time she and the other prisoners were dogged by illnesses. She had rashes, throat infections, and the inescapable stomach trouble. At the end of August, she summarised a few weeks illness with "Recovered speedily from dysentery. Then had urticharea so was given three calcium injections."

"After two weeks I started running a temperature and had gland trouble. Neck

bandaged and kept in bed. Was to leave but had heavy diarrhoea in the night (ten to 13 attacks) so was kept in."

Food rations altered. On March 6 she wrote: "Rations definitely atrocious. Not enough to feed a mouse."

The first signs of apparent heroics are modestly mentioned in August 1944. "A day of excitement of the wrong kind. Trouble with Mrs. Dixey and Mackintosh sawing planks in wall to aid escape instead of fire. Five of us questioned (mainly myself) and stood in sun for an hour and then questioned again.

"Ray collapsed in sun and taken to hospital. Dixey fainted and fell over a parapet on her head. I also received an hefty smack on the left cheek from Nippon Ishimaiso for no other reason that appearing annoying I suppose, because Itosan's Malay and mine are not alike, I know just enough to be dangerous.

"The others spoke none or little and I was chief mutt and centre of questions. Returned to camp eventually quite a heroine for no reason except being dragged into trouble not of my own making. Who would be a Captain? Anyway it at least impressed my flock on the importance of obedience and penalty if they disobeyed."

Hunger and malnutrition were gripping Mrs. Jennings severely by March 1945, two months before her death. On March 30 she wrote: "Re-read Clarice's and Linnie's letters. Oh for news. Wish I could think less of food. My nights are filled with restless longing for home food, particularly meat. System craves it."

There were no more entries in the diary after April 6. The camp was moved to Lubbock Linggau, near Bencoolen, Sumatra, where she died at 9.25 a.m. on May 12, aged 35. Her grave was marked by a wooden cross with her name burned on it. The main killer was malnutrition. When she was captured she weighed 11 stone. Mrs. Jennings was a little over six stone at her death.*

When the remaining prisoners were freed, Mr Jennings went hoping to meet his wife, but Mrs. Hinch broke the sad news and gave him the diary, her wedding ring, which Mrs. Hellewell has as a memento, and his cigarette case.

Mr Jennings remained in Malaya as a building inspector, re-married and retired to New Zealand where he died about five years ago, leaving a widow and two children.

Before he left England he left a plaque in Otley Wesleyan Chapel. It marks her death and ends simply.

"Through faith in Christ she lived nobly and died bravely."

**she was actually 37 when she died*

The details of the diaries and documents deposited with the Imperial War Museum include the following summary:

'Overall the diary gives a remarkable insight into the conditions in the camps at Palembang and later (from 19 October 1944) at Muntok on Bangka Island, particularly into the tensions induced by close incarceration. Mrs. Jennings was patently a God-fearing woman who believed in and practised the Christian virtues of kindness to one's neighbour and forgiveness towards one's enemies, but repeatedly throughout the diary, she indicates that she was often abused and misunderstood in her sincere efforts to help her fellow internees. Although matters improved for her in this respect when she moved to a different 'Kongsi', or communal group, the difficulties were soon propounded by her election as 'Captain' of her block (5 April 1944). In this capacity she was responsible to the Japanese for the actions and discipline of members of her block, the more selfish element of which tended to identify her with the Japanese and accordingly defied her. On at least one occasion this led to severe Japanese recriminations against Mrs. Jennings as block representative (14 August 1944). Although even her closest friendships were sometimes spoiled by these tensions, she found one loyal 'soul-mate' in 'Pip', whose help and companionship consistently made her life more tolerable. In November 1944 an epidemic of an unidentifiable disease ravaged the camp and the dead listed in Mrs. Jennings diary include many people described in earlier entries. Mrs. Jennings own health, never good even at the best points of her internment, suffered a steady decline from this time onwards. The description of worsening deprivation in the camp, the records of deaths and her desperate appeal for a normal life and a return to her husband (17 March 1945) give the diary a final overwhelming note of pathos. A note is added at the end of the diary recording Mrs. Jennings'death.

'Also included in the archives is the letter from 'Pip' (Miss Elizabeth Meyer), to Captain C.O. Jennings describing in pathetic and very moving terms her friendship with Mrs. Jennings and the last moments of her life.'

In 1950 Captain Jennings published a book about his wartime experiences in Singapore. The book, *"An Ocean Without Shores" (Hodder & Stoughton, 1950*), is dedicated to 'Midge', the nickname of his wife Margery Jennings. The final sentence in the book is, *'He gave me the greatest news – the only news I then wanted to hear – when he said ,"Skipper, your wife is safe and a prisoner here in Palembang."* Sadly, before he had a chance to see his wife again, she died.

Ronald Kay (1917-1941)

Merchant Navy (S.S.Stanwold) - Third engineer - Died 27 February 1941 (Age 24) - Hartlepool(Stranton) Cemetery (Plot 10 Div. B.C. of E. Grave 684) - Son of George and Ellen Kay, husband of Esther Kay, of West Hartlepool.

Ronald Kay, Merchant Navy (born 14 March 1917) was at Prince Henry's from September 1928 (Form Upper 3B) until February 1932 (Lower 5A), when his family left the district. Originally from Middlesbrough, he lived on The Oval, Newall, Otley and his father, George, was a coal trimmer. George married Ellen E. Ridsdale in 1916 in Wharfedale. The couple moved to Middlesbrough, where Ronald was born, but then moved back to Otley.

Ronald was given a W.R.C.C. *'Special Place Award'* tenable for 4 years and 2 terms, and previously attended North Parade Elementary School. He showed some promise by being awarded first prize in his form in 1929 and fourth prize in Lower 4A in 1930. The only evidence of his athletic ability was fourth place in the Under 14 High Jump at Sports Day 1930. He left school to join the Merchant Navy as an apprentice.

Ronald married Esther Lyver in 1937 in Hartlepool and their daughter, Annie I. Kay, was born there in 1938. He was third engineer on the *S.S. Stanwold*, which was sunk as a result of enemy action. He was reported missing, but his body was later washed ashore and he was brought to his home at West Hartlepool, where he was buried in March 1941.

The following article was published in the *'Wharfedale and Airedale Observer'* on 21 March 1941:

'A former Otley Prince Henry's Grammar School pupil, Ronald Kay, aged 23, who died as the result of enemy action, was buried at West Hartlepool on Saturday. Mr Kay was in the Merchant Service and was the third engineer in a ship which was recently sunk by enemy action in the English Channel. He was reported missing, but his body was later washed ashore and he was brought to his home at West Hartlepool for burial. He would have been 24 on Friday last. Until he was 16, Mr Kay lived with his grandmother, Mrs. Fred Ridsdale, 73, The Oval. He attended Otley North Parade School, and on winning a County Minor scholarship went to the Grammar School. Soon after leaving school he joined the Merchant Service, and had made good progress. The ship on which he met his death was the first on which he had served in his higher rank as third engineer. He was on board one of the ships in the Jervis Bay convoy incident, and took part in the rescue efforts. Mr Kay leaves a widow and a daughter aged two.'

The *S.S. Stanwold* was originally built in 1909. After various changes of ownership and name, at the beginning of the war she was fitted with a ship's wireless and renamed *Stanwold*. On 26 February 1941 she was in convoy, carrying coal from Southend to Cowes, Isle of Wight. Her cargo shifted and at 11.30 hours she reported steering problems due to a heavy list to port. At 04.20 hours on the following day, she was reported as being sighted with a list to starboard.

No further communication was received. Some bodies were washed ashore some days later at Pevensey Bay. The captain, his crew of 19 and 2 gunners were lost. The wreck lies at a depth of 40 metres.

The *Stanwold* had been discussed in Parliament in 1938 after a question about an attack by *'an armed insurgent trawler in the Straits of Gibraltar.' (Hansard 11th July 1938)*

'Yes, Sir. According to a report now received from the Naval authorities, the master of the steamship "Stanwold" stated that he was interrogated by an armed trawler in General Franco's service on 22nd June when approximately eight miles south-west of Europa Point. He signalled the ship's name but apparently did not reply to further questions, whereupon the trawler signalled to him to halt and fired one round of blank, without, however, attempting further to enforce compliance with this order or otherwise interfering with the steamship "Stanwold."

Hartlepool (Stranton) Cemetery

The Hartlepool (Stranton) Cemetery contains war graves of both world wars. The Second World War graves are sited together in the War Graves Plot, a piece of ground set aside by the local authorities during the early months of the War. There are 260 identified casualties either buried or commemorated on the site, 132 of them being victims from the Second World War. *(Commonwealth War Graves Commission)*

Bernard Dallah Lilley (1922-1945)

Royal Air Force Volunteer Reserve (272 Squadron) - Flying Officer - Service Number: 154285 – Died 3 January 1945 (age 22) - Malta Memorial (Panel 18, Column 1) - Son of George Francis and Florence Mary Lilley, of Leeds, Yorkshire.

Flying Officer Bernard Dallah Lilley, R.A.F.V.R. (born 30 November 1922) was at Prince Henry's from September 1933 (Form Upper 3B) until October 1938 (Lower VI) when his parents left the district. His father, George Francis Lilley, was a tailor. He married Florence Mary Smith in 1920. The family lived in Pool-in-Wharfedale before moving to Otley, and Bernard attended Pool National School from 1929-1933. He was given a W.R.C.C. Special Place Award to run from September 1933 until he left school.

He was not athletic, though he did come fourth in the Obstacle Race (Under 12) on Sports Day 1934. His talents lay elsewhere, particularly in the academic side of school life. He won form prizes in each of the years he was at school:

1933 Upper 3B	1934 Lower 4A	1935 Upper 4A	1936 Lower 5A	1937 Upper 5A
First	Second	First	First	Second

He obtained his School Certificate in 1937. In 1936 he was elected to the Committee of the Natural Science Society and joined the Magazine Committee in 1938. He was also a member of the League of Nations Union, delivering a report, with P. Jackson, on their attendance at the Nansen Pioneer Camp in Summer 1938. He took parts in two school plays; playing Ford in a selection from '*The Merry Wives of Windsor*' in 1937 and Captain Absolute in '*The Rivals*' in 1938. He was said to have given *'satisfaction in this long and not altogether easy part, especially at the second (Saturday) performance.'*

As a member of the R.A.F.V.R. he worked his way up from Aircraftsman to Flying Officer. He completed his navigation course in Canada and came out top of his class of 29 in both marks and character assessment. In a letter to '*The Otliensian*' he said *'I was practically adopted as a brother and son by a family there and did quite an appreciable portion of my study in the comfort of their home.'*

He failed to return from operations over Germany and was presumed killed. He is commemorated in the Commonwealth Air Force Memorial at Floriana, Malta.

Malta Memorial

The Malta Memorial commemorates 2,301 airmen who lost their lives during the Second World War whilst serving with the Commonwealth Air Forces flying from bases in Austria, Italy, Sicily, islands of the Adriatic and Mediterranean, Malta, Tunisia, Algeria, Morocco, West Africa, Yugoslavia and Gibraltar, and who have no known grave. Their names are displayed on 19 panels on the memorial. It is situated in the area of Floriana and stands just outside the main entrance to Valletta, and was unveiled by Her Majesty Queen Elizabeth II on 3 May 1954. (*Commonwealth War Graves Commission)*

Mark Lupton (1908-1943)

Royal Air Force Volunteer Reserve (410 Squadron, R.C.A.F.) - Sergeant-Observer - Service Number: 1456999 - Died 23 January 1943 (Age 34) - Runnymede Memorial (Panel 157) - Son of Mark and Sarah Ann Lupton; husband of Laura Mary Lupton, of Skellow, Yorkshire.

Sergeant–Observer Mark Lupton, R.A.F.V.R. (born 19 June 1908) was at Prince Henry's from September 1920 (Class 3A) until July 1923 (Lower 5) when his family moved to Malton, and Mark transferred to Malton Grammar School. In Otley the family lived in Ivy Cottage, Newall and his father, Mark, was a Station Master. Mark senior married Sarah Ann Standidge in 1901 in Wharfedale. Mark junior had previously attended Welbeck Street Council School, Castleford, and on entering Prince Henry's was awarded a W.R.C.C. County Minor Scholarship tenable for three years. From Malton Grammar School he went on to Leeds University.

At School he made a major contribution to the development of cricket in the early 1920s. Against Bottrell's XI in June 1922 he *'captured 5 wickets for 3 runs, and also did the "hat trick".'* Against the Old Boys in 1923 he took 6 wickets for 8 runs and School won by 7 wickets. Against Roundhay in the same season *'Lupton was responsible for our opponents' small total.'* Had he stayed at Prince Henry's he might have also been a force in Rugby, being identified as one of *'our junior players of promise from whom we hope to get recruits for the 1st XV.'*

Mark junior married Laura Mary Wood in Gilling, Yorkshire on 8 September 1934. He joined up at the beginning of the War and both he and his brother John were commissioned as pilots. He was described in *'The Otliensian'* as having *'a most happy disposition, and will be well remembered by earlier Old Scholars. He often visited Otley after moving to Malton. In civil life he was an elementary school teacher at Skellow, near Doncaster. He volunteered for the R.A.F. in 1940.'*

No.410 'Cougar' Squadron was a Royal Canadian Air Force night fighter squadron that was formed at Ayr on 30 June 1941, to defend central Scotland and the north east of England against German raiders. It remained in the north for the next two years, upgrading to the Bristol Beaufighter and then the de Havilland Mosquito during that period.

On 20 October 1942 the Cougars moved from Scorton to Acklington in Northumberland. The move was accompanied by the re-equipment of the squadron with Mosquitoes, the most modern type of night fighter. Immediately after arrival at Acklington, a dual-control Mosquito was delivered and intensive training began. By 3 December, conversion was well advanced, and the first Mosquito sorties were made that night. The Beaufighters remained in service for a month longer, the last sorties being made on 4 January. By the end of that month, the squadron was wholly equipped with the Mosquito II. Both December and January were active months, totalling 93 operational sorties.

In February 1943, with the threat of German raids diminishing, the squadron moved south to Lincolnshire, from where it began to carry out intruder missions to France and the Low Countries.

After a spell of defensive work from September 1943, the squadron moved to the southwest, operating over the Normandy beaches. In September 1944 No.410 Squadron moved to France, and spent the rest of the war providing night fighter defences over the advancing Allied armies.

Sergeant Lupton was posted 'killed in action' when flying as a Navigator on 23 January 1943. The aircraft was a de Havilland Mosquito NF.Mk II (HJ919) which crashed into the sea 2 miles off Seahouses, Northumberland while on a training flight from R.A.F. Acklington. The aircraft, piloted by Sergeant Garth Gibson Mills (R.C.A.F: R/113366), who was also killed, stalled while low flying and was written off. There were only two people on board, the pilot (Mills) and Lupton – the radar/radio observer. A search for the aircraft was arranged, they located pieces of wreckage 2 miles south east of Seahouses, but there were no survivors.

The Runnymede Memorial

The Runnymede Memorial lies overlooking the River Thames on Cooper's Hill at Englefield Green between Windsor and Egham on the A308, 4 miles from Windsor. The Air Forces Memorial at Runnymede commemorates by name over 20,000 airmen who were lost in the Second World War during operations from bases in the United Kingdom and North and Western Europe, and who have no known graves. They served in Bomber, Fighter, Coastal, Transport, Flying Training and Maintenance Commands, and came from all parts of the Commonwealth. Some were from countries in continental Europe which had been overrun but whose airmen continued to fight in the ranks of the Royal Air Force. (*Commonwealth War Graves Commission*)

James Edward Mason (1917-1943)

Royal Artillery (122 Field Regiment) - Gunner - Service Number 963864 - Died 27 December 1943 (Age 26) - Kanchanaburi War Cemetery (2.G.74) - Son of Mr and Mrs. J M Mason; husband of Jean E Mason, of Otley, Yorkshire

Gunner James Edward Mason, Royal Artillery (born 10 May 1917) lived at 7 Booth Street, Burley-in- Wharfedale. He attended Burley National School and entered Prince Henry's in September 1928 (Class Upper 3B) on the award of a W.R.C.C. County Minor Scholarship tenable for 5 years. His father, James Mounsey Mason, was a Fish Merchant, though the 1911 Census lists him as a stonemason.

James senior married Annie Brooksbank in 1907, the marriage being registered in North Bierley. James left school in July 1933 (Upper 5A). Before joining the Army in 1940 he was an architect and surveyor on the staff of St James' Hospital, Leeds.

Although he received an 'honourable mention' in the form prizes for 1929 he will be *'well remembered for the prominent part he took in School games.'* In Summer 1931 he was described as *'a stylish batsman, who so far has been out of luck. His main fault is walking across his wickets. An excellent fielder and a splendid catch.'* In 1932 he was awarded his cricket colours and the cricket prize and *'batted well for 53'* in the School vs Otliensians match. His batting average was 23.5 from 6 innings (2 not out), which placed him top of the averages. In Summer 1933 it was reported that *'the success of the 1st XI has been mainly due to the excellent bowling of Clapham, Mason and Bolton.'* Over the season Mason took 13 wickets at an average of 5.85.

In Lent 1932 his profile in Rugby read *'another recruit from the second XV, has been well worth his place. Is a good all-round forward and dribbles well.'* He was awarded his Rugby colours at the end of the season. In Lent 1933 his profile read, *'Mason J.E. has been our only outstanding forward. He has hooked well in the tight scrum, and cannot be blamed for our failure to get the ball, and he has done more than his share in the loose.'* After leaving school he continued to play Rugby with the Otliensians and Ilkley, and cricket with Burley. In Summer 1934 he was the second highest scorer for the Otliensians Rugby XV with 70 points. (see photograph – Charles Leslie Harrison)

Gnr. J. E. Mason.

He married Miss Jean Eileen Hewitt (1919-2003) on 14 November 1940 at Burley Parish Church. He was taken prisoner in Malaya in 1943 and died from malnutrition in December 1943, though confirmation of his death was not received until July 1945.

122 Field Regiment Royal Artillery was a Territorial regiment formed in Bradford on 1 June 1939. It had headquarters opposite Valley Parade Drill Hall and units in Halifax and Heckmondwike. It had two batteries, 278 and 280.

On 3 January 1941 the Regiment embarked at Glasgow in the ironically named Canadian Pacific liner *'Empress of Japan'* and arrived in Malaya on 11 March to become part of the 12th Indian Brigade. When the Japanese invaded Malaya the following December, 278 Battery was sent up country to face them and fought its way all down the Peninsula to rejoin 280 Battery in the short battle for Singapore Island.

The three and a half years of captivity in inhuman conditions cost the Regiment dearly. Its members were scattered all over the Far East. Many were sent as slave labour to build the infamous Burma/Siam Railway on which it was reckoned that one prisoner died for every sleeper laid.

Today 41 soldiers of 122 Field Regiment lie buried in the Kanchanaburi War Cemetery in Thailand. Another 13 are buried at Chungkai. There are graves of 17 others in Kranji Cemetery, Singapore and the Kranji Memorial to those with no known grave lists another 43.

Others from the Regiment were shipped in appalling conditions to Korea and to mainland Japan and 10 are buried in the War Cemetery at Yokohama. Out of the original complement of 500 men, 122 Field Regiment lost 132, including 3 who died before war started in the Far East. Effectively, the Regiment ceased to exist with the surrender of Singapore. It was never re-formed and came to be called *'The Forgotten Regiment'* by the survivors.

Kanchanaburi War Cemetery

The Kanchanaburi War Cemetery is the main prisoner-of-war cemetery associated with victims who died during the construction of the Burma Railway and is in the town of Kanchanaburi, Thailand, 129 miles northwest of Bangkok. It is only a short distance from the site of the former Kanburi, the prisoner-of-war camp through which most of the prisoners passed on their way to other camps. The cemetery contains the remains of 6,842 identified prisoners-of-war, including 5,084 casualties of the Second World War. 6,982 prisoners-of-war (identified and unidentified) are buried there, mostly Australian, British and Dutch. (*Commonwealth War Graves Commission*)

The Burma-Siam Railway

The Burma-Siam railway, also known as the 'Death Railway' is 258 miles long and was built using forced labour between June 1942 and October 1943. It was driven by the need for improved communications to support the large Japanese army in Burma following the loss of an effective sea route to Allied shipping. Two forces, one based in Siam, and one in Burma, worked from opposite ends of the line, the two sections meeting on 17 October 1943.

British, Australian, Dutch and American prisoners-of-war, a total of over 61,000, were used to build the railway. In addition about 180,000 Asian labourers were brought from Malaya, the Netherlands East Indies, Siam and Burma. An estimated 80,000 to 100,000 Asian labourers and 16,000 Allied prisoners-of-war died as a direct result of the project. Most of the deaths were from sickness, malnutrition and exhaustion.

The graves of those who died during the construction and maintenance of the Burma-Siam railway (except for the Americans, whose remains were repatriated) were transferred from camp burial grounds and isolated sites along the railway into one of three cemeteries at Chungkai and Kanchanaburi in Thailand and Thanbyuzayat in Myanmar.

The most famous part of the railway is probably bridge 277 over the Khwae Yai River, made famous in a novel and film as *'The Bridge Over the River Kwai'*. The film has been criticised because it does not show what the conditions and treatment of the prisoners was really like. In the early days life was not unpleasant for the workers. Food was inexpensive and reasonably plentiful. Local families and monks gave the prisoners fruit and at night prisoners would sneak out of the camp to get food. However, as the Japanese government put pressure on to finish the railway, conditions became much worse. Food supplies became much more irregular and inadequate. Away from the large camps men sometimes lived for weeks on only a daily ration of rice with a little salt. The supplies that did reach the camps were usually insufficient and of low quality.

The food was just sufficient to keep people alive until a prisoner became ill. Vitamin deficiency diseases, malaria, cholera and dysentery attacked the prisoners. 80% of the prisoners in a single camp might be sick, but were often still forced to work.

After the railway had been completed, 32,000 prisoners continued to maintain it, often repairing the damage done by Allied raids. Many prisoners died in these raids because the camps were next to the railway track. In one raid alone 95 were killed and 300 wounded.

Arthur Miller (1913-1943)

Royal Army Pay Corps - Private - Service Number: 7671995 - Died 1 June 1943 (Age 30) - Burley-in-Wharfedale (St Mary) Church Cemetery (Grave 5244) - Son of John and Alice Miller, of Burley-in-Wharfedale; husband of Catherine Miller

Private Arthur Miller, Royal Army Pay Corps (born 11 January 1913) lived on Fenton Street, Burley-in- Wharfedale. His father, John Miller, was an Asylum Attendant at Scalebor Park Hospital, Burley-in-Wharfedale.

John married Alice Denby in 1911. Arthur attended Burley National School before being admitted to Prince Henry's in May 1924 (Class Lower 3A). He left in March 1929 (Upper 5B). In 1939 he married Catherine Stable in Wharfedale. They were both employed on the clerical staff of William Walker & Sons (Otley) Ltd.

He joined the Army in 1940, and died in a military hospital, after being ill for about seven weeks, during which time he had two operations. At school he was *'of a quiet and retiring nature ... and will be remembered as a cousin of the Hintons. A native of Burley-in-Wharfedale, he settled in Otley on his marriage.'* One of his chief interests was swimming, in which he had achieved a high degree of efficiency. He was also an adept ice-skater. His hobby was sketching.

On 5 June 1943, he was buried in St Mary's Church Cemetery, Burley-in-Wharfedale, where there are 9 identified Commonwealth War Dead. His address at that date was given as 45 Lawn Avenue, Burley-in-Wharfedale.

Anthony Alan Morton (1918-1944)

Royal Berkshire Regiment: 1st Battalion Wiltshire Regiment - Lieutenant - Service Number: 293001 - Died 19 April 1944 (Age 26) - Rangoon Memorial (Face 15) - Son of Charles Thornhill Morton and Frances Ellen Morton; husband of Marion Joan Morton, of Menston, Yorkshire

Lieutenant Anthony Alan Morton, Royal Berkshire Regiment (Secondary Regiment – Wiltshires) (born 6 January 1918) was at Prince Henry's from September 1929 (Class Upper 3A) until July 1936 (Sixth Form). In 1929 he was awarded a W.R.C.C. County Minor Scholarship tenable for two years and two terms. He lived on Charles Street, Otley; his father was an overlooker. Anthony had previously attended Otley Westgate Council School and when he left Prince Henry's in 1936 he became a Bank Clerk with Barclay's Bank.

His father, Charles Thornhill Morton, was born in 1880 in Ravensthorpe, Yorkshire. In 1908 he married Frances Ellen Haigh in Wakefield and in the 1911 Census the couple were living in Sandal Magna, and Charles was listed as a Power Loom Turner. Anthony was born in Wakefield in 1918. He married Marion Jane Walter in 1941 in Wharfedale. Marion was the sister of John F.S. Walter who died 6 August 1945, and whose name also appears on the Prince Henry's Roll of Honour (see below).

A.A. Morton threw himself into all aspects of the School from an early age. In his first year he was awarded a form prize for second place in Upper 3A and in August 1931 was third in a competition for pen and ink sketches and watercolours at Otley Flower Show. He had a fine career as an actor, played Rugby for the First XV, was Secretary for the Natural Science Society, the Literary, Historical and Debating Society and the Boxing Club. His acting credits consisted of:

1930	5 episodes from *'Alice in Wonderland'* by the Junior School	Played the part of the March Hare
1933	*'As You Like It'* by William Shakespeare	*'Morton, as "the melancholy Jaques" was in quiet restraint to the livelyTouchstone.He acted the mood of contemplation which "sucked melancholy" out of woodland situations and incidents. The "all the world's a stage" speech was given effective and dramatic gesture, and was impressively appropriate to the utterance of such a melancholy philosopher. Again, his duel of manners with Orlando was artistic; and his words to Rosalind defining his "melancholy compounded of many simples" expressed the quintessence of his* acted disposition.'

1934	*'She Stoops to Conquer'* by Oliver Goldsmith	*'Much of the success of the play depends upon the liveliness of Tony Lumpkin, Morton, in this role, proved to be truly boisterous, and soon won the applause which he deserved. Particularly amusing was his by-play with Constance Neville and the scene in which Tony convinces his mother that Mr Hardcastle is a highwayman.'*
1935	*'Pickwick v Bardell'* – based on *'Pickwick Papers'* by Charles Dickens	*'Morton as Mr Pickwick, Margaret Atkinson as Mrs. Bardell and Edna Wood as her friend, all performed well the difficult task of silently portraying varying emotions.'*
1936	*'The Boy Comes Home'*, a war play	*'A.A. Morton surpassed himself as the choleric uncle.'*
1938	Old Scholars production of the comedy *'Aren't We All?'* by Frederick Lonsdale.	*'The two servants, Morton, the butler at the Mayfair house, and Roberts, the butler of Grenham Court, were played by Mr Douglas Waye and Mr Anthony Morton respectively. Both presented finished performances, and in this excellence of the smaller characters lay part of the virtue of the production.'*

As a member of the Rugby 1stXV he was awarded his colours in 1936; his team criticism in that season read *'is hard working. A strong tackler, but in attack often tries to "bullock" through instead of opening out play for the backs.'*

He was a founder member of the Boxing Club; *'The activities of the Boxing Club, which came into being at the beginning of this term, commenced with a meeting for the election of officials. P.H.Cribb was elected captain and A.A. Morton secretary. Mr Evans and Mr Davison agreed to give instruction. The Club nights were fixed for Mondays and Thursdays. The membership to date is just over twenty, and progress has, so far, been highly satisfactory.'*

In 1934 he was elected Secretary of the Natural Science Society and, at the second meeting of the term, gave a lecture:

'The second meeting of the session was held on November 1st, when A. A. Morton favoured the Society with a lecture on 'Airships'. The lecturer first summarized the history of dirigibles from the time of the balloon, and then passed on to the subject of present-day airships, paying special attention to Britain's position in the field of their development. Mr Morton concluded by making speculations regarding the possible future of the airship. The Chairman W. Berwick, after thanking the Lecturer for his most interesting and instructive lecture, dissolved the meeting.'

In 1935 he became joint Hon. Secretary of the Literary, Historical and Debating Society. In the same year he passed his School Certificate with Matriculation and obtained a Distinction in Geography.

On 23 August 1941, at St John's Church, Menston, he married Marion Joan Walter (ex P.H.G.S. student) and in Autumn 1942 Mrs. Morton gave birth to a son, Charles C. Morton.

He was called up in December 1939, and was in the Royal Army Pay Corps until July 1942, when he went to O.C.T.U. as a prospective infantry officer in the Indian army. He sailed for India in September 1943, where he finished his training. He received his commission as Second Lieutenant in May 1943, and was later promoted to Lieutenant. He was reported wounded in Burma on 15 April 1944, and later missing, believed wounded, in Burma on 19 April 1944.

The Rangoon Memorial

The Rangoon Memorial is situated in the Taukkyan War Cemetery, which is about 35 kilometres north of Yangon (formerly Rangoon). The Memorial bears the names of almost 27,000 men of the Commonwealth land forces who died during the campaigns in Burma (now Myanmar) and who have no known grave. (*Commonwealth War Graves Commission*)

The following remembrance notice was published in the *'Yorkshire Post and Leeds Intelligencer'* on 19 April 1948:

'MORTON – Remembering "Tony" Lieutenant Anthony Alan Morton, Royal Berkshire Regiment, dear husband of Joan Morton. Presumed killed in action in Burma, April 1944.'

Ian Rochester Naylor (1926-1945)

Royal Naval Volunteer Reserve (H.M.M.T.B.494) - Midshipman- Service Number:D/ *JX287428 - Died 7 April 1945 (Age 18) - Portsmouth Naval Memorial (Panel 90, Column 2) - Son of Arthur R. and Nellie Naylor of Guiseley, Yorkshire.*

Midshipman Ian Rochester Naylor, R.N.V.R. (Born 11 May 1926) was at school from September 1934 (Form Upper I) until November 1943, when he left the Sixth Form to go directly into the Navy. He joined Prince Henry's when he was 8 years old, after spending two years at Guiseley Council School. He lived on Tranmere Park, Guiseley, and his father, Arthur Rochester Naylor (1885-1976), was a Worsted Coating Manufacturer, and assistant adjutant to the headquarters of the 29th(Otley) Battalion, West Riding Home Guard. Arthur married Nellie Asquith in North Brierley in 1924. In 1937 Ian was awarded a W.R.C.C. County Minor Scholarship tenable for his school career.

He made major contributions in athletics and rugby. In the 1941 Annual Sports he won the 880 yards, and came second in the mile. In 1942 he was fourth in both the 440 yards and the 880 yards, and second in the mile. He performed even better in 1943, winning both the 880 yards and the mile, coming second in the 440 yards and third in the high jump. His time for the mile was only slightly over 5 minutes.

At the end of the 1942 Rugby season he was described as *'a strong well- built forward who is always in the thick of play. His main fault is in trying to pick up the ball when dribbling would be more profitable. His footwork needs more control.'* In 1943 the criticism read *'has speed, fine physique and is an excellent tackler. Weak in dribbling. Unfortunately we were without his services for more than half the season for health reasons.'* In 1944 *'Naylor I.R. and Walter D., both of last year's team played until Christmas when they left school, Naylor to go into the Navy and Walter the Merchant Navy. They both have our good wishes.'*

He went straight from school in November 1943, to join the Royal Navy under the "Y" scheme at the minimum age of 17½ years. He was a former member of the 1st Airedale Sea Cadets from 1940 to 1943 and left with the rank of petty officer. On joining the Royal Navy his first training was received ashore and he was selected as 'commission worthy.' After only eight months service in the Royal Navy he qualified as a midshipman, an unusual achievement for someone who was only 18 years of age. From *H.M.S. Ganges* he passed out top of his division; on completing his sea time he took a first-class pass and was placed in the same class after completing a ten-week course at the Officers' Training Establishment.

He was drafted to an active flotilla of M.T.B.s in September 1944. The M.T.B.s were used to protect convoys against attack from 'E' boats. He was reported 'missing' in early April 1945.

The report of his death was announced in '*The Otliensian*' with the following tribute:

'Of all our casualties none has affected the School more than the loss in a recent naval action of Midshipman Ian R Naylor, R.N.V.R. He entered the School in 1934 in Form I and left the Sixth Form to go directly into the Navy in November 1943, so that he was known to all above the present Third Form. He was in every way an ideal pupil – of fine character, splendid physique, proud of the School and anxious to do all he could for it. He was immediately commissioned on completing his preliminary training and then, after specialist training, at once went into action with a M.T.B. flotilla. Between September 1944 and April of this year, he took part in many engagements off the Dutch and German coasts. It was in the last of these, on April 6th, 1945, that his boat was rammed and sunk by an E-boat, with the loss of three officers and twelve ratings. As we knew him so recently and so intimately, his loss has brought home to the School more keenly the significance of our casualty list.'

Portsmouth Naval Memorial

Portsmouth Naval Memorial is situated on Southsea Common, overlooking the promenade, and is accessible at all times. After the First World War, an appropriate way had to be found of commemorating those members of the Royal Navy who had no known grave, the majority of deaths having occurred at sea where no permanent memorial could be provided. An Admiralty Committee recommended that the three manning ports in Great Britain – Chatham, Plymouth and Portsmouth – should each have an identical memorial of unmistakable naval form, an obelisk, which would serve as a leading mark for shipping. The memorials were designed by Sir Robert Lorimer, who had already carried out a considerable amount of work for the Commission, with sculpture by Henry Poole. The Portsmouth Naval Memorial was unveiled by the Duke of York (the future George VI) on 15 October 1924. After the Second World War it was decided that the naval memorials should be extended to provide space for commemorating the naval dead without graves of that war, but since the sites were dissimilar, a different architectural treatment was required for each. The architect for the Second World War extension at Portsmouth, was Sir Edward Maufe (who also designed the Air Forces memorial at Runnymede) and the additional sculpture was by Charles Wheeler, William McMillan and Esmond Burton. The Extension was unveiled by Queen Elizabeth, the Queen Mother on 29 April 1953. Portsmouth Naval Memorial commemorates around 10,000 sailors of the First World War and almost 15,000 of the Second World War – a total of 24,587 identified casualties. (*Commonwealth War Graves Commission*)

In Spring 1945 Ian Naylor's parents presented to the School, in his memory, a new cup for the Boys' Open Mile race. At the Upper School Speech Day in November 1945, the Headmaster, Mr Wilde said:

'It is not easy to speak of this or that individual where all have paid the same heavy price, said Mr Wilde, but I will refer, for special reasons, to two of our former scholars of whom we are bound to think today. You will have noticed a new trophy among our sports awards. Ian Naylor who set up a school record in the open mile in 1943, left us in November of that year to join the Royal Navy under the Y scheme. Sixteen months later, before his 19th birthday, he was lost while navigating a motor torpedo boat in a gallant and hard-fought battle against German E boats in the North Sea. There can scarcely be a boy or girl in the room who did not know and admire him. The cup, which will be awarded today for the first time, was presented by his family in his memory, and we accept it gladly, but with great sorrow.' ('Wharfedale and Airedale Observer', 30 November 1945)*

**the second person Mr Wilde spoke about was Margery Jennings*

MTB 494 – Killed in Action – 7 April 1945

Name	Rank	Age	Burial
Jack May (RNVR)	Lieutenant Commanding Officer MTB 494	-	Crayford (St Paulinius) Churchyard Row 22 Grave 4
Ian Turner Macfarlane (RNVR)	Sub-Lieutenant MTB 494	21	Portsmouth Naval Memorial Panel 90 Column 2

Ian Rochester Naylor (RNVR)	Midshipman Third Officer MTB 494	18	Portsmouth Naval Memorial Panel 90 Column 2
Victor Marcus Wheeler	P/MX 543586 Petty Officer. Motor Mechanic	28	Portsmouth Naval Memorial Panel 89 Column 3
Jeffrey Slater	D/KX 139149 Leading Stoker	24	Plymouth Naval Memorial Penel 94 Column 3
Frank Crowder	C/JX354779 Able Seaman	23	Wallasey (Frankby) Cemetery Sec. G. Grace 510
Anthony Worcester Dandie	C/JX 378644 Able Seaman	20	Lowestoft (Beccles Road) Cemetery Sec. 25. Grave 534
Charles Augustus Holland	P/JX/262015 Able Seaman	23	Orpington (St Mary Cray) Cemetery Grave 1399
George Rudolph Shoesmith	C/JX 559374 Leading Seaman	19	Chatham Naval Memorial Panel 81 Colimn 1
Leslie Frederick Vine	P/SSX 35669 Able Seaman	22	Poole Cemetery Sec. 3. Grave 13587
Douglas Charles Chudley	P/JX 700850 Signalman	18	Lowestoft (Beccles Road) Cemetery Sec. 25. Grave 532
Charles Simmons	P/KX 153796 Stoker First Class	-	Portsmouth Naval Memorial Panel 89 Column 3
Arthur Treece	P/JX 402999 Telegraphist	-	Portsmouth Naval Memorial Panel 89 Column 2

The final operation of MTB 494 is described in Chapter 19 of the book *'AIR-SEA RESCUE IN WORLD WAR TWO'* – by Alan Rowe (with the collaboration of Andy Andrews), published in 1995 by Alan Sutton Publishing Limited. **(**direct quotes are shown in italics.)

German E-boats, based at the Hook of Holland, were a threat to east coast convoys right up to the end of the War. Anti-E-boat flotillas, made up of a frigate and a group of MTBs and MGBs aided by specially equipped Wellington aircraft, were used to intercept the E-boats before they could attack a convoy.

On 6 April 1945 six E-boats slipped out of Den Helder to make a final gesture of defiance in a war which was effectively already lost. Conditions were good – no moon, a smooth sea and good visibility – enabling them to reach the convoy route without being intercepted. However, before they could do any damage they were attacked by the destroyer *H.M.S. Cubitt* and turned north into a trap set for them by MTBs 781 and 5001, which soon intercepted them, tried to ram them, exchanged fire, and forced the E-boats to attempt to escape to the south-east.

Unfortunately, MTB 5001 was hit by a shell and soon became a mass of fire. MTB 781 abandoned the chase and went to its aid. Forty minutes later MTB 5001 blew up and sank, with the loss of three ratings killed and others wounded. The E-boats headed for home, but were tracked by Wellington, J.524, which directed a unit of three MTBs to intercept them.

'In the leading British boat, MTB 494, the Senior Officer, Lieut. Jack May, headed for the first of the E- boats as they approached his bows from right to left. He had just opened fire, preparing to ram, when he himself was rammed amidships by the second in line. Although the boat was badly damaged, his guns' crew continued to fire.

'In MTB 493, Lieut. A.D.Foster had just enough time to observe the exchange of fire between the leaders before another wake appeared fine to starboard and the third E-boat was sighted less than fifty yards away. Instinctively, Foster drove at full speed into the port quarter of this boat, then went full astern to pull his boat away and crashed the engines into full speed ahead again. Passing through its wake, he turned to port and pursued it at close quarters, pouring shells and bullets into the stricken enemy. At a range of only twenty-five yards, he observed five six-pounder hits on the E-boat. Then, suddenly, his ship stopped with a crunching shock, as the already damaged bow ploughed into the submerged hull of MTB 494. From now on he found it impossible to go ahead; the ship would go astern only.

'MTB 494, though virtually cut in two, had continued firing to the last, and now several men were in the water around the wreck. Lieut. Foster, unable to manoeuvre properly to reach them, had to call to them to swim towards him. After one man had been picked up, a red Very light was seen coming from an E-boat lying stopped about two hundred yards away. Not knowing whether this was a signal to others to come to the attack, Foster moved astern, clear of the wreck and the survivors, and illuminated the enemy with rocket star-shell, opening fire again upon the enemy craft. The latter, however, did not return his fire and continued sending up red Very lights, so 493 ceased firing.'

MTB 497, commanded by Lieutenant Harrington (D.S.O.) took his boat into the rear of the enemy line, opening fire on two E-boats that were crossing his bows. Another E-boat tried to ram him, but he took avoiding action and fired a number of shells into the E-boat. He then abandoned the chase and returned to the scene of the battle. As 497 passed the wreckage of 494 cries of distress were heard and Harrington searched for survivors, picking up three of her crew.

Harrington took one of the damaged German E-boats in tow, but despite his efforts it sank before daybreak. The MTB losses had been heavy, but two or probably three E-boats had been sunk and the others damaged by gunfire. It was the last E-boat attack of the war.

On the following day HSL 2558 went to investigate a life-raft spotted by a patrolling Catalina flying- boat. The life-raft contained the bodies of Lieutenant Jack May and three of his crew.

'What had happened to them following the sinking of 494 no one can now tell. Perhaps they had been badly wounded and put in the raft by their comrades soon after the

boat was hit. Perhaps they had been too weak to call for help or had even succumbed to their wounds before 497 came back to pick up the few survivors. One can only hope that they did not lie suffering for hours, hoping in vain for rescue. The HSL had the sad task of bringing back the last of 494's dead, which, in addition to Lieutenant May, included the First Lieutenant, the Midshipman and eleven members of the crew. The German prisoners told their captors that, although the ship was cut in two and sinking, the gunners kept up their fire to the last. Only a few weeks after they gave their lives, so heroically, and in some ways so unnecessarily, all the rest of us were celebrating the end of the war in Europe.'

On 12 May 1945 the German E-boats left their base for the final time. On 13 May 1945, displaying white flags at their mastheads, they sailed up the river and moored in Felixstowe harbour. Their officers came ashore and formally surrendered, five weeks too late for Ian Naylor and the crew of MTB 494.

Harold Newell (1912-1944)

Royal Air Force Volunteer Reserve - Flying Officer - Service Number: 143589 - Died 27 April 1944 (Age 31) - Leeds (Lawnswood) Crematorium (Screen Wall, Panel 2) - Son of Norman and Elizabeth Newell, of Otley; husband of Mary Newell, of Otley

Flying Officer Harold Newell, R.A.F.V.R. (born 11 September 1912) lived at Hillcrest, Pool Bank, Pool- in-Wharfedale, and later on The Crossways, Otley. His father, Norman Newell, was a Chauffeur. He married Elizabeth Marley in Wharfedale in 1911. Harold attended Bramhope Council School and was awarded a W.R.C.C. County Minor Scholarship tenable for 4 years on his admission to Prince Henry's in September 1924 (Class Upper 3A). He left in July 1928 (Upper 5A) to become a Clerk. He obtained his School Certificate in 1928. He joined the R.A.F. as ground crew and moved up through the ranks to become a Flying Officer in 1943. He married Elizabeth Birkett in Wharfedale in 1937.

The '*Wharfedale and Airedale Observer*' published 5 May 1944 reported on the death of Flying Officer Newell as follows:

OTLEY R.A.F. OFFICER – SHOOTS HIMSELF AT BOLTON ABBEY

A verdict that he shot himself with a Service revolver while the balance of his mind was temporarily upset was returned by the Deputy Craven Coroner (Mr H. Wright) at a Skipton inquest on Monday on Flying Officer Harold Newall, aged 31, of the R.A.F., whose body was found in the Valley of Desolation at Bolton Abbey on Thursday night.

Evidence of identification was given by his father-in-law, Ernest Birkett, of 192, Bradford Road, Otley, who said deceased married his daughter in August 1937. They lived next door to him until his son-in- law joined the R.A.F. in 1940, when their home was broken up.

Wanted Divorce

Flying Officer Newell had done a good deal of operational flights. Their married life was happy, but about four months ago Newell wrote to his wife asking her to divorce him. She wanted to meet him to see if they could bridge their difficulties, but he still maintained that he wanted a divorce.

In January his wife got a separation order with a view to taking divorce proceedings later. Subsequently they had not met, but they had had three telephone conversations, in one of which Newell repudiated what he had written before, and said it was untrue.

His wife had suggested that they should meet to see if they could come to an understanding, but no meeting had taken place.

Left Two Letters

P.S. Marsh stated that two letters were found in Newell's pocket. One was addressed to the Air Ministry and the other to the Coroner. In the former he resigned his commission 'because he was going to take his life'; the other letter dealt with domestic matters.

Leeds (Lawnswood) Crematorium

The crematorium is in the Lawnswood area to the west of Leeds-Otley Road. 94 identified casualties are commemorated there. (*Commonwealth War Graves Commission*)

Norman Nicholson (1923-1944)

Royal Air Force Volunteer Reserve (1657 H.C.U.) - Sergeant Navigator - Service Number: 1624728 - Died 29 May 1944 (Age 21) - Otley (Newall-with-Clifton and Lindley) Ceme tery (Sec S. Grave 156) - Son of Donald and Annie Nicholson, of Otley, Yorkshire.

Sergeant Norman Nicholson, R.A.F.V.R, (born 24 April 1923) entered Prince Henry's in September 1934 (Class Upper 3B), after attending Otley North Parade Elementary School from 1928-1934. He lived on St. Clair Street, Otley and his father, Donald Nicholson (1900-1973), worked as a Leather Worker. Donald married Annie Smith in 1922 in Wharfedale.

Norman received a W.R.C.C. County Minor Scholarship in 1934, tenable for his total school career. He left school in July 1939 (Upper 5A); his occupation on leaving being listed as '*Candidate for Air Force*'. In fact he was employed at the Guiseley firm of Crompton, Parkinson Ltd. before taking a civilian appointment as a meteorologist at an air station and later joining the R.A.F.

He played the part of Tom in a one-act play *'The Paragon'* in 1937 and he passed his School Certificate in 1939.

N. Nicholson

He was a committee member of the newly inaugurated Model Aero Club when it was founded in February 1939.

'The Prince Henry's Grammar School Model Aero Club was inaugurated on February 22nd. The Headmaster was elected President. Mr Lewis was elected Vice-president and Mr F. V. Houlgate Hon. Secretary. The Committee chosen consist of: B. H. Moore, G. Weston, J. Lund, N. Nicholson, G. Watkinson and P. Jennings.

'On March 4th the first meeting for erecting and flying the model aeroplanes was held and there was a very good attendance. The Club will start a library consisting of air stories at some future date. The Club meets every Friday afternoon and Saturday morning.'

The '*Wharfedale and Airedale Observer*' published 2 June 1944 reported that:

'Sgt. Nicholson, who is 21, volunteered for the R.A.F. in September 1942, and passed out as a navigator last November. He intended making the Air Force his career, and prior to joining the service was a member of Otley A.T.C. Squadron, where he had a 100 per cent attendance record, never missing a parade from the time the Corps was formed to entering the Services. He was formerly employed as assistant chemist at Crompton Parkinson Ltd., and was an old scholar of Prince Henry's Grammar School. His younger brother, Arthur, is serving in the R.A.F. as Flight Engineer.'

He was killed in a flying accident on 29th May 1944 and is buried in Otley.

Rank	Service	Name	Age	Service No.	Buried
Flying Officer	R.A.F.V.R.	William Arthur Churchill Yates	24	149373	Whitchurch (Pantmawr) Cemetery
Sergeant	R.A.F.V.R.	Sidney Sterry	37	1121985	Hull Northern Cemetery
Sergeant	R.A.F.V.R.	Norman Nicholson	21	1624728	Otley (Newall with Clifton)
Sergeant	R.A.F.V.R.	Joe Carter	33	1458092	Brighouse Cemetery
Sergeant	R.A.F.V.R.	Granville Wood	22	1549835	Colne Valley (Slaithwaite)
Sergeant	R.A.F.V.R.	Thomas Reuben Farley	20	1897257	Aldershot Civic Cemetery
Sergeant	R.A.F.V.R.	John Walker Grainger	19	2213920	Cambridge City Cemetery

(RAF Bomber Command Losses Volume 8: Heavy Conversion Units & Miscellaneous Units 1939-1947 – W R Chorley)

The Heavy Conversion Units (H.C.U.) trained crews to operate heavy bombers who had previously learned to fly in smaller aircraft at Operational Training Units. Nicholson was part of the crew of Stirling I R9298 that took off from Shepherds Grove for night circuit practice. On approach to landing the plane was shot down from 1000 ft. at 02.39 by an enemy intruder and crashed into a hangar, wrecking a Stirling I (R9283 XT-H) and Mk.III LK506. Debris from the stricken aircraft also fell onto the night-flying equipment.

The same crew had been involved in a previous accident on 9 May 1944 when their Stirling I (BF 432–L), after a training flight from Stradishall, ended at 14.00 with the aircraft just off the right of the runway with its undercarriage broken. Sadly, none of those involved would live to see the end of their course.

The funeral was reported in the '*Wharfedale and Airedale Observer*' on 9 June 1944:

'Cadets of the Otley and District Squadron A.T.C., with their band of nine pipers and six drummers, attended the funeral at Otley on Friday of Sgt-Navigator Norman Nicholson, of the R.A.F., an ex- cadet of the squadron, who was killed in active service. Sgt. Nicholson, who was 21, was the eldest son of Mr and Mrs. D. Nicholson, of St. Clair Street, Otley.

'The squadron, 70 to 80 strong paraded under the command of Flt-Lieut. A. E. Turton, Commanding Officer, and lead the cortege from the house to the cemetery. They slow marched to the music of the bagpipes and muffled drums, and on entering the cemetery gates formed two ranks, halted, turned inwards and stood to attention while the hearse, bearing the flag-draped coffin, had passed. At the close of the service cadets gathered round the grave, and from a distance, Cpl. R. Fisher piped a lament. This gave a most impressive finish to the funeral. Members of the squadron also acted as bearers.'

Otley (Newall-with-Clifton and Lindley) Cemetery is on the Pool Road out of Otley to the east. There are 54 identified casualties buried there, including four Old Scholars of Prince Henry's who died in the Second World War.

His brother, Sergeant Flight Engineer Arthur Nicholson, also serving with the R.A.F., was reported "missing" in March 1945. He had been on fifteen operational trips, was an old Scholar of Otley Modern School and had worked at Dawson, Payne and Elliott, Ltd, Otley.

George Kenneth Nield (1911-1941)

Intelligence Corps - Lance Corporal - Service Number; 7687379 - Died 4 January 1941 (Age 29) - Oldham (Hollinwood) Cemetery (Sec H.11. Grave 9) - Son of John Henry and Helena Jane Nield, of Oldham. B.A. Hons (Manchester)

GEORGE KENNETH NIELD

Lance Corporal George Kenneth Nield, Intelligence Corps, (born 21 March 1911) was the first member of staff to join up and the first to be killed on active service. He joined Prince Henry's in March 1935 as an Assistant Master teaching French and English. He was educated at Oldham Municipal High School, from where he went to Manchester Victoria University, graduating in 1933 with a B.A. (Class II Honours) in French. He obtained his Teacher's Certificate in 1934. His teaching practice was undertaken at Ashton-under-Lyne Secondary School, where he taught French plus Junior/Middle English and Latin. He later taught French at Oldham Municipal High School and English at the Oldham Municipal Evening School of Commerce. His letter of application for Prince Henry's expressed an interest in music – a member of Oldham Secondary School Orchestra, qualified to teach singing.

His father, John Henry Nield (1868-1934) married Helena Jane Pugh (1873-1954) in 1892. In the 1911 Census John Henry was listed as a Commercial Clerk, born in Staleybridge, Cheshire. George's death was registered in Hendon, Middlesex.

In April 1940 he joined the Field Security Police. The *'In Memoriam'* entry in the Summer 1941 issue of *'The Otliensian'* reads:

'The School learnt with very deep regret at the beginning of this term that Mr Nield had met with a fatal accident while on duty on the 1st of January. Mr Nield had left us in April 1940, to join H.M. Forces. He entered the Field Security Police where his qualifications in French would have been of great use but for the unexpected course which the war took last summer. As it was, Mr Nield was doing valuable work in the army as his Commanding Officer testified and had every prospect of advancement before him. With us Mr Nield had already shown his ability not only as a linguist but as a most gifted pianist. He joined our Staff in 1934, having graduated with honours in French at the University of Manchester. He might well have looked for every success in his career if he had been spared to pursue it. He was held in friendly regard by all and we offer our deep sympathy very sincerely to his mother and to his brother and sister.'

The *'Wharfedale and Airedale Observer'* (10 January 1941) reported that:

'From later information it is learned that Mr Nield died in hospital at Edgeware,

Middlesex, on Saturday at 7.30 p.m. The accident occurred about 10.30 p.m. on New Year's Day. He was on duty at the time, and had a passenger on the machine who received only slight injuries. It is understood that his machine hit the kerb and Mr Nield was thrown off. His head struck a lamppost. The inquest was held at Hendon Town Hall on Tuesday.'

His mother, Mrs. Helena Nield, donated her son's collection of gramophone records to the school. '*They will remain a tribute to the keen interest Mr Nield took in the School's music and to his love for classical compositions. Two recitals of selections from the records have already been given during the School dinner hour, and it is hoped to continue these at fortnightly intervals during the winter.'*

The Field Security Police were formed in 1937 as a wing of the Corps of Military Police. In July 1940 the F.S.P. wing was separated from the C.M.P. and became the Intelligence Corps. It seems likely that Nield's skill in foreign languages would have been utilised in this branch of the services.

Oldham (Hollinwood) Cemetery contains the graves of 79 identified casualties from both World Wars.

Harry Overend (1921-1944)

Royal Air Force Volunteer Reserve (613 Squadron) - Flying Officer, Pilot - Service Number: 146439 - Died 19 November 1944 (Age 23) - Burley-in-Wharfedale (St Mary) Church Cemetery (Grave 134) - Son of Walter and Dora Overend, of Barnsbury, London.

H. Overend

Flying Officer Harry Overend, R.A.F.V.R. (born 26 August 1921) lived on Lawn Road, Burley-in-Wharfedale. His father, Walter Overend, was born in Bingley in 1888 and married Dora Dix in Islington in 1915. In the 1911 Census he lived on Fenton Street, Burley-in-Wharfedale and was listed as a manufacturer's clerk. He died in 1935.

Arthur attended Burley Main Street Council School from 1928-1934 before being admitted to Prince Henry's in October 1934 (Class Upper 3A). He left in December 1936 (Lower 5C), when his family moved to London.

Mrs. Overend and her son later moved to Stoke where Harry was on the staff of Barclay's Bank Ltd. when he joined the R.A.F. shortly before the outbreak of war. He spent two years in Canada, where he became an instructor, and returned to this country to fly Mosquitoes. He was killed in a flying accident.

613 (City of Manchester) Squadron was formed at Ringway on 1 March 1939 as an Auxiliary Air Force army co-operation unit equipped with Hawker Hinds. They later flew Hectors and Lysanders before re-equipping with American built Curtis Tomahawk aircraft in the army co-operation role. They also flew Mosquito fighter-bombers specialising in precision daylight attacks, and famously bombed the Gestapo HQ in The Hague. From 1943 to 1944 the Squadron was based at Lasham Airfield, but later moved to Cambrai for the rest of the war.

Following a service at St John's Methodist Church, he was buried in St Mary's Church Cemetery, Burley-in-Wharfedale, where there are 9 identified Commonwealth War Dead.

Eric George Paul (1915-1941)

Royal Air Force Volunteer Reserve (103 Squadron) - Sergeant-Wireless Operator/Air Gunner- Service Number 1112339 - Died 21 September 1941 (Age 25) - Otley (Newall-with-Clifton and Lindley) Cemetery (Section S, Grave 24) - Son of Albert George and Annie Helga Paul of Otley.

Sgt. E. G. Paul

Sergeant Eric George Paul, Royal Air Force Volunteer Reserve (born 16 October 1915 in Bath, Somerset) was at School from September 1928 (Upper 4A), following the award of a W.R.C.C. Special Place Award tenable for 4 years, 1 term. He had previously attended Alexandra Street Elementary School, Goole, and Ripon Grammar School. He lived on Boroughgate, Otley and his father, Albert George Paul (1891-1970), was a Monumental Mason. Albert married Annie Helga Bishop in 1915 in Chepstow, Monmouthshire.

In 1931 Eric was joint winner of the *'Miss Barker Memorial Art Prize'* and his work was displayed in the Art Exhibition of 1932. On leaving school, he trained to become an architect. He obtained his School Certificate (with Matriculation) in 1932, and entered the VIth. Form, but left before completing the course.

He was training as an architect with Messrs. Bain and Richardson, of Leeds, when he was called up. He was very interested in aviation and was a member of the Bradford Aviation Club. He joined the R.A.F. and was promoted Sergeant about three months before his death, which occurred while on an operational flight.

After its original formation in 1917 and disbanding in 1919, 103 Squadron was reformed in 1936 as the threat from Germany increased. The Squadron was re-equipped with the new Vickers Wellington bomber and commenced operations against Germany from December 1940. Night raids on Germany over the next three months were followed in spring and summer 1941 by raids on U-boat bases and pens along the French Atlantic coast, and key German shipping at Brest. After being based at Abingdon, then at Honington and later at Newton, the Squadron moved to Elsham Wolds in July 1941, from where over the winter of 1941 raids in force were concentrated against Germany.

On the 20/21 September 1941 34 aircraft were recalled from a mission to target Frankfurt, because of worsening weather. Some flew on and bombed the targets. No aircraft were lost, but 3 crashed in England.

Wellington IC – R1539 PM- crashed near Holbeach, 7 miles E.N.E. of Spalding, Lincolnshire, after trying to make an emergency landing in fog. Of the crew of six, five were killed; the only survivor was Sgt Bennett.

Rank	Service	Name	Age	Service No.	Buried
Sergeant (Pilot)	R.A.F.V.R.	Anthony Hughenden Rex	20	1154916	Bristol (Arnos Vale) Cemetery
Sergeant (Pilot)	Royal Canadian Air Force	George Kenneth Proctor	25	R/69896	Sutton Bridge (St Matthew) Churchyard
Pilot Officer (Observer)	R.A.F.V.R.	Alan Geoffrey Stanes	19	68760	Edgware (St Margaret) Churchyard
Sergeant W.Op/ Air Gunner	R.A.F.V.R.	Eric George Paul	25	1112339	Otley (Newall with Clifton) Cemetery
Sergeant W.Op/ Air Gunner	R.A.F.V.R.	Ernest George Birch Lennon	N/A	1183441	Streatham Park Cemetery
Sergeant	R.A.F.V.R.	Bennett	N/A	N/A	Injured – Survived

(*R.A.F. Bomber Command Losses, Vol. 2, 1941 by W.R. Chorley,)*

The '*Wharfedale and Airedale Observer*,' published 26 September 1941, reported that his parents had received a letter from an R.A.F. friend of their son, who wrote:

'Our own crew was not on duty that particular night, but one of the wireless operators from another crew reported sick and Eric was asked to take his place. Consequently he was not flying with his own crew when he was killed. We had all learned to admire and respect him, not only for his ability to do his job, but for the cheerful way in which he did everything. His cheerfulness, and particularly his enthusiasm, earned him the goodwill of everyone on the station.'

Otley (Newall-with-Clifton and Lindley) Cemetery is on the Pool Road out of Otley to the east. There are 54 identified casualties buried there, including four Old Scholars of Prince Henry's who died in the Second World War.

Harry Pickard (1916-1944)

Royal Navy (H.M. Submarine, Stratagem) - Petty Officer - Service Number: P/JX 137672 - died 22 November 1944 (Age 28) - Portsmouth Naval Memorial (Panel 81, Column 2) - Son of Enoch and Edith Pickard.

P/O.
H. Pickard

Petty Officer Harry Pickard, Royal Navy (born 22 August 1916 in Sculcoates) was at Prince Henry's from September 1928 (Class Upper 3A) until September 1930 (Lower 5C). He was awarded a W.R.C.C. County Minor Scholarship tenable for 4 years in 1928. He lived on Castley Lane, Pool-in- Wharfedale and attended Pool National School. His father, Enoch Pickard, was a Lithographer. Enoch married Edith Rogerson in Bradford in 1910. On leaving Prince Henry's, Harry moved to Aireborough Grammar School. He joined the Royal Navy at the age of 15 and spent the seven years before his death in the submarine service.

H.M.S. Stratagem was a S Class Submarine built at Cammell Laird Shipyard, Birkenhead. She was launched on 21 June 1943 and commissioned on 9 October 1943. On 10 November 1944 she sailed from Trincomalee, Ceylon, to patrol the Malacca Straits. On 19 November 1944 she torpedoed and sank the Japanese tanker 'Nichinan Maru', which was part of a convoy of five Japanese ships, escorted by three small destroyers. The destroyers attempted to counter-attack, but Stratagem managed to leave the area and by the morning of 22 November was in a position about three miles south-west of the port of Malacca.

Just after noon on 22 November the submarine was spotted by a Japanese aircraft that directed a destroyer to where she had dived. The destroyer dropped depth charges which caused the submarine's bow to strike the bottom. She was plunged into darkness and the forward part began to flood. Attempts to close the watertight doors to the forward compartment failed and the crew were forced to attempt to make their escape. Ten of the men in the compartment are known to have left the submarine alive although only eight were picked up by the Japanese. The other men on board, from a total crew of 48, including Harry Pickard, did not survive. Only three men ultimately survived the treatment they were subjected to in the prisoner-of-war camps. One of these men, Lieutenant D. C. Douglas has written an account of the loss of the submarine and the treatment he received from the Japanese after the sinking. (http://w.w.w.cofepow.org.uk/ships-strategem.htm)

Portsmouth Naval Memorial

Portsmouth Naval Memorial is situated on Southsea Common, overlooking the promenade, and is accessible at all times. After the First World War, an appropriate way had to be found of commemorating those members of the Royal Navy who had no known grave, the majority of deaths having occurred at sea where no permanent memorial could be provided. An Admiralty Committee recommended that the three manning ports in Great Britain – Chatham, Plymouth and Portsmouth – should each have an identical memorial of unmistakable naval form, an obelisk, which would serve as a leading mark for shipping. The memorials were designed by Sir Robert Lorimer, who had already carried out a considerable amount of work for the Commission, with sculpture by Henry Poole. The Portsmouth Naval Memorial was unveiled by the Duke of York (the future George VI) on 15 October 1924. After the Second World War it was decided that the naval memorials should be extended to provide space for commemorating the naval dead without graves of that war, but since the sites were dissimilar, a different architectural treatment was required for each. The architect for the Second World War extension at Portsmouth, was Sir Edward Maufe (who also designed the Air Forces memorial at Runnymede) and the additional sculpture was by Charles Wheeler, William McMillan and Esmond Burton. The Extension was unveiled by Queen Elizabeth, the Queen Mother on 29 April 1953. Portsmouth Naval Memorial commemorates around 10,000 sailors of the First World War and almost 15,000 of the Second World War – a total of 24,587 identified casualties. *(Commonwealth War Graves Commission)*

Geoffrey Claude Pickles (1924-1945)

Royal Naval Volunteer Reserve (H.M.S. Glory, 837 Squadron) - Sub-Lieutenant (A) - Died 16 April 1945 (Age 20) - Cambletown (Kilkerran) Cemetery (Division 4, Grave 625) - Son of John and Evelyn Pickles, of Otley, Yorkshire.

Sub-Lt. Pickles.

Sub-Lieutenant Geoffrey C. Pickles, Royal Navy Volunteer Reserve – Fleet Air Arm (born 26 June 1924) was at School from September 1935 (Upper 3A) until July 1940 (Lower VI). He lived on Bridge Avenue, Otley, and attended North Parade Elementary School from 1929-1935. His father, John Pickles, was a Pleasure Boat Proprietor – Bridge Avenue being situated near the River Wharfe. In 1920 John married Evelyn Dawson in Wharfedale.

'He (Geoffrey) will be well remembered by his contemporaries for his happy spirit and his great ability as a wing-forward in the School XV.' In the Spring 1939 issue of '*The Otliensian*' it was noted that he had joined the team at Christmas, *'and is now one of our best forwards. Excels in loose play.'* A year later he was described as *'a fine loose forward, always up with the play and an active defender. A good goal kicker.'* Against Ilkley Grammar School in 1940, *'Our dogged resistance was led by Pickles and Lund, whose loose play fully merited their colours which*

they received at the end of last season.'

He was also a Prefect, vice- captain of the Cricket XI, and in 1937 took part in a one-act play, 'The Knave of Hearts' – *'G Pickles as the Chancellor, being worthy of special mention.'*

He received an 'honourable mention' in the prize lists in both 1937 (Upper 4C) and 1938 (Lower 5) and passed the School Certificate in 1940, before joining the Sixth Form. On leaving School he found employment in clerical work. He joined up in February 1943, and was commissioned after training.

He trained as an observer, received his wings the same year, and was commissioned as temporary midshipman, to be promoted three days later, to the rank of temporary acting Sub-Lieutenant. He was made Sub-Lieutenant shortly after, and was serving on an aircraft carrier when reported missing in April 1945.

H.M.S. Glory was a Colossus Class Light Fleet Air Craft Carrier built by Harland and Wolff at Belfast, launched on 27 November 1943, with build completed on 17 November 1944. After trials she was commissioned for service on 21 February 1945 and began sea trials on 23 March 1945. Flying trials were held in April 1945, before she became operational and left the Clyde on 14 May 1945 to sail to the Mediterranean. It was on *HMS Glory* that the Japanese surrender was signed. In 1952 she served in the Korean War before being placed on Reserve from 1956-61, and eventually being sold for scrap in August 1961.

It was during the trial period that Geoffrey C. Pickles was killed in an air crash. He was flying a Barracuda MX794 with Sub/Lt. Arthur Snape and Leading Aircraftsman William George Ryan when his aircraft crashed in the sea off the north coast of the Isle of Islay. All three crew members were killed. Pickles' body was washed up on Kintyre and he was buried in the Cambletown Cemetery in Argyle. The other two crew members are commemorated on the Lee on Solent memorial. The log for the Squadron states that *'On their first 'Navex' from the ship, Sub.Lts. Snape and Pickles, together with L/Airman Ryan, do not return. The Squadron went out for three days scouring the sea for them, from Ireland across to the Hebrides, but to no avail, they were lost.' (David W. Earl, aviation historian, as listed in web-site dedicated to the* ***'Trafford War Dead'****, and specifically to Arthur Malcolm Snape)*

G. C. Pickles

As a member of 837 Squadron, had Pickles survived he would, later that month, have sailed on *H.M.S. Glory* to become part of the British Pacific Fleet, becoming part of the 16th Carrier Air Group. The squadron returned to the U.K. in October 1947.

He was buried with full naval honours in Kilkerran Cemetery, Cambeltown on 5 September 1945. The letter from the Admiralty containing the news stated that his body had been recovered on 3 September.

The Cambeltown Cemetery

The Cambeltown Cemetery, containing 103 identified casualties, is in Argyllshire. The great majority of the War Graves are in a reserved plot at the eastern end of the cemetery, and on a hill behind these graves the Cross of Sacrifice has been erected. *(Commonwealth War Graves Commission)*

Harold Pullan (1921-1944)

Royal Air Force Volunteer Reserve (76 O.T.U.) - Flying Officer/Pilot - Service Number: 152542 – Died 16 May 1944 (Age 22) - Ramleh War Cemetery (5.C.13.) - Son of Albert and Mary Pullan; husband of Mabel Pullan, of Stockton-on-Tees, Co. Durham.

H. Pullan.

Flying Officer Harold Pullan, R.A.F.V.R. (born 28 August 1921) from Chevin Side, Otley entered Prince Henry's in September 1933 (Form Upper 3A) and left in July 1938 (Upper 5B). His father, Albert Pullan (1893-1965) was a currier (leather dresser) and married Mary Russell in Otley in 1920. Harold was granted a W.R.C.C. *'Special Place Award'* tenable for his total school career in 1933. Harold had attended Otley National Elementary School from 1928-1933. His occupation on leaving school was as a Post Office Engineer, working in Bradford.

His early promise as an athlete was evidenced when he came second in the Obstacle Race (12-14) at Sports Day in 1934. In 1937 he came second in the Long Jump (Open) and third in Throwing the Cricket Ball. In 1938 he was joint second in the 100 yards (Open) and third in both the Long Jump (Open) and Throwing the Cricket Ball. By this time he was Vice Captain of the Cricket XI and had received his Cricket colours. But his main skill was in Rugby.

He was playing for the First XV in the 1936-37 season, scoring a try against Belle Vue Secondary School in the first match of the season. He was awarded his Rugby colours at the end of that season, and was appointed vice-captain for season 1937-38. He scored tries in almost all the matches during the season:

9 October	Belle Vue S.S. (home)	*The scoring was opened by H. Pullan.*
16 October	West Leeds H.S. (home)	*As a result of a good run by H.Pullan, J.Robertshaw went over for the winning try.*

3 November	Yorkshire Wanderers (home)	*As a result of a quick heel near the opponents' line H. Pullan went through for a try.* *In the second half School obtained a lead over the visitors when H. Pullan went through to score again.*
20 November	Morley G.S. (away)	*School retaliated well, scoring an unconverted try through H. Pullan*
18 December	Bingley G.S. (home)	*Scorers on our side were H. Pullan (2)*
22 January	Ilkley G.S. (home)	*Conspicuous in the backs were H. Pullan and K. Temple.*
5 February	Thornton G.S. (home)	*Scorers were A. Moore (3), K. Temple, H. Pullan*
26 February	Belle Vue S.S. (away)	*The backs played very well, H. Pullan and E. Anderson being conspicuous. Scorers were H. Pullan (3)*

His team profile in 1936-37 read *'has been an excellent forward. Works hard and is quick on the ball. Has been very valuable in going down on the ball in defence',* and in 1937-38, as stand-off, *'Has excellent hands and an eye for an opening. Also has a good side-step and cuts through smartly. Chief weakness is failure to fall back in defence. As vice-captain has done good work in developing the play of the backs.'*

He later played for Otley, and had a trial with Yorkshire.

He also showed promise on the academic side. He was awarded form prizes in Upper IIIA (fourth), Lower 5C (first) and Upper 5B (first) and obtained his School Certificate in 1938.

Harold Pullan joined the R.A.F. in November 1939 as a member of the ground staff and worked his way through the ranks to become a Flying Officer. He trained as a pilot in Canada and gained his wings in August 1943, returned to the U.K. and was posted to the Middle East. In 1941 he married Mabel Salmon, the marriage being registered in Stockton-on-Tees, where, on his death, his wife and two-year-old son were living. Eventually he became a member of 76 O.T.U. (No. 76 Operational Training Unit) based at R.A.F. Aqir in Palestine. The unit was formed in October 1943 to train night bomber crews using Wellingtons. The unit disbanded on 30 July 1945. He died, together with the other members of his crew, in a flying accident on 16 May 1944. They are buried together in the Ramleh War Cemetery in Israel.

Rank	Service	Name	Age	Service No.	Buried
Sergeant	R.A.F.V.R.	John Richard Pettit	21	1809850	Ramleh War Cemetery 5.C.14
Sergeant	R.A.F.V.R.	William Jardine	22	1341579	Ramleh War Cemetery 5.C.16
Sergeant	R.A.F.	Eric Thomas Stephenson		637887	Ramleh War Cemetery 5.C.15
Sergeant	R.A.F.V.R.	Harold Pullan	22	152542	Ramleh War Cemetery 5.C.13

Ramleh War Cemetery

The cemetery is located at Ramleh (now Ramla) in Israel, and dates from the First World War. During the Second World War the cemetery was used by the Ramla Royal Air Force Station and by various Commonwealth hospitals posted in turn to the area for varying periods. It contains the graves of 4,420 identified casualties, 1,168 from the Second World War. *(Commonwealth War Graves Commission)*

Three months after Harold's death his brother Private Brian Pullan, Lincolnshire Regiment was killed in action in France. He was 19, had been in the Army since November 1943 and went out to France in June 1944. He had been a member of the Home Guard, and was a keen football player, for which he had won several medals. He was educated at Otley, North Parade School. A third, and older brother, Arthur, had been serving with the R.A.M.C. since the outbreak of war.

Thomas Rathmell (1922-1942)

Royal Navy (H.M.S. Niger) - Able Seaman - Service Number: D/JX 287428 - Died 6 July 1942 (Age 19) - Plymouth Naval Memorial (Panel 66, Column 2) - Son of James Arthur Rathmell (deceased) and Lily Rathmell of Menston, Yorkshire

A/B. T. Rathmell

Able Seaman Thomas Rathmell R.N. (born 21 September 1922), came from the Viewlands Estate, Chevin End, Menston. He was at Prince Henry's from September 1934 (Form Upper 3A) until October 1936 (Lower 5C). He had previously attended Otley, North Parade Elementary School from 1926-1934. He received a W.R.C.C. 'Special Place Award' in September 1934, tenable for the remainder of his school career, but his amended admission form indicates that he '*broke his agreement with the W.R.C.C. owing to his parents' poor financial position*.' In fact, his mother was his guardian, his father having died, and it seems likely that Thomas left school and obtained employment as a Clerk, in order to support his widowed mother. His father, James Arthur Rathmell, was born in North Rigton in 1886. In the 1911 Census he was a farm manager at High Snowden, Askwith, near Otley.

In 1911 he married Lily Bateson. James Arthur died in 1924. During his first year at School Thomas was awarded second prize in his form and played the part of Abu Hassan – a Maker of Songs – in the play "*Twice is too Much*".

He was described as being '*well-built physically, giving promise of becoming a good athlete, and it was no surprise to hear that he had been attracted to the Navy.*'

On leaving school he worked at the Greenbottom Dyeworks, at Yeadon. He joined the Navy before he was 19. He was returning to England from Russia when his ship was sunk. He was initially reported as missing, but it was later confirmed that he had been killed in action on 6 July 1942.

H.M.S. Niger was a Halcyon-Class Minesweeper, launched on 29 January 1936. The ship was adopted by the town of Swadlingcote, Derbyshire, following a successful Warship Week, National Savings Campaign in February 1942. In May 1940 she had taken part in the evacuation of the British Expeditionary Forces from Dunkirk, evacuating some 1,500 men.

In April 1941, after flotilla duties in the North Sea involving escort and mine clearance, she joined the Iceland Escort Force and was deployed for convoy escort and anti-submarine patrols. In December 1941 she was nominated for detached service in North Russia for local escort and minesweeping duties in the Barents Sea area. In January 1942 she was under refit in preparation for her new role. The refit included *'Arcticisation'* during which her bow structure was strengthened and additional insulation provided for deckheads and internal bulkheads. Over the following months she played her part in the escort of Russian convoys.

Convoy QP13 (35 ships) left Murmansk on 27 June 1942. *H.M.S. Niger* led a column of merchantmen in bad weather with visibility reduced to under one mile. At 19.10 the convoy was split into two columns to pass through the gap inshore of the British minefield of Straumness. The bad weather had made it impossible to take bearings and H.M.S Niger mistook an iceberg as a sighting of land.

Unfortunately she had led the convoy into a British minefield off Iceland. She was mined at 22.40 hours in 5th July 1942, as were four of the six merchantmen she was escorting. The Commanding Officer, 8 officers and 140 ratings lost their lives. Unfortunately as well, *H.M.S. Niger* was carrying the survivors from the cruiser *H.M.S. Edinburgh*, which had been sunk earlier. In total 417 people died out of the 600 personnel carried on the seven vessels.

Source: Article from the World Ship Society's publication **'WARSHIP' THE WAR OF THE HALCYONS 1939-1945, R A Ruegg** (supplemented with additional information)

Plymouth Naval Memorial

The Memorial commemorates those members of the Royal Navy with no known grave, the majority of deaths having occurred at sea where no permanent memorial could be provided. After the First World War an Admiralty committee recommended that identical memorials should be built at Chatham, Plymouth and Portsmouth. The memorials were in the form of obelisks, which would also serve as identification marks for shipping. After the Second World War it was decided that the naval memorials should be extended to provide space for commemorating the naval dead without graves of that war, but since the three sites were dissimilar, a different architectural treatment was provided for each.

The Plymouth Memorial commemorates a total of 23,186 casualties; 7,251 sailors of the First World War and 15,933 of the Second World War. The Memorial is situated centrally on the Hoe, which looks directly towards Plymouth Sound. It is accessible at all times. *(Commonwealth War Graves Commission)*

The following notice was published in the *Yorkshire Post and Leeds Intelligencer* on 24 August 1942:

Presumed Dead

'A.B. Thomas Rathmell (19), Royal Navy, Chevin End, Menston. Previously reported missing at sea. An old boy of Otley, Prince Henry's Grammar School.'

George William Saunders (1920-1944)

Royal Artillery (70th Field Regiment) - Gunner - Service Number 922251 - Died 5 July 1944 (Age 24) - Caserta War Cemetery (I.B.20) - Son of Mr and Mrs. S. Saunders, Nurses' Home, Farnley Lane, Otley.

G. W. Saunders

Gunner George William Saunders, Royal Artillery, (born 12 May 1920) came from Clifton, near Otley and was at School from September 1931 (Upper 3B) until July 1936 (Upper 5B). He previously attended Clifton Elementary School from 1925-1931. His father, Stephen Edward Saunders, was a joiner, who married Minnie Stephenson in 1912. George's parents were awarded exemption from payment of fees, tenable for his school life.

He had *'a quiet, but most attractive character.'* He had *'a strong physique with a quiet and gentle manner.'* He played 1st XV Rugby and was *'a vigorous and powerful member of the pack.'* He was a promising violinist and a founder member of the school orchestra playing at School Concerts and plays in 1935; *'during the interval music was provided by the newly formed school orchestra consisting of M Bartle, D Mudd, Saunders and Robinson. Through the efforts of Miss Baxter the orchestra has already reached a promising standard.'* On leaving school he worked at Lingard's, drapers, in Bradford.

He volunteered for service with the Otley Battery of Territorials in 1939, before the outbreak of war, and went to France in 1940. He later took part in the fighting in North Africa and Italy. He was killed in an accident in the Middle East in July 1944.

Caserta War Cemetery

Caserta War Cemetery is located near the Caserta Nord exit from the autostrada A1 (Roma to Napoli). The cemetery contains 768 Commonwealth burials of the Second World War, 755 have been identified.

On 3 September 1943 the Allies invaded the Italian mainland, the invasion coinciding with an armistice made with the Italians, who then re-entered the war on the Allied side. Allied objectives were to draw German troops from the Russian front and more particularly from France, where an offensive was planned for the following year. The Royal Palace at Caserta served as headquarters for the Allied armies in Italy for the greater part of the duration of the Italian campaign, and the 2nd General Hospital was at Caserta from December 1943 until September 1945. Some of those buried here died in the hospital, others as prisoners of war before the Allied invasion. *(Commonwealth War Graves Commission)*

Jack Lawrence Smith (1918-1945)

Royal Engineers & Royal Air Force - Died 9 November 1945 (Age 26) - Otley (Newall-with- Clifton and Lindley) Cemetery - Son of Angelo Thomas Smith and Edith Mary Smith, Otley.

Sapper Jack Lawrence Smith, Royal Engineers (born 23 October 1918) lived at Oatlands, Pool Road Otley and attended North Parade Elementary School before moving to Prince Henry's in September 1929 (Class Upper 3B) following the award of a W.R.C.C. County Minor Scholarship. He left in December 1934 to become a builder, possibly working for his father A.T. Smith, Joiner and Builder. Angelo Thomas Smith (1881-1968) married Edith Mary Berryman (1881-1941) in Chertsey in 1902.

In the 1931 School Concert *'J Smith pleased the audience with 'The Swallows'. He shows remarkable promise as a soloist.'* In the 1932 Concert *'two delightful solos were sung by Jack Smith and Robert Crawshaw.'*

The 'Valete!' section of the magazine shows that he played 1stXV Rugby. It also appears likely that he was awarded first prize in his form in 1933 and second prize in 1934. He left at the age of 16 to train as a builder's quantitative surveyor at Bradford Technical

College. He played Rugby for Otley and was a keen swimmer, winning several trophies and holding both the bronze and silver medals of the Royal National Life Saving Society.

'*The Otliensian*' of Spring 1940 notes that '*At least two Old Scholars are now serving in France. These are Jack Smith and Charles W. Kerby, and Joseph Towers will most probably have joined them by the time these notes are read.*'

Smith was called up with the militia in September 1939, and joined the School of Military Engineering at Ripon, with the Royal Engineers. He saw service in France, though at the time of Dunkirk was home on leave in England. In 1941 he was transferred to the R.A.F. for training as a pilot, but in the last week of his course he met with an accident, sustaining head injuries. After convalescence he was recalled for Army service, from which he was discharged in 1945. He was awarded the 1939-45 Star.

His three brothers also served with the Forces. Major Fred A. Smith was with the Royal Corps of Signals, Captain Ronald Smith served in Burma, and Harold Smith was discharged from the Royal Air Force in 1945. Their sister, Angela, was in the W.R.N.S.

He died on 9 November 1945. An inquest held at Otley on 12 November 1945 returned the verdict '*that the deceased died from a self-inflicted head wound whilst the balance of his mind was deranged owing to injuries received in an aircraft crash, and personal worries resulting therefrom.*'

The '*Wharfdale and Airedale Observer*' (16 November 1945) reported on the inquest:

'Dr William H Galloway of Otley, in a statement to the police on November 9 said he was called by 'phone to Newall Hall about 10 a.m. on November 9. In the cellar he found Jack Smith lying on his left side. By his side was a small bore rifle. He was unconscious and died before he could be removed to hospital. When he examined the body he found a gunshot wound in the left temple, surrounded by a powder burn, which was indicative of a shot fired at very close range. "I am convinced that the wound was self inflicted and that the rifle could have been fired by himself," said the doctor.

'Answering questions by the Coroner, Dr. Galloway said deceased had recently been in the Otley surgery and was attended by his partner, Dr. Rhodes. He had overheard the conversations which took place and gathered "he was mainly complaining of headaches, sleeplessness and a muddled head."

'Dr Galloway said that he understood that deceased had been involved in a flying accident whilst he was in the R.A.F., and had received a bad fractured skull. He was in jeopardy of his life for a long time. Such injuries would, in his opinion, cause him to suffer from the things he complained of. The accident would tend to make him worry.

'Mrs. M. Smith in a statement, said the deceased was her step-son, and was living at Newall Hall. About 8.10 a.m. on Friday November 9 she saw him in the kitchen near the fireplace. He appeared his usual self. She went upstairs expecting him to get his breakfast which was on the table. About 9.30 a.m. she heard what she took to be someone sobbing. Passing the top of the cellar steps she heard the same sound coming

from the cellar. In the cellar she found her step-son unconscious. Nearby was a rifle. She telephoned another step-son and asked him to come, and bring a doctor with him. She covered her step-son with a rug, took a hot water bottle down, and then came upstairs to wait for the doctor.

'In a statement made later, Mrs. Smith said that the deceased, whilst serving with the R.A.F. was involved in an aircraft crash in 1941 and he sustained head injuries. Some time after the accident he was transferred to the Army and was discharged in February of this year. Since then he had been receiving treatment from a psychiatrist.

'Answering the Coroner Mrs. Smith said little things had worried her step-son since his accident. She said his work as a surveyor was "getting him down" because of the closeness of figures involved. He could not work things out as he thought he ought to be able to and he was losing sleep. He could not concentrate on anything for very long.

'Mr A. T. Smith, father of the deceased, said, in a statement, that about December 16 1941 he received a telegram from the R.A.F. to the effect that his son was in hospital. He went, with his daughter, and was informed that he had been in an accident while performing night flying duties. The doctor at first declined to give an opinion on his chances of living, but later said he had a "fifty- fifty" chance of recovering from his head injuries. His son was in hospital for six months, and after a period of convalescence, he was claimed by the Royal Engineers.

'While with the Army, said witness, his son obtained a number of leaves and complained of pains in he head. He was eventually discharged with a disability pension.

'Mr Smith said his son was a surveyor in civilian life and he knew he was worrying about figures in his job. He had complained recently to the doctor about "rumblings in the head."

'Before he was injured in the flying crash his son was a "very bright lad", and never worried.

'Evidence was also given by Miss Margaret Mary More, North Scales, Walney Island, assistant librarian, the fiancée of the deceased who was staying at Newall Hall at the time of the tragedy.'

The funeral service was held at Otley Parish Church, followed by interment in Otley Cemetery. He was buried with military honours and three volleys were fired at the graveside. He was buried in the same grave as his mother, Edith Mary Smith, who pre-deceased him in 1941.

John Ramsden Smith (1913-1943)

Royal Air Force Volunteer Reserve - Sergeant/Navigator - Service Number: 1459381 - Died 19 February 1943 (Age 29) - Aireborough (Guiseley) Cemetery (Section B Grave 80) - Son of Reuben and Sarah Ellen Smith, of Guiseley Yorkshire

L.A.C. J. R. Smith

Sergeant-Navigator John Ramsden Smith, R.A.F.V.R. (born 14 June 1913) lived on Butt's Terrace Guiseley. His father was a Motor Haulage Contractor. After attending Guiseley Council School, John was admitted to Prince Henry's in April 1926 (Class 3C), and left in July 1929 (Lower 5A) to become a Draughtsman, though the commentary on his death in *'The Otliensian'* notes that he became a surveyor for the Central Electricity Generating Board at Leeds. His father, Reuben Smith (1885- 1964), married Sarah Ellen Ramsden in 1909. In the 1911 Census the family was living at Cassfield, Guiseley and Reuben was listed as a 'stationary engineer'.

John was a keen sportsman and an enthusiastic member of the Otley and South Leeds Golf Clubs, and the Leeds Polar Bears' Swimming Club. He was also a popular member of Guiseley Amateur Operatic Society, something that may have come out of his performance as MacConnachie, the Court Official in the play *'Rory Aforesaid'* in 1929.

He joined the R.A.F. in 1941, and shortly before his death was expecting to complete a special course to become a navigator-radio operator.

He was accidentally killed on active service on 19th February 1943 and is buried in the Aireborough (Guiseley) cemetery which stands on the Guiseley-Menston boundary on Netherfield Road and contains the graves of 7 identified war-time casualties.

A report of his funeral was published in the '*Wharfedale and Airedale Observer*' dated 26 February 1943:

'The esteem in which L.A.C. Smith was held was reflected in the number of mourners who attended the service at the Parish Church, conducted by the Rector, Archdeacon Lowe. Many organisations with which he was associated were represented, including the British Legion, the Women's Section of the Legion, the Otley and South Leeds Golf Clubs, the Guiseley Operatic Society and the Leeds Polar Bears' Swimming Club. Along the route taken by the funeral cortege from the house to the church, many blinds were drawn, and in places people lined the thoroughfare, standing with bowed heads. The coffin was draped with the Union Jack and uniformed men of the R.A.F. acted as pall-bearers. There were many touching tributes of respect. At one point on the way to the church, members of Guiseley Veterans' Parliament were grouped with bare heads, and near the lychgate at the church two R.A.F. sergeants stood at the salute while the coffin was carried past them. The two sergeants were friends from L.A.C. Smith's unit, and had made the journey to Guiseley to pay their final personal tributes to a good comrade.'

Aireborough (Guiseley) Cemetery

Alfred Peter Sully (1920-1940)

Royal Air Force (107 Squadron) - Sergeant/Observer - Service Number: 581542 - Died 30 August 1940 (Age 20) - Bergen-Op-Zoom War Cemetery (32.B.2.) - Son of Alfred and Gladys Sully of Otley, Yorkshire.

Sergeant-Observer Alfred Peter Sully (born 12 June 1920, birth registered in Croyden, Surrey) was the son of Alfred Sully, manager of an Employment Exchange, and lived in Pool Road Otley. Alfred Sully (1882-1949) married Gladys Helena Bewers in Croyden in 1917. Alfred junior attended Otley National School from 1929-1932 and joined class Upper 3A at Prince Henry's on 13 September 1932, aged 12. He spent 4 years at

P.H.G.S., moving on to Leeds College of Commerce from class Upper 5B on 29 July 1936. He became sports champion at Leeds College of Commerce, and was also an expert swimmer. He was a civilian clerk in the Otley police headquarters when he joined the R.A.F. in July 1939.

His main claim to fame at school was as an athlete. At the time he was the only boy to win the Championship in his first year as a senior, and the first to win the Senior Championship for two years running. His Sports' Day record is shown below:

1933	*100 yards (Under 14) Fourth Place*	*220 yards (Under 14) Third Place*		
1934	*100 yards (Under 14) Third Place*	*220 yards (Under 14) First Place*	*High Jump (Under 14) Second Place*	*Long Jump (Under 14) First Place*
	Novelty Obstacle Race Second Place	*Junior Championship Second Place*		
1835	*100 yards (Open) Second Place*	*100 yards (14-15) First Place*	*220 yards (Open) First Place*	*440 yards (Open) First Place*
	High Jump (Open) Joint Second Place	*Long Jump (Open) Joint Fourth Place*	*Throwing the Cricket Ball (Open) Joint First Place*	*Senior Championship First Place*
1936	*100 yards (Open) Second Place*	*220 yards (Open) First place (28 seconds)*	*440 yards (Open) First Place (64.4 seconds)*	*Long Jump (Open) Second Place*
	High Jump (Open) Fourth Place	*Throwing the Cricket Ball (Open) First Place*	*Senior Championship First Place (retained)*	

The early athletics' careers of Sully and P.W.Barber (see earlier obituary) were closely linked. Barber won the Junior Championship in 1934 with 10 points to Sully's 9, but as a Senior Sully was clearly the best. Both students joined the R.A.F. on the outbreak of war and both died within three days of each other in 1940. Sully was soon promoted sergeant on qualifying as an Observer. The life appealed to him, *'as he told us on his visits to School when on leave.'*

Peter Sully

Outside school Sully competed in many open sports meetings and had many successes in 200-yard races. He returned to School on Sports Day, 1938, when he won the 'Old Boys' Race'. He was also a keen and able swimmer and played in the School Rugby 1stXV. In 1936 he was awarded the Bronze Medal of the Royal Life-Saving Society. He took over at fullback in the 1stRugby XV after the first choice player left school at Christmas 1934. The player profile said that *'He fields the ball well and has a strong kick, but does not always find touch. At present he lacks sense of position.'*

He showed some ability as an actor; in the 1933 School

Concert he had a small part in the play *'Katawampus'*, described as a 'pleasant comedy.' In 1935 he played the part of Albert, 'a daring cockney' in the play *'A Night at the Inn'*, the story of a gang of thieves who steal a jewel from the head of an idol and are pursued by the priests of the god to a lonely country inn. At Easter 1936, he was a member of the cast of *'The Bishop's Candlesticks'* – 'an exciting drama' which again involved convicts!

Mr R. Pratt J.V. Offermann S.A.V. Irwin J.Ineson
A.P. Sully C.W. Kerby J.E. Garside R.S. Howard B.F. Palmer K. Whitley

Otley Prince Henry's Grammar School Rugby Team
SEASON 1934–35.

K. Rhodes J. Towers T.E. Thornton (Capt.) K.J. Payne E.F. Wear
E. Findlater H. Rigg

In 1935 he gave a lecture to the Literary, Historical and Debating Society on *'South Africa'*:

'With the help of a large collection of photographs and slides he took us on a trip from Southampton through the Channel Islands to Durban. He then went on to illustrate some of the main features of such important towns as Ladysmith, Johannesburg and Pretoria. We hope that Sully's example will be followed by other members of our society who are in the lower forms.'

Although not particularly academic, he did win the third prize in the Fanny Barker Memorial Art Prize examination in 1935.

On Thursday 29 August 1940 twenty Blenheims were despatched in daylight to attack enemy held airfields at De Kooy, Bergen/Alkmaar and shipping off Den Helder. Weather conditions forced the abandonment of the mission in most cases, but seven crews pressed home their attacks on De Kooy and Alkmaar. One aircraft, Blenheim N3620 of 107 Squadron, Wattisham, suffered severe flak damage and was shot down at 04.30 at Balgzand, a large tidal flat located at the tip of mainland North-Holland, northeast of Den Helder. Flying Officer E.R.Berry, Sergeant A.P. Sully and Sergeant H. Bentham were killed and are buried in Bergen Op Zoom War Cemetery. News was received from German sources through the International Red Cross at Geneva that the body of Sergt. Observer Sully was washed ashore, though the place was not mentioned. Sergeant Sully was the first Otliensian to be killed in the Second World War.

Rank	Service	Name	Age	Service No.	Buried
Flying Officer	Royal Air Force	Ernest Reginald Berry	23	39959	Bergen-op-Zoom War Cemetery
Sergeant	Royal Air Force	Alfred Peter Sully	20	581542	Bergen-op-Zoom War Cemetery
Sergeant	Royal Air Force	Henry Bentham	18	552444	Bergen-op-Zoom War Cemetery

(RAF Bomber Command Losses Vol. 1 1939-1940 by W R Chorley – page 195)

Bergen-op-Zoom Cemetery

Bergen-op-Zoom is a town in the Dutch province of Noord-Brabant, 40 kilometres northwest of Antwerp. The War Cemetery is 3 kilometres east of the town and contains 1,284 Commonwealth burials and commemorations of the Second World War, 116 of the burials are unidentified. *(Commonwealth War Graves Commission)*

The connection with Peter Barber continued with the creation of the Battle of Britain Chapel in Westminster Abbey, both their names being inscribed on the Roll of Honour listing the aircrew of the R.A.F. who fell during the Battle of Britain.

Sully and Barber died within 3 days of each other in 1940 and the following article was published in the '*Yorkshire Evening Post*' on 7 September 1940:

'Two Otley airmen who have been taking part in bombing raids over Germany are reported missing. They are Sergeant-Observer Alfred Peter Sully, elder son of Mr A. Sully, manager of Otley Employment Exchange, of Pool Road, Otley, and Sergeant-Wireless Operator Barber, youngest son of Mrs. Barber of Bloomfield House, Otley.

'Sergeant-Observer Sully was a civilian clerk at Otley police headquarters before joining the R.A.F. in July 1939. A letter from his commanding officer states that he was taking part in a flight over Holland and Belgium.'

Geoffrey Elliott Thompson (1920-1943)

Royal Air Force Volunteer Reserve - Aircraftman 2nd Class - Service Number: 1356432- Died 8 November 1943 (Age 23) - Ambon War Cemetery, Indonesia (10.B. 9) - son of Roland and Annie Thompson, of Guiseley, Yorkshire.

Aircraftman Second Class Geoffrey Elliott Thompson, R.A.F.V.R. (born 19 January 1920) lived on Ashtofts Mount, Guiseley. His father, Roland Thompson (1892-1953) was a Coal Factor's Manager, who married Annie Elliott in 1918. Geoffrey went to Guiseley National School and moved to Prince Henry's in September 1930 (Class Lower 2A). He left in July 1937 and became an Organ Maker with the firm of Harrison and Harrison, Durham. He was one of the assistant organists at Guiseley Parish Church. The '*Otliensian*' noted that '*he was most popular with his contemporaries and took a full part in school activities.*

He was a wireless instructor in the R.A.F., and was officially posted as missing in April 1943. In June 1943 his parents received information from the International Red Cross that he was a prisoner of war in Japanese hands in a prison camp in Java. He died in captivity in Java. An article in the '*Wharfedale and Airedale Observer*' (26 October 1945) notes that '*friends of his in Boston (Lincs), a few days ago wrote saying that a message had been received from his closest friend, now on his way to this country from the Far East, that Geoffrey had died, and that he was with him at the end.*'

Ambon War Cemetery

The Ambon War Cemetery was constructed on the site of a former Dutch army camp used to hold Australian, American and Dutch prisoners-of-war captured during the invasion of the town of Ambon, situated on the Latimor Peninsula on the southern shore of Ambon Bay. The Cemetery contains Australian soldiers who died during the Japanese invasion of Ambon and Timor, plus those who died in captivity in one of the many camps constructed by the Japanese on the Moluccas Islands, including many British prisoners who were transferred from Java to the islands in April 1943.

The total number of graves in the cemetery is over 2,000, over half Australians. Most of the 800 British casualties belonged to the Royal Navy and Royal Air Force; nearly all the naval dead were originally buried at Makassar. All the graves are marked with bronze plaques mounted on concrete pedestals and set in level turf. There are 1,956 Commonwealth burials of the Second World War here, 357 of these are unidentified. *(Commonwealth War Graves Commission)*

Ten years after his death the following was published in the '*Yorkshire Evening Post*' (7 November 1953):

Roll of Honour

'Remembrance of Geoffrey Elliott Thompson eldest son of Mrs. and the late Roland Thompson, died Java, November 8 1943: - 6 Esholt Avenue, Guiseley.'

Gordon Edmund Waddington (1922-1943)

Royal Air Force Volunteer Reserve (183 Squadron) - Flight Sergeant - Service Number: 1379975 - Died 15 November 1943 (Age 21) - Runnymede Memorial (Panel 139) - Son of Leonard and Dorothy May Waddington of Birstwith, Yorkshire

Flight Sergeant Gordon Edmund Waddington, R.A.F.V.R. (born 8 June 1922) lived at 'Plympton', Harecroft Road, Otley and attended Otley National School from 1929-1934. He was awarded a W.R.C.C. County Minor Scholarship tenable for his school career and entered Prince Henry's in September 1934 (Class Upper 3A). He left school in November 1937 (Upper 5B), when his parents moved away from Otley, and transferred to Knaresborough Grammar School. His father, Leonard Waddington (1885-1949), was a Motor Engineer, who married Dorothy May Gilmour in 1922 in Wharfedale.

In his first year at Prince Henry's he played Giafar, the Caliph's Vizier, in the play *'Twice as Much'*. In the 1936 Sports Day he came third in the 100 yards (12-13) race.

'The Otliensian' announced that *'Flight Sergeant Gordon E Waddington, R.A.F., is reported missing, presumed killed. Gordon E Waddington (1934-7) had a bright and happy nature and showed great promise during the time he was with us.'* His Typhoon 1b (JP932) was on a shipping reconnaissance when it was hit by enemy flak south west of St Mathieu. He had had a lucky escape on 4 November 1943 when his Typhoon 1b (JP897) had crashed on landing at Predannack. (*RAF Fighter Command Losses Vol. 2: Norman Franks)*

183 Squadron was formed at Church Fenton on 1 November 1942 as a Typhoon squadron. Because of early difficulties with this aircraft, the squadron did not become operational until 5 April 1943 and did not fly its first mission until 19 April 1943, after which it was involved in fighter-bomber attacks against coastal targets and enemy airfields. In September the squadron moved to Cornwall, from where it attacked enemy shipping and airfields. In November rockets replaced bombs, and were used for the rest of the war. From February 1944 it began attacks against communication targets in preparation for the forthcoming invasion. The squadron moved to Normandy soon after D-Day and was used to support the army's advance towards Germany. In January 1944 it supported US forces during the 'Battle of the Bulge' and shortly before VE-Day it moved onto German soil. The return to Britain led to a change of aircraft to Tempest IIs, which were flown until November 1945, when the squadron was disbanded by being re-numbered No 54.

The Runnymede Memorial

The Runnymede Memorial lies overlooking the River Thames on Cooper's Hill at Englefield Green between Windsor and Egham on the A308, 4 miles from Windsor. The Air Forces Memorial at Runnymede commemorates by name over 20,000 airmen who were lost in the Second World War during operations from bases in the United Kingdom and North and Western Europe, and who have no known graves. They served in Bomber, Fighter, Coastal, Transport, Flying Training and Maintenance Commands, and came from all parts of the Commonwealth. Some were from countries in continental Europe which had been overrun but whose airmen continued to fight in the ranks of the Royal Air Force. (*Commonwealth War Graves Commission*)

John Francis Stansfield Walter (1922-1945)

Royal Electrical and Mechanical Engineers - Sergeant - Service Number: 7634808 - Died 6 August 1945 (Age 23) - Labuan War Cemetery (P.C. 13) - Son of Geoffrey Charles and Marion Walter, of Menston, Yorkshire

Sergt. Walter.

Sergeant John F.S. Walter, R.E.M.E., (born 25 April 1922) was at School from May 1932 (Form I) to June 1937 (Upper 4A). Previously he attended Grange Road Council School, Bradford. He lived in Menston and his father, Geoffrey Charles Walter (1897-1976) was a Bank Official. He married Marion R. Stansfield in 1918. John was the third of four children who attended Prince Henry's – Marion Joan (b. 1919), Patricia Grace (b.1921) and David Anthony (b. 1927). On leaving school he became a professional soldier, initially as a private with the Royal Army Ordnance Corps (R.A.O.C) and later, on promotion, transferring to R.E.M.E.

In 1940 he was engaged to Dorothy Newton from Bramhope. One of his sisters was married to Anthony Morton (*see previous obituary*), another married Peter Henry Cribb (*see 'Decorations'*)

He went from school at the age of 15 to the Army Technical School, and later to the Military Academy, Woolwich. He went abroad in November 1941, and arrived in Java in February 1942, just before the Japanese closed in on the island. No news was received of him since then until March 1943, when the War Office informed his parents that he was a prisoner of war in Japanese hands and interned in a camp in Borneo.

His relatives had received postcards indicating that he was still alive, but unfortunately he died of starvation shortly before the end of the war. *'He was popular with Staff and scholar alike and called to see us on his last leave before leaving for the Far East.'*

Labuan War Cemetery

Labuan is a small island in Brunei Bay, Malaysia, off the coast of northwest Borneo. The War Cemetery, the largest in Malaysia, is situated less than 1 kilometre from the airport and about 3 kilometres from the island's main town, Victoria. It contains the graves of 1,788 identified casualties. The total number of burials is 3,908. *(Commonwealth War Graves Commission)*

The following information is from the ***Australian Government, Department of Veterans' Affairs web-site:***

'After the fall of Singapore several thousand British and Australian prisoners of war were sent to camps in Borneo, mainly in the Sandakan area on the eastern coast of North Borneo, where they were employed in aerodrome construction. In October 1943, most of the officers were separated from their men and sent to Kuching. Thereafter conditions at Sandakan greatly worsened; the men were starved, beaten and overworked by their captors. In February 1945, the Japanese, anticipating the Allied landings in North Borneo, decided to move the prisoners of war westwards to Ranau, more than 160 miles inland from Sandakan. More than 2,000 British and Australian servicemen took part in the "Death March to Ranau". Those who fell, sick or exhausted, on the journey were killed; the survivors who reached Ranau were made to perform superhuman work on starvation rations. Only six survived Sandaken and the death marches.

'When the Australian Army Graves Service entered Borneo, they followed the route from Sandaken to Ranau and found many unidentifiable victims of these infamous marches. These and other casualties from battlefield burial grounds and from graves throughout Borneo were taken in the first instance to Sandakan, where a large number of prisoners of war were already buried. This flat coastal area, however, was subject to severe flooding and it proved impracticable to construct and maintain a permanent cemetery. The Sandakan graves, numbering 2,700, of which more than half were unnamed, were therefore transferred to Labuan War Cemetery, specially constructed to receive graves from all over Borneo.

'Labuan War Cemetery is about two miles from Victoria, on high ground overlooking the harbour. It is the only war cemetery in North Borneo and contains, as well as the graves from Sandakan, about 500 from Kuching where there was another large prisoner of war camp. The total number of burials is 3,908. The preponderance of unidentified graves is due to the destruction of all the records of the camps by Colonel Suya, the Japanese commandant, before the Australians reached Kuching, his headquarters. When apprehended Suya committed suicide rather than face questioning on his conduct of the Borneo camps.'

William Thomas Watson (1912-1944)

West Yorkshire Regiment (Prince of Wales Own):Secondary Regiment:- Durham Light Infantry - Lieutenant - Service Number; 200775 - Died 23 April 1944 (Age 32) -Rangoon Memorial (Face 7) - Son of William Thomas Watson and Amy Watson; husband of Frances Watson, of Wakefield, Yorkshire

Lieutenant William Thomas Watson, West Yorkshire Regiment (Prince of Wales Own): attached to the Durham Light Infantry (born 16 April 1912 in Llanrhaiadr, Denbigh, Wales) lived in Lindley Wood, Otley where his father was a Gamekeeper. He was only at Prince Henry's for two years, having moved into the area from Fakenham. He was admitted in September 1928 (Class Upper 5A), left in July 1929 before being re-admitted in January 1930 and finally leaving in July 1930 (Sixth Form) to attend Becketts Park Training College, Leeds. He was awarded a W.R.C.C. County Minor Scholarship in 1928, tenable for one year. He obtained a Teacher's Certificate in 1932 and worked as an Assistant Schoolmaster for Morley Education Authority.

The '*In Memoriam*' comment in '*The Otliensian*' notes that he '*will be well remembered by his contemporaries as he was a most active member of the School as prefect, and member of the Rugby XV and Cricket XI. His family left the district shortly after he left school. He joined the army early in the war and held the rank of Lieutenant in the Durham Light Infantry when recently killed in action in Burma.*'

He was made a Prefect on joining the School in 1928 and immediately set about taking an active part in sport and drama. His Rugby profile in 1929 reads '*Has picked up the game well and made one of our best forwards. Gets the ball well at the line out, but sometimes throws it back when men are covered.*' He was awarded his colours at the end of the season.

In the play *'The Grand Cham's Diamond'*, '*Miss J E Benson as "Mrs. Perkins" and W T Watson, as her rather timid husband, showed considerable cleverness in the study of their rather difficult parts... W.T. Watson displayed great ability – for all the action was left to "Mrs. Perkins" – in quite literally standing and staring.*'

He passed his School Certificate with Matriculation and a Distinction in Chemistry and was given a 'honourable mention' in the Upper 5A class prize list in 1929. He left at the end of the 1929 school year and immediately got involved with the Old Scholars Association being elected to the Committee and taking part in the Dramatic Society production of "Eliza Comes to Stay." He re-entered school in January 1930 and joined the Sixth Form; although he was only to remain for two terms, he still found time to play Cricket for the 1stXI, though perhaps with more enthusiasm than skill according to his profile – '*Though not conspicuous in the batting averages, Watson is a great hearted enthusiast and trier. Nothing in the field which comes within his reach is too 'hot' to attempt to stop.*'

On 4 August 1938 he married Frances Burdett in Wakefield. They had one daughter,

Ruth Burdett Watson, born 11 January 1941. He joined the Territorial Army on 14 October 1940 and was posted to the Chemical Warfare Training Battalion, Royal Engineers. He was discharged on 8 August 1941, having been granted an emergency commission as Second Lieutenant in the West Yorkshire Regiment. He embarked from Liverpool on 13 April 1943 and arrived in India on 12 June 1943. He was posted to the 2ndBattalion Durham Light Infantry on 23 August 1943. He may have been wounded because he was in hospital from 27 February 1944 to 3 March 1944. He was killed in action in Burma on 23 April 1944.

The Rangoon Memorial

The Rangoon Memorial is situated in the Taukkyan War Cemetery, about 35 kilometres north of Yangon (formerly Rangoon). The Memorial bears the names of almost 27,000 men of the Commonwealth land forces who died during the campaigns in Burma (now Myanmar) and who have no known grave. (*Commonwealth War Graves Commission*).

Eric Frederick Wear (1917-1942)

Royal Air Force Volunteer Reserve(148 Squadron) - Sergeant, Observer - Service Number: 999231 - Died 24 April 1942 (Age 24) - Catania War Cemetery, Sicily (Coll. Grave IV.L.24) - Son of J.E. Wear of Burley-in-Wharfedale, Yorkshire

Sgt./Obs. Wear.

Sergeant-Observer Eric Frederick Wear, R.A.F.V.R., (born 23 October 1917) lived on Main Street, Burley-in-Wharfedale and, after attending Burley National School was admitted to Prince Henry's in September 1928 (Class Upper 3B). On leaving in March 1935 (Sixth Form) he took articles as an architect and immediately these were completed he joined the R.A.F. His father, James.E. Wear (1885-1966) was a Clerk; he married Sarah A. Iles in 1916 in Wharfedale.

Eric played both 1stXV Rugby and 1stXI Cricket for School. He was one of the backs to *"show promise of development"* in the 2ndXV in 1934, though he had already played for the 1stXV and scored a try against West Leeds in October 1933. His team criticism in 1935 read *"Has been very disappointing. He has a useful turn of speed, but fails to make full use of it. His chief fault is in failing to take passes, due to his talking his eye off the ball. Tackling is much improved."* In spite of this rather negative comment he seems to have done well in some of the games:

6 October 1934	Ilkley Grammar School)	*A strong and determined runner was Wear, the right-wing three quarter, who also showed a marked improvement in defence.*
13 October 1934	Morley Grammar School	*Wear scored after a good run.*

15 December 1934	Roundhay Grammar School	*Half-time came and went without a score, Wear being the only one who crossed the opponents' line in a sharp dribble.*
19 January 1935	West Leeds High School	*West Leeds went ahead with an improved try, School replying with unconverted tries by Wear and Towers.*
2 February 1935	Thornton Grammar School	*Wear dropped a neat goal.*

(1st XV photograph – see Alfred Peter Sully)

In the 1933-34 Cricket season he had a batting average of 5.75 from 4 innings, but against Yeadon & Guiseley Secondary School he scored 17, '*being the only player to reach double figures*.' His batting average improved to 7.40 from 5 innings in the following season with 20 of his 37 runs coming in the match against Harrogate Grammar School, which School won by 20 runs. He was described as a '*useful change-bowler*' and took 3 wickets from 13 overs at an average of 14.67 per wicket.

He competed in Sports Day in 1934, finishing fourth in the 220 yards (Open) and third in Throwing the Cricket Ball, and in 1935 when he managed third place in both the 440 yards (Open) and Throwing the Cricket Ball.

In 1934 he was awarded third prize in his form and in 1935 he passed his School Certificate with Matriculation.

He was studying architecture at Leeds College of Art when he joined the R.A.F.V.R. in October 1940. He took part in several operational flights over Germany before being posted to the Middle East in 1941.

He was reported missing on an operational flight in April 1942. He was a member of the crew of a Wellington IC (DV 573) that took off from Luqa at 20.40 on 23 April 1942, to attack Comiso, Sicilly. The plane was shot down over the target; none of the crew survived.

Rank	Service	Name	Age	Service No.	Buried
Flying Officer	R.A.A.F. (Australian)	Roderick McMillan Harper	29	402442	Catania War Cemetery
Sergeant	R.A.F.V.R.	George Henry King	25	933276	Catania War Cemetery
Sergeant	R.A.F.V.R.	Eric Frederick Wear	24	999231	Catania War Cemetery
Sergeant	R.A.F.V.R.	Raymond Tucker Perrin	28	1167487	Catania War Cemetery
Sergeant	R.A.F.V.R.	Thomas Pellow Hosking	22	926519	Catania War Cemetery
Flight Sergeant	R.A.F.V.R.	Herbert Charles Powell	32	1378440	Catania War Cemetery

(RAF Bomber Losses in the Middle East and Mediterranean Volume 1 1939-1942 by David Gunby and Pelham Temple)

148 Squadron was formed at Andover, Hampshire in February 1918 and went to France as a night- bombing squadron. It was disbanded in June 1919 but re-formed

at Scampton in June 1937 as a long-range medium-bomber unit. As a result of the European crisis it was re-mustered as a heavy night-bomber unit in September 1938 and by March 1939 was flying Wellington Is.

A few days after the start of the Second World War, 148 Squadron moved to Harwell and, equipped with Wellingtons and Ansons, became a training squadron in No 6 Group. In December 1940 it again became a bomber squadron, equipped with Wellingtons and based in Malta, from where it played a valuable role in the North African and, later, the Italian campaigns. The squadron carried out attacks on Axis bases in Italy and Libya, initially from Malta and later from Egypt. This period ended on 14 December 1942 when No 148 became a special duties squadron.

Catania War Cemetery

Catania War Cemetery lies 7 kilometres south-west of Catania. On 10 July 1943, following the successful conclusion of the North African campaign in mid May, a combined allied force of 160,000 Commonwealth and American troops invaded Sicily as a prelude to the assault on mainland Italy.

The Italians, who would shortly make peace with the Allies and re-enter the war on their side, offered little determined resistance, but German opposition was vigorous and stubborn. The campaign in Sicily came to an end on 17 August when the two allied forces came together at Messina, but failed to cut off the retreating Axis lines. The War Cemetery contains burials from the later stages of the campaign, from Lentini northwards. Many died in the heavy fighting just short of Catania and in the battle for the Simeto river bridgehead. There are 2,135 Commonwealth burials of the Second World War, 113 of them unidentified. (*Commonwealth War Graves Commission*)

Stanley Whitaker (1914-1944)

Royal Air Force Volunteer Reserve (625 Squadron) - Flying Officer - Service Number: 168796 - *Died 23 October 1944 (Age 30) - Runnymede Memorial (Panel 209) - Son of Mrs. R. H. Whitaker, of Acton Middlesex.*

Flying Officer Stanley Whitaker, Royal Air Force Volunteer Reserve (born 17 September 1914) was at School from September 1927 (Form Upper 3A) until July 1933 (Form VI). He lived on Granville Mount in Otley and his father, Sam Whitaker (1877-1941) was a fitter, probably at a printing machine works. Sam married Ruth Hannah Boothroyd in Wharfedale in 1910. Stanley had previously attended Westgate Elementary School, Otley. On entry to Prince Henry's he was given a W.R.C.C. '*Special Place Award*', tenable for 3 years and 2 terms. He left School to become an accountant.

He was a Prefect and played for both the First XV Rugby team – colours awarded in 1933 and the First XI Cricket team. His player criticism for Rugby in 1933 read '*has improved, but still shows lack of judgement. He throws himself into the game more, but is too often losing ground for his team by getting offside.*' In spite of this he was

P/O S. Whitaker.

given favourable write-ups in three match reports in the 1932-1933 season. In Cricket he was a moderate batsman; his average in 1933 was 6.0. from four innings, though 17 of these runs came in one innings against Roundhay. On leaving School he played Rugby for the Old Scholars (Otliensians) and was a Committee Member for that organisation in both 1936 and 1937.

On the academic side he was awarded form prizes in 1928 – 'honourable mention' in Form 3A – and in 1929 – third prize in Form Upper 4A, and was joint winner of the French Travelling Scholarship (with Margaret Parsons) in 1933. He passed his School Certificate with Matriculation in 1932, and entered the Sixth Form. He had a brief part in the play *"Thread O'Scarlet"* in 1931, playing the 'traveller'. After he had left School, he still found time to return to give a lecture on *'Brussels'* to the Literary, Historical and Debating Society, an organisation for which he was Honorary Joint Secretary from 1932-1933.

He volunteered for the R.A.F. in September 1941, and went to Southern Rhodesia to continue his training in February 1942. He was commissioned shortly after passing out as Sergeant Bomb Aimer.

625 Squadron was formed at Kelstern, Lincolnshire, on 1 October 1943, as a heavy-bomber squadron equipped with Lancasters. Between October 1943 and April 1945 the Squadron flew 3385 sorties, mainly involving targets in Germany, with a total of 66 aircraft lost.

On 23 October 1944 Whitaker took part in a 1,055 aircraft and massively damaging raid on Essen. This was the largest number of aircraft deployed on any target up to that time. 4,538 tons of bombs were dropped, over 90% being high explosive. 3 Halifaxes and 5 Lancasters were lost, including the Lancaster B III (PB531 CF-H) with the following crew:

Rank	Service	Name	Age	Service No.	Buried
Flying Officer	R.A.F.V.R.	Owen Henry Morshead	21	150313	Runnymede Memorial Panel 202
Sergeant	R.A.F.V.R.	James Hardman Porteous	N/A	1369004	Runnymede Memorial Panel 236
Sergeant	R.A.F.V.R.	Derrick Rowley Owen Pugh	21	1581750	Runnymede Memorial Panel 236
Flying Officer	R.A.F.V.R.	Stanley Whitaker	30	168796	Runnymede Memorial Panel 209

Sergeant	R.A.F.V.R.	Percy Alfred William Black	20	1606715	Runnymede Memorial Panel 225
Sergeant	R.A.F.V.R.	Leslie Johnson	19	2204527	Runnymede Memorial Panel 232
Sergeant	R.A.F.V.R.	John Crawford McConkey	29	1899023	Runnymede Memorial Panel 233

(Royal Air Force Bomber Command Losses of the Second World War, Volume 5 -1944- by W.R.Chorley)

The aircraft was lost without trace and all 7 members of the crew are commemorated on the Runnymede Memorial.

The Runnymede Memorial

The Runnymede Memorial lies overlooking the River Thames on Cooper's Hill at Englefield Green between Windsor and Egham on the A308, 4 miles from Windsor. The Air Forces Memorial at Runnymede commemorates by name over 20,000 airmen who were lost in the Second World War during operations from bases in the United Kingdom and North and Western Europe, and who have no known graves. They served in Bomber, Fighter, Coastal, Transport, Flying Training and Maintenance Commands, and came from all parts of the Commonwealth. Some were from countries in continental Europe which had been overrun but whose airmen continued to fight in the ranks of the Royal Air Force. (*Commonwealth War Graves Commission*)

Norman Percy Winterburn (1922-1943)

Royal Air Force Volunteer Reserve (156 Squadron) – Sergeant – Wireless Operator/Air *Gunner – Service Number: 1439760 – died 29 September 1943 (Age 21) – Otley (Newall-with Clifton and Lindley) Cemetery (Sec. M Grave 190) - Son of George Horace and Edith Anne Winterburn, of Otley, Yorkshire.*

N. .P. Winterburn

Sergeant Norman Percy Winterburn, R.A.F.V.R. (born 8 May 1922) lived on Walkergate, Otley; his father, George Horace Winterburn (1894-1947) was a Council Workman, who married Edith Anne Mennell in Wharfedale in 1922. Norman attended Otley National School from 1929-1933 and entered Prince Henry's, on a W.R.C.C. Special Award tenable for his school career, in September 1933 (Class Upper 3B). He left school to work in Garnett's Paper Mill in March 1937 (Lower 5A).

Although the comment made in "*The Otliensian*" on his death in a flying accident states that he '*was very keen on games, though not strongly built*', there is no evidence that he took part in Sports Days or played for School teams. He did receive form prizes for third place in both 1933 and 1934. He was a keen philatelist.

He was called up for duty in October 1941, and had been on seven operational flights including two raids on Berlin, attacks on Nuremberg and Peenemunde and a raid over Lille.

156 Squadron was first formed in October 1918, but disbanded in November 1918, without having become operational. In February 1942 it was re-formed at Alconbury, as a medium-bomber squadron equipped with Wellingtons. When the Pathfinder Force was formed in August 1942, with the object of securing more concentrated and effective bombing by marking targets with incendiary bombs and flares dropped from aircraft flown by experienced crews and using the latest navigational equipment, No 156 was one of the four squadrons selected to form the nucleus of the force. It remained with the Pathfinder Force for the rest of the European war and, still flying Wellingtons at first and then Lancasters, played a major part in Bomber Command's offensive.

On 29 September. 1943, 352 aircraft, including 213 Lancasters, (10 from 156 Squadron) flew from Warboys to target Bochum. The raid was successful in terms of accurate and concentrated bombing.

Five Halifaxes and four Lancasters were lost, including Lancaster EE118 which crashed in bad weather at Wimbotsham, 2 miles from Downham Market, Norfolk. The crew comprised:

Rank	Service	Name	Age	Service No.	Buried
Flight Sergeant	R.A.F.V.R.	Frederick Henry Ray	26	1391599	Carisbrooke Cemetery
Sergeant	R.A.F.V.R.	William Alf Lineham	19	1815307	Cambridge City Cemetery
Flying Officer	Royal Canadian Air Force	Sydney Kent Smith	21	J/14174	Cambridge City Cemetery
Sergeant	R.A.F.V.R.	David Robert Booker	NA	1413457	Tenby (St Mary) Church Cemetery
Sergeant	R.A.F.V.R.	Norman Percy Winterburn	21	1439760	Otley (Newall with Clifton and Lindley) cemetery
Sergeant		A.S.W. Orchard	NA		Injured – broken leg, survived

(Royal Air Force Bomber Command Losses of the Second World War, Volume 4 – 1943 – by W.R. Chorley)

He was buried in Otley Cemetery on 4 October 1943. The '*Wharfedale and Airedale Observer*' reported that '*The coffin was draped with the Union Jack and cadets of the Otley and District A.T.C. squadron acted as pall bearers.*'

Otley (Newall-with-Clifton and Lindley) Cemetery is on the Pool Road out of Otley to the east. There are 54 identified casualties buried there, including four Old Scholars of Prince Henry's who died in the Second World War.

Prisoners of War

Eleven former students of Prince Henry's Grammar School were prisoners of war during the Second World War. Six of these Otliensians, including one woman – Margery Jennings – were prisoners of the Japanese. The Germans captured the other five. Four of the six Japanese prisoners of war died in captivity. All five of the prisoners interned in Germany or German occupied countries, returned home at the end of the War. In some cases the proof that relatives were PoWs came as a relief following news that their loved ones were 'missing in action'. It could take months for postcards posted after capture to arrive home.

A Prisoners of War Club for the Wharfedale district, covering Otley, Ilkley, Burley, Menston and the rural villages was founded at a meeting held in Otley on 15 July 1942. Nearly 50 relatives of war prisoners and helpers attended. The Vicar of Otley, in presiding, explained that the object of the Club was to provide an opportunity for relatives of prisoners of war to meet periodically to discuss the latest news from the prison camps, exchange information received in letters, provide help for men in need of comforts and clothing, and obtain news of those men posted as missing.

An important part of the work of the Club was to provide parcels for the men in the camps. It was suggested that every prisoner should receive a parcel from his relatives every three months. The Club had access to a parcel-packing centre in Leeds, and articles for parcels could be bought through the Club, free of purchase tax. Razor blades were five for 7½d., pyjamas were 6s. 6d., shorts 6s., soap 2d. per tablet, chocolate 9d. per ½lb., handkerchiefs 4½d. each and towels 5d. each. At the first meeting it was announced that the Christmas Gifts Committee of the Otley Comforts Fund was willing to provide gifts of knitted garments for relatives to send to war prisoners. However, the greatest need was for funds to buy the articles sent in the parcels and at each meeting relatives, friends and helpers donated money, which was used to subsidise the cost of parcels. Members gave what they could afford, but the lists of subscribers show that at most meetings each person donated something; this must have proved difficult at a time when the main breadwinner was a prisoner of war.

One of the most popular items received by prisoners of war was parcels of cigarettes, paid for from Club funds. Letters to the Prisoners of War Club and to relatives make regular reference to these parcels. An article published in the *'Wharfedale and Airedale Observer'* on 8 December 1944 states that:

P. OF W. THANKS FOR CIGARETTES

'Mrs. Booth, hon. secretary of the Otley and Wharfedale Prisoners of War Club, has received several more postcards from prisoners thanking the club for gifts of cigarettes.

Captain the Rev. Charles King, a former curate of Otley Parish Church writes: "Please accept my thanks for another two parcels of cigarettes. The devil, they say looks after his own. I don't know about that, but the people of Wharfedale are certainly very kind to their adopted sons. As my old landlady used to say, "Thee get thee feet under t'table," and I seem to have done so very thoroughly. Have started 'soft ball'. At the moment it's too 20th century."

Driver Geoffrey Carr, of 81 The Crossways, Otley, writes: "I had a very pleasant surprise a few days ago when I received 200 cigarettes from you. I need hardly write of the pleasure these parcels bring us, but believe me, they are a blessing for which I myself am very grateful. Thanks a lot."

'Sgt. Jack Crossley, of 57 The Crossways, Otley, writes: "Since October 2, I have received four more parcels, each of 200 cigarettes. Please give my very grateful thanks to the P.O.W. Club members and donors."

'Horace Gibson, of Chevin End, Menston, writes: "Many thanks for the 200 cigarettes received on October 11. I would be very grateful if you would thank all concerned for the gift, which comes at a time when they are very scarce. Yours are the first I received in Italy, and also the first in Germany. I am hoping it won't be long now before I am back again."

Flt-Sgt. Peter Craven writes, "During the past few days I have received two cigarette parcels from the P.O.W. Club. I would like to express my sincere thanks to all concerned for their great kindness and consideration.'

In a letter read out at the meeting on 12 January 1945, a local prisoner of war, John L. Whitworth was quoted as follows - *"I have received two more cigarette parcels, making six in all, since I arrived in Germany. I wish to convey sincere thanks to all contributors and organisers of the club, from all the boys here who share in these parcels. A cigarette makes a big difference to the boys in this life and certainly creates a more pleasant atmosphere for 'no smokes' is the prisoners nightmare."*

German Prisoner of War Camps

There were several types of PoW camps in Germany and German occupied countries. ***Oflags***, were camps for officers, while ***Stalags*** were for both officers and enlisted men. Some of the Stalag camps were more properly named ***Stalag Luft,*** run by the Luftwaffe and initially intended to house air force prisoners. There were also camps known as ***Marlags*** – intended for captured naval servicemen.

Before being sent to a camp a captured prisoner of war would pass through a transit camp, known as a ***Dulag***, where they were interrogated and their details processed. Under the terms of the Geneva convention prisoners were only obliged to give their name, rank and serial number, though interrogating officers would often try to get more information from servicemen through tricks and clever questioning. Prisoners would then be transferred to a prisoner of war camp, transported usually by train. This could take some time depending on the distance and on the number of times the train stopped because it had to give way to passing troop trains. According to the Geneva

Convention trains carrying prisoners of war should be marked to identify them as being exempt from attack by foreign aircraft; in many cases this marking was not carried out and trains were strafed and prisoners were killed or injured.

Conditions in the transit camps and on the trains were very poor. Carriages, sometimes no more than cattle trucks, were overcrowded, food was scarce or poor in quality and sanitation was very basic.

Individual camp layouts varied from camp to camp. Some camps had been purpose built, others were converted from existing barracks or training areas. All were enclosed with barbed wire fences and guard towers manned by armed German soldiers ready to shoot anyone trying to escape. Prisoners were usually housed in single-storey wooden huts that contained bunk beds and a charcoal burning stove in the middle of the room.

Generally two meals per day were provided, consisting of thin soup and black bread. Prisoners looked forward to deliveries of Red Cross food parcels that allowed them to supplement their diet through luxuries such as biscuits, chocolate, condensed milk, dried fruit and vegetables.

Daily routine varied from camp to camp, but all prisoners would parade at least once a day for roll call. Some men would be put to work either in the camp or in the local area. In the better camps a range of sports was played and there would be concerts put on by the prisoners, but on the whole, life was boring, prisoners were hungry and could only dream of release and home when the War ended.

Camps were multi-national with prisoners from Commonwealth countries, the USA and Canada, Western Europe, and Eastern Europe. Conditions and treatment were not the same for all prisoners; Soviet troops in particular were badly treated. As the War came towards an end, the Germans became concerned about the Russian advance because many of the camps were situated in the east of Germany and in Poland. In some cases prisoners were marched long distances to other camps in the west; in others the camps were relieved by the Red Army from the east or the Americans and British from the west, and the prisoners repatriated. There were also examples of PoW camps being abandoned by the German guards and prisoners being expected to make their own way back home.

Japanese Prisoner of War Camps

Prisoners in the hands of the Japanese were in camps in Japan, Taiwan, Singapore and other Japanese occupied countries. There were over 140,000 prisoners in Japanese PoW camps and of these one in three died from starvation, work, punishments or disease. Both military personnel and civilians who were in the east after the outbreak of War were interned in camps after being captured during the Japanese invasion of the area. Margery Jennings, a nurse with the Medical Auxiliary Service, was captured in February 1942 on Bangka Island, off Sumatra. She was housed in several camps, and died in a camp in Sumatra before the end of the War.

Camps were encircled with barbed wire or high wooden fencing. Accommodation was usually in barracks and prisoners were given mats to sleep on. Most male prisoners were put to work in mines, fields, shipyards and factories. They worked for 12 hours a day on a diet of barley, green stew and seaweed stew, with meat or fish once a month. They were continuously hungry. Red Cross parcels were not delivered to the prisoners.

OLD OTLIENSIAN PRISONERS OF WAR

	Date of Birth	Rank/Service	Prisoner of War Camp	Future
Robert Peter Geoffrey Barker	22 March 1918	Sergeant – Royal Northumberland Fusiliers Service No. 1463232	Captured 15 February 1942 – camp in Thailand	Liberated 2 September 1945 Died 2006, Bridgend, Wales
William Child	29 May 1920	Gunner – Royal Artillery Service No. 980677	Fossoli of Carpi camp, near Modena, Italy (Camp No. 73). Transferred to Sankt Johann im Pongau, Austria (Camp No 317)	Returned to UK at the end of the War. Died 2005, Chichester.
Jack Crossley	1 June 1920	Sergeant – Coldstream Guards Service No. 2662444	Pupping, Austria (Camp No. 398). Prisoner of War No. 8440.	Returned to UK at the end of the War Died 1989, Claro
Derek Heaton Furness	24 April 1920	Sergeant – Flight Engineer, R.A.F. Service No. 571405	Stalag Lamsdorf (Camp 344), Poland. Furness' Prisoner of War number was 25640.	Returned to UK at the end of the War. Died 2010, Leeds
Jack Ineson	28 July 1917	Lieutenant – Royal Northumberland Fusiliers	Captured by Japanese at fall of Singapore , February 1942. 3 years in a Japanese POW camp.	Returned to UK at the end of the War. Died 1970
Margery Jennings (née Hellewell)	10 November 1908	Civilian - Nurse, Medical Auxiliary Service	Taken prisoner by the Japanese on Bangka Island, off Sumatra, in mid-February1942. Interned in various camps	Died 12 May 1945 Loebok Lingau (Sumatra)
James Edward Mason	10 May 1917	Gunner - Royal Artillery, 122 Field Regiment Service No. 963864	He was taken prisoner by the Japanese in Malaya and died from malnutrition in December 1943.	Died 27 December 1943 Kanchanaburi War Cemetery

Frank Newhouse	25 September 1924	Private – Anti-tank Platoon, Support Company, 10th Parachute Battalion Service No. 14557569	Prisoner of war camp at Limburg. three prisoner of war camps, including one at Dresden POW No. 14188	Freed from the POW camp at Dresden, in March 1945 by the Russians. Returned home May 1945. Died 2009, Wootton Bassett.
Geoffrey Elliott Thompson	10 January 1920	Aircraftsman 2nd Class – R.A.F.V.R. Service No. 1356432	He was reported missing in Singapore, and later known to be a prisoner-of-war in Japanese hands.	Died in captivity in Java – 8 November 1943. Ambon War Cemetery, Indonesia
John Francis Stansfield Walter	25 April 1922	Sergeant – Royal Electrical and Mechanical Engineers Service No. 7634808	Taken prisoner by the Japanese in Borneo. His relatives had received postcards indicating that he was still alive, but unfortunately he died of starvation shortly before the end of the war	Died 6 August 1945 Labuan War Cemetery
Douglas Whiteley	19 October 1913	Driver – Corporal – Royal Army Service Corps Service No. T/133691	Fossoli of Carpi Camp (PoW Camp no73), near Modena in Italy: moved to Stalag 357, Oerbke, near Fallingbostel, Lower Saxony, North West Germany, POW No. 247105.	Returned to UK after the War Died 1992, Bradford

The prisoners who suffered the worst conditions and hardship were those who were forced to build the Burma-Siam railway. PoWs and Asian labourers worked side by side to build the 260-mile railroad by hand. They worked from dawn to dusk, ten days on and one day off, moving earth, building bridges, blasting through mountains and laying track. They survived on a meagre diet of rice and vegetables; illness, malnutrition and disease were common. Of the 61,000 prisoners put to work on the railroad, 13,000 died.

The Japanese ignored the terms of the Geneva Convention. Escape attempts were rare, and those who did try to escape were executed in front of other prisoners. Failure to comply with instructions would merit a beating. Prisoners were forced to learn Japanese in order to understand the commands they were given. The daily roll call involved prisoners calling out their prisoner number in Japanese.

At the end of the War when surviving prisoners were released the lack of food had transformed them into walking skeletons. Mental illness affected prisoners who had been traumatised by the brutality of the guards.

Robert Peter Geoffrey Barker (1918-2006)

The *'Otliensian'* (*Volume XXVI, Spring 1944*), reported that *'Sergeant R. Peter G. Barker is a prisoner of war in Japanese hands.'* The *Summer 1945* issue of the School Magazine expressed the hope that:

'While we cannot hope that these words will be read by those whose names appear below, we wish to remember especially the five Old Otliensians who are prisoners of war in Japanese hands'.

Included in the list was

- ***Sergeant R. P. G. Barker, Royal Northumberland Fusiliers***

Peter Barker (born 22 March 1918) entered Prince Henry's Grammar School at ten years of age on 25 April 1928 (Form I). He had been educated previously at Miss Barret's Private School in Otley. His father, Peter Raymond Barker (1893-1948), was a leather manufacturer, born in Otley, and the family lived at 'Thorncroft' on Burras Lane, Otley. Peter married Margaret E. Clayton in 1915, the marriage being registered in Leeds. Robert was the middle child of three; his sisters Jean and Margaret were born in 1916 and 1925 respectively.

Robert's only mention in the *'Otliensian'* (*Volume XI, Summer 1929*) was third place in the Egg and Spoon Race (Forms I & II). He left school on 23 December 1931 (Form Upper 3B), when his family left the district.

The report that he was *'missing'* was published in the *'Wharfedale and Airedale Observer'* on 10 April 1942:

FORMER OTLEY BOY

'News has been received at Otley, that Peter Barker, the only son of Mr and Mrs. P. R. Barker, formerly of Otley, and now of Fixby, Huddersfield, is among the missing in Malaya. He is a sergeant in the Tank Corps, and it is believed he was serving in Singapore at the time of the capitulation. Sergeant Barker was born in Otley, and is a grandson of the late Mr Robert Barker, of Cambridge House, who was associated with the leather works of William Barker and Sons Ltd.'

His service number was 1463232 and he may have been a member of the 9th Battalion of the Royal Northumberland Fusiliers that landed in Singapore a few days before the fall of the island, and fought a brief but violent battle before the island fell to the Japanese.

The fall of Singapore to the Japanese on 15 February 1942 is regarded as one of the greatest defeats in the history of the British army. Singapore, an island at the southern end of the Malay Peninsula was a vital, strategic military base, and many considered it impregnable. The surrender of Singapore showed the Allies that the Japanese army was powerful and led to three years of misery and appalling treatment for the Commonwealth and British soldiers who were caught there and moved to PoW camps.

The Japanese advance through the Malay Peninsula took everyone by surprise. The Japanese army moved so quickly that the British forces had no time to re-group. The British believed that any attack on Singapore would come from the sea, and all the defences were on the seaward side. But the Japanese attacked through the jungle and mangrove swamps of the Malay Peninsula, and their troops were ordered to take no prisoners because to do so would slow up their advance. There was little aerial support because the R.A.F. had lost nearly all its front-line aeroplanes from Japanese attacks on airfields in Singapore. Britain's naval presence in Singapore was strong and included the battleship *'Prince of Wales'* and the Battle cruiser *'Repulse'*. However, on 10 December 1941 both ships were sunk by repeated attacks from Japanese torpedo bombers.

Only the Army could stop the Japanese advance on Singapore. 90,000 British, Indian and Australian troops were ranged against 65,000 Japanese, but the Japanese were experienced and battle-hardened, and many of the Allied troops had never seen combat. The Allies were soundly beaten at the Battle of Jitra on 11/12 December 1941, and retreated towards Singapore. Captured, wounded Allied soldiers were killed where they lay; those who were uninjured, but had surrendered were also murdered; locals who had helped the Allies were tortured before being murdered. This brutality of the Japanese shocked the British, but the effectiveness of the Japanese advance led to the capture of the Malaysian capital, Kuala Lumpur, on 11 January 1942.

On 31 January 1942, the Allied forces withdrew across the causeway separating Singapore from Malaysia. This was to be their last stand. On 8 February 1942, 23,000 Japanese soldiers attacked Singapore, and Singapore fell to the Japanese army on 15 February 1942. The Japanese took 100,000 men captive in Singapore. Many had just arrived and had not fired a bullet in anger. 9,000 of these men died building the Burma-Siam railway. The people of Singapore fared worse; many were of Chinese origin and were slaughtered by the Japanese.

Peter Barker was one of these men, a Sergeant in the Tank Corps, when he was captured on 15 February 1942 and placed in a camp in Thailand. He was liberated on 2 September 1945 and returned to England. His parents, then living in Fixby, Huddersfield, received a cable, dated 17 September 1945 that stated *'Arrived safely at Colombo. Hope to be home soon.'*

Peter married Lula M. Hazeldon in 1947, in Liskeard, Cornwall, and the couple had two children – Raymond P. Barker (born 1949, birth registered in Huddersfield), and Elaine

M. Barker (born 1953, birth registered in Wharfedale). Robert Peter Geoffrey Barker died in 2006, his death being registered in Bridgend, Wales.

William Child (1920-2005)

Gunner William Child (born 29 May 1920), Royal Artillery (Service No. 980677) was reported missing in the Middle East in 1942, but was later discovered to have become a prisoner of war in Italian hands. The *'Yorkshire Evening Post'* (14 July 1942) announced that he was missing:

W. Child.

'Gunner William Child (22), Royal Artillery: mother lives Ash Tree House, Arthington. Is an old boy of Otley Prince Henry's Grammar School and played cricket with the Arthington club. He was a gardener at Harewood House.'

William Child attended Otley National School (1930-1932) before being admitted to Prince Henry's Grammar School on 13 September 1932 (Form Upper 3A). At that time he lived at Ash Tree House, Arthington and his father, Robert William Child (1894-1972), was a Clerk. Robert married Annie Tempest in 1913 and they had four children – Stanley (born 1915), Harry (born 1916), Douglas (born 1918) and William. William left P.H.G.S. on 29 July 1936 (Form Lower 5A).

He was a gunner in the Royal Artillery and had been in the Middle East since April 1941.

He was a prisoner of war at Fossoli of Carpi camp, near Modena, Italy (P.O.W. Camp No. 73). The Royal Italian Army established the camp in May 1942 for the British, South African and New Zealand military personnel captured in military operations in North Africa. It operated until 8 September 1943 – on the morning of 9 September 1943 the German army occupied the camp, and the prisoners were deported to Germany. From 5 December 1943 to 15 March 1944 the camp became a concentration camp for the internment of Jews. During this period the first two trains left for Auschwitz.

William Child was transferred to Sankt Johann im Pongau – then called Markt Pongau - camp in northwest Austria, close to Salzburg. (Camp No. 317 – Stalag XVIII C). Construction began on this camp in March 1941, which was built to accommodate around 10,000 prisoners. By the end of 1941, the number of prisoners of war had risen to 30,000. The prisoners of war were mostly from France and Russia, many of whom were forced, because of the overcrowding, to live in tents. The prisoners of war had to perform forced labour in nearby factories and in agriculture. The Russian prisoners were exposed to particularly harsh conditions, and the majority of the 4,000 prisoners who died were Russian.

Towards the end of the War, as the Russians advanced west, the Germans decided to move as many British prisoners as possible from the camps in eastern Austria further west into the Salzburg area. They were to move towards Markt Pongau, or even further west towards Landek. Most of these British prisoners were marched on foot from the area around Wolfsberg to Markt Pongau, a distance of 212 km., in 13 days.

The following extract is from the recollections of prisoner of war W. Wynne Mason (***www.stalag18a.org.uk***):

'Although some marching columns did not get as far as Markt Pongau, a sufficient number arrived to bring the numbers to nearly 13,000. Since the capacity of the camp was reckoned by the German authorities as four to five thousand, it needs little imagination to picture the overcrowding of sleeping accommodation and sanitary facilities. A medical officer comments that there were 'sick men lying on the floor in every corner of the hospital.' Though Red Cross supplies were on hand they were insufficient to cope with such a mass of men for any length of time, and the food situation could soon have become serious again. On 2 May the German guards were withdrawn, though fighting was still going on in the adjacent areas where the German forces had refused to capitulate. As in most camps, plans had been made months before for such a situation and a properly organised scheme was immediately put into operation. But by 6 May it was apparent that the controlling of the cosmopolitan mass of men then in camp was becoming increasingly difficult. On that day several hundred prisoners broke out of camp and looted a German goods train. A Swiss representative who had been stationed at the camp for some time reported that order was re-established by the camp leaders without any serious incident with civilians. But it would have been unwise to have risked a repetition. A medical officer was immediately sent up to Salzburg to contact the American forces, and a party of American troops arrived the following day. From then on the food problems at the camp were solved by distributing supplies of American army rations, and arrangements were made for the speedy evacuation of the released prisoners, of whom 700 were New Zealanders. British liaison officers, one of them a New Zealander, were in the camp by 17 May, and on the 20th the ex-prisoners began to move by lorry to the Salzburg airfield for the flight to France and on to England. Most of our men from Markt Pongau and adjacent Arbeitskommandos seem to have reached England by the end of the month.'

Like most of the parents of local prisoners of war, William's mother was a member of the '*Wharfedale Prisoners of War Club*'. When they attended meetings, members would give money to fund the parcels sent to their relatives abroad. Mrs. Child is recorded as regularly giving 10s, and on occasion £1. It must have been difficult for her to attend meetings, living in Arthington, and making donations would have caused some financial concern when her son was not at home to contribute to the household income.

When William returned home he, along with other released prisoners of war, was invited by the Wharfedale PoW Club to a tea for ex-prisoners, their relatives and friends. At this gathering he reported that he was a non-smoker and used to give his parcels of cigarettes to the other prisoners.

The *'Otliensian'* (*Volume XXVII, Summer 1945*) reported on William Child's safe return to the U.K. He died in 2005, his death being registered in Chichester.

Jack Crossley (1920-1989)

The *'London Gazette'*, (22 July 1943) contained details of the award of the Military Medal to Guardsman Jack Crossley (Service No. 2662444), 3rd Battalion Coldstream Guards, attached to the Long Range Desert Group. The theatre of operations was named as *'Middle East Special Operations and Escapes.'*

War Office; 22nd July 1943.
The KING has been graciously pleased to approve
the following awards in recognition of gallant and
distinguished services in the field: —
The Military Medal.
No. 2662444 Guardsman Jack Crossley, Coldstream Guards.

The *'Otliensian'* (*Vol. XXV, Summer 1943*) contained the following comment:

'Corporal Jack Crossley, of The Crossways, Otley, has been awarded the M.M. for what he calls a "job" in January during the North African fighting. Corporal Crossley thus earns the distinction of being the first Otley man to win this award in the present war.'

The recommendation for the award of the Military Medal reads as follows:

'Gdsn. Crossley was the navigator of a patrol which, in Jan. 1943, was detailed to carry out a topographical recce of the country north and west of BUERAT, to prepare "going" maps for the subsequent advance of the 8th Army. The country was alive with enemy patrols, and much of the recce had to be done at night. Although the patrol was frequently chased by armoured cars, Gdsn. Crossley carried on with his navigations with perfect calmness, and was eventually able to produce an accurate "going" map of the whole area. Later he was of use as a guide to a part of the 8th Army during its advance to TRIPOLI. During his next operation, a recce of the area south of the CHOTT DJERID, Gdsn. Crossley's Patrol were attacked at night by a band of well armed Arabs, who caused some casualties to men and vehicles. Crossley displayed great gallantry in acting

as a decoy to draw fire to himself, while the rest of the Patrol got their vehicles unstuck and on the move. His work has always been of the highest order.'

A note on the recommendation reads:

'Awarded M.M. 22.7.43. B.L. Montgomery, G.O.C. Eighth Army, signed the recommendation.'

The Spring 1944 issue of the School Magazine reported that Sergeant Jack Crossley M.M. previously reported missing in Leros, *(Greek island in the Dodecanese)* is now reported a prisoner of war in German hands. He was interned in a camp in Pupping, near Linz. Austria (Camp No. 398). His Prisoner of War Number was 8440. He was later moved to Stalag 378 in Germany, and it was from here that his parents received a letter in November 1943 in which *'he writes cheerfully, and asks his parents to send him his swimming trunks and some civilian clothes.'* – reported in *'Wharfedale and Airedale Observer'*, 4 February 1944.

Another letter, to Mrs. Booth, secretary of the Otley and Wharfedale P.O.W. Club, and sent from Stalag 170 XVII, was published in the *'Wharfedale and Airedale Observer'* on 9 March 1945:

'Today I have had a very pleasant surprise. A cigarette parcel arrived from the P.O.W. Club addressed to me. I don't know what I have done to deserve it, or how I may repay your kindness, but I may state that it arrived at a very appropriate time. We were all absolutely out of smoking material (and that is a very inclusive term.) Every cigarette here is absolutely precious, and not only do I send my most grateful thanks, but my friends, who naturally also benefit, send their thanks in addition. I'm swelled beyond recognition with the importance of belonging to such a local community, which supports its members to this extent. Am I proud of Wharfedale to-day! I'll say I am!'

SERGT. J. CROSSLEY, M.M.

The *Summer 1945* issue of the *'Otliensian'* announced his safe return to the U.K.

Jack Crossley (born 1 June 1920) entered Prince Henry's Grammar School on 10 September 1931 (Form Upper 3B) following the award of a West Riding County Minor Scholarship. He attended North Parade School from 1924-1931. His father, Ernest Crossley, was a labourer and, at that time, the family lived at 4, The Green, Otley. In 1918 Ernest Crossley married Florrie Pickles in Wharfedale.

In the Scout Ambulance Competition held on 18 March 1933, the Parish Church Troop won the shield presented by N.L. Frazer Esq. M.A., the ex-headmaster of Ilkley Grammar School. Four Prince Henrys' scholars were members of the successful team –

Jack Crossley, Norman Graville, R. S. Imeson and M. Smith – the first three being in the same Form. He played Rugby for Otley, the Otliensians and the Coldstream Guards, and was a good swimmer.

In 1935 Crossley won the prestigious '*Fanny Barker Memorial Art Prize*.' In 1936 he passed his School Certificate examination before leaving school on 29 July 1936 to take up employment as an electrical engineer. In 1945 he married Joan Pickard and they had two daughters, Lyn (born 1946) and Jill (born 1947).

He volunteered for the Coldstream Guards in June 1940, going out to the Middle East a year later as a signaller. In February 1942 he transferred to the Long Range Desert Group, employed by General Alexander to create chaos behind enemy lines. Some idea of the work of this group was published in the '*Wharfedale and Airedale Observer*' on 17 December 1943:

'Details of this invaluable group were only released after the fighting in North Africa ended. The men, few in number, were the pick of the seasoned desert fighters of the Eighth Army, and did a very important job in disrupting enemy communications and keeping him in a state of increasing "jumpiness". They used fast motor transport, well-armed with machine guns, and moved by night swiftly and silently. The patrols swept down upon aerodromes, lorry parks or isolated posts, and the men got to work with sticks of dynamite, hand grenades and automatic weapons. They would inflict as much damage as possible and then make off.

'Cpl. Crossley said their work was entirely behind enemy lines, and consisted of road watching for signs of an increase in traffic, German or Italian. They were so close that they could read the numbers on the trucks and also see whether the men were Germans or Italians. Such a job usually lasted a fortnight. The patrol would then return to base, 1000 miles from Cairo. The trip would be about 800 miles in enemy territory with a constant risk of being spotted and 'strafed' from the air or ground. A trip might be anything up to 2000 miles and up to three months in duration. Sufficient food and water supplies were carried for this period, and each vehicle was equipped with armament against air attack. The men wore tropical kit, but on operations, native dress. In the photograph, Cpl. Crossley is wearing the Keffiyeh, the headdress of the Bedouins.

'Cpl. Crossley passed out as a navigator and was in charge of a car. In July 1942 he contracted malaria and was taken ill, 200 miles out in the desert. He was flown by Blenheim to a base hospital and recovered. An officer took command of his truck, and shortly afterwards an Italian plane dive-bombed and machine-gunned it. The truck was burnt out, the officer killed, and Jack's driver seriously wounded. He was eventually brought home to Scotland.

'Before the Germans withdrew from Tripoli Cpl. Crossley went into the city and "borrowed" sheets of the official notepaper of the 20th Italian Armoured Headquarters Corps. On another occasion he bought some Tunisian stamps at a post office in a town occupied by the Germans.

'When the 1st Army landed in North Africa the 8th were over 800 miles away, and as a desert scout, Cpl. Crossley went through enemy occupied territory from Kufra oasis, Ytipoli, Tozeur, Constantine to Algiers (where he met Signaller Granger of Weston) and back.

'The patrols raided desert airfields to destroy axis aircraft and he was in one of these raids when they had to fight their way out. He has been in Morocco and also went on a 1000-mile journey on the Nile.

'Their work in North Africa done, Cpl. Crossley went on an intensive and strenuous course in mountain fighting and learned to ski at the Middle East Ski School for British troops, 7,000ft up in the Cedar Mountains, Lebanon.'

J. Crossley.

Another aspect of the war, and probably the character of Corporal Crossley, was shown in a letter from a Middle East desert oasis to a friend, published in the '*Wharfedale and Airedale Observer*' on 19 June 1942:

'He writes the facilities for swimming are exceptionally good where he is stationed at present.

"We have about ten swimming pools, all about 20 yards across, and they are up to 30 feet deep. The water is pure and clear as crystal, and the temperature about 75 degrees to 80 degrees. This oasis is about six miles long, enclosed by desert, and a huge wall of hills like the Colorado Canyon. It is like a South Sea island. The pools and village supposed to have been built by Cleopatra."

'At the time of writing he states there was no real danger, "except from malaria, snakes, stranding, thirst and heat stroke. 'Course, if we are spotted, things get rough. It is a bit similar to a rugby scrum – kick hard and gallop. This morning we killed a snake and yesterday a chap was bitten by a cobra. These cobras are 7 feet long, and the beetles are as common as flies. They are fully two inches long and about five inches wing-spread, and they buzz about after dark like Stukas. The flies are persistent again with the increasing heat."

'He adds that he is 'quite a colour' and has grown a three-inch beard and a moustache.'

He was liberated by American Forces, and came home on 10 June 1945. He was later employed as an Instructor at a Coldstream Guards Unit in High Wycombe. He was presented with the Military Medal by the King, at an investiture at Buckingham Palace on 20 November 1945.

Jack Crossley died in 1989, his death being registered in Claro.

Derek Heaton Furness (1920-2010)

Sergeant Derek Heaton Furness was born in Lancaster on 24 April 1920. He lived at 1 Kirklands Avenue, Baildon. His father, Harry H. Heaton (1888-1959) was a Wool Merchant. Harry was born in Bradford and in the 1911 Census was listed as a Yarn Salesman. In 1914 Harry married Maggie A. Barker. After attending Mrs. Nicholson's Private School in Baildon, Derek entered Form 1 at P.H.G.S. in April 1929. He left from Form Upper 5B in November 1936 to join the R.A.F. via the apprenticeship scheme, and initially was on the maintenance staff. (Service No. 571405).

Academically, he was awarded fourth prize in Form 1 and third prize in Form 2. In the 1935 Athletic Sports he finished 4th in the 100 yards (15-16 age group).

He was reported missing from an operational flight over Germany in August 1942. In September 1942 it was confirmed that he was a prisoner of war in German hands.

The '*Otliensian*' (*Vol. XXV, Autumn 1942*) reported that:

'Sergt-Flight Engineer Derek Heaton Furness R.A.F., second son of Mr and Mrs. H. H. Furness of 1 Kirkland Avenue, Baildon, previously reported missing from an operational flight over Germany, is a prisoner of war in German hands. Sergt. Derek Furness was mentioned in despatches a few months ago (January 1942) for rescuing the pilot and observer from a burning plane. ('London Gazette,' 1 January 1942)

In *Vol. XXVII, Summer 1945*, it was announced that:

'On behalf of all Old Scholars, the Staff and members of the School, we extend warm greetings to the following on their safe return after being prisoners of war in German hands:

- ***Warrant Officer D. H. Furness R.A.F.'***

His homecoming was noted in the '*Wharfedale and Airedale Observer', 8 June 1945*:

'Warrant Officer Derek Heaton Furness, second son of Mr and Mrs. H. H. Furness of 1 Kirklands Avenue, Baildon, who was mentioned in despatches for rescuing his pilot and observer from a burning plane, has arrived home after three years in a German prison camp. Warrant Officer Furness, who is a member of the Caterpillar Club**, was reported missing after an operational flight over Germany in 1942. He wrote later from a prisoner of war camp in Germany saying that he was safe.'*

**Clearly, he had been promoted to Warrant-Officer while in the P.O.W. Camp.*

***The **Caterpillar Club** is an informal association of people who have successfully used a parachute to bail out of a disabled aircraft.*

In 1946 he married Dorothy I. Stephenson, the marriage being registered in Wharfedale, and the couple had two children – Sheila (born in 1949) and Barbara (born in 1954).

He was based at R.A.F. East Moor, which was located near Helmsley, North Yorkshire, and was a sub-station of R.A.F. Linton-on-Ouse. He was a Sergeant in 158 Squadron when on 6 August 1942 his Halifax II bomber (W1215) crashed in Holland after an operational flight to attack Bochum. The crew had to bale out of the disabled plane by parachute. Two of the crew were killed, one evaded capture and the remaining four were captured and taken to Stalag Lamsdorf (Camp 344), Poland. Furness' Prisoner of War number was 25640.

'158 Squadron: Halifax II W1215 NP-C Op. Bochum 5-6 August 1942. 'T/o 2213 East Moor. Shotdown by a night-fighter (Lt August Geiger, III. /NJG1) and crashed 0128 at Oldebroek (Gelderland), 12 km. NNW of Epe, Holland. The two airmen who died are buried in Oldebroek General Cemetery. It is believed P/0 Phillips R.A.A.F. was trying to crash land in order to save P/0 Marshall, who had been wounded and could not bale out. Sadly, structural failure occurred and the Halifax plunged down, out of control.'

Name	Rank	Service/No	Home	Outcome
Clive Henry Phillips	Pilot Officer: Pilot	R.A.A.F. 402537	Mosman, New South Wales, Australia	Died – buried in Oldebroek General Cemetery, Netherlands
Leslie Vincent Harvey	Pilot Officer: Navigator	R.A.A.F. 400239	Middle Bright, Victoria, Australia	Prisoner of War
Derek Heaton Furness	Sergeant: Flight Engineer	R.A.F. 571405	Lancaster, Lancashire	Prisoner of War
Earl George Price	Sergeant: Bomb Aimer	R.C.A.F. R/84592	Canterbury, New Brunswick, Canada	Evaded Capture
Warwick Arthur Thompson	Sergeant: Mid Upper Gunner	R.A.F. 1310697	Rochford, Essex	Prisoner of War
Joseph Albert Byrne	Sergeant: Wireless Operator/ Air Gunner	R.A.F. 954513	West Ham, Essex	Prisoner of War
John Edwin Marshall	Pilot Officer: Rear Gunner	R.A.F.V.R. 117005		Died – buried in Oldebroek General Cemetery, Neth.

('RAF Bomber Command losses of the Second World War 1942' – W R Chorley)

Sergeant Price evaded capture with help from the Comete Line*. He was back in the U.K. in November 1942 and returned to Canada the following month. Pilot Officer Harvey was later taken to Stalag Luft III where he was held for two and a half years. He was at the Camp during the "*Great Escape*" and the murder of 53 escapees. He returned home to his native Australia in September 1945 after liberation.

**The Comete Line was a resistance group in Belgium and France that helped allied soldiers and airmen get back to Britain. The line started in Brussels where men were fed, clothed and given false identity papers, before being hidden in attics and cellars until being guided by a network of people through occupied France, into neutral Spain and back home via Gibraltar. The Comete Line was created by Andrée de Jongh, a young Belgian woman.*

The same aircraft had made a three-engine landing in the early hours of 27 July 1942 after being attacked by enemy aircraft over Germany having completed a bombing raid on Hamburg. The crew was the same as above except for the Rear Gunner. The aircraft was repaired on site at East Moor and was back in service by 5 August 1942.

Derek Heaton Furness died on 17 September 2010, age 90. The following notice was published in the *'Yorkshire Post'* on 23 September 2010:

'FURNESS DEREK HEATON Peacefully on September 17, at Leeds General Infirmary, aged 90 years. Much loved husband of the late Ina, a very dear father of Sheila and Barbara. Will be sadly missed by all.'

The following information about Lamsdorf Stalag VIIIB 344 Prisoner of War Camp is taken from the web-site (***www.lamsdorf.com***):

'Stalag VIIIB Lamsdorf was a large, German prisoner of war camp located in Poland, near the small town of Lamsdorf. Initially the camp was built to house British and French prisoners in the First World War, though there had been a prisoner camp there during the Franco-Prussian War (1870-71). More than 100,000 prisoners from Australia, Belgium, Britain, Canada, France, Greece, New Zealand, the Netherlands, Poland, South Africa, the Soviet Union, Yugoslavia and the USA passed through this camp. In 1941 a separate camp was set up close by to house the Soviet prisoners. The Soviet Army reached the camp on 17 March 1945.

'In January 1945, as the Soviet armies resumed their offensive and advanced into Germany, many of the prisoners were marched westward in groups of 200 to 300 in the so-called 'Death March'. Many of them died from the bitter cold and exhaustion. The lucky ones got far enough west to be liberated by the American army. The unlucky ones were 'liberated' by the Soviets who held on to them as virtual hostages for several more months. Many of them were finally repatriated towards the end of 1945 through the Black Sea port of Odessa.'

More details about the 'Death March' (also known as the 'Long March') can be found in the book ***'THE LAST ESCAPE - THE UNTOLD STORY OF ALLIED POWS 1944-56'*** **by John Nichol and Tony Rennell.**

The fact that Derek Heaton Furness returned to Britain in 1945, makes it likely that he took part on the above march.

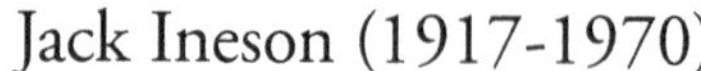

Jack Ineson (1917-1970)

Jack Ineson was born on 28 July 1917 in Hunslet. After attending Otley, North Parade Elementary School he entered Prince Henry's on 12 September 1928 (Form Upper 3B). He lived at 143 Gay Lane, Otley, and his father, Thomas Robert Ineson (1888-1945) was employed as a Tailor's Cutter. Thomas married Eliza A. Kirkby in 1915. On entry to P.H.G.S. Jack was awarded a West Riding County Minor Scholarship. He passed his School Certificate in 1933 and his Higher School Certificate in 1935 and left school on 29 July 1936 (Sixth form) to enter Durham University. He was awarded an Entrance Scholarship (£35) in Geography at Durham University to add to the award of a County Major Scholarship. The '*Otliensian*' noted that:

'We expect excellent things of him when he goes into residence in the autumn to read for a degree as the first part of his preparation for the ministry of the Church of England. Our congratulations and best wishes!'

His original intent at Durham was to pursue a theological career, but he later transferred to geology and graduated in 1939 before joining the Royal Northumberland Fusiliers. His unit was captured by the Japanese in Singapore, and his health was affected permanently by the privation and hardship suffered during imprisonment. He was repatriated in 1945, and returned briefly to Durham before joining the Geological Survey in 1946.

One of the most noticeable features of schools such as Prince Henry's was the enthusiasm shown by many pupils in the extra-curricular activities on offer. It was certainly the case that Jack Ineson threw himself whole-heartedly into these pursuits over the eight years he was at the school.

His contemporaries in Form Upper IIIB, who entered the school at the start of the 1928 Autumn Term are listed below:

Upper IIIB	Bairstow A., Broadbelt W. W., Clapham J. S., Clarkson G. A., Dodgshon H., Firth J. D., Goldsborough H., Hindle Charles N., Ineson J., Kay Ronald, Mason J. E., Payne K. J., Towers J., Wear E. F., Wilkinson C. A.

All fifteen of these boys joined up to fight in the Second World War. John Stanley Clapham, Ronald Kay, James Edward Mason and Eric Wear died in service.

Jack Ineson was clearly gifted academically and won several form prizes, though there was clear competition from his form mates, especially Joseph Towers.

Joseph Towers was also in competition with Jack Ineson in the annual Athletic Sports, though as they got older Joseph's name disappears, (apart from a comeback in 1935 to win the High Jump!) leaving the field clear for Jack.

Form	First	Second	Third	Fourth
Upper IIIB	R. Kay	K. J. Payne	J. Ineson	J. Towers
Lower IVA	J. Towers	K. J. Payne	J. Ineson	R . Kay
Upper IVA	J. Towers	J. Ineson	K. J. Payne	
Lower VA	J. Towers	J. Ineson	K. J. Payne	
Upper VA	J. Towers	K. J. Payne	J. Ineson	K. Greenwood

In 1936 he was awarded the Old Scholars' Prize for the best English Essay. He was also a prefect.

1929:	First	Second	Third	Fourth
100 yards (under 12)	J. Towers (White)	C. MacDonald (White)	J. Ineson (Blue)	L. Harrison (Red)
1930:				
Long Jump (Under 14)	Cooper J. S. (14ft. 7ins.)	Clarkson G. A.	Ineson J. and Thornton T.	
1931:				
100 yards (Under 14)	Ineson J. (12 2/5th seconds)	Newstead J.	Harrison C. L.	Harrison A.
220 yards (Under 14)	Ineson J. (32 1/10th seconds)	Newstead J.	Harrison C. L.	Kerby C.
High Jump (Under 14)	Towers J. (4ft.)	Ineson J. and Newstead J.		Jowett I.
Long Jump (Under 14)	Towers J. (13ft. 1in.)	Mann J.	Ineson J.	
Junior Individual Champion	Ineson J. (7½ pts.)	Towers J. (6 pts.)		
1933:				
100 yards (Open)	C. Hobday (11 1/5 seconds)	C. Cooper	J. Ineson	T. Thornton
220 yards (Open)	C. Hobday (27 1/5 seconds)	C. Cooper	J. Ineson	S. Labram
High Jump (Open)	T. E. Thornton (4ft. 10ins.)	G. A. Clarkson	L. Harrison	J. Ineson
1934:				
100 yards (Open)	C. Cooper (10 4/5 seconds)	T. E. Thornton	S. G. Labram	J. Ineson
440 yards (Open)	T. E. Thornton (59 seconds)	S. G. Labram	J. D. Waye	J. Ineson

High Jump (Open)	T. E. Thornton (4ft. 9ins.)	C. Cooper & J. Towers		J. Ineson & C. A. Wilkinson
Long Jump (Open)	C. Cooper (18ft. 1in.)	J. Ineson & T. E. Thornton		S. E. Cruise
1935:				
100 yards (Open)	Thornton T. E.	Sully A. P.	Ineson J.	Kerby C. W.
220 yards (open)	Sully A. P.	Thornton T. E.	Kerby C. W.	Ineson J.
High Jump (Open)	Towers J.	Sully A. P. & Thornton T. E		Hudson F., Ineson J. & Payne K. J.
Long Jump (Open)	Hudson F.	Thornton T. E.	Ineson J.	Sully A. P. & Kerby C. W.
1936:				
100 yards (Open)	J. Ineson (11 2/5 seconds)	A. P. Sully	J. E. Garside	K. G. Payne
220 yards (Open)	A.P. Sully (28 seconds)	J. Ineson	K. G. Payne	J. Mann
440 yards (Open)	A. P. Sully (64 2/5 seconds)	J. Ineson	K. G. Payne	J. Mann
Long Jump (Open)	J. Ineson (18ft 2in)	A. P. Sully	J. Mann	P. Walker
High Jump (Open)	K. G. Payne (4ft 9in)	J. E. Garside & J. Ineson		A. P. Sully
Individual Championship Boys Senior	A. P. Sully (13½pts.)	J. Ineson (11 pts.)		

Athletics was not Jack's strength, though he showed his competitive spirit each year by entering and picking up points for his House. However, he did eventually succeed in winning two events in the 1936 Sports and being runner-up as Individual Champion to A.P. Sully, another pupil who was to lose his life in the War.

Jack Ineson's main sporting passion was Rugby. His first appearance for the First XV was against Ashville College on 4 February 1933, and the following match report was published in the '*Otliensian*' (*Vol. XV, Lent 1933*)

ASHVILLE COLLEGE Away 4 February:

'A very strong wind blowing along the pitch rather spoilt the handling of the backs, so play became confined to the forwards, of which the School's were rather more dangerous in loose rushes. Playing against the wind in the first half, School were kept on the defence most of the time, and were unfortunate to lose the services of Clapham, who had been playing well up till the time of his injury. After half time, School were on the attack most of the time, and on several occasions had bad luck in not scoring. At last, they were rewarded, after a good cut-through by Underwood, who, on reaching

the full-back, passed to Kay, who scored under the posts. J. Ineson played very well on his first appearance in the first team; other good forwards were Labram, Whitaker and Hobson.'

His end of season critique read *'Has improved greatly of late. Tall and fairly fast, he requires more dash and vigour'.* He was awarded his Rugby colours in December 1934. At the end of the 1933-34 season he was said to have *'Started the season well, but has not developed as much as expected. He is tall and has speed, but is a slow starter'.*

His end of season player criticism for 1934-1935 noted that Ineson *'Is a good, hard-working forward, useful in the line-out and with a dangerous burst in the open.'*

Some extracts from the match reports in the 'Otliensian' included:

13 October 1934: School 30 points: Morley Grammar School 0	*'School were definitely superior in all phases of the game. The forwards gave the finest display so far. Garside hooked well in the set scrums, while Smith, Labram and Ineson were always up with play, and Whitley impressed favourably in his first appearance.'*
2 February 1935 School 42 points: Thornton Grammar School 0	*'For this game Labram and Garside returned to the pack, and Sully was also included at the full-back position. These arrangements proved to be highly successful. With a large share of the ball, due to Garside's good hooking, the three-quarters were able to find the weak spots in the Thornton defence. Rigg caused much anxiety with his dummy and clever cut through. Kerby and Ineson were always in the front of the attack, whilst Labram showed great skill at loose forward. Sully handled the ball well, tackled determinedly and kicked with precision.'*
13 February 1935 School 16 points: Yorkshire Wanderers 0	*'In this, the hardest contested game of the season, School were ably assisted by the valuable services of three Otley players – Mr T. Kilmartin at full-back, Mr H. Evans, the School physical training instructor, at left-centre; and Mr F. A. Smith, an old scholar, as leader of the pack. Great credit is reflected on the pack as a whole, and especially on the fine display given by Mr F. A. Smith and Garside as pack leader and hooker respectively. School obtained almost equal possession from the tight scrums, while the advantage in the loose was if anything in favour of School forwards. Labram, Irwin and Ineson were very prominent.'*
16 March 1935: School 16 points: Bingley Grammar School 3 points	*'Garside hooked well in the set scrums, and along with Ineson made good use of height to secure the ball in the line-out. School were rewarded by a try on the touch-line from Garside, following a smart piece of backing up by the forwards, shortly before the interval.'*

Prince Henry's Grammar School First XV Rugby 1933-1934
J. Smith J. Ineson S. A. Irwin D. Waye S. Greenwood Mr Pratt
F. Lofthouse J. Kettlewood
C. A. Wilkinson T. E. Thornton C. Cooper G. Hobson G. Labram S. E. Cruise K. J. Payne
K. Rhodes J. Towers

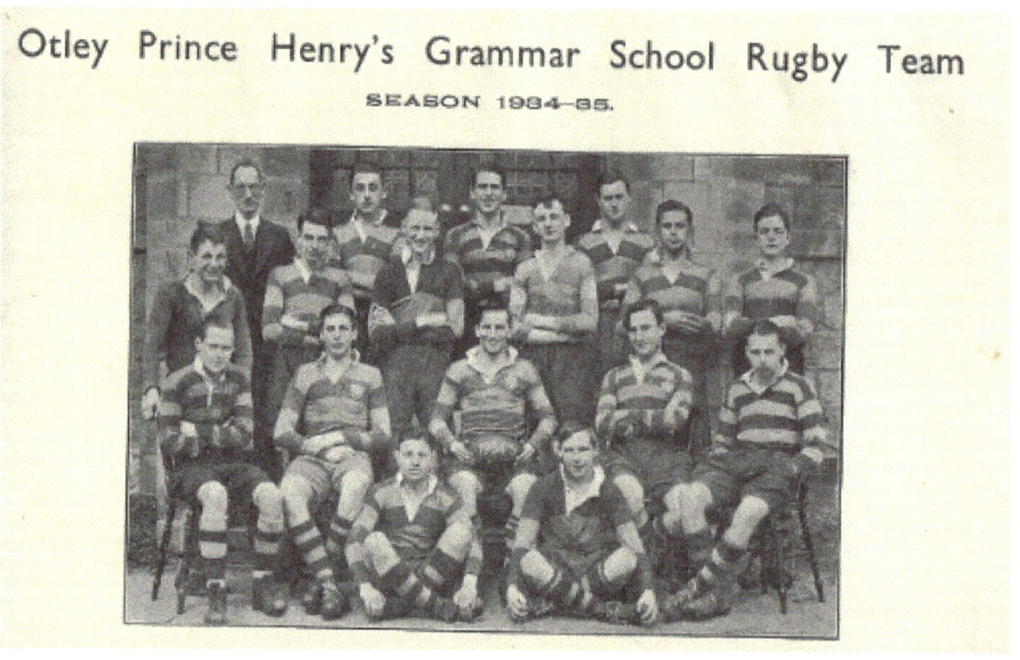

Mr R. Pratt J. V. Offermann S. A. V. Irwin J. Ineson
A. P. Sully C. W. Kerby J. E. Garside R. S. Howard B. F. Palmer K. Whitley
K .Rhodes J. Towers T. E. Thornton (Capt) K. J. Payne E. F. Wear
E. Findlater H. Rigg

In his final season it was said that Ineson *'Has been an excellent forward for two seasons, and his strong running has made him a useful emergency three-quarter.'*

Throughout his school life Jack Ineson was also prominent in the acting field;

Christmas 1929 – Annual School Concert	*'The Junior School opened the programme by presenting five episodes from 'Alice in Wonderland'. Arrayed in excellent costumes, all those who took part contributed towards a very successful performance. J. Ineson gave a clever display as the 'Mad Hatter'.'*
Christmas 1930 – Annual School Concert	*' 'The Swineherd', a short play, which was given several years ago, was again presented and very well received. Marjorie Fozard portrayed the petulant princess of Hans Andersen's fairy tale very well, and Kenneth Payne and Jack Ineson, as emperor and swineherd respectively, gave very creditable performances.'*
Easter 1933 – School Production of *'As You Like It'*	*'In Act II, Scene I, Ineson, as Duke Senior, with the question "Are not these woods more free from peril that the envious court?" strikes the keynote for the rest of the play, that of freedom. The easy passiveness essential to the manner of this character, during his speeches, was rendered by Ineson.'*
Easter 1934 – School Production of *'She Stoops to Conquer.'*	*'Oliver Goldsmith's 'She Stoops to Conquer', a costume play, was revived by the Upper School performance at Easter, and proved very successful, although it has been given here previously.* *The heroine of the play, Kate Hardcastle, is a lively girl with a taste for fun, and Margaret Carr showed that she had caught the spirit of the play in her admirable portrayal of the part. She was well supported by J. Ineson, who succeeded in giving a good portrait of the "modest" Mr Marlow, Kate's suitor, who finds it impossible to converse with any young lady of rank.'*
Easter 1935 - Three one-act plays	*' 'Pickwick v Bardell' brought the programme to an hilarious close. Ineson was good as Mr Winkle, the second witness. He portrayed well a nervous, dandified young man, completely over-awed by the Court, and frightened out of his wits by Buzfuz's questioning.'*

Easter 1936 – Three one-act plays	*"The Bishop's Candlesticks' by Norman McKinnel. An exciting drama, in which the parts of the Bishop and his sister were admirably portrayed by J. Ineson and B. Firth, while K. J. Payne put life and meaning into the Convict's part. Others in the cast were D. Stowe and A. P. Sully.'*

Another area of extra-curricular activity, which was popular, especially with senior students, were the various clubs and societies. Jack Ineson took an active part in the Natural Science Society and the Literary, Historical and Debating Society. He was elected to the Committee of the Natural Science Society in autumn 1932. At the end of the Christmas Term, 1933 he gave a lecture on *'Paper'*:

'He gave very lucid explanations of the various processes involved from the time that the raw materials entered the mills to that when they emerged as finished sheets of paper. He carefully pointed out the differences between the processes used for rags and for wood-pulp, and concluded with a brief account of the manufacture of cardboard. We were unfortunate in not having the epidiascope available, but the lecturer very cleverly sketched various sections of the machinery on the blackboard, and revealed an artistic genius hitherto totally unsuspected. The chairman, J Mann, proposed a vote of thanks to Ineson, and dissolved the meeting.'

He was elected Secretary of the Natural Science Society in October 1934, and at the next meeting he gave a lecture on '*Railways*'.

'A varied collection of lantern slides, kindly lent by the L.N.E.R. Co was shown to illustrate the development of railway engines from the original steam engine invented by George Stephenson to the present day "No 10,000". This series also contrasted the facilities of travelling today and those experienced during the early days of the railways.'

On 7 April 1933 Ineson gave a lecture to the Literary, Historical and Debating Society on '*Otley Parish Church*'.

'Ineson described the position and shape of the church. He then outlined the history of the church, showing that possibly a church had existed since the seventh century. He then illustrated by lantern slides some of the relics found in the church, among which were an old Saxon Cross, and the tombstone of an Ancient British chieftain. Throughout the lecturer revealed a detailed knowledge of his subject. After the questions asked had been answered, the lecture was closed.'

At the first meeting in 1934 a debate was held on the proposition *'That Modern Education is a Fit Preparation for Life'.*

'The proposer of this was Margaret Carr. She was opposed by J. Ineson, and the seconders were M. Dodgshon and Barbara Lewis. The proposers said that modern education developed character and stressed the use in after life of subjects taught

in school. The opposers said that the modern system of "cramming" was injurious to health and stressed the examinations difficulty. There was a good attendance at the meeting, and the result of the voting was an easy victory for the opposers.'

At the meeting held on 5 May 1934, Ineson gave 'a very interesting lecture on '*Scouting*'.

'He showed the development of the movement, pointing out the good work done by the Scouts in the War, and then described the various branches and divisions. The interest of the lecture was greatly increased by the fact that Ineson appeared in uniform and explained why the Scout dress should be chosen as it is. The attendance at this meeting was rather disappointing.'

In 1934, together with another Scout, he represented the Boy Scouts of Wharfedale, at a service at St George's Chapel, Windsor, before which His Majesty the King reviewed the assembly of about 800 scouts.

He enlisted in the Royal Northumberland Fusiliers and received his commission as Second-Lieutenant in July 1940. He left the U.K. *'for an unknown destination'* in November 1941. He was declared *'missing'* in a letter to his parents from the War Office in March 1942, which stated that *'he was serving in Malaya during the hostilities which terminated in the capitulation of Singapore on February 15. Every effort was being made through diplomatic and other channels to trace him.'*

The *'Otliensian'* (*Vol. XXV, Summer 1943*) contained the following article:

PRISONERS OF WAR

'Lieut. Jack Ineson, Royal Northumberland Fusiliers, is a prisoner of war in Japanese hands. He was serving in Malaya when Singapore capitulated in February 1942. As we go to press, we are glad to hear that their relatives have received postcards from Lieut. Ineson and Sergt Walter.'

On 24 December 1942 the *'Wharfedale and Airedale Observer'* published the following article:

'News has been received by Mr. and Mrs. T.R. Ineson of Ash Grove, Otley, that their son, Lieutenant Jack Ineson (25), Royal Northumberland Fusiliers, is a prisoner of war. The official notification states that a letter follows shortly. Mrs. Ineson describes the news as "the best Christmas present she has ever received." It is almost a year since they last heard of him, and just before they received his last letter he was posted 'missing' in Malaya. He was serving in Malaya when Singapore capitulated on February 15.'

Vol. XXVII, Summer 1945 of the *'Otliensian'* noted that:

PRISONERS OF WAR IN JAPANESE HANDS

'While we cannot hope that these words will be read by those whose names appear below, we wish to remember especially the five Old Otliensians who are prisoners of

war in Japanese hands:

- ***Lieut. J. Ineson, R.N.F.'***

In September 1945 Mr and Mrs. Ineson received a letter from their son. The letter was written on 28 August at Bangkok and said, *'At the moment of writing I am in a dockside warehouse patiently waiting – for how long? I am in excellent health and good spirits, food and medical supplies are many comforts – so there is no need to worry.'*

He was the first Otley man to reach home from the Japanese camps after being liberated in September 1945. When he arrived home he was interviewed by a local reporter and the following article was published in the *'Wharfedale and Airedale Observer'* on 26 October 1945:

'Although reticent about his experiences, Lt. Ineson told sufficient to an 'Observer' reporter to show what fortitude our men have faced their difficulties and their long years of separation. In spite of it all, and although leaner than he was, Lieut. Ineson avows himself as fit as he has ever been.

He was taken prisoner on Singapore Island, on February 15, 1942, and for nine months was in a camp in Malaya. Then came a welcome move to Thailand, where conditions were better.

He said there was never anything like a real shortage of food, although the provisions were not western. The officers bought food out of the monthly allowance they were paid by the Japanese government, and they did the cooking. There was no white flour, and rice flour was used in the baking of bread, cakes and pies. The cooks' 'piece de resistance' was 'peanut special' – comprising mainly sugar and nuts.

Improvisation

'At all times, however, there was a shortage of medical supplies, but by improvisation and the use of all possible local resources, the doctors managed somehow.

Recreation, education and amusements were the prisoners' own concern. To keep themselves fit they organised cricket, "rugger", basketball and "soccer," which, in true English tradition they played in the heat of the sun. In the early days they were fortunate in having with them some members of the staff of Rafael's College, Singapore, who had been taken prisoner as part of the Singapore volunteer forces. They were able to lecture and give valuable help in the educational activities. In Lieut. Ineson's last camp there was an orchestra of 26 pieces, the instruments having been made by the men themselves. Some of the men had the scores of well-known pieces, such as Elgar's 'Enigma Variations,' with them when they were taken prisoner, and from these orchestrations were made.

News Service

'The clandestine news service at the camp was good, and although its details remain a

secret, its efficiency is shown by the fact that the prisoners knew all about VE-day very soon afterwards.

Lieut. Ineson was moving to another camp, and was on the outskirts of Bangkok, when he learned of the surrender of Japan. He stayed in the port, and was transported from there to Rangoon by air. At Rangoon he went aboard the 'Corfu' whose passengers were mainly ex-prisoners, but which also had on board fighting men from Burma. On the way home the ship called at Colombo and Port Suez.

He gave a glowing report of the way in which the Red Cross, which had been able to do very little for them during their captivity, had provided for them at the ports of call and had welcomed them at Southampton.'

'The only Otley man that Lieut. Ineson met during his captivity was Pte. M. Spittlehouse, R.A.M.C., of 2 Bank Parade, whose liberation has also recently been announced.

Lieut. Ineson is on six weeks' repatriation leave, after which he will report back for duty.'

He married Mary Ruth S. Wright in 1946, the marriage being registered in Wirral, Cheshire. Jack died in 1970; Mary died in 2000.

An article in the *'Quarterly Journal of Engineering Geology and Hydrology'*, published in 1970 stressed his importance in the field:

'He had gained national and international recognition for his researches into many aspects of the occurrence, behaviour and development of ground-water, and his untimely death has cut short a most distinguished career.'

The extract below is from the book *'200 YEARS OF BRITISH HYDROGEOLOGY'* edited by J.D.Mather: Geological Society Special Publication 225 (published 2004)

'Jack Ineson was born in Otley in 1917. He had many of the characteristics of a Yorkshireman; although not blunt by any means, he was direct and straightforward, did not mince words and was generally unable to tolerate fools gladly. He had a sense of humour, which did not extend to frivolity.

He went to the University of Durham in 1936 with an Entrance Scholarship, intending to read theology but came under the inspiring influence of Arthur Holmes and made what must have been a dramatic switch to geology, graduating with honours in that subject in 1939. During his time at Durham he played Rugby for the University and was Senior Man at University College – a position reserved for a student of undoubted all-round ability and with leadership qualities.

Originally destined to be a petrologist, he began research for a Ph.D. under Holmes but the war intervened and a few months after graduating he enlisted in the army and was commissioned in the Royal Northumberland Fusiliers. Posted to Malaya his unit was captured by the Japanese at the fall of Singapore in February 1942. He spent over three years in captivity, working on the notorious Burma-Siam Railway and it was largely due to his initial good physique and his strength of character that he was able to withstand the experience. But his health was permanently affected by the privation, malnutrition, disease and severe hardship. Whilst in captivity he taught himself Russian with the help of a fellow prisoner – an achievement in itself in the circumstances. He rarely mentioned this period other than occasionally to describe some humorous incident, indeed he disapproved of it becoming known. When he was repatriated he weighed only 36 kg (6 stone) and throughout his life he suffered recurring bouts of malaria and was soon exhausted by physical exertion. But he had the constant support of his wife Mary, who undertook many of the physical tasks associated with domestic life, giving him much freedom to pursue his interests.

Jack Ineson worked hard but had many other interests, not least watching motor racing and following rugby. He was an accomplished pianist and organist and could speak fluent French and German as well as Russian; he translated texts in all three languages.

Those who knew Jack Ineson recognised that he was a rather unique individual. He belonged to the tradition and generation which regarded public service as a duty willingly met. Few who came into contact with him realised or appreciated the underlying health problems that he always had to overcome. But overcome them he did very successfully until his untimely death from a heart attack on June 3rd 1970, whilst travelling home from work.'

His contribution to geology is illustrated by the Ineson Lecture, a 'flagship annual event' held by the International Association of Hydrogeologists, and named after the man who 'will always be associated with introducing quantitative methods in British hydrogeology.

Margery Jennings (1908-1945) - See 'War Dead'

James Edward Mason (1917-1943) - See 'War Dead'

Frank Newhouse (1924-2009)

Frank Newhouse (born, Settle, 25 September 1924) entered Form Upper 3B at Prince Henry's on 11 September 1935 after six years at Bramhope Council School. His family lived at Westgate, Bramhope, and his father, Richard V. Newhouse was a farm labourer. Richard (1901-1979) was born in Kirkby Malham, where his father was also a farm labourer. In 1924 he married Helen Syers, and the couple had three sons – Frank (born 1924), Leonard (born 1926) and Alan (born 1929). Frank was awarded a W.R.C.C. County Minor Scholarship on entry to P.H.G.S. He obtained his School Certificate in 1940 and left from Form Upper 5C in July 1940 to take up a job in farming at Mrs. Bentley's farm in Esholt.

The '*Otliensian*' (*Vol. XXVII, Spring 1945*) announced that:

'Pte. Frank Newhouse, Parachute Regt. of Old Hollings, Guiseley, previously reported missing with the First Airborne Division at Arnhem, is now known to be a prisoner of war in Germany.'

Private Newhouse, who was a paratrooper, joined the Army in 1942, and went to Arnhem with the First Airborne Division in September 1944. His parents were informed on 24 October 1944 that their son was *'missing in North West Europe'* and was known to be suffering from head injuries. Approximately 10,600 men fought at Arnhem, but only 2,398 returned.

The Summer 1945 issue published the *'welcome home'* news:

'On behalf of all Old Scholars, the Staff and members of the School, we extend warm greetings to the following on their safe return after being prisoners of war in German hands:

- ***Pte. F. Newhouse, Parachute Regt.'***

In 1949 he married Sylvia Laurence (marriage registered in Swindon, Wiltshire).

The following article by Bob Hilton is taken from the 'Pegasus Archive' *(**www.pegasusarchive.org**):*

Private Frank Newhouse

Unit: Anti-Tank Platoon, Support Company, 10th Parachute Battalion, Army No.: 14557569.

'Frank joined up for military service on 4th March 1943, and, after his basic training with the King's Own Yorkshire Light Infantry he volunteered for the Parachute Regiment. Unfortunately, due to his young age (18 years and 10 months), he was not accepted. As a result, Frank joined the Royal Artillery, but when he was nearly 19 years old, he applied again to join the Paras. After the completion of his parachute course in October 1943 he was posted to the 156th Parachute Battalion. In January 1944, Frank was transferred to the 10th Parachute Battalion and was assigned to the Anti-Tank Platoon.

'During conversations with Frank he told me that during their training, in the United Kingdom, in the summer of 1944 the Anti-Tank Platoon of the 10th Parachute Battalion had the opportunity to practice with the American issued bazooka. Nearly all the platoon decided that they did not like the long 'tongue' of flame that came out of the back and the fact that it gave away their position when fired, so they opted for the P.I.A.T. as their weapon of choice. He added:

"I'm pleased to hear that my old Sergeant 'Joe' Sunley and our good friend "Shack"

have been able to help - a couple of good lads who looked after me when I joined the Battalion as a very young para. after it returned from the Middle East in December 1943. I rate 'Joe' as the finest man I've ever had the privilege to know. A great LEADER and friend".

Note: 'Joe' Sunley was 6403069 Sergeant Ralph Sunley and "Shack" was 4696760 Private Ralph Shackleton, both of the Anti-Tank Platoon.

"As for my own place in the Battalion, I was a P.I.A.T. (Projectile Infantry Anti-Tank) man attached to 'B' Company".

On Monday 18th September 1944, with the rest of the 10th Parachute Battalion and 4th Parachute Brigade, Frank parachuted onto Ginkel Heath near Arnhem.

"It was a parachute drop into the area. I was excited, not scared. D-Day was in June and we were all geared up for fighting, but we had to wait another few months so we were raring to go".

'In spite of much resistance and heavy fighting, the following day they arrived at the 'Leeren Doedel' (now called the Pinoccio Restaurant). The Battalion launched an attack astride the Ede to Arnhem road with 'B' Company supporting 'D' Company on the right hand side of the road. Various attempts were made to deal with the German tanks and armoured vehicles that were causing the Battalion so many casualties. This involved the anti-tank men trying to get forward and into a firing position that put them within 50 metres of the enemy armour. This, of course, was asking a lot and not surprisingly there were many casualties amongst the PIAT men, with Frank being one of them.

"I got a bit knocked about with a head wound when attempting to tackle some tanks on the Tuesday afternoon (9th September 1944). Spent a while being sheltered and looked after by the Dutch doctors and nurses in the Wolfheze Hospital until this was evacuated, along with 6 others (wounded men)".

'He suffered a serious head wound. With seven others he was taken to the emergency hospital in the Psychiatric Hospital in Wolfheze, where his head wound was treated. On 21st September 1944, his 20th birthday, one of the Dutch nurses who treated him, brought him a bunch of marigolds. One evening the Germans, who were taking over the village, ordered that the hospital be evacuated. Frightened they would be captured, Frank and seven other soldiers escaped by covering themselves in blankets and pretending to be patients. He said:

"We covered ourselves with blankets and pretended to be lunatics along with the rest of them. We had hobnail boots on. But the Germans didn't seem to notice".

'Frank and two soldier friends met up with the Dutch resistance who carried them, hidden under bales of straw, to Ede on a horse-drawn cart. Frank stayed in Ede for a few weeks but he was informed on and captured and was sent to a prisoner of war camp at Limburg. Frank, a father of three, added:

"I went to three prisoner of war camps, including one at Dresden, but the one at Limburg was the worst. There was nowhere to sleep apart from on the ground in marquees and they only turned the water on for an hour a day and there were 1,000 people there. It was an evil, horrible place".

'After being freed from the PoW camp at Dresden, in March 1945 by the Russians, Frank and his comrades made their way to Czechoslovakia where they met some American soldiers who gave them a car and some petrol so they could reach Brussels. They were then looked after and sent back to England, arriving home in May 1945.

'After his period of leave, during which he regained his strength, Frank returned to his beloved Parachute Regiment. In September 1945, he was posted to The Glider Pilot Regiment as Administration Staff. After a while, he was assigned to work at the Parachute Regiment Depot at Aldershot. On the 15th June 1950, much to his regret, Frank was demobilised and returned to civilian life.

'In 1947, Frank, who was originally from Yorkshire, settled in Wootton Bassett where he met his wife Sylvia. She sadly died in 2003.

'In February 1952 Frank returned to military service as part of the Parachute Regiment Reserves. He remained in the Reserves until 1966 and gained the rank of Sergeant. He became a manager at Austin Rover in Swindon after leaving the army.

'Frank Newhouse was a genuine and sincere man, who was always ready to help others. For many years he was Treasurer of the 'Arnhem 1944 Veterans Club'. Frank was particularly proud that, during the annual commemoration service at the Airborne Cemetery, he was able to lay a wreath with two schoolchildren at the Cross of Sacrifice.'

In May 2009, Frank was made a Member of the British Empire in the Queen's Birthday Honours list.

Frank Newhouse, shown with his medals, is to be made a Member of the British Empire

Photograph courtesy of *'This is Wiltshire'* (**www.thisiswiltshire.co.uk**).

At the age of 85 Frank passed away on Saturday 17 October 2009. He leaves behind three children, eight grandchildren and five great-grandchildren.

His M.B.E. was awarded for his voluntary work with the Arnhem 1944 Veterans Club. He also helped to organise an annual reunion of veterans in Arnhem where servicemen were able to pay their respects to fallen comrades.

The camp at Limburg (Stalag XIIA) was a transit camp that processed newly captured PoWs before sending them to other camps. Many British prisoners captured during the Battle of Arnhem were initially sent here and it is likely that at any one time over 20,000 men were interned there. Conditions were notoriously bad, but within a few weeks, after interrogation and documentation, Frank Newhouse would have been moved to Stalag IVB at Muhlberg. The population of the Limburg Stalag was always very high because this was the first port of call for many prisoners captured on the Western Front. Daily rations for each man was a fifth of a loaf of bread with a serving of margarine, occasionally with a bit of filling, for breakfast, followed by coffee after morning roll call, and finally the main and evening meals were watered down soup.

The extract below is taken from the web-site (***www.pegasusarchive.org***):

'Despite these problems and the unwieldy numbers, little was done by the authorities to raise the camp above the lowest common denominator. For the British and Americans, temporary accommodation came in the form of four very large marquees, not wholly dissimilar to circus tents. There was no furniture of any kind inside these structures. Instead the cramped conditions dictated that everyone had to sleep back to back on the floor, which in some instances was cobbled stone, with, if they were extremely lucky, a loose scattering of straw for bedding.

'Between meals, which were only a few notches above starvation rations, there was absolutely nothing in the way of entertainment to occupy the minds of the prisoners. There was no lighting in the camp, and so as soon as it got dark men slept until dawn because there was little point in being awake. The threat of disease, especially diarrhoea, was far from being uncommon, and the camp possessed almost nothing in the way of medical facilities. The stone toilets served several thousand men, and as such created a considerable stench.

'Upon arrival, men who were newcomers to life as a PoW had the basic ground rules of Stalag law spelt out to them, one of which was a warning that they would be shot if they placed as much as a finger upon the tall barbed wire fence that surrounded the camp. For many freshly captured servicemen, Stalag XIIA was their first opportunity to write a postcard home to their family, and although it would take weeks to arrive it was often the case that this would be the first news they would receive that their loved ones, now posted as missing in action, were alive.

'When the time came to leave Stalag XIIA to a more permanent camp, the majority were sent via rail from Limburg station. Depending on their destination this journey could last anything from a couple of days to a week, due to the stoppages caused by

the constant threat of opportunistic strikes by British and American fighters. There were several instances of planes strafing a train which, against the rules set out in the Geneva Convention, carried no markings on it to indicate that it carried PoWs, and as a result some men were killed or wounded.

'The cattle trucks that the prisoners were herded into possessed not even the luxurious comforts that they had become accustomed to at Stalag XIIA. Typically 50 men were packed into each car, and most had to stand throughout the duration of the journey as there was not enough room to get down and sleep, though in some cases it was possible for men to rest in shifts. During transportation very little was provided in terms of food or water. Sometimes men were issued with a large sandwich before departure which they had to make last for a week, whilst others received nothing to begin with, but were given a foul brand of cheese along the way. However, the German guards were willing to trade their own food for any items of the prisoners' kit. Each car contained only one toilet, usually in the form of a deep tin of one description or another. The opportunity to empty this container did not come too often, and as such the already stale air inside each carriage became something to behold. Due to the nature of their diet since arriving at Stalag XIIA, the men often suffered with diarrhoea during transportation.'

Following his capture after the Battle of Arnhem in 1944, Frank Newhouse was taken to Limburg and later transferred to Stalag IVB at Muhlberg, south of Berlin, north east of Leipzig and north west of Dresden. This was one of the largest PoW camps in Germany during World War II, holding up to 16,000 men. The camp was built in 1939 and the first inmates, Polish soldiers captured during the German September 1939 offensive. According to camp records, there were 25,052 prisoners of war at Muhlberg on 1 January 1945 – twice as many as had initially been planned. The majority were Soviet soldiers, who were not subject to the protection of the Geneva Convention, and thus had to endure especially harsh and inhumane conditions, leading to a high death rate.

The Red Army liberated the camp on 23 April 1945, and Frank Newhouse arrived back home in England in May 1945.

Geoffrey Elliott Thompson (1920-1943) - See 'War Dead'

John Francis Stansfield Walter (1922-1945) - See 'War Dead'

Douglas Allison Whiteley (1913-1992)

Douglas Whiteley was born on 19 October 1913 and lived at Brook Cottage, Pool, where his father, J.C. Whiteley (1884-1955) was a Master Butcher, who married Lily Tankard in Wharfedale in 1912. They had five children, Douglas being the eldest. After attending St Wilfred's C. of E. School in Pool he entered Form 1 at Prince Henry's on 15 May 1922. He was 9 years of age. He left school from Form Upper VB in summer 1930. Before the outbreak of war he was employed at Pool Paper Mills, where his grandfather, Mr

Samuel Whiteley, was one of the founders. Douglas played cricket as a bowler for Pool Cricket Club.

He joined the Army in 1939 and saw service in France before the evacuation in June 1940. He was stationed in the Middle East from September 1941. He was taken prisoner by the Italians at Tobruk on 20 June 1942.

The '*Otliensian*' (*Vol. XXV, Autumn 1942*) reported that:

'Driver Douglas Whiteley, R.A.S.C., previously reported missing, is a prisoner of war in Italy.'

He spent 13 months in Italian camps and the rest in Germany before the camp was liberated by the British in April 1945, and from then on served in England until he was demobilised on 5 December 1945 and returned to his pre-war occupation at Pool Paper Mills.

In *Vol. XXVII, Summer 1945,* under the heading 'WELCOME HOME' it was announced that:

'On behalf of all Old Scholars, the Staff and members of the School, we extend warm greetings to the following on their safe return after being prisoners of war in German hands:

- ***Cpl. D. A. Whiteley R.A.S.C.'***

Douglas Whiteley performed well at school in athletics and rugby. He excelled at athletics, becoming junior champion in 1927 and senior champion in 1929. In the Athletic Sports in summer 1927 his record was as follows:

100 yards (under 14)	D. Whiteley (12 4/5 sec)	G. Fairbanks	A. Pickard	G. Cullen
220 yards (Under 14)	D. Whiteley (30 1/5 sec)	G. Fairbanks	A. Pickard	I. Mackenzie
Long Jump (Under 14)	D. Whiteley (14ft 6in)	A. Pickard	I. Mackenzie	C. Barker
Boys – Junior Champion	D. Whiteley (9 points)			

The '*Otliensian*' (*Vol. XI, Summer 1929*) gave details of his performance as Senior Champion, for which he won the Milligan Cup:

'From preliminary heats, held on days previous to Sports' Saturday, had emerged the pupils superior in athletics. One good feature of the Boys' Senior Championship was the keen competition between Douglas Whiteley and Harold Mallinson. In the 100 yards (Open) Whiteley gained first place and Mallinson second, but in the 220 yards

(Open) the positions were reversed, as they were in the 440 yards (Open). In the half-mile, Mallinson was first and Whiteley third. However, Whiteley recovered his place by winning the long jump and the event of throwing the cricket ball. The result of this last event was that Whiteley had 14 points as against Mallinson's 13 points, certainly a very close and memorable finish.'

100 yards (Open)	D. Whiteley (Red) (11 1/5 seconds)	H. Mallinson (Yellow)	S. Myers (Yellow)	H. Cheetham (Yellow)
220 yards (Open)	H. Mallinson (Yellow) (26 1/5 seconds)	D. Whiteley (Red)	G. Barker (White)	S. Myers (Yellow)
440 yards (Open)	H. Mallinson (Yellow) (64 seconds)	D. Whiteley (Red)	S. Myers (Yellow)	C. Barker (White)
Half-Mile (Open)	H. Mallinson (Yellow) (2min 25 4/5 sec)	S. Myers (Yellow)	D. Whiteley (Red)	C. Barker (White)
Long jump (Open)	D. Whiteley (Red) (17ft 6in)	S. Myers (Yellow)	C. Barker (White)	H. Cheetham (Yellow) & A. Mallinson (Yellow)
Throwing Cricket Ball	D. Whiteley (Red) (76 yards)	C. Barker	G. Hinton	K. Pickard
Senior Champion	D. Whiteley (14 pts.)	H. Mallinson (13 pts.)		

He played Rugby for the school and in the 1929-1930 season was mentioned in the match reports on three occasions:

14 September OLD OTLIENSIANS At Home:

'Without playing really well, the School team was definitely superior throughout the game. The two packs were evenly matched, but better handling amongst the backs gave School the victory. Kay opened the scoring with an unconverted try, but the Old Otliensians quickly equalised. Immediately after the interval, the Old Scholars went ahead with an unconverted try, but School played up strongly after this reverse. Whiteley scored a try and Mallinson gave the School the lead by kicking the goal. Just before time, Mallinson clinched the victory for School by scoring an unconverted try.'

RESULT: School 11pts; Old Otliensians 6 pts.

21 September CITY OF LEEDS SCHOOL At Home:

'Though outweighed, the School team was by far the better side, and the result was never in doubt. In the first half, School obtained a lead of 9 points, through tries scored by Barker (G), Whiteley and Woods. After the interval, the City of Leeds team was unable to cope with the School's improved three-quarter play, which resulted in tries by G. Barker (2), C. Barker (2) and Mallinson.'

RESULT: School 24 pts: City of Leeds School 3 pts.

19 October WOODHOUSE GROVE 'A' At Home:

'The game was completely one-sided, the School team being far superior in every department of the game. The Woodhouse side was never dangerous and was quite unable to prevent the School from scoring with annoying regularity. Tries were scored for School by Barker G. (3), Barker C. (2), Whiteley (2), Mallinson (2), Kay, Whitehead and Pickersgill. Mallinson kicked 3 goals.'

RESULT: School 42 pts: Woodhouse Grove A 0

Corporal Douglas Whiteley (Service No. T/133691) was a driver with the Royal Army Service Corps (R.A.S.C.) – the 'T' in the service number refers to 'transport'. The R.A.S.C. was the unit responsible for keeping the Army supplied with all its provisions, excluding weaponry, military equipment and ammunition, which were supplied by the Royal Army Ordnance Corps.

He was a prisoner of war at Fossoli of Carpi Camp, near Modena in Italy (*see William Child*). When the German army occupied the camp in September 1943 and converted it into a concentration camp to house Jews, the prisoners were deported to Germany. Douglas was taken to Stalag 357, Oerbke, near Fallingbostel, Lower Saxony, North West Germany, where his PoW No. was 247105.

In November 1943 his wife received a letter from Cpl. Whiteley; the '*Wharfedale and Airedale Observer*' of 26 November 1943 reported that:

'News has been received by Mrs. Douglas A. Whiteley, 12 Wharfe Crescent, Pool, that her husband Corpl. A. Whiteley who was a prisoner of war in P G 73 Italy, has been transferred to Germany where his address is PoW No 247105 Stammlager IV B.

'In a letter to his wife, Cpl. Whiteley says – "After five weeks of silence I am able to write to you from my new address in a new country. Perhaps by now it may not be such a surprise to you, but at the time it was for us; we were looking forward to Christmas in England. However, our treatment here is of the best and we couldn't wish for better or more food." He says that they have comfortable beds in the camp, and he feels no worse for his long journey. He is still optimistic.'

In 1938 the Germans opened a training area near Fallingbostel, which included two large barrack areas. The workers used to build these barracks were housed in temporary wooden barracks in the village of Oerbke. When the Germans attacked Poland in 1939 large numbers of prisoners were taken and housed in this camp, which became Stalag XIB. When the Germans advanced to the west they needed more camps and 40,000 British, French, Dutch and Belgian prisoners were sent to Stalag XIB.

With the fall of Italy to the Germans in 1943, Italian PoWs arrived at the camp. This included British prisoners of war previously housed in Italian camps. By mid-1944 there were some 96,000 PoWs in the camps and sub-camps of Fallingbostel. In October 1944

400 British paratroopers, captured at Arnhem, arrived in the camp. Each hut contained 400 men, though it had bunks for only 150 and In February 1945 yet more prisoners arrived – Americans captured after the 'Battle of the Bulge.'

March 1945 saw the allies crossing the Rhine, and the British and American armies moved closer to the camps. In early April the Germans decided to relocate camp 357. 12,000 men marched to the northeast with all they could carry in columns of 2,000. There was snow and rain; the men were cold, hungry and tired and scavenged what they could find on the march. During the march the columns were attacked by 9 R.A.F. Typhoons, mistaking them for the enemy, and 60 prisoners were killed and many more wounded. Eventually they made it through to the British lines.

Stalag XIB was liberated on 16 April 1945, the first British PoW camp to be liberated by advancing troops. The British troops remaining were those who had been considered unfit to march by the Germans.

In 1941 he married Barbara M. Marshall, and, after his return from the War, they had three children – John (born 1946), Roderick (born 1951) and Heather (born 1956).

His cousin, Gunner Jack Whiteley, was also a prisoner of war in Italian and, later, German hands. He joined the regular army when he was 17 and fought in the Libyan, Crete and Greece campaigns. He too worked at Pool Paper Mills for a short time prior to joining the Army. He escaped from the Italians at the time of Italy's capitulation, but was recaptured and taken to Germany. He was first taken prisoner at Tobruk on 20 June 1942, which, by a coincidence, was the day on which his cousin Douglas was also captured.

Douglas Whiteley died in 1992, his death being registered in Bradford.

The Wounded

463 old scholars and staff from Prince Henry's Grammar School were members of the Armed Forces during the Second World War. Of these 41 were killed during the war. Eleven ex-pupils were prisoners of war, and four of them sacrificed their lives in Japanese camps. Throughout the war, the *'Otliensian'* published details of the personnel involved in the war, including those ex-pupils who were wounded in the conflict.

Many attempts have been made to calculate total war related deaths associated with the Second World War. The Commonwealth War Graves Commission estimates that in the U.K. and the Crown Colonies there were 383,786 war related deaths, and that the number of wounded was 284,049 from the same area. It certainly seems to be the case that the number of wounded was significantly lower than the number who died, but compiling accurate statistics, especially for the wounded, must be almost impossible. The *'Otliensian'* only lists nine ex-pupils who were wounded and survived, and additional research from other sources adds only two further names to the list – Kenneth William Horner and Frank Newhouse. It is much more likely that news of the death of a local man would have been reported in the local paper and in the school magazine, than news of a wounding, and therefore this list should be regarded as incomplete.

John Douglas Firth (1919-1976)

J. D. Firth

John Douglas Firth was born on 15 May 1916. He attended Westgate Council School before moving to Prince Henry's Grammar School on 12 September 1928 (Form Upper 3B). He lived at 'Netherfield', Bradford Road, Otley and his father, Seth (1890-1958), was in business as a plasterer. John left Prince Henry's on 27 July 1932 (Form Lower 5A) and went to work for his father in the family plastering business of Andrew Firth & Sons, founded by his grandfather. The fact that John left from form Lower 5A suggests that he did not complete the usual number of years in the grammar school, did not take his School Certificate and left to take up employment.

He was in the Royal Artillery and was wounded in Western Europe on 20 January 1945. In 1941 he married Miss Rita Winterburn. His younger brother, Andrew T. Firth, also served in the Royal Artillery. (*see chapter on Military Decorations*)

The following article was published in the *'Wharfedale and Airedale Observer'* on 9 February 1945:

WOUNDED IN WESTERN EUROPE

'Mrs. J. D. Firth of 'Brooklyn', Tranmere Drive, Guiseley, has received official notification that her husband, W/Brd. (Dvr I/C) John Douglas Firth (28), serving with the Royal Artillery, was wounded in Western Europe on January 20 and is now in hospital.

'In a letter written in hospital to his parents, Mr and Mrs. Seth Firth, of "Netherdale", Bradford Road, Otley, he says he is "progressing satisfactorily."

'W/Bdr. Firth joined the Army five years ago in April and before going overseas on D-Day he was an instructor at Scarborough. He married Miss Rita Winterburn, only daughter of Mr and Mrs. H. Winterburn, of Tranmere, Guiseley, during the war.

'He was educated at Prince Henry's Grammar School, Otley, and before joining the Forces was working with his father in the firm of Andrew Firth and Sons, Otley.

His brother, Lieutenant Andrew T. Firth, who left this country to take part in the invasion of Normandy, is hoping to return home on leave in the near future.'

Kenneth William Horner (1915-1987)

Capt. Horner

Kenneth William Horner volunteered for the Royal Marines in February 1940 and rose rapidly through the ranks. In April 1940 he was made corporal and by August 1940 was given full sergeant rank. After training for a commission he was promoted to 2nd Lieutenant in November 1940, and by 1942 had risen to the rank of Captain.

He was born on 9 July 1915 in Otley. His father, William Henry Horner (1886-1944) was born in Leathley. William's father, James, was employed as a machine turner in the Otley printing machine manufacturing industry and William Henry became an apprentice in the same trade. He married Lucy Maston (1888-1968) on 20 February 1909 at Otley Parish Church. However, in the 1911 Census he is listed as a plumber and this was his trade on the admission of Kenneth to Prince Henry's. The family was then living at 15 Queen's Place, Otley.

Kenneth attended North Parade School, but was awarded a Governors' Scholarship and was admitted to form Upper 3A at Prince Henry's in September 1927. He left from Form Upper 5A in July 1931 after passing the School Certificate. He was employed as a journalist with the '*Wharfedale*'.

His journalistic skills were first displayed at a School Concert held in February 1930 when, at a social to raise money for the Playing Fields' Fund, '*Dancing and a sketch entitled "Young Dudley" by Mr Pratt, Mr Nealy and Kenneth Horner, were the principal items on the programme.' ('Otliensian', Vol. XII, Lent 1930).*

He played Rugby for the First XV. His player profile in Spring 1930 read *'Has done hard work in the tight scrums, but is rather slow in the loose. His height has been useful in the line out.' ('Otliensian, Vol. XII, Lent 1930*), and in the following year: *'Is strong and vigorous. His height is useful in the line-out. He has gained several tries by following up, and would make a first-rate forward with a little more speed.' ('Otliensian, Vol. XIII, Lent 1931).*

In the 1930-1931 season the First XV won 12 of the 14 games they played, scoring 253 points and conceding only 40 points. Kenneth scored two tries in each of the matches against Thornton Grammar School and Ashville College.

In 1931 he played the part of Breen in the thriller *'Thread o' Scarlet'*: *'Horner as Breen managed skilfully his "voice-off" passages with the landlord. His sudden reappearances gave a new dramatic thrill to the play, and he died a really dramatic death.' ('Otliensian', Vol. XIII Summer 1931)*

In 1941 Second-Lieutenant Horner was serving with the Royal Marines in the Middle East. From letters home his family learned that he was embarking for *'an unknown destination in the East'* for *'an apparently short voyage.'*

'Mrs. Horner surmised that he was bound for Crete and the announcement shortly after that the Royal Marines had landed in Crete supported her theory. She has followed the terrific struggle in the island with a good deal of anxiety.'

'News was received this week by Mr and Mrs. J. Horner, of the Mechanics Institute, from their younger son, Second Lieutenant Kenneth W. Horner of the Royal Marines, indicating that he was in the battle for Crete, and was among the men safely evacuated from the island.' ('Wharfedale and Airedale Observer, 6 June 1941)

A later article suggests that 'he took part in the Crete campaign, where he was wounded.' ('Wharfedale and Airedale Observer, 8 January 1943).

In April 1941 the Germans invaded Yugoslavia, which fell in twelve days. They then rapidly overran Greece and seized Crete. On 20 May 1941 German paratroops landed on Crete. Many were killed by British and Commonwealth troops, and by the Greek population, but they succeeded in capturing an airfield, which allowed more soldiers and equipment to be landed.

2,000 Royal Marines were landed on the island to man anti-aircraft and coastal defence batteries at Suda Bay and the aerodromes at Malemi and Heraklion. They succeeded in shooting down German fighters, troop carriers and parachutists, and on several occasions used A.A. guns against enemy troops on the ground. A stubborn rearguard action by the Australians, backed up by the marines, allowed many of the Allied troops to escape. The Royal Navy evacuated thousands of troops from Crete to Egypt, and those left behind surrendered and became prisoners of war. Only 900 marines escaped, and among them was Kenneth Horner.

Herbert Kerby (1906-1968)

Herbert Kerby was born in Otley on 9 September 1906. At the time of the 1911 Census the family was living in Bloomfield Square, Otley. His father, Charles Henry Kerby (born 1878 in Hoxton, London) was employed as a warehouseman, and Herbert had one brother and two sisters. His youngest brother, Charles Watkinson Kerby, was not born until 4 February 1918.

Herbert attended the Otley National School, but in 1920 became a pupil at Prince Henry's Grammar School, but only stayed until 26 July 1922 when he left to become a pattern designer at Duncan, Barraclough Ltd., Otley. He was a former captain of the National School Old Boy's football team, and occasionally played for the Otley first and second teams. In 1933 he married Clara Holmes in Otley. Herbert died in 1968.

He was twice wounded during the war as evidenced by the following article which was published in the '*Wharfedale and Airedale Observer*' on 28 January 1944:

Otley B.S.M. Wounded in Italy

'During recent fighting on the Fifth Army front in Italy a field battery of the Royal Artillery commanded by Major J Welsh, M.C., of 15 Croft Avenue, Otley, suffered casualties in killed and wounded among whom was Battery-Sergeant-Major Herbert Kerby, an Otley man.

'Mrs. H. Kerby, of 19 Weston Lane, received a letter from her husband on Saturday, following an official notification, in which he said that he had been wounded and was now in hospital. He had undergone an operation, as a result of which a piece of shrapnel two inches long had been removed. The wound was not serious and although he was weak from loss of blood, he hoped to be back on active service soon.

'This is the second time that B.S.M. Kerby has been wounded. In March of last year there were a number of casualties among Wharfedale men serving with a R.A. regiment in Tunisia, and Kerby was wounded in the shoulder by shrapnel.

'B.S.M. Kerby, who is 36, is the second son of Mr and Mrs. C. H. Kerby, of 3 Newall Avenue, Otley. He was called up at the outbreak of war with the Otley Battery of Territorials and saw service in France. In June 1942, he was promoted from Sergeant to Sergeant-Major, and went to North Africa with the First Army at the end of that year.'

His younger brother, Charles, was also an old scholar of P.H.G.S. He transferred from Otley, North Parade in September 1930, having been awarded a W.R.C.C. scholarship. He left from the Lower VI in May 1936, having passed the School Certificate in 1935. He joined the Royal Engineers shortly before the outbreak of the war, went out to France in November 1939 and took part in the rear-guard actions at St Valery and Le Havre. He was posted to the Middle East in January 1941 and later took part in the successful advance of the 8th Army from El Alamein to Italy. He was promoted to Sergeant.

Frank Mackintosh (1921-2001)

S/P Mackintosh

Michael Frank Mackintosh was born on 1 September 1921 and lived in Bramhope. He attended Arthington Church of England School from 1926-1932 and was awarded a W.R.C.C. Minor Scholarship to Prince Henry's Grammar School. He joined the school on 12 September 1933 (Form Upper 3A) and left on 29 July 1937 (Form Upper 5B), after passing his School Certificate.

In summer 1936 he was awarded third prize in form Lower 5C, but his main claim to fame lay in the sporting field. In athletics he was perhaps unfortunate to compete against two of the best athletes in Barber and Sully, but in coming 4th in the 100 yards (Under 14) at the summer 1934 Sports Day, he was described as *'showing promise'*. In summer 1935, taking part in the Under 14 events, he came 3rd in the 100 yards, 4th in the 220 yards, 1st in the High Jump and 4th in the Long Jump. In summer 1936 he won the Senior Obstacle Race. He was also a playing member of the School Rugby XV and cricket XI.

On leaving school he was employed at Messrs. F. Smith & Co, Insurance Brokers, Otley. He joined the R.A.F.V.R. in 1940, when he was 18 years of age, received his training in England and was awarded his 'wings' in October 1941. In February 1942 he went out to the Middle East with 148 Squadron, based in Egypt. On 31 May 1942 he was second pilot for an operation against Derna aerodrome. The pilot was Flying Officer Bill Astell and the rest of the crew was Pilot Officer 'Bish' Dodds (navigator), Sgt. 'Tiger' Philby (wireless operator) and Sgt. Fred Hooper and Ft.Sgt. Ian Robinson (gunners). They dropped their first stick of bombs, but were then attacked by a Me. 109 night fighter.

In June 1942 his parents, then living at 7 Moorland Road, Bramhope, received official intimation that their son was missing in Libya after an operational flight. However, they received a cablegram from their son on 5 July 1942, saying that he was *'safe and well.'* The cablegram did not say that he had, in fact, been wounded, and the full story was not known until the following article was published in the *'Wharfedale and Airedale Observer,'* on 18 December 1942:

BRAMHOPE PILOT'S ADVENTURE – REMARKABLE STORY OF DESERT ESCAPE

'Sergeant-Pilot Frank Mackintosh, R.A.F.V.R, son of Mr and Mrs. J. Mackintosh, 7 Moorland Road, Bramhope, has been invalided home from the Middle East after remarkable experiences, and is now in a West Coast hospital.

'Frank, who is 21, had been in the Middle East since early this year, and whilst out on a bombing sortie over Derna in May, his plane was shot down by night fighters. Shortly before the attack he had handed over the controls to the co-pilot, who came down with the plane and eventually succeeded in reaching the British lines, an exploit for which he was decorated.

During the attack Frank was seriously wounded in both arms. A pocket torch and a steel mirror, both of which were in his left-hand breast pocket, were shattered by shrapnel, but they prevented the shrapnel from entering his body, and are believed to have saved his life. His tunic front was shot away and his right arm hung useless.

'He baled out and how he succeeded in opening his parachute he does not know, but he landed safely and hid in a cave near an enemy hospital. The shattered torch is now in his mother's possession.

A short while after he met an uninjured member of the crew, who bandaged his wounds. Owing to loss of blood Frank remained in the cave to rest and finally persuaded his pal to leave him and make good his escape. He attempted to do so but was captured with three others.

'For three weeks Mackintosh lived in the cave, hiding from German search parties, who had found his abandoned parachute and were scouring the surrounding district. He would not give himself up, despite the pain from his wounds, and the tantalizing sight of the nearby hospital.

Helped by Arabs

'During this period of hiding he was looked after by the Senussi Arabs, who fed him on goat's milk and water every other night. These friendly natives provided him with the means of escape, and one of his many adventures was a sixty-mile ride on a camel travelling by night, escorted by the Senussi. They took control of a lorry and made their way slowly towards the British lines.

'He was eventually rescued by Captain Eric Townsend of the Royal Army Medical Corps, a Skipton officer, who was awarded the Military Cross for his rescue. This officer had been out far into the desert with a Commando patrol which, subjected to dive-bombing and machine-gunning out in the open, returned by night to Siwa. Word was received that a wounded airman was being looked after by the Senussi in the Jebel, and Captain Townsend at once volunteered to return and find this airman. He was successful in locating Mackintosh, and after attending to his wounds brought him safely in.

'Mr Arthur Townsend was informed by his son that he had rescued a wounded Bramhope airman, and he immediately wrote a letter to Mr Mackintosh, informing him that his son was safe, putting as the address "To the parents of a boy now serving in the Middle East – Bramhope."

'Captain Townsend wrote a personal letter to Mr and Mrs. Mackintosh giving full details, and saying what a brave boy Frank had been, never once complaining.

'A Sister at the hospital in Cairo where Sergeant-Pilot Mackintosh had been taken, also wrote enclosing the 'Egyptian Mail' for September 23, which published a photograph of Frank, his right arm in plaster of Paris, and holding the shattered torch which saved his life.

Return Home

'Sergt.-Pilot Mackintosh came home on November 18 for fourteen days' leave and then went back to hospital for special treatment. He has had ten operations upon his right arm, and is to have another shortly. He speaks highly of the treatment he received in Cairo, and said everyone was very kind. His Wing-Commander informed his parents that he was missing and gave no hope for his safety, but fortunately this letter arrived after the good news that he was safe. The Wing-Commander, who is now himself missing, said that Frank was due for promotion to Flight-Sergeant. Mr and Mrs. Mackintosh also received a cablegram from their son, after his rescue, saying that he was 'safe and well,' without informing them that he had been wounded.'

In spite of his injuries he was able to return to restricted flying. After leaving the R.A.F. he became a head of department at a school in Scotland. After several operations he kept his injured arm and, despite significant pain and the fact that one arm was two inches shorter than the other, he taught cricket as well as other subjects. It is likely that if he had been picked up by the Germans, his arm would have been amputated.

A more detailed description of the crash, the baling out and Frank's eventual return to base is contained in the book ***'FREE TO FIGHT AGAIN, R.A.F. ESCAPES AND EVASIONS, 1940-1945'*****, by Alan W. Cooper** (pub Pen and Sword Books, 2009). Quotes from Mackintosh published in the book are included below in italics:

The attack put the starboard engine out of action and set the wing on fire. The remaining bombs were jettisoned, but another attack by a German fighter resulted in Mackintosh being badly wounded in the elbow.

He baled out at 2,000 feet, landed badly with bombs falling all around him, and for a few seconds was unable to move. Eventually he set off to the south-east and after 15 minutes met Fred Hooper, who used his hospital training to bandage Frank's arm. They moved off together on a desert track, but soon had to stop because Frank was not feeling well. He persuaded Hooper to leave him and go on alone. Moving on very slowly, Frank came across his burnt-out aircraft, *Wellington AD653-R for Robert*. He made sure that no one was trapped inside and continued on.

The official records show that Flying Officer Astell and Pilot Officer Dodds had no time to bale out and crash-landed the plane. They destroyed all the important equipment and set out on a desert track. Frank walked on for about two or three hours, but as dawn broke he had to stop for a rest and lay down in the sand. He became very cold and realized that he must keep moving, but had some difficulty in doing so. There was a wadi nearby and he could hear the sound of sheep and goats and Arab voices. He knew that the Senussi Arabs had helped other airmen to evade capture behind enemy lines and decided to approach them and hope they were friendly.

'The wadi was very deep but there was no sign of the enemy. At the bottom were three tents. Outside one an Arab was tending to the sheep and goats. By this time my legs were very unsteady and I was staggering about, and the Arab, when he saw me, looked alarmed so I greeted him in Arabic telling him I was English and I needed food and water, and asked if he was a friend of the English. He replied the English were good and the Italians bad. He then led me down to the farm and into a tent where I was greeted by all present including the Sheik, Braiham Haarak, an old man with a grey beard.

'A young girl gave me a glass of goat's milk, then another Arab entered the tent. He was Yadem Abdual Mustafa Said and he spoke some English. He removed the bandages from my arm, washed the wound, applied some form of powder and then freshly bandaged my arm. I was offered food but declined as I had no appetite but did accept another welcome glass of goat's milk. The Arabs put their heads together discussing my case. Yadem then said he was taking me somewhere I could hide in the day so I left the tent accompanied by Yadem and Braiham who rode a horse. By now I could hear aircraft engines being tested on the ground and I then saw several German fighters in the air. The two Arabs took me to a cave at the side of the Wadi where they placed a blanket on the floor for me to lie on; in the circumstances it seemed very comfortable. Then a boulder was rolled into the entrance and I was again alone.'

He could hear aircraft overhead, and in the evening Yadem came and took him to a nearby farm. Frank had difficulty in standing and Yadem was concerned that he might die and would be better advised to be taken to the nearest German hospital. This gave Frank the incentive to stand and reach the farm safely. The next day he was moved to a different cave and Yadem again brought him milk and water. At the same time four German armoured cars stopped in front of the cave and then moved off towards the farm. They were looking for an 'English major', who had been shot down at Derna. Frank's name had been clearly marked on his abandoned parachute.

'Braiham said he had not seen me but would keep his eyes open as he wanted the reward he would get if he found me. I reminded Yadem that he would be rewarded if he got me back to the British lines and he replied, "I want no reward, my reward is getting you back to your English comrades, no more." They hated the Italians because of the way they treated the Arabs, and disliked the Germans because they were friends of the Italians.'

The next cave was 10 kms. away and Frank suggested that when dusk fell he would attempt to reach the British lines at Gazala. However, he was persuaded by Yadem that he was not yet well enough and would be better to wait a few more days.

'Later Yadem came and made me up some lemonade and said they had a plan for my escape. They were going to take me to a British patrol but to do this they would have to borrow a camel and I would have to sign a chit to enable them to borrow one. We set off and all the village came out to see us off. They told me the next time I flew over to drop them tea and sugar. After one day's travel we came to another Arab encampment

where I was made welcome, and in the roofs of the tent were letters from RAF and Army personnel who had passed through.'

After a few more days camel-riding they finally reached a wadi where they met a British officer and two signal-men, members of the Long Range Desert Group. A signal was sent to Cairo arranging for a patrol to collect them. The patrol took three days to reach an oasis where a Red Cross plane had been sent to pick them up. However, this plane was destroyed in an air raid and another one was sent which flew Mackintosh to a R.A.F. hospital in Cairo. He arrived in Cairo on 26 June 1942, almost four weeks after being attacked. He later learned that Bill Astell had managed to make it back to Cairo. The rest of the crew were captured by the Germans and three of them were PoWs for the duration of the war. Pilot Officer Dodds was also a PoW in Italy, but later escaped.

In 1956, when Frank, still in the R.A.F., was stationed at Dyce, Yadem came to England as a corporal in the Libyan army. He managed to trace Frank and their reunion was reported in the Scottish press.

'BLOOD BROTHERS' YADEM, MIKE REMEMBER...

'Flight-Lieutenant Mike Mackintosh and his "blood brother" Yadem Abdhul Mustapha – Senussi tribesman who saved his life 14 years ago – spent a lazy day at the R.A.F. officer's Aberdeen home yesterday, recalling old times.

Flight-Lieutenant Mackintosh was the sergeant-pilot of a bomber shot down over the desert in North Africa in 1942. He was wounded and was found by Yadem, then a shepherd, who took him to his tribe.

They dressed his wounds and hid him in caves from the German patrols before taking him 160 miles to a New Zealand long-range desert patrol. Before they parted Mike gave Yadem his name and address.

Letters Returned

'They wrote to each other, but their letters never arrived. Said Flight-Lieutenant Mackintosh yesterday: - "Yadem had joined the Libyan army and all my letters were returned 'address unknown'."

But Yadem became a corporal, was picked to attend a mechanical course in the United Kingdom, and promptly set about tracing his "blood brother."

'He sought the help of the Air Ministry, the B.B.C. and the British Legion, and eventually traced Mike to Aberdeen.

Yadem, on Saturday, met Mrs. Mackintosh and Mike's two children and attended the Battle of Britain air display at Dyce Airport, where Mike was officiating in the airfield control tower.

May Return

'Last night Yadem – after a day of reminiscing at the Mackintosh home at The Hedges, Milltimber, Deeside – left for Birmingham to continue his mechanical course. "But if he can get some leave at the end of his course he'll probably return for a longer visit," said Flight-Lieutenant Mackintosh.'

Michael Frank Mackintosh died, aged 79, in May 2001. His death was registered in Sutton, Surrey.

Frank Newhouse (1924-2009) - (See 'Prisoners of War')

James Alfred Bernard Nottage (1921-2008)

Gunner Bernard Nottage was born on 24 October 1921. He was awarded a W.R.C.C. Minor Scholarship and attended Prince Henry's Grammar School from September 1932 (Form Upper 3B) until May 1938 (Form Lower VI). He passed the School Certificate with Matriculation in 1938, and throughout his school career did well academically:

Form Upper 3B	Form Lower 4A	Form Upper 4A	Form Lower 5A	Form Upper 5A
Progress Prize	1st Prize	2nd Prize	2nd Prize	3rd Prize

He was a Prefect from 1937-1938. On leaving school he was employed on the staff of the Caledonian Insurance Co., Park Lane, Leeds. He joined the Royal Artillery in July 1941. His younger sister, Kathleen May Nottage joined the Civil Nursing Reserve in August 1942. In April 1943 his parents, Mr and Mrs. A. J. Nottage, of Athelstan Lane, Otley, received official intimation that Bernard had been wounded in action in North Africa and was in hospital. Although his injuries were not serious he spent some time at a Convalescent Depot in the Middle East.

J. A. B. Nottage

His military career to date was described in an article published in the *'Wharfedale and Airedale Observer'* on 29 June 1945, when he was home on short leave after three year's active service overseas:

'During these years Gunner Nottage has served as a Surveyor with the Royal Artillery, and has had many varied experiences and taken part in notable engagements. He first went into action in the great Artillery barrage at El Alamein in October 1942, continuing through the victorious desert campaign to Tunis. He holds the Africa Star and Eighth Army clasp.

Proceeding to Italy he was there almost two years of active service, taking part in the advance upon Naples, the shelling of Cassino and the drive to Rome. Transferred to France in the closing weeks of the campaign in Europe his regiment took part in the assault upon Dunkirk and fired their final shells into that famous port on the afternoon of VE-Day.

'Apart from injuries caused by German mines near the Mareth Line, which necessitated a short stay in hospital, Gunner Nottage has enjoyed excellent health, and made the most of the opportunity to visit places of historical interest and famed in other ways. These include Jerusalem, Bethlehem and other places in the Holy Land; Naples, Rome, Florence, Durban (South Africa), Paris etc. Contact with people and places have proved an absorbing interest.

At present he is serving at a dispersal camp in Germany, where over 100,000 German prisoners of all ranks and ages are being dealt with.'

James Alfred Bernard Nottage died on 30 June 2008, his death was registered in Leeds.

Harold Rhodes (1923-)

Harold Rhodes was born on 3 February 1923. His father G.W. Rhodes was a council worker. Harold attended Westgate Council School from 1930-1934 and won a W.R.C.C. Minor Scholarship to Prince Henry's Grammar School. He was admitted to P.H.G.S. in September 1934 (Form Upper 3A) and left in April 1939 (Form Upper 5B). He left to enter the cloth-finishing department at Duncan, Barraclough & Co. Ltd., Otley.

He was not particularly academic, and there are few mentions of him in the '*Otliensian*'. He was commended for submitting an article for the school magazine in the Autumn 1936 issue, but the article was not printed. He was awarded the Bronze Medallion of the Life Saving Society in 1938, perhaps something that persuaded him to join the Royal Navy, and played Rugby for the First XV in his final year at school. His team comment read *'a big, strong forward, with some speed, but rather lacking in mobility. With power to side-step, he would be a good player.'*

He joined the Royal Navy as an Ordinary Seaman, in February 1942 and was on convoy duty on a light cruiser when he was wounded in November 1942. His injuries were stated to be not serious. His younger brother, George H. Rhodes, was also in the Royal Navy. An account of a meeting of the two brothers, both now Able Seamen, in the Pacific was published in the '*Wharfedale and Airedale Observer*' on 16 March 1945:

OTLEY BROTHERS MEET IN THE PACIFIC

'Two Otley brothers, serving on different ships in the Royal Navy, have met in an Eastern port with the Pacific Fleet. They are Able Seaman Harold Rhodes (22) and Able Seaman George H. Rhodes (19), sons of Mr and Mrs. G. W. Rhodes, 1 Newall Avenue, Otley.

'George, who joined the Navy in 1943, in a letter home writes: "I just missed Harold at our last port, but I am glad to say I have caught up with him at last. I went on board to see him yesterday and then we went ashore to celebrate. Today he came on to us and we had tea together – peaches and cream."

Harold joined the Navy in 1942 and has served continuously on the same light cruiser. In 1942 he was wounded in action, but his injuries were not serious. In a letter home he says he was present at the operations off the Burma coast which resulted in the capture of Akyab. He also took part in the landing at Ramree and Cheduba Islands.

"We carried out bombardments when the Army required them," he said.

'George attended Otley Modern School and before the war was apprenticed to Mr M Nelson, plumber, North Avenue, Otley. Harold is a former pupil of Prince Henry's Grammar School and was in the cloth-finishing department at Duncan, Barraclough and Co. Ltd.'

Edgar Robinson (1924-1977)

Driver Edgar Robinson (R.A.S.C.) was born on 15 June 1924 and was one of twin sons of Mr Walter Robinson, the first Headmaster of Prince Henry's Grammar School after it's re-opening in 1918. Edgar was admitted to the Preparatory Department (Form 1) of Prince Henry's on 14 April 1932, when he was still only 7 years of age. He left in May 1937 (Form Upper 3B) after the death of his father. His mother moved the family to Halifax, and Edgar attended Crossley and Porter School.

Edgar participated in Sports Day in 1934 when he came second in the 60 yards (Under 10) and first in the Egg and Spoon Race (Forms 1 & 2). A comment in the *'Otliensian'* notes that he *'shows promise'*, and this was fulfilled when at the 1935 Sports Day he came second in the 70 yards, and first in both the Obstacle Race and the Egg and Spoon Race. In summer 1936 he was awarded second prize in Form 2, and the following year, fourth prize in Form Lower 3.

In April 1943 he joined the General Service Corps. At the time his brothers, L/Sgt. Philip B. Robinson was serving with the R.A. in India, and Cpl. Edward W Robinson with the R.A.S.C. respectively. Edgar transferred to the R.A.S.C. and was wounded in Western Europe on Boxing Day 1944. The Spring 1945 issue of the *'Otliensian'* announced that *'he has now returned to his unit.'*

Edgar Robinson died in 1977, his death being registered in Leeds.

John Reynard Robinson (1920-2007)

L/Sgt. Robinson

Lance Sergeant John R. Robinson (R.A.) was born on 10 February 1920. His father, Reynard Robinson (1872-1958), was a joiner, who married Mary Hannah Burnell (1875-1959) in Wharfedale in 1899. They had ten children, 7 girls and 3 boys.

John attended North Parade School, Otley and from there moved to Prince Henry's in September 1931 (Form Upper 3A). He passed his School Certificate in 1935 and left on 14 February 1936 (Form Upper 5A) to take up employment as a clerk, though he was later employed by Messrs. Winder, of Tranmere Park, Guiseley, as a body-builder of caravans.

He was called up on the outbreak of war with the Otley Battery of the Territorials, and served for some time in France. In December 1942 he went to North Africa. In March 1943 his parents, then living at 1 Duncan Avenue, Otley, were informed that John, their youngest son, had been wounded in North Africa. In an airgraph sent to his parents in early April 1943, he said that he was wounded by shrapnel in his left shoulder, but was now O.K. and hoped to rejoin his unit in a short time.

He was de-mobbed in March 1946, at which time he was with the 70th Field Regiment of the Royal Artillery. He had served in North Africa, Italy, Greece and Austria.

John Robinson died on 6 March 2007.

Frederick George Thomlinson (1918-1996) See - 'Military Decorations'

Thomas Wolf (Wolsey) (1924-)

Thomas Wolf was born on 25 August 1924. He was admitted to Prince Henry's on 26 April 1939 (Form U4A) and left from U5A after passing his School Certificate on 25 July 1941. It seems likely that his family came to England from Germany because on his admission form Thomas' previous schools were listed as 'Montesori, Germany', and 'Kaiser Karl's Gymnasium', which may have been in Aachen. His father was a woollen manufacturer, and in 1939 the family was living at 'Hazeldene', Burras Lane, Otley.

In the Autumn Term, 1939, Thomas joined and became a committee member of the Model Aero Club. He was artistic enough to design a poster for display in local shops during 'War Weapons Week' in 1941, and won the prestigious 'Fanny Barker' Art Prize, presented to him at the Speech Day held in November 1941. When he left school he became a '*Designer*.'

In 1944 he joined the Pioneer Corps, as a Private, and the Spring 1945 issue of the *'Otliensian'* announced that he had been wounded, though no further details were given. By this time he was known as Thomas Wolsey, having changed his name after joining the Army.

Military Decorations

Throughout the War the *'Otliensian'* published lists of Old Otliensians serving with the Forces, and included those who received awards for gallantry. Members of His Majesty's Forces who served in the war received campaign medals, some of which depended on the theatre of war in which they served. Personnel who had their service cut short by death, wounds or capture by the enemy, still qualified for these medals. The reverse of most campaign medals issued by the British government was plain and the medals were unnamed. The criteria for the award of the individual campaign medals were very specific and differed according to the service involved – Army, Royal Navy, Royal Air Force, Merchant Navy – and the operational area covered. Medals are worn suspended from their own specific ribbons, the colours of which have been designed to have a symbolic significance related to the particular medal.

CAMPAIGN MEDALS

Most Armed Service Personnel received the **War Medal 1939-1945** which was awarded to all full time British and Commonwealth service personnel wherever and whatever their service.

The second medal that was awarded to the majority of the Armed Forces Personnel who fought in the Second World War was the **1939-1945 Star**. This star was awarded for service undertaken between 3 September 1939 and 2 September 1945, with different criteria depending on which of the services was represented:

A series of campaign medals were awarded for specific service in a range of theatres of war:

- Africa Star
- Atlantic Star
- Burma Star
- France and Germany Star
- Italy Star
- Pacific Star
- Air Crew Europe Star

These campaign stars also carried clasps, usually referred to as 'bars', that were single-faced metal bars carried on a ribbon attached to the medal to indicate the recipient's service in a particular campaign or battle. The clasps carried side flanges to enable them to be attached to the medal and riveted to each other, so that new ones could be attached as earned.

The final campaign medal issued to British and Commonwealth forces in the Second World War was **The Defence Medal**. It was instituted to recognise both military and some types of civilian service, including, but not confined to, civilian personnel who worked as members of, but not confined to:

- Home Guard
- Royal Observer Corps
- Fire Brigades
- Civil Defence Messenger Service
- Police
- Coast Guard

The qualifying time varied according to the threat and the area served; for the UK it was 1,080 days, served during the period of active hostilities in Europe between September 1939 and May 1945; for overseas non-operational in an area deemed to be closely threatened or subject to air attack, it was 180 days.

GALLANTRY AWARDS

The Otliensians who qualified for the award of campaign medals would have received them at the end of the war. Announcements of the award of gallantry awards were published during the war in the *'London Gazette'*, and King George VI at Buckingham Palace often presented recipients with their awards.

<table>
<tr><th>(Final)Rank
Name
Service No.</th><th>Award</th><th>Service
Regiment/
Squadron</th><th>Date
(Gazette)</th><th>Date of Birth</th><th>Date of Death
(Registered)</th></tr>
<tr><td>Pilot Officer
Eric Reginald Anderson
(1505663)</td><td>Distinguished Flying Cross</td><td>Royal Air Force</td><td>1945</td><td>25 November 1921</td><td>9 March 2010
(Leeds)</td></tr>
<tr><td rowspan="3">Lieutenant-Colonel Reginald Walker Atkinson
(11761)</td><td>Mentioned in Despatches</td><td rowspan="3">Royal Corps of Signals:
23 Indian Divisional Signals</td><td>16 December 1943</td><td rowspan="3">20 December 1907</td><td rowspan="3">1977
(Richmond)</td></tr>
<tr><td>Mentioned in Despatches</td><td>5 April 1945</td></tr>
<tr><td>Order of the British Empire</td><td>28 June 1945</td></tr>
</table>

<table>
<tr><td>Lieutenant-Colonel Harry Ayrton (54347)</td><td>Member of the British Empire</td><td>Royal Army Service Corps</td><td>28 May 1943</td><td>8 July 1909</td><td>18 March 1986 (Andover)</td></tr>
<tr><td rowspan="3">Wing Commander Peter Henry Cribb (33360)</td><td>Distinguished Flying Cross</td><td rowspan="3">Royal Air Force</td><td>1942</td><td rowspan="3">28 September 1918</td><td rowspan="3">20 June 2011 (Australia)</td></tr>
<tr><td>Distingished Service Order</td><td>11 May 1943</td></tr>
<tr><td>D.S.O. with Bar</td><td>March 1945</td></tr>
<tr><td>Sergeant Jack Crossley (2662444)</td><td>Military Medal</td><td>Coldstream Guards; 3rd Battalion</td><td>22 July 1943</td><td>1 June 1920</td><td>1989 (Claro)</td></tr>
<tr><td>Lieutenant Andrew Trevor Firth (289499)</td><td>American Bronze Star</td><td>Royal Artillery</td><td>20 March 1947</td><td>4 June 1922</td><td>1999 (Leeds)</td></tr>
<tr><td>Sergeant – Flight Engineer Derek Heaton Furness (571405)</td><td>Mentioned in Despatches</td><td>Royal Air Force</td><td>1 January 1942</td><td>24 April 1920</td><td>17 September 2010</td></tr>
<tr><td>Flight Lieutenant Douglas Harold Halliwell (169406)</td><td>Distinguished Flying Cross</td><td>Royal Air Force Voluntary Reserve: 199 Squadron</td><td>25 May 1945</td><td>1 October 1920</td><td>1989 (Grantham)</td></tr>
<tr><td>Flying Officer Frederick Victor Houlgate (54598)</td><td>Croix de Guerre</td><td>Royal Air Force – 570 Squadron</td><td>September 1945</td><td>26 January 1923</td><td>1999 (Canada)</td></tr>
<tr><td>Major C. Vernon Light (87378)</td><td>Mentioned in Despatches</td><td>Royal Army Medical Corps</td><td>1944</td><td>9 June 1911</td><td>2 March 1990 (Leeds)</td></tr>
<tr><td>Corporal Brian Hardy Moore (2601498)</td><td>Mentioned in Despatches</td><td>Royal Corps of Signals</td><td>4 January 1945</td><td>16 May 1923</td><td>2003 (South Somerset)</td></tr>
<tr><td>Flying Officer John Robertshaw (149279)</td><td>Distinguished Flying Cross</td><td>Royal Air Force</td><td>20 February 1945</td><td>19 August 1921</td><td>17 September 1994 (Shipley)</td></tr>
<tr><td>Sergeant Thomas Fenton Scott (7397663)</td><td>Mentioned in Despatches</td><td>Royal Army Medical Corps</td><td>24 August 1944</td><td>18 January 1911</td><td>1998 (Huddersfield)</td></tr>
</table>

Second Lieutenant Frederick George Thomlinson (329144)	Croix de Guerre with Silver Star	Kings Own Yorkshire Light Infantry	15 December 1944	16 October 1918	1996 (Ryedale)
Flying Officer Peter Walker (1064007)	Distinguished Flying Medal	Royal Air Force: 78 Squadron	18 May 1943	1 January 1920	???

Eric Reginald Anderson D.F.C. (1921-2010)

Flying Officer, Eric Reginald Anderson was born on 25 November 1921 in Otley. His father, Reginald Anderson (1897-1990) was born in Bramhope and in 1921 he married Lilian White (1894-1996), the marriage being registered in Leeds. Eric entered Prince Henry's (Form Upper 3B) in autumn 1932.

He gave notice of his proficiency in athletics by winning the 100 yards (Under 12) in a time of 13.6 seconds in the summer 1933 Sports. In summer 1935 he was the Individual Junior Champion.

JUNIOR ATHLETIC SPORTS	1	2	3	4
100 yards (under 14)	Anderson E.	Brearley D.	Mackintosh F.	Mallinson D.
220 yards (Under 14)	Anderson E.	Brearley D.	Harrison H.	Mackintosh F.
High Jump (Under 14)	Mackintosh F.	Anderson E.	Wood E.	Mallinson D.
Long jump (Under 14)	Mallinson D.	Anderson E.	Brearley D.	Mackintosh F.
Individual Champion (Junior)	Anderson E.	Brearley D.		

In 1937, competing in the Open events and probably younger than his rivals, he again had some success:

	1	2	3
100 yards (Open)	D. G. Brearley (11 2/5 seconds)	E. R. Anderson	A. D. Walker

440 yards (Open)	A. Walker (59 4/5 seconds)	T. R. Robertshaw	E. R. Anderson
High Jump (Open)	T. Robertshaw (4ft. 7in.)	E. R. Anderson & A. Walker	

But he left the best to his final year when in summer 1938 he became Individual Senior Champion and was awarded the Milligan Cup. He set a new record in the 220 yards, with a time of 25.6 seconds, 0.6 seconds better than the time set by H. Mallinson in 1930.

	1	2	3
100 yards (Open)	E. R. Anderson (10 4/5 seconds)	H. Harrison & H. Pullan	
220 yards (Open)	E. R. Anderson (25 3/5 seconds)	D. H. Mallinson	H. Harrison
440 yards (Open)	E. R. Anderson (59 seconds)	N. Rhodes	D. H. Mallinson
880 yards (Open)	D. H. Mallinson (2min 28 3/5 seconds)	L Aveyard	E R Anderson
High Jump (Open)	E. R. Anderson (4ft. 11in.)	A. W. Moore	
Individual Championship Senior	E. R. Anderson (13 points)	D. H. Mallinson (9 points)	

Eric Anderson played both Cricket and Rugby for the School. His performances in Cricket were not strong; his batting average in 1935-36 was only 3.00, though he did score 16 runs in a 6 run defeat to R. Whyte's XI in May 1938. His Rugby career was more memorable. In the Lent 1937 issue of the '*Otliensian*' (*Vol. XIX*) he was said to be *'improving. He is inclined to tackle high and lacks confidence in making a dash for the line.'* His position in the team was left wing, showing his sprinting prowess.

In the following year he was awarded his Rugby colours and had moved to Left-Centre where he was said to be *'Strong, speedy and well-built. Very good in defence, but often weak in taking passes.'*

'Our congratulations go to the following on being awarded their School colours:

- *RUGBY – E. R. Anderson, A. Firth, N. B. Robinson, K. S. Temple, R. Watkins'*

In autumn 1937 he was appointed as a Prefect:

'The following School appointments have been made this term –

PREFECTS – Boys: Eric R. Anderson, Joseph Mann, James A. B. Nottage, Thomas R. Robertshaw, Frank Secker. Girls: Margaret Atkinson, Marjorie S. Bennett, Margaret Bramley, Lucy H. Stowe, Muriel Keighley, Sheila G. Hay, Eileen M. Wall'

His academic ability was limited to an 'honourable mention' when he was in Form Upper 5A, but in 1938 he did pass the School Certificate with Matriculation and attained a distinction in English Language. He left school from the Lower VI in summer 1938.

He volunteered for the Royal Air Force in 1940 and trained in California, where he gained his 'wings' in October 1942. On 29 November 1943, whilst still a Sergeant, he was the pilot of Halifax Bomber DT776 that took off from Riccall on a night circuit practice. A tyre burst on landing and the plane swung and its under-carriage collapsed. No one was injured.

(R.A.F. Bomber Command Losses, Vol. 8, by W.R. Chorley)

He began operational duties at the start of 1944, and received his commission as Pilot Officer in April 1944, by which time he had been on 12 trips, including raids on Berlin, Stuttgart, Nuremberg, Essen and several French targets.

In Spring 1945 (*Vol. XXVII*) the '*Otliensian*' announced the award of the D.F.C. to Eric Anderson:

'Flying Officer Eric R. Anderson R.A.F. has been awarded the D.F.C. The official citation refers to Flying Officer Eric Anderson as a pilot and captain who has completed very many sorties, involving attacks on well-defended targets in Germany and, more recently, on targets in Northern France. He has displayed outstanding determination and his coolness and courage under enemy fire has greatly inspired his crew. On one occasion, when over Bourg Leopold, Flying Officer Anderson saw one of the Bomber force being attacked by a fighter. Drawing closer he manoeuvred to a good position and his gunners opened fire. As the enemy aircraft turned to meet the challenge another burst of fire was delivered which caused the fighter to fall towards the ground with quantities of smoke pouring from it.'

In 1945 he married Carella Margaret Lockett, eldest daughter of Mr and Mrs. R. Lockett of Trevanson, Wadebridge. The bride was a nurse at the Bristol Royal Infirmary.

Eric Anderson died on 9 March 2010, his death being registered in Leeds.

Reginald Walker Atkinson O.B.E. (1907-1977)

Lieutenant-Colonel Reginald Walker Atkinson (born 20 December 1907), Royal Corps of Signals was awarded the O.B.E. (Military Division) for operations in Burma. He lived at 27 Hamilton Terrace, Otley. His father, Fred Atkinson was a mechanic. In 1905 he married Annie Walker, the marriage being registered in Wharfedale. The 1911 Census listed the family as living at 16 Market Place, Otley where Fred was an Iron Turner at a Printers and Annie was a pawnbroker's assistant. They had two children, Reginald (aged 3) and his younger sister Louisa (aged 0). After attending Otley National School, Reginald was awarded a West Riding County Minor Scholarship and entered Prince

Henry's Grammar School on 16 September 1919 (Form 3B). He was part of the second intake into the re-opened school. He left on 25 July 1923 (Form Upper 5) to become a draughtsman-surveyor with Dawson, Payne and Elliott Ltd, Otley, and later joined the Army, where he worked his way through the ranks, becoming a Lieutenant Colonel in 1943.

Whilst at P.H.G.S. he played rugby for the 1st XV and Cricket for the 1st XI. He ran in the 220 yards (under 14) race on Sports Day in 1921, finishing fourth in a field of 32.

He scored 18 runs in a game against Shipley Salts School on 27 May 1922 during a season in which School won all of its matches, though they fared less well in the following season. He later played for an Army XI at Lords.

The '*Otliensian*' of Summer 1922 commented as follows on the team's performance over the season: *'the season has witnessed a marked improvement in the quality of our cricket. Not only have we won all our games, but in the winning we have shewn real cricket. Our batsmen are learning to appreciate the superiority of correct strokes over those of the "agricultural or mowing" variety; in the field too, intelligent anticipation of strokes has helped as much as keenness. Altogether a most successful season, and only one of many to come when every boy regards Saturday afternoons on the field as a pleasure rather than a duty. To Baldwin, Hellewell, Atkinson, Watkinson and Mainprize (N), belongs the credit for our scores; whilst the task of controlling our opponents' scores has been well carried out by Webb, Thistlethwaite, Lupton (M) and Baldwin. Lupton (M) and Thistlethwaite both accomplished the "hat trick" the latter making with his fourth ball a successful start towards a double event.'*

He was awarded his School rugby colours in 1923, when he played scrum-half for the 1st XV. His profile described him as '*quick and active. His short kicks have been useful in defence.*'

He joined the ranks of the R.C.S. in February 1926, and some time later went to Egypt, where he served for over five years. He came home in 1935 as a Sergeant. On 8 August 1936 he married Miss Hilda Margaret Neesham of West Hartlepool. One year after his marriage he went to India, where he was awarded a commission, and made Lieutenant. In November 1941 he was made Captain; in 1942 promoted to Major; and in 1943 to Lieutenant Colonel. He made the Army his career and worked his way up from the ranks to a position of high responsibility.

The award of the O.B.E. was confirmed on 28 June 1945 while he was still a Major (Service No. 11761) with the 23rd Indian Divisional Signals, based in Burma. He returned to England from Bombay on the '*Circassia*', landing in Liverpool on 31

December 1950. The award citation, dated 19 October 1944 reads:

'T/Lt-Col R.W.ATKINSON has held the appointment of O.C. 23 Ind. Div. Sigs, since 19 Mar 43. During the operations in the IMPHAL area from March – August 44 he carried out his duties to my entire satisfaction. This officer is an enthusiast and his drive and tireless energy and his cheerfulness in difficulties inspired the whole of the Divisional Signal personnel with the result that their work was first class. As C.S.O. he had many difficulties to contend with apart from the Japs. The terrain over which the Brigades operated, mountainous and with thick jungle, and latterly the monsoon conditions all added to the difficulties of inter-communication and it speaks highly for the Signal personnel – so thoroughly trained by him – that in spite of these conditions they were always able to maintain communication.

'Lt.Col. ATKINSON never spared himself and was perfectly willing and able to work 24 hours a day when the occasion demanded it. I consider that his careful and skilful planning, his ability to look ahead and ensure that the necessary signal stores were in the right place at the right time and his selfless devotion to duty were in the greatest measure responsible for the undoubtedly high standard of signal efficiency maintained in the Division in action under definitely difficult and arduous conditions.'

The citation also records that he had previously been twice mentioned in despatches on 16 December 1943 and 5 April 1945, on both occasions in Burma.

The *'Otliensian'* (*Vol. XXXIX, Summer 1957*) reported that:

'Colonel Reginald Walker Atkinson, O.B.E. of the Royal Signals, has been granted the acting rank of Brigadier. Brigadier Atkinson, on leaving school, decided to make the Army his career and joined as a private soldier. We remember how well he could wield a cricket bat and dance a Highland fling. It is understood that he will shortly retire to live in Richmond, though he will continue to give the Army the benefit of his wide experience by accepting a civilian attachment at Catterick Camp.'

He died in 1977 at Richmond, North Yorkshire.

Harry Ayrton M.B.E. (1909-1986)

Harry Ayrton was born on 8 July 1909 at Ashfield Place in Menston, and was baptised at St John the Divine Church, Menston, on 8 August 1909. His father, Burton Ayrton (born 1882 in Halifax, died 1965 in Worth Valley), married Alice Broughton in 1908. In the 1911 Census the family was living at Derry Hill, Menston and Burton was listed as a Station Porter. They had two sons, Harry, the eldest, and his younger brother Stanley. Their father saw action in the Boer War, and took part in the 1914-18 war. On Harry's entry to P.H.G.S. his father's occupation was given as a Signalman.

Harry entered Prince Henry's (Form 3A) on 13 January 1922. He had attended Menston Council School and lived on Main Street, Menston. He left school on 27 June 1924

(Form 4A) and entered a 'Textile Trade School'; his school record shows that the '*agreement was broken but penalty paid'* – this shows that he was allowed to leave school early on the understanding that agreed penalty fees were paid by his parents.

He performed well in the 1922 Athletic Sports:

JUNIOR BOYS	1	2	3	4
High Jump (Under 13)	H. Ayrton	E. Condradi	C. Hodgson	H. G. Allsop
100 yards (Under 14)	F. Greetham	H. Ayrton	W. Hixon	W. Hindle
220 yards (Under 14)	F. Greetham	W. Hixon	H. Ayrton	M. E. Midgley
Long Jump (Under 13)	H. Ayrton & A. Mawson		F. Knowlson	F. Thackery

After leaving school he worked for some time as a clerk for Robert Jowett & Sons, Bradford.

He joined the Army as a private in 1932. His father had been a soldier with the King's Royal Rifle Corps, and Harry also joined the Greenjackets (K.R.R.C). Harry served in Shanghai and Hong Kong, and went to France early in the war, being evacuated from Dunkirk. He worked his way through the ranks and in May 1943 was granted a commission and was promoted to the rank of Captain. At the time he was serving in India with the R.A.S.C. In 1944 he was promoted to the rank of Major, and by August 1945 had attained the rank of Lieutenant Colonel. He left the Army after the war, and went into business, but in the early 1950s he applied to re-enter the Army and finally retired in 1962.

In the Summer 1945 edition of the '*Otliensian*' (*Vol. XXVII*) it was reported that:

'M.B.E. (Military Division)

Major Harry Ayrton, R.A.S.C., has been awarded the M.B.E.'

This was a late acknowledgement of the award of the M.B.E. in 1943, which was published in the *'London Gazette'* on 28 May 1943:

No. 54347 Warrant Officer Class I Staff Sergeant Major Harry Ayrton, Royal Army Service Corps.

On 15 October 1938 he married Kathleen Mary Anderton:

'The wedding took place at St. John's Church, Menston, on Saturday, of Mr Harry Ayrton, eldest son of Mr. and Mrs. B. Ayrton of Derry Hill Road, Menston, and Miss Kathleen Mary Anderton, only daughter of Mr. and Mrs. T. Anderton of Ashfield Homestead Estate, Menston.'

Harry and Mary had two daughters, Pamela (1939-1988) and Wendy Lois (1947-2005). Harry died on 18 March 1986, age 76, in the Memorial Hospital, Andover, Hampshire. His occupation was given as a Catering Contractor (retired). Mary died in the Royal

Hampshire County Hospital, Winchester on 12 December 2002, aged 89.

His progress through the ranks can be followed in a series of articles published in the *'Wharfedale and Airedale Observer'*:

'Wharfedale and Airedale Observer', 21 May 1943 -
PROMOTED TO CAPTAIN

'Staff-Sergt-Major Harry Ayrton (33) elder son of Mr and Mrs. Ayrton, Derry Hill, Menston, has been granted a commission and promoted to the rank of Captain.

He is serving in India with the R.A.S.C. Capt. Ayrton, a native of Menston, is an old scholar of Prince Henry's Grammar School, Otley. After leaving school he worked for some years as a clerk on the staff of Robert Jowett and Sons, Bradford, and joined the Army 11 years ago. He served in Shanghai and Hong Kong, and went to France early in the war, being evacuated from Dunkirk. He has been in India about a year. He is married and has one small daughter.'

'Wharfedale and Airedale Observer', 3 March 1944 -
MENSTON OFFICER PROMOTED MAJOR

'Captain Harry Ayrton (34) elder son of Mr and Mrs. Ayrton, Derry Hill, Menston, has been promoted to the rank of Major. Serving in India with the R.A.S.C., he was promoted last year from the rank of Staff-Sergt-Major.

'Wharfedale and Airedale Observer', 24 August 1945 -
MENSTON MAN PROMOTED

'Mrs. H. Ayrton of Menston has received a cable from India to say that her husband has been promoted to Lieut-Colonel.

Lieut-Colonel Ayrton M.B.E. is only 36 years of age. He is the elder son of Mr and Mrs. B. Ayrton, Derry Hill, Menston. He is a regular soldier. After joining up some 14 years ago as a private, he saw service in the Far East before the outbreak of war in 1939. He took part in the Dunkirk invasion, and since has been serving in India.

His home is in Menston having married the only daughter of Mr and Mrs. T. Anderson of the Homestead Estate. They have one child, a little girl five years old.'

Harry's brother, Warrant Officer Stanley Ayrton, served in the Royal Engineers. He spent four years with the 50th Division in the Western Desert. He came home on leave in March 1945 having been the only member of his unit to draw a ticket under the 'leave ballot scheme.' After his leave he went back to Trans-Jordan and later Syria and Iraq before returning to England on home service in October 1945 and finally being demobilised on 23 December 1945. After demobilisation he re-opened the plumbing business he ran in Menston before the war.

Peter Henry Cribb D.F.C., D.S.O. with Bar (1918-2011)

Peter Henry Cribb was born on 28 September 1918 in Bradford and entered Form Lower 5A in Prince Henry's on 13 September 1932, having previously been at Bradford Grammar School (1928-1932). His father, Charles Bertram Cribb (1870-1947) was a retired Stuff Merchant, and the family lived at 'Nokassen', Cleasby Road, Menston. Charles married Ethel Bown in 1904 and in the 1911 Census they were living at 5 Cunliffe Villas, Bradford and Charles was listed as a Manager in the Lining Department in a Stuff Merchant. At the time they had four children and were able to employ a Nursery Governess and a Domestic Servant. Peter left school on 29 July 1935, from the Sixth Form. He entered R.A.F. Cranwell as a Cadet.

He passed his School Certificate with Matriculation in summer 1934. His only academic form prize was awarded in summer 1933 when he was placed third equal. He played Rugby for the First XV, but his only mention in the '*Otliensian*' was in Lent 1936 when it was noted that both he and Robertshaw *'Have had places in the pack since Christmas and have shown considerable promise'.*

In summer 1934 he won the Royal Life Saving Society: Silver Medal and went on to gain his First Class Instructor's Certificate in the following year. To gain this award he had to supervise a swimming class:

'Cribb P. H., who holds the Silver Medal, is in charge of the boys' class. We wish him success in his attempt to win the Instructor's Medal. The class, though small, is very keen, and there is every prospect of the results being highly satisfactory. (We have just been informed that all candidates have been successful – EDITOR) Result, 100 per cent success.' (Vol. XVII, Summer, 1934)

In summer 1936 he was elected captain of the newly formed Boxing Club. A.A. Morton was elected as Secretary and *'Mr Evans and Mr Davison agreed to give instruction. The Club nights were fixed for Mondays and Thursdays. The membership to date is just over twenty, and progress has, so far, been highly satisfactory.'*

Peter Cribb was also a keen actor. At Easter 1934 he shared the part of Mr Hastings in '*She Stoops to Conquer*' with Douglas Waye - Cribb acting on the first night, and Waye on the second. In the following year in '*The Boy Comes Home*' he played the double part of the Boy.

' 'The Boy Comes Home', a war play. P. H. Cribb played the double part of the Boy excellently, and A. A. Morton surpassed himself as the choleric uncle. L. Stowe was very

good as the terrifying Mrs. Higgins, and D. Irving and E. Wood also took part.'

At Easter 1936 in the play *'A Night at the Inn'*, he:

'was good as "the Toff" – a gentleman crook. The rest of the gang provided interesting contrasts – Sully as Albert, a daring cockney; Hudson, as Bill, a real tough; and Hymas, who was outstanding as the highly strung, timid Sniggers. Irwin was most impressive as the idol, and Atkinson, Anderson and Watson made admirable stealthy Indian priests and died most realistically.'

His interest in flying was shown by two lectures he gave to the Natural Science Society. The first in 1933 was on *'Model Aeroplanes.'*

'The next meeting was addressed by P. Cribb, who dealt with 'Model Aeroplanes'. After a survey of the types of models and how they are built, the lecturer dealt with more intricate points, such as balance, stability, and speed. Those present were able to examine the lecturer's own models, and the various unassembled parts which he brought with him. Kay from the Chair thanked Cribb for his fascinating lecture.' ('Otliensian' Vol. XV, Lent 1933)

The second in 1934 was on *'Imperial Airways.'*

'Two meetings have been held during the past term. At the first, the Lecturer was P. H. Cribb. It will be remembered that Cribb gave us an exceedingly good talk on 'Model Aeroplanes' last year, and while his lecture on 'Imperial Airways' took a somewhat different form, it was equally enjoyable. It consisted of a series of lantern slides, kindly lent for the occasion by Imperial Airways Ltd. Descriptions and explanations were provided by the Lecturer. A series of statistics were first shown, demonstrating the remarkable growth of air traffic in recent years. Next came illustrations of the various types of aeroplanes in use by Imperial Airways Ltd., and of Croyden Aerodrome. Finally a most charming set of aerial photographs was shown. These were of various towns and cities visited by Imperial Airways machines. At the close of the lecture, a vote of thanks proposed by the Chairman, S.E. Cruise, was heartily carried.' ('Otliensian' Vol. XVI, Summer 1934)

Peter Cribb married Patricia G. Walter in 1939. They had two children, Michael Bruce Cribb (born 1941) and Rosemary Cribb (1942-2001). Peter and Patricia were later divorced and both remarried in 1949 – Peter to Vivienne Janet Peniston Perry, and Patricia to Ewart W. Macdonald. Peter and Vivienne had three children - Julian Hilary James Cribb (born 1951), Andrew Charles Adrian Cribb (born 1956) and Simon Peter Cribb (born 1958 in Germany).

He was commissioned as Pilot Officer in 1938, and promoted to acting Squadron Leader in January 1942. In September 1942 he was promoted to Acting Wing Commander, by September 1944 he held the rank of Group Captain, and from February 1945 that of Wing Commander.

The *'Otliensian'* followed Peter Cribb's career closely. The award of the D.F.C. was recognised with pride in Summer 1942 *(Vol. XXIV)*:

'Acting Squadron Leader Peter Henry Cribb (No 35 Squadron), whose "devotion to duty, regardless of the opposition, has set a fine example to all", has been awarded the D.F.C. Acting Squadron Leader Cribb has taken part in many attacks on enemy targets, including Oslo, Aalborg, Stavanger, Bremen and Hamm. Hearty congratulations and best wishes from all Old Scholars!

The School was proud to learn of the award of the D.F.C. to Acting Squadron Leader P. Cribb who, we believe, is the first Old Scholar to receive a military decoration. To him we extend our warm congratulations, and to all Old Scholars, wherever they may be serving, we send greetings and sincere wishes for their speedy and safe return.'

The presentation of the D.F.C. was noted in Autumn 1942 (*Vol.XXV*):

'Wing Commander Peter Henry Cribb has received from H.M. the King at a recent investiture the Distinguished Flying Cross awarded to him this summer. Mrs. Peter Cribb (nee Patricia Walter), also an Old Scholar, was present at the investiture. Wing Commander Cribb, who is a Path-Finder, has made more than fifty operational flights since the war began, over Norway, Denmark, Germany, Holland, Belgium, Italy and France. His exploits include a low level attack on the German battleship, 'Tirpitz'.'

The Pathfinder Force was formed because early in the war bomber crews had little or no way of gauging the accuracy of their bombing.

'At the time the Pathfinders were formed, the aircraft had virtually no radio or electronic aids to navigation or bombing which were effective over enemy territory. This meant that finding the target depended almost entirely on map reading and dead reckoning, using very shaky forecasts of winds. If, as frequently happens in Europe, the night was dark and the coastal features and targets well obscured by cloud, the odds were heavily against even the most determined crew pinpointing the target.'

*(Peter H Cribb, as quoted in **'THE PATHFINDER COMPANION', Sean Feast, 2012**)*

In some instances bombers were missing their targets by as much as seventy or eighty miles, and, being unable to find their primary targets, ended up bombing secondary or even tertiary targets. When cameras were fitted to planes to verify claims that targets had been hit they confirmed that results were poor. Even with a full moon only two out of five operations found their targets.

At first target marking was tried, where a group of planes dropped flares to improve the bombing accuracy of the planes that followed. However, it was eventually agreed that an elite, dedicated force be set up using the best pilots and navigators, and the

Pathfinder Force was formed, with the aim of marking the targets for the bombers that followed.

Cribb visited his old school early in 1943, and the award of the D.S.O. was noted (*Summer 1943, Vol. XXV):*

'It was with particular pleasure that the School received a visit last term from Wing-Commander Peter Cribb D.S.O., D.F.C., who addressed us after prayers one morning. Since Christmas there have also been several talks and lectures on various aspects of the war by outside speakers who have thus been the means of relating our school life to the world in which we live.

'Wing-Commander Peter Henry Cribb D.F.C., of Menston was invested with the D.S.O. on May 11th 1943. The citation stated: "Wing-Commander Cribb has an outstanding record as a captain of an aircraft and has displayed exceptional qualities of leadership in many sorties against the enemy. He has attacked his targets with unfailing regularity and accuracy. Wing-Commander Cribb has a thorough knowledge of air warfare and his high qualities, combined with his consistent keenness have set a high example to all.'

The award of the bar to the D.S.O. was noted in the Summer 1945 issue (*Vol. XXVII*):

'Group Captain Peter H Cribb, D.S.O., D.F.C., R.A.F., has been awarded a bar to the D.S.O.'

'The Yorkshire Post and Leeds Intelligencer' (24 March 1945) contained an article confirming the award of the bar to the D.S.O.:

'A Bar to the D.S.O. has been awarded to Acting Group Captain Peter Henry Cribb D.F.C. This officer has commanded his squadron for a considerable period with distinction and gallantry and has also proved himself to be an outstanding captain of aircraft. Since the award of the D.S.O. he has raised the squadron to a high pitch of efficiency. He recently operated over many of the most heavily defended targets in Germany. Born near Bradford, he was educated at Bradford and Prince Henry's Grammar School, Otley. His home is at Menston.'

The final magazine entry was as late as Summer 1957 (*Vol. XXXIX*):

'Group-Captain Peter H. Cribb has been appointed Commanding Officer at R.A.F. Oldenberg, Germany. For the last four years he has been Group-Captain Plans and Policy at Bomber Command H.Q.'

Peter Henry Cribb died on 20 June 2011 in Western Australia; his obituary was published in the *'Daily Telegraph'* on 22 June 2011.

Air Commodore Peter Cribb

'Air Commodore Peter Cribb, who has died aged 92, was one of the most successful and gallant master bombers of the Pathfinder Force; he flew more than 100 wartime operations, including one when he made an unauthorised raid on Hitler's retreat at

Berchtesgaden.

'Cribb was already a veteran of more than 70 missions when he returned to operations in May 1944 to fly the Lancaster. He attacked targets in the run-up to D-Day, often acting as the master bomber directing the main force against rail yards and gun emplacements.

'In July he was put in command of the newly formed No. 582 Squadron and flew 16 daylight sorties in support of the Normandy landings. On July 18 he was the deputy master bomber when more than 1,000 aircraft pulverised the German panzer divisions in front of Montgomery's stalled army at Caen.

'Cribb also controlled more than 700 bombers which attacked the V-7 sites before the bombing campaign resumed its efforts against major oil targets in Germany.

'On October 3 he was master bomber for the attack on the sea walls of Walcheren Island. Coastal gun batteries dominated the approaches to the important port of Antwerp; the aim was to breach the walls and flood the island, most of which was reclaimed polder below sea level.

'As the first to arrive at the head of 252 Lancasters, he orbited the target and directed eight separate waves of bombers, correcting the aiming point with flares and markers to widen the initial breach. The sea poured in, forcing the German defenders to abandon their carefully prepared positions. Cribb was the last to leave the target after a brilliantly controlled attack, which allowed Canadian ground forces to capture the island and opened Antwerp to the Allies. Newspapers hailed the achievement with the headline "R.A.F. sinks an island."

'On promotion to group captain at the age of 25, Cribb was appointed to command the Pathfinder airfield at Little Staughton in Bedfordshire, and shortly afterwards he was awarded a Bar to an earlier D.S.O. Frustrated at being desk-bound, he flew unofficially on a number of operations. On April 24 1945 he learned that a force of Lancasters was to bomb Hitler's Bavarian retreat at Berchtesgaden, but the Lancaster squadron on his airfield was stood down.

'Determined not to miss this final attempt to eliminate Hitler, Cribb commandeered a Lancaster and some bombs and made up a crew from the senior executives on his station. He took off at dawn, catching up with the main force as it was approaching the target. He dropped his bombs and obtained an excellent aiming point photograph.

'Anxious to get back to Britain before anyone realised what he had been up to, Cribb returned on a direct route at top speed – but to no avail. Air Vice-Marshall Donald Bennett, head of the Pathfinder Force, had tried to contact him and his deputy, only to be told that they were airborne on "a 10-hour navigation exercise." It was said that, when he learned the truth, Bennett "hit the roof".

'The son of a wool merchant, Peter Henry Cribb was born in the Yorkshire Dales on September 28 1918 and educated at Prince Henry's Grammar School, Otley, before

gaining a cadetship to the R.A.F. College, Cranwell, where he trained as a pilot.

'Cribb joined No 58 Squadron to fly the Whitley bomber, and on the outbreak of war flew convoy patrols before the squadron reverted to the bombing role. He was involved in attacks of German-occupied airfields in Norway and Denmark.

'Following the German blitz into the Low Countries, he bombed road and rail systems being used to transport reinforcements, and during a hectic period in June he flew numerous sorties in support of the British Expeditionary Force. After completing 25 operations he was rested.

'In December 1941 Cribb was promoted to squadron leader and joined the R.A.F's first Halifax squadron, No 35, as a flight commander. He attacked major industrial targets in Germany before turning his attention to the German battleship Tirpitz, which was at anchor in a fjord near Trondheim.

'Bad weather and a smoke screen severely hampered the low-level attack and the force returned the following day. As he approached in poor visibility, Cribb's Halifax hit the sea and the tail wheel was ripped off. After he had landed the intelligence officer asked him at what height he had delivered his attack. Cribb replied: "I don't know. The altimeter reads in feet. Not fathoms."

'Cribb flew on the first 'Thousand Bomber' raid, against Cologne of the night of May 30 1942, and on the attacks on Essen and Bremen that followed. Shortly afterwards he was awarded a D.F.C.

'No 35 became one of the founder squadrons of the Pathfinders, and Cribb – who was rated an "exceptional" pilot – flew on the first raid mounted by the new force when he attacked Flensburg on the night of August 18/19 1942. He went on to attack the heavily defended targets on the Ruhr, often returning with the Halifax damaged by enemy gunfire. By January 1943 he had completed 60 operations and was awarded his first D.S.O.

'During this period he shared a bleak Nissen hut with his Canadian colleague, "Shady" Lane. The winter of 1942-43 was especially cold, and both men were anxious to avoid being the last into bed, and thus responsible for switching out the lights. Eventually Cribb circumvented this problem by shooting them out instead with his .38 revolver. Due to the cold and an alcoholic haze, he frequently missed. In the morning his batman would wake him with a cup of tea and inquire: "Shall I reload, sir?"

'Cribb was given command of the Bomber Development Unit, working closely with the eminent scientist R.V. Jones to develop new bombing, navigation and electronic countermeasure aids. He frequently flew on operations unofficially to test new equipment and tactics. In May 1944 he returned to the Pathfinder Force to start a third tour of operations.

'In May 1945 he left for Ceylon, from where he flew Liberators on mercy missions to drop food and medical supplies to the P.o.W. camps spread across the Far East. He

served in India and commanded the airbase at Peshawar during the difficult period of Indian Partition.

'After a period with Coastal Command and at the Air Ministry, on technical intelligence duties, he served at HQ Bomber Command, responsible for operational plans and policy at a time when the V-bombers were entering service. He was appointed C.B.E.

'In 1957 Cribb was sent to Germany, where he commanded three fighter stations and took every opportunity to fly the Meteor and Hunter fighters. In 1961, on promotion to Air Commodore, he served in Aden as the senior air staff officer, having responsibility for operations in the Radfan and along the Yemen border.

'Two years at the M.o.D. left him disillusioned with the Wilson government's defence cuts, and disdainful of "the ponderous bureaucratic existence in Whitehall". Accordingly, he resigned in 1967.

'Cribb moved with his family to Western Australia, where he was manager of one of the state's first giant iron ore mines before starting his own business in Perth. He was active as a Rotarian, magistrate and charity worker.

'A keen sportsman in his youth, Cribb played rugby for the Yorkshire Wanderers, once breaking his nose during a warm-up match against the All Blacks. In later life he was a blue-water yachtsman and game fisherman. A modest man, he never spoke of his wartime experiences unless pressed to do so and then only to relate the episodes he had found amusing.

'Peter Cribb died on June 20. He married, in 1949, Vivienne Perry, who survives him with their three sons. A son by an earlier marriage also survives him.'

Jack Crossley (Military Medal) – see 'Prisoners of War'

Derek Heaton Furness – see 'Prisoners of War'

Andrew Trevor Firth (American Star) (1922-1999)

Andrew Trevor Firth achieved the distinction of being awarded an American decoration – the Bronze Star Medal:

'awarded to any person who, after December 6, 1941, while serving in any capacity with the Armed Forces of the United States, distinguishes himself or herself by heroic or meritorious achievement or service, not involving participation in aerial flight.'

He was born on 4 June 1922, and entered Prince Henry's Grammar School in September 1933 (Form Upper 3B). He lived at 'Netherfield', Bradford Road, Otley and his father, Seth (1890-1958), was in business as a plasterer. Seth married Amy Womersley in 1915, and their first child, John Douglas Firth (1916-1976) also attended Prince Henry's.

Andrew's grandfather, also named Andrew, who founded the business of Andrew Firth & Sons, plasterers, came originally from Eccleshill, Bradford, but Seth and his four brothers and two sisters were born in Yeadon.

Lt. A. T. Firth

John was also in the Royal Artillery, and was wounded in Western Europe on January 20 1945. (*see 'Wounded'*)

At the end of his first year, Andrew was awarded a prize for fourth place in Form Upper 3B – first prize went to Bernard Lilley, 3rd prize to Norman Winterburn, both of whom were later killed in the war. In 1935 he was again placed fourth in Lower 4A, in 1936 was joint-third in Form Upper 4A, and in 1937 was third in Form Lower 5A. In summer 1939, just before the start of the war, he passed his School Certificate and in the following year gained the Higher School Certificate and entered Leeds University as a Law student, articled to Messrs. Ernest Hind and Co., solicitors, Bradford. He also joined the University Training Corps, and was a member of the local Home Guard. The old scholar's letter from Leeds in autumn 1941 noted that *'at odd times the beaming face of A.T. Firth greets us as he bounces from one lecture on Law to another (by way of the Union coffee room.)'*

The *'Otliensian'* published in Summer 1942 announced that Andrew had joined the Royal Artillery as a Gunner (Service No. 289499). He was awarded his L.LB. Degree in summer 1943 and was accepted by the O.C.T.U where he was commissioned as Second Lieutenant. In spring 1944 he became engaged to Nora Cornforth Armitage, the happy event coinciding with his promotion to Lieutenant. In 1945 he was promoted to Captain in the Royal Army Education Corps. He was married at Baildon Parish Church on 27 April 1946. He was demobilised in November 1946.

Like many of his contemporaries at Prince Henry's, Andrew took an active part in extra-curricular activities. He played both Rugby and cricket for the school, eventually captaining both the First Rugby XV and the First Cricket XI. He was awarded his Rugby colours in 1938, when his team criticism noted that as a forward he *'has improved greatly and is a good all round player, always ready to help in defence.'* In 1939 he was said to have *'played well both in the pack and as a centre. Lacks speed but has tireless energy and uses his weight,'* and in 1940 as captain that he *'has been a good leader. Works hard in scrums and loose play. Tackling and kicking have been invaluable in defence.'*

At cricket he was something of an all rounder, scoring 17 runs out of the school's total of 53 against Roundhay in 1939, and taking 4 wickets at a cost of 20 runs against Ilkley in 1940.

His name features only once in the Sports Day results, when he was placed third in the Discuss in 1939, but in the same year he was third in the Boys' Swimming Championships. He may have been a participating member of the Boxing Club; he was certainly thanked in 1938 for designing a new head for the Club's notices.

He also took a keen and active interest in the non-sporting societies. In the annual Christmas Concert in 1934 he was one of the Three Merchants in the play '*Twice as Much*.' In 1937 the Dramatic Society produced a selection from Shakespeare's '*Merry Wives of Windsor*,' in which Andrew played the part of Bardolph. In 1938 he took the part of Sir Lucius O'Trigger in '*The Rivals*':

'A. Firth's natural breeziness was well suited to Sir Lucius, who was portrayed with life and with an accent which was not the less comical because it was, we believe, linguistically non-existent!' ('Otliensian' Vol. XX, Summer 1938)

His portrayal of Sir Peter Teazle in The Literary, Historical and Debating Society's production of '*School for Scandal*' in 1939 was especially commended by the Chairman, Mr Leech.

His career in the Law had its foundations in his membership of the more 'academic' School societies, but may well have started when on 21 October, 1938 a House Speaking Competition was held:

'This was an innovation, but was greatly appreciated. Teams of three had to speak on subjects introducing the House Colour, such as 'White Elephants' and 'Yellow Press.' The result was 1. Fawkes 2. Cave 3. Fairfax 4. Duncan; and the "individual championship" was won by A. Firth, whose speech on 'Blue Devils' was awarded 41 marks out of a possible 50.' ('*Otliensian' Vol. XXI, Autumn 1938*)

He was an active member of the 'League of Nations Union', Treasurer of 'The Literary, Historical & Debating Society', and Hon.Sec. of the 'Magazine Committee.' The 'League of Nations Union' at school was short-lived, but at the March 1939 meeting, Andrew may well have spoken on the merits of 'Fascism', only months before the outbreak of war against Germany.

'.....the old arguments for and against Communism, Fascism and Democracy were brought forward in new guises, in the form of election speeches. N. King, A. Firth and R. Whitaker were the speakers, and they sought to persuade their audience that the form of government which they spoke for was the best for the welfare of the nation.' ('Otliensian' Vol. XXI, Spring 1939)

Andrew won his first legal argument at a meeting of the Literary, Historical and Debating Society held on 14 December 1939:

'At this meeting a mock trial was held. The case was taken from Dorothy Sayers's 'Trial of Martin Burdock', in which a body is stolen, so that Martin may benefit from a clause in his father's will.

The case was tried before N. Q. King as Judge. The Clerk to the Court was Robert

Whitaker, The Counsel for the Prosecution was S. Simmons, assisted by M. Wilkinson, while A. T. Firth and A. Laverack were for the Defence. The result of the trial was that Martin (P. Jackson) was acquitted on the charge of stealing his father's body.

'During the present term no meetings have taken place to date because of the difficulties of transport and the early falling of night.' (*'Otliensian' Vol. XXII, Spring 1940*)

In 1939 he was made a Prefect, and on leaving the School in summer 1940 he received an 'honourable mention' and was awarded the Chairman's Prize for the boy who had '*exercised the best influence*.' His links with the School were to continue, firstly on his election as Joint Hon. Sec. to the Otliensians in 1940. After the war he was elected as a Councillor to the Otley Urban District Council. He became a Governor of the School in 1954, was elected Chairman of the Staffing Committee in 1961 and became Chair of Governors in 1971, in succession to another old scholar, Mr Midgley.

Andrew Firth died in 1999, at the age of 77, and was buried in Otley Cemetery.

On 6 July 1945 the '*Wharfedale and Airedale Observer*' published the following article noting that the then Lieutenant Firth had been chosen as one of the first forty British officers to enter Berlin:

'He goes in the capacity of an Intelligence Officer which is entirely separate from the routine occupational forces who follow later.

Lieut. Firth landed on the beaches in Normandy the day following D-Day. He volunteered for special duty with the 6th Airborne Division and commanded a troop of the new "Centaur" tanks, fitted with 95mm howitzers, one of the British secret weapons, and just removed from the secret list. He held a Captain's command as Forward Observation Officer with the Canadian Parachute Regiment of the 6th Airborne Division.'

'When the 6th Airborne Division came back to England, he rejoined his training unit and fought with them in trying to help the 1st Airborne Division escape from Arnhem across the Rhine. Here he acted as Divisional Artillery Officer for the 101st US Airborne Division and fought with the Canadians up to the Maas to free Antwerp for shipping. His last action was the freeing of the left bank of the Meuse at Venlo and Hoermund. He was appointed to a staff post as Intelligence Officer early in the New Year at the time of Runstedt's break-through into Belgium.'

On the collapse of Germany he was among the first British officers to enter Berlin, where he was employed in the Education Branch of Headquarters and where his work was rewarded by promotion to Captain. As a result of his military record following D-Day he was awarded the United States Bronze Star Medal with the following citation:

'This officer distinguished himself many times during the critical days of the German offensive in the Ardennes for his outstanding and meritorious achievements in planning and carrying out operations against enemy saboteurs and agents dropped by parachute on Allied vital points.'

Douglas Harold Halliwell D.F.C. (1920-1989)

Flight Lieutenant Douglas Halliwell (born 1 October 1920 in Barton upon Irwell, Lancashire) joined Prince Henry's in September 1935 (Form Upper 4A) together with his younger brother Kenneth (see 'War Dead'). The family lived at Hawthorn Villas, Bingley Road, Menston. His father, Harold Halliwell, was a salesman. Harold married Florence Mary Stephens in Salford in 1919. The only reference in the *'Otliensian'* to Douglas at school was that he finished third in the Obstacle Race in the Junior Boys Sports in summer 1936. He left school later in 1936 (Form Lower 5A), attended Bradford Technical Institute, and was employed as an engineering draughtsman at Messrs. Knowles Ltd, Bradford.

He joined the R.A.F.V.R. as an air gunner and ended up a pilot. During the war he rose through the ranks to become a Flight Lieutenant with 199 Squadron. His service number was 169406. The *'Otliensian'* (*Vol. XXVII, Summer 1945*) included the following statement:

'Flight Lieutenant D H Halliwell, R.A.F., who has taken part in 94 operational duties in Bomber Command, has been awarded the Distinguished Flying Cross.'

The notification of the award of the D.F.C. appeared in the *'London Gazette'* on 25 May 1945.

199 Squadron was founded in November 1917 and disbanded in June 1919. It was reformed in November 1942 as a bomber squadron based at Blyton, Lincolnshire. Between December 1942 and April 1944, flying Wellingtons and later Sterlings, the squadron undertook regular bombing and mine laying missions. On 1 May 1944 they moved to North Creake, Norfolk, and became No. 199 Bomber Support Squadron. From June 1944 until May 1945 they flew Stirlings and later Halifaxes. The last operational mission in World War II was on 2/3 May 1945 when Halifaxes flew 17 successful bomber support sorties in connection with a main force attack against Kiel.

After the war he was promoted to the rank of Squadron Leader and was based for a time in Libya, where he was the station commander.

The announcement of Douglas's engagement was published in the *'Yorkshire Post & Leeds Intelligencer'* on 25 March 1950, and he was married later in the same year.

'The engagement is announced between Flight Lieutenant DOUGLAS HAROLD HALLIWELL, D.F.C., R.A.F., elder son of Mr and Mrs. H. Halliwell of "Cordova", Bargrange Avenue, Shipley, and CONSTANCE JOYCE, younger daughter of Captain A.H. PARSONS, M.B.E., and Mrs. Parsons of "Lyndene", Birchwood Drive, Keighley'

His younger brother, Sergeant Pilot Kenneth S. Halliwell, aged 22, also an old scholar of Prince Henry's, lost his life in a flying accident in Italy in April 1945. (*see 'War Dead'*)

Douglas Harold Halliwell died in 1989, his death being registered in Grantham, Lincolnshire.

Frederick Victor Houlgate (Croix-de-Guerre) (1923-1999)

Flying Officer F. V. Houlgate

Frederick Victor Houlgate was born in Hunslet on 26 January 1923. His initial education was at Headingley National School, Leeds. His father, Frederick Houlgate (1891-1976) married Elizabeth Baddley in 1922. In the 1911 Census Frederick senior was living with his family in Leeds and was listed as a Compositer. When Frederick Victor entered Prince Henry's on 28 May 1934 (Form Lower 3) the family was living at 61 Leeds Road, Otley, and his father was described as a Linotype Operator. Frederick Victor left Prince Henry's on 27 July 1939, after passing his School Certificate, to become a Draughtsman.

His first mention in the *'Otliensian'* came in Autumn 1937 (Vol.XX) with the foundation of the Boxing Club:

'The first meeting of the Boxing Club took place on November 9th, when the Headmaster was elected President, David Sully vice-president, and Victor Houlgate secretary.

Although the Club started late in the term there has been quite a good attendance. Most of the older members have attended regularly and still are keen; but we need many other members, particularly from the junior school. We are deeply grateful to Mr Evans and Mr Davison for assisting us in the "Noble Art" F.V.H. Hon Sec.

In 1938 he was elected as a member of the Geographical Society, and on 24 January 1939 he gave a lecture on *'An Air Journey to Africa'*. He was also a member of the Literary, Historical and Debating Society and in autumn 1938 he gave a short lecture on *'The Production of a Modern Newspaper'* which he illustrated with specimens of type and sections of tape from news machines.

His early interest in aircraft was evidenced in 1939 when he helped to set up, and became the Honorary Secretary of the Model Aero Club.

'The Prince Henry's Grammar School Model Aero Club was inaugurated on February 22nd. The Headmaster was elected President. Mr Lewis was elected Vice-president and

Mr F. V. Houlgate Hon. Secretary. The Committee chosen consist of: B. H. Moore, G. Weston, J. Lund, N. Nicholson, G. Watkinson and P. Jennings.

'On March 4th the first meeting for erecting and flying the model aeroplanes was held and there was a very good attendance. The Club will start a library consisting of air stories at some future date. The Club meets every Friday afternoon and Saturday morning.' F. V. H. Hon. Secretary

He was not as involved with sport as he was with clubs and societies, but he was said to have '*played in occasional first team games and gave promise of being very useful if available next season*', in reference to school Rugby. His only success in athletics came in summer 1939 when he came fourth in throwing the discuss.

He left school from Form Upper 5B in summer 1939, and went straight into the R.A.F. (Service No. 54598). He was trained under the Empire Training Scheme in Canada. The scheme was the result of an agreement signed on 17 December 1939 between Canada, the UK, Australia and New Zealand, making Canada the focus of a British Empire wide scheme to instruct aircrew. Canada was well endowed with air training space beyond the range of enemy aircraft, excellent climatic conditions for flying, immediate access to American industry, and relative proximity to the U.K. via the North Atlantic shipping lanes. At its peak there were 107 schools and 184 ancillary units at 231 sites. Victor Houlgate was at Calgary during 1942-43.

The total number of graduates from the Scheme, which lasted until 31 March 1945, was 131,553 pilots, navigators, bomb aimers, wireless operators, air gunners and flight engineers. Almost half the total aircrew employed on British and Commonwealth flying operations were products of the Scheme. Canadian graduates numbered 72,835, providing crews for overseas R.C.A.F. squadrons and for individual crew members of R.A.F. squadrons. Canada thus provided a major commitment to the air war overseas, particularly to Bomber Command, and this exacted a heavy toll in Canadian casualties.

In 1945 he was awarded the Croix de Guerre:

Croix de Guerre for Leeds Airman

'Flying Officer Frederick Victor Houlgate, son of Mr F. Houlgate of 'The Yorkshire Post' composing staff, and Mrs. Houlgate, has been awarded the Croix de Guerre. Flying Officer Houlgate was educated at Prince Henry's Grammar School, Otley, and went straight from school into the R.A.F. He received his training under the Empire Training scheme in Canada.' ('Yorkshire Post and Leeds Intelligencer', 4 October 1945)

His son, Brian Houlgate, has provided the following summary of Victor's R.A.F. career:

'The Croix de Guerre was, I believe, given to a percentage of selected aircrew in recognition of 'support to the Maquis' during Special Operations Executive missions with 38 group (in his case 570 Squadron). Those missions were often long, solo, night missions over enemy territory to drop agents and supplies. He flew Albemarles, towing gliders for the airbourne assault in the early hours of the D-Day invasion of Normandy.

After the Squadron converted to Stirling IVs he did multiple runs into Arnhem during Operation Market Garden, where many of his squadron mates were shot down. His own aircraft was damaged by anti-aircraft fire on his second flight to Arnhem and his bomb-aimer badly injured (he survived, and I had the opportunity to visit him and another of their crew mates in Belfast some months after my father died). He flew paratroops for the Rhine crossing and later to Norway for the disarmament of German forces after the surrender. The crew was then sent to a transport unit in Egypt from late 1945 to 1946, flying Stirling Vs and Dakotas.'

570 Squadron was formed on 15 November 1943 and began training using Albermarle aircraft to tow gliders and drop parachutists. In February 1944 their first operational sorties involved dropping supplies of arms to the French Resistance. The Squadron played a prominent role on the first night of the Normandy landings, by carrying the pathfinders and advance parties whose job was to mark out the landing zones ahead of the arrival of the main force. Several hours after the initial landings had taken place ten of 570 Squadron's aircraft towed Horsa gliders across the Channel to Normandy. On the following evening, 6 June, 20 more of 570 Squadron's aircraft, each towing a Horsa glider, carrying soldiers and equipment of the 6th Airlanding Brigade, flew back to Normandy. All of these aircraft returned successfully to base, but two Sterling aircraft from 620 Squadron and four Horsa gliders crashed in the grounds of the Chateau de Grangues, near Ranville. One of these gliders (Chalk no 90) was towed by the aircraft flown by Pilot Officer Houlgate of 570 Squadron. The two aircrew and all the passengers were killed on impact. The glider having landed on top of dense woodland. (***www.591-antrim- parachute.info/Grangues-crashes.html)***

In July 1944, the Squadron's Albermarle aircraft were exchanged for the more powerful Sterlings. These aircraft played a major part in Operation Market Garden in the week beginning on Sunday 17 September 1944 and ending on Sunday 24 September 1944. The following extract is taken from the Pegasus archive web-site: *(**www. pegasusarchive.org/arnhem/batt-570.htm**)*

'570 Squadron had two tasks to perform on the First Lift of Operation Market Garden, on Sunday 17th September. Twelve of their Stirlings were to tow Horsa gliders to Arnhem while eight more carried elements of 1st British Airborne Corps HQ to Nijmegen. The Arnhem contingent delivered all of their charges without loss, although one aircraft sustained slight flak damage, however only seven Horsas arrived at Nijmegen as one Stirling had crashed on takeoff due to engine failure. The glider that this aircraft had in tow was airborne at the time of the crash and so it was able to put down safely, and although the Stirling was a wreck, all aboard survived, though one man was injured.

'On Monday 18th September, the Squadron brought in a further ten Horsas, one of which safely cast-off when its tug aircraft was shot down, killing all six aircrew and one passenger. On the same day, a further fifteen aircraft participated in the first resupply mission, during which one Stirling was damaged and two were shot down; resulting in a fatality. 570 Squadron also carried out an SOE/SAS mission on this day, with one Stirling

delivering twenty-four supply containers and two packages to SOE agents operating to the south of Orleans, while another aircraft dropped the same number of containers to SAS troops in the area.

'On the 19th September, the Squadron delivered a single Horsa to Arnhem whilst seventeen other aircraft brought in supplies, each carrying twenty-four containers and four packages. Flak over the route was severe, especially over the drop zone, and although all supplies were dropped it was felt to be an unsatisfactory outing as the accuracy of the drop was doubtful. Furthermore, three Stirlings were shot down and most of the remainder had sustained some form of damage, though only two of any great note, one of which was on fire when it landed at Harwell.

'Sixteen aircraft completed the resupply flight on Wednesday, resulting in one aircraft being badly damaged and forced to land prematurely at Benson, with flat tyres and damage to both engines. Eleven Stirlings flew to Arnhem without loss on Thursday 21st September, but on Saturday 23rd, four of the fourteen aircraft involved in the resupply effort were lost and a further two were compelled to make forced landings, one at Antwerp and the other at Manston. Fatalities were suffered on three of the four Stirlings shot down; in total fifteen aircrew and four RASC despatchers were killed, with only three crew and two despatchers escaping from these aircraft.

'On the same day, 570 Squadron received eight new aircraft to replace their losses. A resupply effort was to have taken place on Sunday 24th September, but this was cancelled due to high winds. 570 Squadron played no further part in Operation Market Garden, which had cost them eleven aircraft and the lives of twenty-three aircrew and four despatchers. Sixteen men who had bailed out were taken prisoner, though a further eighteen men shot down over Arnhem returned to the Allied lines when the 1st Airborne Division withdrew on the 25th/26th September.'

When the War ended, 570 Squadron flew troops of the 1st Airborne Division to Norway to oversee the German surrender. From then, until it was disbanded on 8 January 1946, the Squadron undertook transport duties across Europe, the Middle East and India.

In 1950 Victor Houlgate married Stella M Cook, the report of the wedding being published in the *'Yorkshire Post & Leeds Intelligencer'* on 18 April 1950:

Hereditary Freeman of York marries

'Flight Lieutenant Frederick Victor Houlgate, only son of Mr and Mrs. F. Houlgate, of Headingley, Leeds, and Flamborough, was married to Miss Stella Maureen Cook, only daughter of Mr and Mrs. S.E. Cook, of Church House, Wellesbourne, Warwick, at St Peter's Church, Wellesbourne, on Saturday.

The bridegroom, a wartime pilot who holds the French Croix de Guerre for dropping supplies to the Maquis, is personal assistant to Air Vice-Marshall R.O. Jones, Air Officer Commanding 24 Group, R.A.F. As a member of the Houlgate family he is a hereditary Freeman of York.

'The Rev. C.G. Evas, assisted by Squadron Leader Knight, senior chaplain to the 24th Group, conductend the service. There was a guard of honour of fellow officers of the bridegroom. The best man was Mr Ray Tisdale, of Kenilworth.

'The bride, given away by her father, wore a gown of white needleran lace, with a lace train from the waist. A long tulle veil was held by clusters of white camellias. She carried a shower bouquet of white iris, lilac, freesias and camellias.

'The bridesmaids, two friends of the bride, Miss June Cole and Miss Brenda Clift, wore gowns of white moire faille.'

After the War he became personal assistant to Air Vice-Marshall R.O. Jones, Air Officer Commanding 24 Group, R.A.F. In 1948 he was promoted to Flight Lieutenant. He retired from the R.A.F. in 1957 and emigrated with his family to Canada. He died in 1999.

Event:	1	2	3
100 yards (Open)	E. Shackleton	J. L. Marshall	B. H. Moore
220 yards (Open)	E. Shackleton	J. L. Marshall	B. H. Moore
High Jump (Open)	J. S. Mounsey (4ft. 10in.)	B. H. Moore	H. S. Brearley, E. Hudson & S. Watkinson

Charles Vernon Light (1911-1990)

Charles Vernon Light was born in Otley on 9 June 1911 and entered Prince Henry's on 27 April 1920, after attending the private Selborne School, Otley. His father, Charlie Light, (1883-1957), was Assistant Clerk to the Board of Guardians, and the family lived at 4 Valley Drive, Otley. Charlie married Martha Annie Hare in North Bierley in 1911. Charles left school on 20 December 1922 (Form Upper 3A) and transferred to Woodhouse Grove School. He married Eva Gertrude Blackburn in Cheltenham, Gloucester in 1941. Charles Vernon Light died on 2 March 1990, his death being registered in Leeds.

He was only 8 years old when he entered the Preparatory Department at Prince Henry's, and only 11 when he left. The only references in the *'Otliensian'* refer to a third prize in Form IIC in summer 1920, and fourth prize in Form IIA in summer 1922.

The report of his wedding in the *'Yorkshire Post & Leeds Intelligencer'* on 5 April 1941 gives some indication of his career after he left Woodhouse Grove and joined the Royal Army Medical Corps.

LIGHT-BLACKBURN

'The wedding took place at All Saints' Church, Cheltenham, on Wednesday, of Miss Eva Gertrude Blackburn and Captain Charles Vernon Light, R.A.M.C. Both bride and bride-groom have been serving with a General Hospital unit. Miss Blackburn received her

training at Leeds General Infirmary and Captain Light was in practice up to the outbreak of war in Halton.

'Among the bridesmaids were Miss Margaret Blackburn, sister of the bride, and Miss Morris, a Sister also trained in Leeds and serving with the same hospital. Major J.M.P. Clark, a Leeds orthopaedic surgeon with the hospital, was best man, and Captain W.S.A. Oakes, who was on the staff of St. James's Hospital, Leeds, was groomsman. The Rev. H.N.Hodd, C.F., chaplain to the hospital and vicar of Emmanuel, Leeds, officiated.'

During the Second World War he served in the R.A.M.C. in France, and in 1941 moved to Malta, where he was based during the siege of Malta (1941-1943). He later moved to Greece, becoming a Lieutenant Colonel.

In the *'Otliensian'* (*Vol. XXVI, Spring 1944*) it was reported that Major C. Vernon Light, R.A.M.C., had been mentioned in despatches – *'for gallant and distinguished services in Malta'*, where he served as medical officer in command of a hospital. His service number was 87378.

In acknowledging his award the *'Wharfedale and Airedale Observer'* of 5 November 1943 reported that:

'Major Light joined a medical unit of the Territorial Army formed before the outbreak of war, in March 1939, by Colonel P. Whalley, in Leeds, and which was mobilised on the outbreak of hostilities. He went to France in February 1940, served in a military hospital at Etaples, and after the capitulation, escaped by the last boat to leave Boulogne.

'For some time he was on the staff of a military hospital in the south of England and then went to the Middle East, arriving at Malta in July 1941.He has been stationed at Malta ever since, a period of over two years, and served throughout the "siege". He went out as Captain and was promoted Major in April this year.

'Major Light is an old boy of Woodhouse Grove School, where he matriculated, and afterwards graduated at Leeds University where he studied medicine and gained the degree of M.B., Ch.B. He served as House Surgeon and House Physician at Leeds Infirmary and also as House Surgeon at Leeds Maternity Hospital. Later, to gain experience, he went to Japan as ship's surgeon.

He is a skillful batsman and for several seasons played cricket with the Otley team and later for the Leeds club at Headingley. He played lacrosse for Yorkshire for several seasons and captained the side.'

After his death in 1990 the following obituary was published in the *'British Medical Journal'* (9 June 1990):

'Charles Vernon Light was brought up in an atmosphere of service to the community, for his father was a local government officer in Otley and the surrounding dales villages. In 1954 Vernon joined his family's general practitioner in Otley. His knowledge and love of the people and the district, which never diminished, and his energy and dedication

helped the practice to develop rapidly. He was quick to see the advantages of group practice and was innovative in the use of nurses and ancillary help in the 1950s. The team, which he led energetically, wisely, and courteously, expanded and integrated closely with local hospitals. He enjoyed being a clinical assistant in the radiotherapy unit at Cookridge Hospital, where his nous and commonsense approach were highly valued in the high tech environment. Vernon had a well-developed sense of humour, a remarkable memory, and a gift for mimicry so that he was an excellent raconteur and always good company, especially on sporting occasions. Having played league cricket for Leeds and having captained Yorkshire's lacrosse team, he delighted in his collection of cricket memorabilia and pictures and was president of Otley Cricket Club, 1956-72 and of Otley Rugby Union Football Club 1966-8. He retired in 1985 and bore his last, mercifully short, illness gallantly.'

Brian Hardy Moore (1923-2003)

B. H. Moore

Brian Hardy Moore was born on 23 May 1923 in Chorlton, Lancashire. He lived on Old Lane, Bramhope. His father, George I. Moore was a Commercial Representative, who married Florence J. Willmot in Lambeth in 1918. During the war he worked for the Air Ministry. Brian entered Prince Henry's on 1 October 1936 (Form Lower 4A), together with his older brother Anthony. His previous school, from 1932-1936, was the Municipal Secondary School, Derby. He left Prince Henry's on 26 July 1940, from Form Upper 5C, to take up an apprenticeship at the North Eastern School of Wireless Telegraphy in Otley. He died in 2003, the death being registered in South Somerset.

At first he seems to have been overshadowed by his brother Anthony who was a good swimmer and a member of both the 1st Rugby XV and the 1st Cricket XI. Anthony left school in summer 1938 and Brian became more active within school. He was awarded a bronze life-saving medallion in summer 1938 (Anthony was awarded his First Class Instructor's Certificate at the same time!).

Brian was not particularly academic, but he received a 'honourable mention' in Form Lower 5B in summer 1938, and first prize in Form Upper VC in summer 1940. A note on his admission form says that he failed his School Certificate in 1939, but he passed in summer 1940.

He was a member of the Committee of the newly formed Model Aero Club in spring 1939 and joined the Literary, Historical and Debating Society in the same year.

'The date of the next meeting was Thursday, the 23rd of November. 'Rory Aforesaid', a play in one act, was read before the Society by G. Cheshire, R. Whitaker, N. Q. King,

M. Barford, B. Moore and R. Garside. It was followed by "a novel dramatic interlude", presented by Miss Hodd and Mr Leech. Eleven famous literary and historical scenes were put before the Society in dumb show.' ('Otliensian' Vol. XXII, Autumn 1939)

'On Tuesday, September 10th, a business meeting was held at which N. Q. King was elected secretary; S. M. Simmons, treasurer; B. H. Moore steward; M. Boyington, stewardess; and G. Clarke, additional committee member. When, later in the term, B. H. Moore left School, G. E. Weston was elected steward.' ('Otliensian' Vol. XXIII, Autumn 1940)

NOTE – this throws doubt on his actual leaving date, which was listed as 26 July 1940 on his school record: it appears that he returned to school in September 1940, but left later that term.

He took part in the Athletic Sports in summer 1940:

He also followed his brother into the First XV Rugby team. In spring 1939 it was noted that:

' MOORE, B.H. and PAYNE, H.J. have been tried as hookers, and both have had some success in spite of having to depend for support on a light pack.'

In spring 1940, *'MOORE, B.H., has also improved and is always found in the thick of the fray.'*

In the away match against Thornton, it was reported that:

'Never before in any match did our forwards play with such vigour; all played excellently, Moore, Lund, Roberts and Bramley being outstanding for their tenacity and power in bursting through the opposing side'

In the *'Otliensian'* (*Vol. XXIV, Summer 1942*), included in the list of Old Otlensians in H.M. Forces was Signalman Brian H. Moore, Royal Core of Signals.

He served in India and Burma for three years and by the end of the war was attached to the British Embassy in Chungking.

The Supplement to the *London Gazette* on 4 January 1945 contained the following:

War Office, 4th January, 1945

'The KING has been graciously pleased to approve that the following be Mentioned in recognition of gallant and distinguished service in the field: 2601498 Sigmn. (actg. Corpl.) B. H. Moore, Royal Corps of Signals'

The 'Mention in Despatches' is the lowest form of recognition that was announced. It did not carry a medal but was a communication of an act of gallantry or service. Moore's Superior Officer would write a written report to be sent to the high command, in which there was a description of what the soldier had done to merit his recognition.

From 1920 the Army authorised the issue of an oak leaf emblem decoration, to be worn on the left breast of the dress uniform, to soldiers mentioned in despatches.

The following article was published in the *'Wharfedale and Airedale Observer'* on 14 September 1945:

'Mr and Mrs. B. H. Moore of Wayside, Old Lane, Bramhope have received news this week that their younger son, Corporal Brian Hardy Moore, Royal Corps of Signals, has been mentioned in despatches, the citation stating "For gallant and distinguished service in the field."

'Cpl. Moore has served in India and Burma for three years and is at present attached to the British Embassy in Chungking, where he broadcast a message to his parents early this year.

He was formerly at the North Eastern School of Wireless Telegraphy at Otley and is an old scholar of Prince Henry's Grammar School.'

2nd-Lieut. A. W. Moore

The announcement of his brother's commission in the Royal Engineers was published in an article in the *'Wharfedale and Airedale Observer'* on 26 June 1942.

GRANTED A COMMISSION

'Second-Lieutenant Anthony W. (Tony) Moore, elder son of Mr and Mrs. B.H. Moore, of Wayside, Old Lane Bramhope, and an old boy of Prince Henry's Grammar School, has been granted a commission in the Royal Engineers.

'Second-Lieutenant Moore was studying to be a Civil Engineer, and at the time of enlistment in March 1941 was a junior assistant in the L.N.E.R. Engineer's Office at Staningley. As a school boy he was good at all forms of sport and played for Prince Henry's cricket and football teams. He also won the bronze and silver medallions of the Royal Life Saving Society for swimming. Later he played for the Otliensians for several seasons. Whilst in the O.C.T.U. he won a heavy-weight boxing contest, and also played water-polo for the R.Es

'Second-Lieut. Moore's brother, Brian, has recently joined the Royal Corps of Signals, and his father works for the Air Ministry.'

John Robertshaw D.F.C. (1921-1994)

Flying Officer John Robertshaw was born on 19 August 1921 in Bradford. His father, George Herbert Robertshaw, was born in 1895 and in the 1911 census was listed as a Wool Merchant's Apprentice. He married Alice Oxtoby in 1919. Both John and his older brother Thomas attended Prince Henry's, John being admitted to Form I in 1930. In summer 1930 he was awarded second prize in Form I – his brother was awarded first prize in Form II. John was reasonably academic, though he is not mentioned again as a prize winner until his fourth prize in summer 1934 when he was in Form Lower 4A. He repeated this feat in summer 1935 in Form Upper 4A. He obtained his School Certificate and went into the Sixth Form, though he left school in summer 1938 after a year in the Lower Sixth.

His main interest was in sport, especially cricket and rugby, though for some reason he seems to have taken a liking to running in the Obstacle Race and Throwing the Cricket Ball in the Athletic Sports.

Event	1	2	3	4
1935: Obstacle Race	Robinson E.R.	Watson D.	Robertshaw J.	Mann J.
1936: Throwing the Cricket Ball	Sully A.P.	Garside J.E.	Walker A.D.	Robertshaw J
1937: Obstacle Race (Open)	Robertshaw J.	Mallinson D.	Smithies A.	
1937: Throwing the Cricket Ball	Robertshaw J. (74yds 2ft 3in)	Walker A.	Pullan H	
1938: Obstacle Race (Open)	Robertshaw J.	Marshall L.	Watson D.	

His brother Thomas was an excellent swimmer; John did attain a bronze medal from the Royal Life-Saving Society in 1935, but the two brothers did not compete in swimming. Instead, John concentrated on cricket and both brothers played Rugby in the 1st XV.

John played a few matches for the 1st XI in summer 1935, but became a regular in the following season. His batting average of 0.50 shows that his talents were more as a bowler.

The Autumn 1936 issue of the *'Otliensian'* included:

***'Cricket** – Colours were awarded to the following – J. E. Garside, C. Moon, K. J. Payne, H. Rigg, J. Robertshaw, K. Temple. K. Temple headed the batting averages with an average* *of 11.7 per innings. J. Robertshaw took 36 wickets at an average cost of 7.4 runs per wicket, while J. E. Garside captured one less at an average cost of 8.5 runs per wicket. Record: 1st XI: Played 11, Won 5, Lost 6. 2nd XI: Played 5, Won 2, Lost 3. Cave House carried off the House Cricket Championship, winning all their matches.'*

4 of these wickets came in the match against rivals Ilkley Grammar School on 16 May 1926, Garside taking the other 6 wickets and dismissing Ilkley for 94 runs – unfortunately Prince Henry's could only score 33!

Robertshaw's good bowling form continued into the 1936-1937 season.

'During the present season the 1st XI has played four matches, two having been cancelled. The batting at the beginning of the season was very disappointing, but it has steadily improved. The greatest weakness, however, is in the bowling where J. Robertshaw is the only bowler of any ability, and at present there is a vacancy for a good length bowler.

'The match with Harrogate G S at home was lost by 4 runs. After dismissing the visitors for 39 (Rigg 6 for 12), School could only muster 35 runs (Foulds 19)

'The second match, with Roundhay at home was won by 3 wickets. The visitors again batted first and were dismissed for 47 runs (J. Robertshaw 9 for 18), and School replied with 48 for 7.

'The Yeadon & Guiseley away match was drawn. The home side batted first and had scored 102 when the last wicket fell. School were lucky to play out time after scoring 76 for the loss of 7 wickets (Wood 33 not out, J. Robertshaw 20)

'The "Derby" match away against Ilkley resulted in a win for Ilkley by 9 runs. The home side won the toss and batted first scoring 106. School batted brightly, but were 44 runs short of victory when the last two men came together. When this partnership was broken School had made 97 (Walker 23)'

BATTING AVERAGES

	Innings	Not Out	Highest Score	Total Runs	Average
Wood	4	1	33 not out	62	20.66
Foulds	4	0	19	38	9.50
J. Robertshaw	4	0	20	37	9.25

BOWLING

	Overs	Maidens	Runs	Wickets	Average
Rigg	14.2	4	21	6	3.50
J. Robertshaw	59.5	20	112	24	4.66

In summer 1938 *'J. Robertshaw and H. Pullan were appointed as Captain and Vice-Captain respectively of the Cricket XI.'*

John started playing Rugby for the first XV at the end of 1935, when it was mentioned in the '*Otliensian*' that Cribb C.B. and Robertshaw J., '*Have had places in the pack since Christmas and have shown considerable promise.*'

Both John and his brother Thomas were awarded their rugby colours during the 1936-37 season. John was a forward, his brother played at full-back. Their end of year criticisms read:

ROBERTSHAW J	'*Has ideal build for a forward. Is strong and vigorous in loose play, and uses his weight in the scrum.*'
ROBERTSHAW T R (full back)	'*Has improved enormously and has been one of the most reliable members of the side. His fielding and long touch-finding have been excellent. His only weakness is poor positioning.*'

In autumn 1937 John Robertshaw was made First XV Captain.

9 October 1937: Belle Vue S.S. (home)	'*The scoring was opened by H. Pullan, other try scorers being T. Robertshaw and J Robertshaw (2).*'
16 October 1937 West Leeds H.S. (home)	'*Before half-time D. Mallinson, playing a good game, touched down near the posts. After this West Leeds scored again, thus equalising, but they failed to hold the lead, when, as a result of a good run by H. Pullan, J. Robertshaw went over for the winning try.*'
3 November 1937 Yorkshire Wanderers (home)	'*Later Mr Evans scored a fine try under the posts, which J. Robertshaw converted. In the second half School obtained a lead over the visitors when H. Pullan went through to score again; J. Robertshaw converted. School held the lead for some time, but towards the end of the second half the visitors scored again.* *In the backs H. Pullan played well, whilst in the forwards D. Mallinson was conspicuous.*'
20 November 1937 Morley G.S. (Away)	'*Morley opened the scoring in the first few minutes, but School retaliated well, scoring an unconverted try through H. Pullan. In the second half School were pressing all the time and tries were scored by R. Watkins and J. Warrington. J. Robertshaw converted one.*'
18 December 1937 Bingley G.S. (home)	'*The visitors were never dangerous, their only score coming from an interception by one of their players. Scorers on our side were: H. Pullan (2), E. Anderson (2), L. Aveyard (2), R. Watkins and J. Robertshaw (3). J. Robertshaw converted 7 tries.*'
22 January 1938 Ilkley G.S. (Home)	'*In the second half Ilkley were outpaced completely, but put up a fight until the final whistle. Other scorers were L. Aveyard (2), T. Robertshaw and K. Temple. J. Robertshaw converted 2 tries. In the forwards D. Mallinson played well, whilst conspicuous in the backs were H. Pullan and K. Temple.*'

5 February 1938 Thornton G.S. (Home)	*'A. Moore played a good game, scoring 3 tries. Scorers were A. Moore (3), K. Temple, H. Pullan, D. Mallinson, H. Harrison (2) and E. Anderson. J. Robertshaw kicked a penalty goal and converted 4 tries.'*
26 February 1938 Belle Vue S.S. (Away)	*'The backs played very well, H. Pullan and E. Anderson being conspicuous. Scorers were H. Pullan (3), E. Anderson, D. Watson, L. Aveyard and K. Temple. J. Robertshaw kicked one penalty goal and converted 2 tries.'*

John Robertshaw as Captain, was said to have *'got the best out of the team by keen and inspiring leadership. He is a most competent forward who should make his mark when he enters club football.'*

In 1936 John Robertshaw was appointed as a prefect and was a Committee member in the Natural Science Society. He left Prince Henry's in summer 1938 from the Lower VI, at the same time his brother left from the Upper VI.

He joined the R.A.F. at the outbreak of war, and served in Egypt for eighteen months.

The Spring 1945 (*Vol. XXVII*) issue of the *'Otliensian'* announced that:

'Flying Officer John Robertshaw, R.A.F., who served for eighteen months in Egypt before returning to this country, has been awarded the D.F.C.'

The news of the award was published in the *'Wharfedale and Airedale Observer'* on 23 February 1945:

MENSTON OFFICER WINS D.F.C.

'Flying Officer John Robertshaw of Fern Lea, Main Street, Menston, son of Mr and Mrs. G. H. Robertshaw has been awarded the Distinguished Flying Cross. His parents were notified of the award by telephone on Monday evening.

'F. O. Robertshaw is an old scholar of Prince Henry's Grammar School, and joined the RAF at the outbreak of war. He served in Egypt for 18 months, and is now back in this country. His wedding to Miss Margaret Wood, also an old scholar of Prince Henry's is to take place tomorrow (Saturday) at St John's Church, Menston.

'His father holds the rank of Pilot Officer in the Otley and District Squadron A.T.C'

John was actually a member of the R.A.F.V.R. and served with 462 (Royal Australian Air Force) Squadron. His service number was 146279. The announcement of the award of the D.F.C. was published in the *'London Gazette'* on 20 February 1945.

462 Squadron was formed in Egypt in September 1942. Equipped with Halifax bombers, the unit operated against Rommel's forces in North Africa throughout 1943 and 1944. The squadron was nominally a 'R.A.A.F.' squadron, but as late as August 1943 only

a quarter of its 600 personnel were R.A.A.F. members. The R.A.A.F. endeavoured to have more Australian servicemen posted to the squadron, but with little success and eventually 462 Squadron was re-designated 614 Squadron R.A.F.

Five months later No 462 Squadron reformed in England - and this time around the unit was allocated a much greater proportion of Australian personnel. Again equipped with Halifaxes, the Squadron participated in day and night attacks against German industrial cities, while at the same time, supporting the Allied ground forces fighting their way across France.

By the end of 1944 and following the fitment of specialised radio and radar jamming equipment, the Squadron, now part of the 100 (Bomber Support) Group, began operations to disrupt the highly organised German air defence system. The Halifaxes also carried small loads of incendiaries, target markers and bombs, which were dropped to further confuse the enemy.

No 462 Squadron disbanded at Foulsham on 24 September 1945.

On 24 February 1945 John married Barbara M. Wood, also an old scholar of Prince Henry's, in Menston. They had five children. John Robertshaw died in Shipley on 17 September 1994, age 73.

Thomas Fenton Scott (1911-1978)

Thomas Fenton Scott was born on 18 January 1911 in Otley. He entered Form Upper 3A on 12 September 1922, and left school on 5 April 1927 from Form Upper 5. He moved into an occupation involving clerical work. The family lived at 5, Jennett's Crescent, Otley and his father, also Thomas Fenton Scott, was a Printer's Engineer. His father was born in 1881 in Otley and in the 1911 Census was listed as an Iron Turner, living at 27 Union Street, Otley. In 1908 he married Ida Bellerby. Thomas Fenton Scott junior died in 1978, his death being registered in Huddersfield.

He received a mention in the *'Otliensian'* (*Vol. V, Spring 1923*) as the first prizewinner in an examination held by the Congregational Union of England and Wales, for which he was presented with a gold medal following a visit to London. The letter, dated 20 January 1923 read:

'DEAR FENTON

I write to inform you that you have come out first in the Honours List of the Lower Junior Division in the recent Examination on 'Grenfell of Labrador', and will, therefore be entitled to a medal or a parcel of books to the value of a guinea. Please let me know which of these you prefer. The distribution of prizes will take place in the City Temple on Friday May 11th.

Let me heartily congratulate you upon your success. I hope that many still greater distinctions are before you.

Yours sincerely, ARTHUR HALLACK

MASTER FENTON SCOTT
5, Jennett's Crescent. Otley Yorks'

In summer 1923 he was awarded third prize in Form Upper 3A, and in 1924, the English prize in Form 4A. His strengths seemed to lie in English – both written and spoken. He was a librarian and member of the Literary, Historical and Debating Society. His first lecture, given when he was in Form Lower 5A was on *'Habits of Red Indians'.*

T. F. Scott

'The lecture was rather short but very interesting. He explained how the Indians lived, how their villages were set out, and how an Indian thinks that when he has done sufficient work for the day he makes his wife do the rest.'

At Christmas 1925 he gave a paper on *'David Livingstone'.*

'The lecturer described Livingstone's expeditions in detail, pointing out the tremendous difficulties which beset the explorer, and illustrating his journeys by means of a map on the blackboard. Mr Scott was a new speaker, but he gave a most interesting lecture.'

And in October 1925:

'Mr Scott read a paper on 'Michael Angelo'. He gave a delightful outline of the career of this great master, the joys and sorrows brought into it, and the influence of the artist-poet upon his followers.'

On 24 March 1927 he opposed the motion *'That singing is of no Educational Value'* in a debate, which was defeated by 24 votes to 27.

He was also a keen actor, taking the part of Old Gobbo in the Easter 1925 production of *'The Merchant of Venice'*. He was said to have *'assumed the tremulous garrulity of the old man very ably.'*

At Easter 1927 he took part in *'She Stoops to Conquer'*:

'C. Conradi, R. Biss, A. Oliver, G. Mainprize and F. Scott played the double role of servants to Mr Hardcastle and of drinking friends to Tony Lumpkin. F. Scott also showed that he had made a study of the play in his interpretation of Sir Charles Marlow, whilst Miss Hardcastle's maid was personated by Ragna Lambert.'

Nor did his acting career end when he left school, because in 1928 he took part in the Old Otliensians' production of *'A School for Scandal'*:

'Mr F. Scott as Joseph Surface, gave a very good performance indeed in the difficult

role of a man constantly called upon to dissimulate his true feelings; and the contrast between him and his brother, Charles Surface, taken by Mr G. Marshall, was as marked as Sheridan meant it to be. The rollicking, drinking scene was very effective. If the remainder of the cast had smaller parts, the acting was nonetheless good.'

His sporting career was rather more limited, though he did compete in the Under 14 High Jump, and played occasionally for the 1st XV Rugby team in 1927, but does not seem to have continued to play in later seasons. *'Hixon and Scott T.F. (three-quarters) and Greenwood C. and Lawson have played on odd occasions, and will be useful recruits for next season.'*

	1	2	3	4
High Jump (Under 14)	R Braithwaite	C Condradi and F Scott		A Oliver

He left school, from Form Upper 5, in April 1927.

The Spring 1946 issue of the *'Otliensian'* reported that Sergeant T. Fenton Scott had been mentioned in despatches. Notification of the award was published in the *'London Gazette'* on 24 August 1944 (page 3935). At the time T.F. Scott (Service No. 7397663) was a Corporal in the Royal Army Medical Corps, based in Italy. He was later promoted to Sergeant.

The following article was published in the *'Wharfedale and Airedale Observer'* on 10 November 1944:

OTLEY CORPORAL MENTIONED IN DISPATCHES

'Corporal Thomas Fenton Scott (33), of Otley, serving as a clerk with the R.A.M.C., headquarters staff in Italy, has been mentioned in dispatches.'

News of his honour has been received by his wife, living at 114 Westgate, Otley. In his letter home, Corporal Scott says 'You might be interested to know that I have been mentioned in dispatches for service in Italy. All I can say is I have done no more than my job – my little bit towards bringing this war to an end.

'Corporal Scott is the eldest son of Mr and Mrs. T. F. Scott, of 24 Bradford Road, Otley. Exactly four years ago this December, he married Miss Phyllis Carter, youngest daughter of the late Mr and Mrs. B. Carter, of Otley, at Otley Parish Church, joining the forces the following year, and has served in Madagascar, India, Iraq, Middle East, Sicily and Italy.'

Frederick George Thomlinson (Croix-de-Guerre) (1918-1996)

'Lieutenant Frederick George Thomlinson (born 16 October 1918), Kings Own Yorkshire Light Infantry (Service No. 329144), was awarded the Croix de Guerre, with Silver Star, while serving with the British Liberation Army.' ('Otliensian' Vol. XXVII, Summer 1945)

Frederick was at Prince Henry's Grammar School from 13 September 1932 (Form Upper 3A) until 19 December 1934 (Lower 5C), when he left to take up farming. His father, W.H. Thomlinson, was a farmer living at Newland House, Arthington. Frederick attended Harewood School (1929-1932) before going to Prince Henry's. In 1948 he married Joan Pullein. He died in 1996, his death being registered in Ryedale, Yorkshire.

He joined the King's Own Yorkshire Light Infantry as a Private in September 1939, serving in Norway and Iceland. He went to France shortly after D-Day, where he was wounded in the arm, and while serving in France was promoted from sergeant to second lieutenant.

He was presented with the Croix de Guerre for an action in August 1944, the date of the citation being 15 December 1944.

'On 29 August 1944 on the outskirts of the FORET DE BROTONNE, the leading platoon was held up by close range fire from enemy machine guns in an orchard and 2nd Lt. Thomlinson's platoon was ordered to carry out an attack from a flank. The enemy positions were very strongly constructed. Although under heavy mortar fire he quickly assessed the position and led his platoon forward and assaulted the enemy position from a flank. When his platoon was held up by wire 2nd Lt. Thomlinson again went forward and personally cut a gap, although in full view of the enemy who were close enough to throw grenades from their trenches.

'When a gap had been cleared, 2nd Lt. Thomlinson led a charge which carried his platoon up to the enemy posts, killing 2 and wounding 5 and capturing an enemy machine gun.

'2nd Lt. Thomlinson shewed outstanding qualities of leadership during the attack. His complete disregard of danger and coolness were an inspiration to his platoon and enabled the company to continue its advance.'

Another action led by Thomlinson was reported in the *'Wharfedale and Airedale Observer'* published on 6 April 1945 under the heading *'Arthington Officer in Night Attack.'*

'When a battalion of the Kings Own Yorkshire Light Infantry were given the task of capturing the town of Klundert in Holland, it was considered necessary for the success

of the operation that a certain farm should be occupied in order that it might be used as a firm base for the attack. A platoon which was commanded by Lieut. F. G. Thomlinson of Newland House, Arthington, was therefore sent forward to occupy it. Whether the farm contained enemy or not was unknown.

'The platoon which set out under cover of darkness made their way over the 1,000 yards of ground which lay between their company's positions and the farm, without incident. On arrival it was found that a wide irrigation ditch ran right the way round the building, traversed at one point by a narrow plank bridge. As a section led by L/Sgt. A. N. Harvey of Ferndale, S. Wales, began to make their way across they were challenged, and a second later fired on from the house.

'Immediately Lt. Thomlinson put one section down in a fire position in front of the house, and despatched another to the rear to serve as a "cut-off" for any Boche attempting to escape at the back. Meanwhile, L/Sgt. Harvey's section continued towards the house, through the doors and windows of which they hurled grenades.

'Boche who started to run out of the back door of the building, were instantly met by concentrated fire from the "cut-off" section. Bolting back again into the house, they received a burst of Sten fire from L/Sgt. Harvey, who was by this time himself inside the farmhouse. Realising that they were trapped, the 18 Boche who had been occupying the position surrendered. A further six were later discovered cowering in an outbuilding, and these too were taken prisoner.'

Peter Walker (D.F.M.) (1920-)

Pilot Officer Peter Walker, (Service No. 1064007), born 1 January 1920, was the first Old Scholar to be awarded the Distinguished Flying Medal (D.F.M.) As a member of a Halifax bomber crew he made many operational flights over Germany and Italy with great success.

The official citation included the statement:

'His cheerfulness and presence of mind in times of stress contributed in no small measure to the successes obtained by his crew.' (*'Otliensian' Vol. XXV, Summer 1943*)

He was at Prince Henry's Grammar School from 11 September 1930 (Form Upper 3B) until 22 December 1936 (Sixth Form), when he left to join the Civil Service, with the Air Ministry in London. He lived in Creskeld View, Bramhope, with his mother; his father, a farmer, was deceased. He attended Bramhope Council School and was awarded a West Riding County Minor Scholarship to

P.H.G.S.

He was clearly an intelligent scholar, winning form prizes in Upper 3B (2nd), Lower 4A (2nd), Upper 4A (2nd), Lower 5A (2nd) and Upper 5A (1st). In each case H. Rigg beat him to the First Prize, except in Upper 5A where he managed to push Rigg into second place. He passed his School Certificate in 1935, with Matriculation and distinctions in History, French, Chemistry and Geography, and joined the Sixth Form where, in the Lower Sixth, he won prizes for French and Geography.

He displayed some proficiency at athletics and Rugby, finishing in fourth place in the 100 yards (14-15) in 1934 and fourth place in the Long Jump (Open) in 1936. He was described as showing *'considerable promise'* in the report on the 2nd XV in 1935 and his *'Valete!'* entry indicates that he did play for the 1st XV, though there is no mention of him in the Rugby Reports or team criticisms.

He was a member of 78 Squadron. The award of the D.F.M. was listed in the *'London Gazette'* on 18 May 1943 (page 2201). The Distinguished Flying Medal was established in 1918 and was awarded to non-commissioned officers of the Royal Air Force. The award was in recognition of the *'valour, courage and devotion to duty performed whilst flying in active operations against the enemy.'*

78 Squadron was formed in 1916, disbanded in 1919 and reformed in 1936 as a heavy bomber squadron. It begin in 1940 by flying Whitleys, but converted to Halifaxes in 1942 and continued with them for the rest of the European war. Among the highlights of No 78's war record was its participation in the historic 1,000-bomber raid on Cologne on 30/31 May 1942; the raid on Peenemunde on 17/18 August 1943; and the attack on the coastal gun battery at Mont Fleury on 5/6 June 1944, in direct support of the Normandy landings. Over the period of the War No. 78 Squadron flew 6,337 sorties, made 302 bombing raids and bombed 187 different targets. The Squadron destroyed 31 enemy aircraft, damaged 35 and suffered the loss of 182 aircraft.

The award of the D.F.M. was noted in the 4 June 1943 issue of the *'Wharfedale and Airedale Observer'*:

D.F.M. FOR BRAMHOPE MAN

'Sergeant-Flight Engineer Peter Walker, son of Mrs. Walker, Creskeld View, Bramhope, has been awarded the Distinguished Flying Medal. The citation states that as a member of a Halifax bomber crew he has done numerous operational flights over Germany and Italy with great success, and his cheerfulness and presence of mind in times of stress contributed in no small measure to the successes obtained by his crew.

'Sgt. Walker, who is 23, is a native of Bramhope, and was educated at Bramhope School and Otley Prince Henry's Grammar School. On leaving school he entered the Civil Service and was with the Air Ministry in London. During a recent leave he gave a talk to cadets of the Otley and District A.T.C. Squadron on flight-engineering.'

In the 18 June 1943 issue his promotion to Pilot Officer was announced:

BRAMHOPE MAN BECOMES PILOT OFFICER

'Sergeant Flight Engineer Peter Walker, son of Mrs. Walker, Creskeld View, Bramhope, who was recently awarded the Distinguished Flying Medal for his part in numerous operational flights over Germany as a member of a Halifax bomber crew has been promoted to Pilot Officer, P/O Walker, who is 23, is a native of Bramhope and entered the Civil Service on leaving Prince Henry's Grammar School, and was with the Air Ministry in London. His elder brother has been in the Army since 1940; he is a sergeant. Their father, the late Richard Walker, was a well-known native of Stainburn, where he was a farmer.'

During and After the War

Before the war and during the war the age range of pupils at Prince Henry's ran from 7-10 in the Preparatory Department and from 11-18 in the main school. The extent to which pupils took notice of and understood what was happening in the war would vary according to age and circumstances, but the further away the events and the less personal the impact, the less the interest. Censored letters from ex-pupils were read out in assembly, stressing the fact that there were many advantages to being abroad, such as visits to historical and tourist sites, mentioning meeting up with fellow Otliensians, and applause would ring out to acknowledge the award of a medal or a citation for bravery. Talks in school from old scholars in the Forces would bring the war closer to home, and as pupils got older they would become more aware of the causes for which old scholars were fighting and dying. Casualty figures announced on the radio would shock the pupils, as would announcements made in assembly about the death of old scholars, particularly those who had been at school in the more recent past, or those with relatives still at the school.

There would be euphoria at the 'victories' – the Battle of Britain, the African campaign, the sinking of the Bismarck, the D-day invasion – and concern at the 'setbacks' – Dunkirk, Singapore, Pearl Harbour. Pupils at Prince Henry's were certainly aware of the difficulties on the Home Front associated with the war and they were encouraged to do their bit by saving, collecting salvage, growing vegetables, helping on local farms, contributing money and 'comforts' to those worse off than themselves, and enlisting in youth organisations and even the Home Guard. The Editorials in the '*Otliensian*' encouraged the view that, in spite of the setbacks, the sacrifices and the problems of the war, pupils ought to be grateful for what they had rather than what they had not.

Most written reminiscences of life for children in wartime Britain come from young children living in cities that were bombed. Memories therefore include air-raids, playing on bomb sites and time spent in shelters, either at home or in communal shelters provided by local authorities. Another common recollection is evacuation to safe, reception areas, especially to rural towns and villages. For many young children the war years were an adventure, even though many of the things we now take for granted – safety, clothes, fuel, food, home and family – were disrupted, and life became hard for many families.

Evacuation was advisory, not compulsory, but fear for children's safety, especially in the early years of the war, meant that mass movement of children occurred. Children were labelled, separated from concerned mothers, sent off to unknown destinations on trains and buses, often to rural areas, and housed with strangers. There are stories of harsh discipline and abuse, but many children were housed with kind families, in tranquil, often affluent, areas. Some children spent almost the entire war as evacuees, though the quiet of the 'Phoney War' meant that by January 1940 about 60 per cent of evacuated children had returned home, against government advice. The fall of France and the Blitz led to a second widespread wave of evacuation, including movement of children overseas. However, the majority steadily returned home as the threat from German bombing diminished.

For many children family life changed dramatically because fathers, older brothers and other relatives joined H.M. Forces and were sent abroad. Fathers would 'disappear' for four or five years; some would be killed, others seriously wounded. This loss of a male influence could have a serious impact on the behaviour of children at a time when fathers had a more disciplinary approach to bringing up children. The return of fathers on demobilisation could lead to difficulties, especially when younger children had never seen their father, or servicemen found it difficult to readjust to civilian life after the pressures of fighting abroad. Family life would also be affected by the fact that during the war more women went out to work and would largely have to fend for themselves and their children.

The material demands of the war – weapons, aircraft, ships, and food – required significant changes in the structure of British industry. The major change was the mass mobilisation of women into essential jobs in armaments, aircraft production and agriculture, work previously undertaken mainly by men. Many women experienced wage-earning for the first time in their lives, being no longer dependent on a husband's wage. Women also joined the armed services. They were not sent directly into combat, but their work was essential and often dangerous – helping to operate radar stations, manning fighter operations rooms, driving lorries and ambulances, manning searchlights and anti-aircraft guns, commanding harbour launches and signalling. For many women the war was liberating and led to social changes that would continue to develop after the end of the war. Life would never be the same again.

The children of Otley and the surrounding villages, including those at Prince Henry's had a different wartime experience than those from the towns and cities that were bombed or more likely to be bombed. Wharfedale was a 'safe' area and therefore there was a net influx of evacuees from the local urban area and from further afield. Pupils from schools in Leeds were evacuated to Wharfedale, the girls from Roundhay moving to Otley and being taught for one term at Prince Henry's. The impact on the pupils of Prince Henry's was a shift system of education where local pupils were taught in the mornings – including Saturday – and the Roundhay girls in the afternoon. Not all pupils from Roundhay came to Otley, but those that did not choose to come received no education because their school was closed. By January 1940 the vast majority of the girls had returned to their homes and to their school. Evacuees from further afield remained in the area, and the Governors and Headmaster took every opportunity to point out to the local authority that classroom space was insufficient given the large number of pupils in attendance. However, from January 1940 onwards, apart from some reduction in the length of the summer holidays – compensated for by a longer half term – lessons continued as normal, and there is no evidence that the education of the pupils suffered. The Headmaster, Mr Wilde, in his Speech Day Report for 1944 announced that the 1939 intake, *'our war babies,'* had performed well in the School Certificate examinations.

A national report from April 1940 estimated that only 50 per cent of children were in full-time education. The fact that in schools such as Prince Henry's there was just about 100 per cent attendance meant that in urban areas the actual figure was much less. Six of the staff – all male – joined the Forces during the War – Messrs. Chapman, Davison, Denham, Evans, Nield and Watson. Again, the impact on the quality of education does not appear to have suffered. Replacements were recruited and some internal adjustments were made. Mr Pratt took over as Boys' physical education Instructor and Miss Horsley took over the teaching of physics from Mr Denham. This provided a bonus for the school because the 1944 Education Act resulted in the closure of the Preparatory Department that had been run by Miss Horsley, and she found a ready appointment in the teaching of physics and mathematics.

The emphasis at school was as far as possible on normality. The changes to the building must have brought some early excitement to the life of the school - blast walls, black-out, shatter proof windows, the digging of a trench by some of the staff and the older pupils. The need to carry gas masks, practices at putting them on and the movement to air raid trenches and shelters brought home to pupils the significance of the war and the potential dangers. However, when no gas attacks or air-raids came and when the danger of invasion seemed to have disappeared, life at school returned to normal – lessons, homework, and exams. Pupils and staff got used to the war.

It might have been expected that a wave of patriotism would develop within the school and that the *'Otliensian'* would become a medium through which such a wave could be encouraged. The school magazine certainly became a means by which the impact of the war on old scholars was communicated. There were regular up-dates on ex-pupils who had joined H.M. Forces, those who had died serving their country, prisoners of war, the wounded and those who had received awards and decorations. Old scholars wrote to the Headmaster, and other members of staff, about their experiences and meetings with ex-pupils. Occasionally there were visits to the school from old scholars in H.M. Forces to talk to the pupils. The reports of those old scholars missing or killed in action must have had an effect on the pupils at school during the war. The death of Mr Nield, a member of staff, would bring home to pupils the closeness of the war and the fact that it affected everyone in some way. Some pupils may well have taken advantage of the fact that two members of staff – Mr Padgett and Captain Shaw – had fought in the Great War, to ask their views on the progress of the war, and so to 'waste' lesson time.

The start of the war seems to have brought about the biggest changes, but even then the emphasis was on the fact that such changes were nothing compared to those suffered by other people in Britain and overseas. The Editorial in the first *'Otliensian'* published after the start of the war stressed the need to make the best of things without complaint:

'This term has been one of many changes, and these have caused some measure of inconvenience to each one of us. Unfortunately it is all too easy in such circumstances to develop a feeling of self pity to an alarming extent. Free Saturday mornings and after-school society meetings are now pleasures of the past, and the result is that we tend

to feel justified in grumbling, which is nothing more than a form of self-indulgence of particularly evil character. It has been said that the English are a nation of grumblers, and certainly we seem to extract a peculiar type of pleasure from grumbling, and it is extremely probable that if conditions suddenly reverted to normal, many of us would mourn our lost afternoons!

'The most dreadful things we have to contend with are rising half an hour earlier, a terrible wrench, or losing one of our many forms of entertainment; and after all there are worse things in France. We should not forget, however, that sometimes it is easier to face danger of a spectacular nature than to keep one's temper when compassed about by constant petty invitations.

'The present situation must not be regarded as a suitable excuse for slackening of diligence on our part. We must realise that Hitler has quite enough to answer for without being taxed, and in many cases unjustly, with our own shortcomings. Let us not be entirely without mercy. If we would only remember that the majority of man's troubles are caused by his own thoughtlessness, short-sightedness and mere foolishness, grumbling would soon be a thing of the past.' (Vol. XXII, Autumn 1939)

The memories of many children alive in cities during the war include playing on the sites of bombed out houses and businesses. In spite of the fact that these sites were unsafe they still attracted children looking for hide-outs, locations for war games and war memorabilia such as shrapnel. Things were very different in rural areas such as Otley. At Prince Henry's the start of the Autumn Term in 1940 was a fortnight earlier than usual and a range of activities was organised to fill the time. Some outside speakers were invited into school to give talks and *'Sergeant Todd's lecture on A.R.P., was made especially interesting by the handing round of relics of bombs which had been collected by the lecturer.' ('Otliensian' Vol. XXXIII, Autumn 1940).* This was as close to a 'bomb' that Prince Henry's pupils would come over the length of the War. Sergeant Todd may have collected his 'relic' following the air-raid on 19 August 1940.

'Wharfedale had its first air-raid of the war, in the early hours of Monday August 19, when a single enemy 'plane dropped several high explosive and about 60 incendiary bombs in the vicinity of Otley Chevin. There were no casualties, and farm stock escaped unhurt. The noise of the explosion was heard over a wide area.

Four days later, another bomb was dropped, almost in the same place.

A week later enemy 'planes were again over the district, and a bomb dropped in the Arthington district.' ('Wharfedale and Airedale Observer', 27 December 1940)

Leeds and Bradford suffered several bombing raids, though the impact was small compared to many other cities and ports. The worst air raid in Leeds was on 14/15 March 1941 when over the two days there were 9 raids, 77 people were killed, 327 injured and over 8,500 buildings damaged. Ex-pupils living in Otley could hear the sounds of the Bradford and Leeds air-raids, and also have memories of German planes flying over Otley on their way to bomb Manchester, Liverpool and Barrow-in-Furness.

The siting of the AVRO factory at Yeadon might have attracted air-raids that would certainly have been seen and heard in Otley and could have resulted in peripheral damage.

In fact the factory was never bombed, some local people suggesting that the Germans did not even know it was there. It was certainly the case that the huge factory was camouflaged to look like farmers' fields when seen from above. On Monday 19 August 1940 a single enemy plane dropped several high explosives and about 60 incendiary bombs in the vicinity of Otley Chevin. There were no casualties. There were other incidents, though in most cases the suggestion was that the German pilots were 'lost' and that the intended targets were cities such as Liverpool and Barrow-in-Furness. The following quotation is from the book *'Mother Worked at Avro,' by Gerald Myers:*

'On 1st September, 1942, a reporter from a local newspaper wrote in his notebook "shortly before midnight an enemy plane flew up the Wharfe Valley and dropped flares in the Pool and Ilkley districts. Tracer bullets were seen and the whole district was illuminated. A few minutes later (11.45 p.m.) the sirens sounded but the plane did not return and there was no further activity. 'Raiders passed' sounded at 12.20 a.m.

The last two sentences of this unpublished report proved to be prophetic, for, never again did an enemy aircraft come within striking distance of the factory.'

Pupils at Prince Henry's, especially those living in Otley, would be used to seeing soldiers in the town. One ex-pupil remembers meeting soldiers in the town and inviting them round for tea. He also notes that the pubs in Otley regularly ran out of beer!

Remains of Farnley Camp, 1959.

There were Army camps at Farnley and at the Old Showground, on Pool Road. The Pool Road Camp was at one time the headquarters of the local searchlight unit. The government declared the camp redundant in September 1946 and offered it to the

Council. However, the housing crisis at the time led to squatters taking over the site and moving in to the abandoned huts. The camp at Farnley was used from November 1914 when the soldiers of the 12th King's Own Yorkshire Light Infantry occupied it. The following description of the camp is from *'Kitchener's Army: The Raising of the New Armies, 1914-1916,'* by Peter Simkins

'Each hut housed 30 men .... They were raised from the ground on concrete piles, had a double thickness in walls and floors, were covered with stout felting, and were absolutely weatherproof.... Other buildings in the camp included a cookhouse fitted with the best known pattern cooking range and boiler for 1,000 men, a library, recreation room, gymnasium, store rooms, canteens, regimental offices and guard rooms, and a well appointed rifle range. The camp was lit with electricity transmitted through overhead wires, and water was laid on from the Farnley Hall mains. For training purposes the camp was most excellently situated, for we had on one side arable land and undulating pasture, and on the other the hilly country and moors. Another advantage was the absence of any very large town close at hand, so that the counter attractions to military discipline were not too powerful.'

During and after the Second World War the camp continued to be regularly occupied by the Army. An article in the *'Wharfedale'* on 7 March 1941, noted the departure of a unit of the Royal Engineers who had been billeted in the town over winter.

'They appeared to be a happy band of men, with a good spirit pervading all ranks, and they dropped into the life of the town in a very homely way. They carry with them the good wishes of the townspeople. They will be missed more particularly at the Y.M.C.A. in Boroughgate, where Miss Hunter and her helpers had a special morning session to cater for their needs.'

In May 1941 the 9th Battalion of the Royal Tank Regiment moved to Farnley to train on the moors in Churchill tanks. The tanks were delivered by train via Otley and Pool railway stations, and then by road to Farnley. To get to Farnley from both stations they had to cross the bridges over the River Wharfe and there was some concern that the tanks might damage them.

In the winter of 1942-1943 the 90th company of the Royal Army Service Corps was stationed there, and about 20 of the men eventually married Otley girls. The company newspaper took the title of the *'Otley Observer.'* In May 1944, before they moved south in readiness for D-day, Canadian troops were based at the camp. Their presence was utilised fully in the arrangements for the 'Salute the Soldier' savings week. Colonel W.E. Morgan, of the Canadian Army, took the salute and gave the opening address. Their band played in the parade and a French-Canadian male voice choir performed in a concert at the Mechanics' Institute.

It was normal to see service men from Farnley Camp in Otley. Many were catered for at the Y.M.C.A. Services Canteen situated in Boroughgate, and later in the old Grammar School buildings in Manor Square. For six and a half years the canteen was in the charge of Miss Hunter, a Governor of Prince Henry's and daughter of Mr F. T. Hunter, one of the original pre-1909 Governors and Chairman of the Governing Body. The following article was published in the '*Wharfedale and Airedale Observer*' on 27 September 1946:

Served in France

'Miss Hunter has always had the welfare of Servicemen and ex-Servicemen very much at heart. In 1915 she went out to France to join Miss Jessie Wilson, formerly of Otley, in a canteen at Harfleur, where the Otley Howitzer Battery was stationed for a time. After the signing of the Armistice, Miss Hunter and her friend moved into Belgium and then to Germany, and experienced many difficulties, as only troop trains were on the move, and there were no arrangements for women workers. Miss Hunter was for two years in charge of a canteen in Germany, serving with the Army of Occupation.

'She says canteens in those days were fewer, and were more appreciated than in the recent war. She is in a good position to express an opinion because for the past six and a half years, she has been in charge of the Y.M.C.A. Services canteen at Otley, formerly in Boroughgate, but now in the old Grammar School building in Manor Square.

Boroughgate Canteen

'At the peak of war, just before D-day, the Boroughgate canteen gave a very big service. It was a common occurrence for over 1,000 troops to be served during one evening, and at week-ends this figure was greatly exceeded. Now the numbers are much smaller, but the interest of voluntary workers has also flagged now that the war is over, and Miss Hunter devotes much time and effort to keeping the canteen open for locally stationed men.'

Pupils would also have been aware that from 1944 until 1948 there was a Prisoner of War Camp situated on Weston Lane. The building of the Weston Estate housing development in the late 1940s destroyed most of the physical evidence of the Camp. It was common to see PoWs being marched through Otley from the station to the camp. Prisoners of war were used to help unload trains, work at the hospital as gardeners and porters, and work on the land at local farms. There was even a suggestion that prisoners should be used to dig the foundations for the new houses being built in Otley, and help to fill in the air-raid trench at Prince Henry's. Discipline at the camp was fairly lax, especially as the war neared its end. Pupils at Prince Henry's would have been curious to see the 'enemy', and on Sunday afternoons local families would walk up to see the camp. Friendships developed and it was not unusual to push cigarettes through the fence as gifts to the PoWs. In contrast some youngsters were ordered by their parents to stay well away from the camp.

When local people are asked about their war-time memories many of them put rationing at the top of the list.

Food rationing was introduced in Britain on 8 January 1940 and finally ended on 30 June 1954 when meat was removed from the ration. As soon as war was declared the Ministry of Food came into being. The intention was that rationing would bring fair shares for everyone and stop the profiteering that was a feature of the early years of the war. Ration books began to be distributed in November 1939, and two months later rationing started. Every man, woman and child had a ration book, with coupons that were required before rationed goods could be bought. Housewives had to register with particular retailers. Weekly limits were set on quantities of sugar (12oz. per person), butter (4oz. per person), bacon and/or ham (4oz. per person).

The authority of the Ministry of Food was delegated to 19 Divisional Food Offices. Under these were 1,500 local Food Control Committees, appointed by local authorities, with representatives both of the consumer and the retailer.

The meat ration, introduced in March 1940, was 1/10d. per person per week at first, but it fell to 1/2d. on 13 January 1941 where it remained for the rest of the war. In May 1940 the sugar ration was reduced to 8oz per person per week, though in June 1940 the allowance was doubled for four weeks to allow for jam making at home. Cooking fats were rationed in July 1940, as was tea (2oz.); while preserves and cheese were added to the list of rationed goods in March and May 1941.

From 1 December 1941 a 'points' system was introduced for the rationing of tinned goods, dried fruits, cereals, pulses, syrup, treacle and biscuits. Priority allowances of milk and eggs, free orange juice and cod liver oil were given to those most in need, including children and expectant mothers. Some housewives would save up their points for special occasions, such as Christmas, but supplies of foodstuffs could not be guaranteed.

The introduction of the 'points' system coincided with the arrival of 30,000 tons of canned meats, canned fish and canned beans from abroad. All the items were given a points value and 'Points Coupon Books' were distributed to ensure that the food was available in equal shares to everyone who wished to buy.

'The basis of the new system of distribution is a pink-coloured "Points Coupon Book" – 'the pink 'un.' It contains a number of coupons all dated and some marked 'A', some 'B', and some 'C.' The four 'A' coupons dated November 17 to December 14 are each worth one point; the four 'B' coupons bearing the same date are each worth one point, and the four 'C' coupons are each worth two points. This adds up to 16 points, so that in the first four weeks of the Scheme each consumer will have 16 points to spend.

What the Coupons are Worth

'When the housewife goes shopping she will find all the items in the new food have been given a value in points as follow:

Sixteen points per lb. net – Solid packed canned meats i.e. tongue, briskets, luncheon meat, stewed steak and rabbit; certain types of canned fish i.e. salmon, sardines, crayfish and lobster.

Twelve points per lb. net – All other canned fish i.e. mainly herrings and pilchards.

Eight points per lb. net – Certain home produced and Eire canned meat products i.e. ready meals, meat rolls and galantines.

Four points per lb. net – Canned beans in sauce or gravy, home produced or imported.

'The scheme will give the consumer freedom to shop for the new foods where and when she likes. She will not have to register, and she will not have to restrict her purchase to one shop and she will be permitted to spend her coupons how she pleases on a wide variety of foods.

To give the new system a good start it was essential that the shops should be well stocked. This has meant a huge job of transport; 30,000,000 lb. of fish and 10,000,000 lb. of baked beans are being delivered to the retailers on condition that no sales are made until November 17.' ('Wharfedale and Airedale Observer,' 7 November 1941)

Not all foods were rationed. Fruit and vegetables were never rationed, but were often in short supply, especially tomatoes, onions and fruit shipped from overseas. Some exotic fruits like bananas and lemons disappeared almost totally from wartime Britain. The following article was published in the '*Wharfedale and Airedale Observer*' on 29 November 1940:

ONIONS SNAPPED UP AT OTLEY – LEMONS, ORANGES AND BANANAS

'There were onions on sale in Otley yesterday, but only for a short time.

A small consignment was delivered to several shops in the town in the morning, and the news quickly spread. One trader, who received 3 stone of onions, was sold out within an hour. Other traders had a similar experience.

'Onions are not the only commodity which are scarce, however. Discussing the general situation in foodstuffs yesterday, Mr Walter Moss, an Otley provision merchant, said there were a few lemons on sale, but oranges were scarce at the moment, and bananas had almost disappeared.

There were some fine English apples on the market, and he advised housewives to buy a few of the "keeping" varieties, such as Bramley Seedlings, now, and keep them in a cool place in store for Christmas.'

The government encouraged people to grow their own vegetables in their own gardens and allotments, under the slogan 'Dig For Victory.' At a public meeting held by Otley Urban Council on 29 September 1939 it was agreed that applications would be favourably considered for the provision of allotments in the town, and that vacant allotments would be let free for the remainder of the year. A decision on allowing poultry to be kept on council owned housing estates was deferred but was later agreed, under certain conditions, at a meeting held on 19 January 1940. It was pointed out that '*the conditions would not debar anyone desirous of poultry keeping; a far greater difficulty would be obtaining feeding stuffs for them.'*

The government also mounted a massive publicity campaign, with 'Food Facts' advertisements printed each week in the press, 'Food Flash' films being shown in cinemas, and radio programmes. Housewives became extremely inventive, creating meals using the limited number of ingredients at their disposal. Dishes were given names that had nothing to do with what they were made from.

In fact, this 'food planning', based on the nutritional needs of the people, with priority rationing for mothers and children, resulted in a decline in infant mortality and an improvement in other indicators of nutritional well-being. Parents were encouraged to promote healthier children through slogans such as *'Milk – The Backbone of Young Britain,'* and *'Carrots keep you healthy and help you to see in the blackout.'*

However, sometimes shortages meant that consumers were unable even to obtain the 'ration'. In January 1941 a shortage of meat supplies in the Wharfedale district led to Otley butchers closing their shops for three days a week. An official of the Otley Butchers' Association said *"We were told to restrict our customers to 1s. 1d. per head, but the supplies we received only ran to about 7¼d. per head, and we could not give our registered customers the rations they were supposed to have."*

"Run" on Tinned Meat

'There was little meat available on Saturday, and butchers were hard pressed to supply customers with a joint for the week-end. The result was that housewives 'raided' the provision shops for tinned meats. Chickens and rabbits had a ready sale, and retailers reported that more customers than usual had taken up the bacon ration.

A leading provision merchant said it was evident on Saturday that there was a shortage of meat. Cooked meats went very quickly and extra supplies had to be made available.

He suggested that, in view of the big demand for tinned meats, it might be advisable for the Ministry of Food to release a further supply of corned beef and similar canned meat to replenish the traders' depleted stocks. If there was another breakdown in the meat supplies, what was going to happen?

Value of Reserves

'The present position in Wharfedale, he said, showed the wisdom of housewives keeping a reserve. A lot of comment had been made about "hoarding", but there is a big difference between hoarding and keeping a sensible reserve. It was in just such an emergency as this that the reserve kept the household going.' ('Wharfedale and Airedale Observer,' 10 January 1941)

Another impact of rationing which caused concern was queuing. In April 1941 the Bakers and Confectioners' Section of the Otley Chamber of Trade recommended that shopkeepers dealing in foodstuffs should not open their shops to the public until 9 a.m., with a view to *'effecting a more equitable distribution of foodstuffs, and the avoidance of early morning queues.'* Shopping problems for women war workers were also noted in the following article published in the *'Wharfedale and Airedale Observer'* on 3 October 1941:

WOMEN WAR WORKERS – OTLEY MOVE TO EASE SHOPPING PROBLEM

'The problem of fair supplies for women war-workers was discussed by the Otley & Wharfedale Joint Food Control Committee at a meeting on Monday.

It was pointed out that, particularly in cases where married women were going into war work, many shoppers were placed at a disadvantage in procuring their fair share of unrationed goods by reason of the fact that their attendance at work prevented them from doing their shopping during the day.

It was decided that a sub-committee comprising Mrs. Johnson, Mrs. Connal and Mr S. Wilkinson, should meet representatives of Otley Chamber of Trade to discuss the possibility of setting up some system of unofficial rationing of these commodities, in order that this disadvantage to war-workers may be overcome.'

Certain other key commodities were also rationed – petrol in 1939, clothes in June 1941 and soap in February 1942. Sweets and chocolate were rationed from 27 July 1942, at 2oz. per person per week.

For clothes rationing each person was granted an allowance of 66 coupons per year, estimated to ensure that each person could buy, on average, one new set of clothes per year. In March 1942 this was reduced to 60 coupons per person, and these coupons had to last for fourteen months instead of twelve. Children's clothing generally had a lower coupon value than adults because it needed less material. Uniforms for H.M. Forces could be bought coupon free. Coupons were even required to purchase wool, and this restricted the 'comforts' produced for servicemen abroad.

Even baby clothes were rationed as announced in an article in the '*Wharfedale and Airedale Observer*' on 15 August 1941:

BABY CLOTHES RATIONED – RICH AND POOR ON EQUAL FOOTING

'Rich babies will be no better off than poor ones under new clothes rationing arrangements announced this week. All baby garments are now rationed.

Hitherto, made-up garments for children under four have been coupon-free. Consequently, mothers with money to spare have been able to buy their babies plenty of clothes, while other mothers trying to save by making clothes themselves have had to give up coupons for materials.

To do away with this unfairness, the Board of Trade first decided to give each expectant mother 50 coupons, but this plan still favoured mothers able to buy garments ready-made. So all-in rationing was the only answer.

In addition to the expectant mother ration of 50 coupons, babies born and registered before the end of November will receive the ordinary civilian clothing card of 40 coupons.

Babies born during December, January and February, will get 30 and those born during March, April and May, 20. In the next ration year, babies will be rationed the same way as adults.

Splitting Coupons

'Coupon ratings for baby garments are not exorbitant. The highest is six for a fully-lined woolen or fur overcoat. Most other articles need only one or two. A pair of socks or a bib can be obtained for a third of a coupon. Baby welfare experts helped the Board to work out these rates.

"The worst off are babies born in June and July, before the expectant mother ration was introduced," an official said.'

Women were encouraged to take better care of clothing, prolong its life and make new items from old clothing and materials such as curtains or bedding in the 'Make Do and Mend' campaign. Wool from unraveled knitted items was reused, socks were darned. Some brides to be made their wedding dresses from discarded parachute silk.

At the end of December 1941 a *'British Restaurant'* opened near the bus station on Bondgate. This was a government scheme designed to combat the severity of rationing by selling basic meals at reasonable prices, off ration. Volunteers, usually members of the Women's Voluntary Service (W.V.S.), staffed it. Members of the Urban Council, officials and their wives attended the official opening of the Otley British Restaurant. The meal consisted of Scotch broth (price 2d.), stewed steak and kidney, carrots and potatoes (6d.), syrup sponge and custard or jam tart (2d.), and a cup of tea (1d.). The full meal cost 11d., but each course could be purchased separately, or repeated.

British Restaurant.

British Restaurants had their critics, but Mr Wilkinson, Chairman of the Council, suggested that *"No one need feel embarrassed in utilising the facilities available, because it is provided out of taxpayers' money. You all have a stake in the restaurant. Use it. From today it is intended that all expenditure and overhead charges should be met out of income, and there is no question of profit-making."*

The end of the war did not bring an end to rationing; in fact cuts were made to the basic ration, bacon went down from 4oz. to 3oz., cooking fat from 2oz. to 1 oz., and part of the meagre meat ration of 1/2d. had to be taken in corned beef. Bread, which was never rationed in wartime, was put on the ration in July 1946.

One way to get rationed goods without coupons, usually at greatly inflated prices, was on the 'black market.' Shopkeepers sometimes kept special supplies 'behind the counter' and 'spivs' sold goods often obtained illegally. By March 1941, 2,300 people nationally had been prosecuted and severely penalised for fraud and dishonesty. Local cases included a farmer who was fined £12 plus costs for selling milk containing water, and an Otley man sentenced to 12 months' imprisonment for involvement in the theft of 45,000 clothing coupons.

It was not until the early 1950s that most commodities came 'off the ration'. The last item to be derationed was meat in 1954. Rationing in one form or another lasted for fourteen years, with some children never having known anything different. However, rationing discouraged waste and, even though portions were small and variety poor, allowed everybody – rich and poor alike – to survive on what they had. Price controls meant that high demand did not lead to high prices that could only be afforded by the rich.

Everyone was encouraged to 'do their bit' for the war effort, and this included school children. The government produced posters, leaflets, film and radio broadcasts to get its message over to the public. People were encouraged to *'Dig for Victory'*, to *'Lend a Hand on the Land,'* to *'Save Kitchen Waste to Feed the Pigs.'* They were warned of the dangers of *'Careless Talk'*, and of the need to *'Make do and Mend'* and to salvage materials for the production of tanks, ships, aircraft and armaments via slogans such as *'Still More Rags wanted for salvage,'* and *'Bones are still needed to make Glue for housing and Fertiliser for food.'*

One of the most successful campaigns of the War involved the significant increase in National Savings. An employee of the National Savings Committee, artist Phillip Boydell, created the 'Squanderbug,' a cartoon bug that appeared in press advertisements and posters as a menace who encouraged shoppers to waste money rather than buy war savings certificates and bonds. The Squanderbug was described as *'Alias Hitler's Pal, known to be at large in certain parts of the Kingdom, usually found in the company of useless articles, has a tempting leer and a flattering manner.'*

Posters with the slogan *'Is Your Journey Really Necessary?'* reminded people to save fuel that could be better used for the transport of troops and war supplies. Posters were also used to keep up morale and wartime spirits. They made it clear that everybody was in this war together and everybody had a part to play. This helped the public to feel involved and to feel that their contribution to the war effort was helping to bring victory nearer.

There were many ways in which the pupils of Prince Henry's 'did their bit,' and they must have felt proud when targets were met, competitions won and concerts performed. These additional activities provided pupils with an alternative to the routine of the school day and for most students would have been much more interesting than normal lessons. There was constant pressure on pupils to join the National Savings Scheme and evidence that the number of savers grew significantly during the war. The annual, themed, 'Savings Weeks' provided opportunities to boost saving and to take part in competitions to design posters, make model planes and warships for display in local shop windows. There were also successes in handwriting and painting competitions. Local schools took part in concerts during the 'Week', displaying their talent for instrumental music, dancing and both solo and choral singing.

Winners of '*The Sea in Wartime*' essay competition held in connection with '*Warship Week*' in March 1942 were:

SENIORS

1. *K. McCulloch (Age 14 years, 11 months), 'Lynton', Otley Road, Bramhope.*
2. *G.W. Pearson (14 years 11 months), 21 Caxton Road, Otley.*

JUNIORS

1. *Anne Taylor (14 years 9 months), 'Easby', Pool Bank, Pool.*
2. *Mary McLennan (13 years), 13 Mount Pisgah, Otley.*

In his report to the Governors in May 1943, Mr Wilde said that:

'the school was playing its part in the coming 'Wings for Victory' Week. The pupils had taken part in all the competitions, they were producing a play in the schools' concert, decorating a shop window, providing a guard during the day for the A.T.C. headquarters, and also providing a speaker at the indicator when the school children undertook the marking-up ceremony.'

Pupils at Prince Henry's played a significant part in 'digging for victory'. Parts of the playing fields were converted to the production of crops and vegetables, the sale of which raised funds for war charities. The formation of a Gardening Club provided a nursery for kale, cabbage, Brussels sprouts and other greens for planting in the school field. In both holidays and term time parties of boys were provided to help local farmers. Pupils and staff attended 'harvest camps', spending much of their time picking potatoes, but also making the most of their limited leisure time. The school workshop was used to make 'instruments of war.'

The collection of 'salvage' was important in providing materials to assist the war effort. At Prince Henry's a 'War Effort Club' was set up to collect wool, waste paper, silver paper, bones and clothes. The wool was used to knit blankets that were distributed to members of the Forces through organisations such as the Otley Christmas Comforts fund and the Merchant Navy knitted comforts fund. Money was raised through the annual Garden Party when forms put on plays, displays and side-shows; in one year the money raised was distributed to St Dunstan's, Aid to Russia, Dr Barnardo's, Otley Christmas Comforts, the Hull and Liverpool Air Raid Distress Funds and the Otley Y.M.C.A.

Most school children prefer holidays to school days, and look forward to trips away from their hometown. However, during the war in order to prioritise military and freight traffic, and to maximise rationed fuel supplies, the government tried to impose restrictions on civilian travel and produced posters asking, '*Is Your Journey Really Necessary*?' Local authorities were encouraged to provide homegrown entertainment through 'Holidays at Home.' Otley U.D.C. organised summer 'Stay-at-Home' holiday programmes from 1942 – 1944.

The 1942 programme, to be held in the last week of July and the first week of August, was described in the '*Wharfedale and Airedale Observer*' on 24 July 1942 as:

'Otley's "Stay-at-Home" holiday programme opens tomorrow, and spread over the next fortnight is a series of social and sporting events, which promise a unique experience for Otley folk.

The programme offers a wealth of entertainment, and the variety of it is a tribute to the hard work of the men and women who have co-operated on the committees responsible for arranging the events. A grand effort has been made to make it a really interesting holiday for those who are patriotic and comply with the Government's wish that they should stay-at-home.

'There should be fun and entertainment in plenty in what is almost a non-stop show. Each day (except Thursday) will have a centre of attraction, something to see and somewhere to go, and on most days Otley people will be able to pick and choose from several events. Given fine weather there should be no difficulty about creating a real holiday spirit. Provision has been made for unkindly weather, and many of the entertainments will be held in the Mechanics' Hall.'

Youngsters, including pupils at Prince Henry's, were catered for by a swimming gala, a tennis tournament, boat rides on the Wharfe, children's entertainment in the Mechanics' Hall, pony rides and Punch and Judy shows.

On the August Bank Holiday the most notable feature was the quietness of the roads:

'The expiry of the last opportunity for pleasure motoring on the Friday evening led to

an absence of cars from the road on the Saturday and following days, which created an atmosphere strangely quiet. Those almost endless processions of cars which pour along the main roads during the whole of a peace-time Bank Holiday week-end were missing; the road was given up to buses, business vehicles and bicycles.

'On the moorland roads, always the delight of the holiday motorist, it was possible to walk with complete enjoyment, and there were no cars parked alongside the grass. Those visitors who did come into the valley had to make use of either the buses or trains, or their own feet as transport.' ('Wharfedale and Airedale Observer', 7 August 1942)

A similar programme was organised for the summer holidays in 1943. Mr K. Milligan, Chairman of the Urban Council, explained that last year's 'Holidays at Home' programme had been a great success and the Government had requested the Council to make similar arrangements this year. The cost to the rates last year was only £105, and in addition £85 was raised for charitable institutions. Added attractions were a children's pet show, *'calculated to have an appeal somewhat wider than the ranks of the juveniles for whom it has been arranged'*, and a children's sports day, organised by the Schools Sports Association.

The first part of the stay-at-home holiday was described as an *'unqualified success'*, bringing *'maximum enjoyment to those who have wisely obeyed the Government's urge not to travel.'*

'Aided perhaps by favourable conditions, the generous variety of events has created an atmosphere little less authentic then the genuine seaside holiday and indeed has offered some of the amenities of that traditional summer treat.'

However, it was also reported that *'railway travel, nothing like normal times, has nevertheless stepped up, and last week-end a fair number of local people set off to holiday resorts. The number of bookings for this week-end is higher, due to the fact that most of the local places of employment are closing down for the coming week.' ('Wharfedale and Airedale Observer', 30 July 1943)*

The summer 1944 programme included a swimming gala, a children's sports day held on the Cross Green Rugby field, a children's fancy dress competition, a mounted gymkhana, with open pony riding and leaping, a cycling gymkhana and a pet/flower show. The sports day results for entries from Prince Henry's students included:

Girls, 13 years	90 yards	3. M. Pratt
Girls, 12 years	80 yards	1. S. Moss 2. S. Pickles
Girls, 10 years	60 yards	1. H. Padgett
Girls, open	100 yards	3. S. Moss
Girls, 9-11 years	Skipping	2. H. Padgett
Girls, 12-14 years	80 yards	3. B. Metcalfe

Girls	Senior Relay	2. P.H.G.S.: B. Metcalf, M. Pratt, S. Moss, S. Pickles
Boys, 14 years	100 yards	1. R.A. Butland 2. R. Leeming 3. W. H. Lambert
Boys, 13 years	90 yards	2. G. Hellewell
Boys, 12 years	80 yards	3. N. Mackie
Boys, 14 and under	220 yards	1. R. A. Butland 2. R. Leeming
Boys, 12-14	60 yards	1. A. Smith 2. G. Hellewell
Boys	Senior Relay	1. P.H.G.S.: Butland, Leeming, Lovack, Lambert

'On Wednesday evening spectators lined the Bridge and banks of the Wharfe to see Geoffrey Thomas of Prince Henry's Grammar School, win the 'Vavasour' cup river race. Last year's cup holder, Gerald Baxter, was second, and Slater third. The race is approximately a quarter of a mile and ends below the Bridge.

Mr J. Nicholson, a member of the Otley Swimming Club, presented the cup to the winner and congratulated him on his success.

Before the race pupils of Prince Henry's Grammar School, with Miss Bowden in charge, demonstrated life saving land drill, and showed various methods of release and rescue in the river.' ('Wharfedale and Airedale Observer,' 11 August 1944)

The holiday-at-home fortnight, aided by good weather, was a huge success. The second Monday was described in the '*Wharfedale*' as a time when:

'Otley holidaymakers were joined by thousands from neighbouring towns and the crowds in the town and by the river reached a new war-time peak. The Green and Wharfemeadows, viewed from the Bridge, looked for all the world like a section of the beach during the height of the season at pre-war Blackpool.'

Otley Urban Council decided not to provide an extensive 'Holidays at Home' programme in 1945, expecting that '*all who possibly can will try and get away this summer.*'

During the war, another holiday very different to previous years was Christmas. Metal shortages meant that toys for children were made from wood, recycled or homemade, and paper shortages reduced the number of books available as gifts. The biggest impact was shortages of food due to rationing or unavailability. In some years food rations were increased for the Christmas period, but there were still only a small number of turkeys available in each year. As shortages worsened 'mock' alternatives to turkey, goose, marzipan and cream were offered and recipes were produced that tried to simulate the real thing – usually without success. Christmas 1941 was the first 'on the ration'. Weekly rations at the time were four ounces of bacon and/or ham, six ounces of butter and/or margarine, two ounces of tea, eight ounces of sugar, two ounces of cooking fats and meat to the value of 1s/10d. Clothing and textiles were rationed from June 1941, and by Christmas rationing was at its height. There were no turkeys, chocolates or fruit and cigarettes, cigars and tobacco were in short supply.

The following article refers to food supplies available in Otley in Christmas 1942:

TINNED TURKEY AND PUDDINGS

'There is a good deal of misunderstanding about supplies of Christmas puddings and tinned turkey which recent pronouncements have led many people to expect would be available at Christmas-time.

After the first announcement there was a rush to place orders. One local provision merchant received within a week no fewer than 500 orders, and at that time he had not a tin in his shop.

He added that the actual allocation of Christmas puddings and tinned turkey did not amount to one tin per 100 customers. To overcome a vexing position he is, like some other traders, allocating his small quota to poorer people and old couples whose rations do not allow of much in the way of luxuries.' ('Wharfedale and Airedale Observer', 18 December 1942)

Things were no different for the festive season in 1943. People began to save their coupons months in advance of Christmas, but shortages were still common.

FIFTH WAR CHRISTMAS

'Most people have completed their preparations for this, their fifth Christmas of the war, although the comparative dearth of goods in the shops has set pre-Christmas shoppers something of a problem. Rationing allows no margin for an extra celebration in the way of additional seasonal delicacies, and the housewife's ingenuity must again be exercised. Needless to say, no displays of turkeys or other birds have been seen. Choice of gifts, too, is somewhat limited, although we are all grateful that things are not as bad as they might have been. The appeal for early posting has had a good effect, although the postal workers are having a busy time with staffs much depleted compared with pre-war years. Parties have been held in various local schools, and, here too, austerity has ruled out some of the erstwhile festivities. At Prince Henry's Grammar School, the cast and helpers of the Shakespeare festival, had a party, but the usual celebrations have been suspended owing to war-time conditions.' ('Wharfedale and Airedale Observer,' 24 December 1943).

Shortages were still at their height at Christmas 1944, when it was said that there was:

'No chance of turkey, chicken or goose - not even the despised rabbit. If we can get a little mutton that is the best we can hope for. A few Christmas puddings are about. There are shops with three puddings and 800 registered shoppers.' ('Mass Observation', by Vere Hodgson)

Christmas 1944 was probably the most joyless of the war, in spite of the fact that the Allied Forces in Europe were pushing the Germans back. The Ministry of Food announced Christmas treats – an extra 1½ pounds of sugar, 8 pennyworth of meat, and half a pound of sweets. Alcohol was at its scarcest that Christmas.

There were still rationing problems at Christmas 1946 when the '*Wharfedale*' gave some details of the supplies of festive food likely to be available in the local shops:

A CHRISTMAS ROUND-UP – THE LOCAL FOOD POSITION

'Meat – For Christmas the meat ration is increased from 1s. 2d. to 2s. for an adult and 8d. to 1s. for a child. The full ration can be drawn this week-end, or the extra ration can be left until Monday or Tuesday. Otley butchers will hand over their counters something like £500 more meat than usual. A quarter of the meat allocation in Otley will be pork, and half of it beef or mutton. The other quarter will be corned beef.

Poultry – You will be lucky if you see a bird of any sort in a shop. The demand is good but the supply meagre indeed. One Otley shop, stacked in pre-war days with turkeys, geese, ducks and chickens has not had one bird to sell. The trader added "We are not likely to have anything either – not even a rabbit."

Puddings – The supply has been better than expected but has not met the demand. Not everyone will have managed to buy one. Prospect of getting one now is very small.

Cakes – Local shops have been able to make very few; less than ever in fact, and casual inquirers have been told "They are all sold" Mince pies will make an appearance this week-end. Again, there will be few of them, and it will be a case of first come first served.

Tinned Fruit – Tins of imported and home-grown fruit are available, strictly on a one-per-household basis. Most of these have already been snapped up but some are reserved for Friday shoppers. One Otley shop, with an allocation of imported peaches, apricots, pears and fruit salad of one to six customers, settled the problem by letting customers take a lucky dip. The unlucky ones got home-canned plums or rhubarb.

Fruit and Nuts – In the last few days there have been more plentiful supplies of oranges, apples and grapefruit, but they are scarce now. There are also a few pears, pomegranates at 1s. 6d. each and tangerines from 4d. each. Some nuts offered – walnuts at 6s. 6d. a lb., chestnuts at 2s. 6d. a lb. Picked Tunis dates have arrived in very short supply – and on points.

Etceteras – Good demand for ample supplies of berried holly at 1s. 6d. to 2s. a lb. Mistletoe is scarce at 5s. a lb. (a good sized bunch will run to about 2s.) Christmas trees have sold well at 1s. 6d. a foot, and there are still many left in the shops.' ('Wharfedale and Airedale Observer,' 20 December 1946)

Families were likely to be separated at Christmas because of overseas postings or evacuation. Christmas messages could be sent to the Forces, but had to be sent up to three months in advance. Parcels containing presents, often including Christmas pudding and cake, were also sent. Most towns and villages in Wharfedale sent comforts to the troops at Christmas.

In Otley the 'Christmas Gifts for Forces' scheme started in 1939. Money was raised by private subscriptions, house-to-house collections, flag days and other activities. It was decided to send each serving man and woman a 10/- note sent by registered post, with a greeting card printed with the town's coat of arms, and bearing the words '*The townspeople of Otley send you greetings and good wishes.*' Money gifts were not sent to officers, who received instead a box of cigarettes costing approximately 10/- (200 cigarettes). Almost 300 parcels were distributed. It was decided to leave the distribution of knitted goods and other articles until the New Year.

'A letter was read from the secretary of the War Service Guild of Roundhay Girls' High School, who are "sharing" Otley Prince Henry's Grammar School. This stated that scholars at the School had knitted three pairs of gloves, ten pairs of mittens, four pairs of socks, 15 scarves and four pull-overs. "We trust Otley men will find these articles serviceable and that you will accept the gift as a token of gratitude for the kindness the people of Otley have shown to the school," stated the letter.' ('Wharfedale and Airedale Observer,' 1 December 1939)

Scores of letters of appreciation were sent to Mr Dacre, Secretary of the Comforts Fund Committee, and to the Editor of the '*Wharfedale and Airedale Observer.*' At Christmas 1940 about 673 parcels were sent, each containing a greeting card, knitted comforts and a 10/- note. The breakdown published in the '*Wharfedale and Airedale Observer,' 11 April 1941* gives an indication of the numbers from Otley serving in the Forces. 673 gifts had been made:

'Six of these were to prisoners of war. For these men a sum of 15s. had been paid to the family of each, with a request that a parcel should be sent through the Red Cross, and he believed that in every case a parcel was sent. Cash gifts of 10s. each went to 12 women in the Women's Services, 27 men in the Royal Navy, 78 in the Royal Air Force, 523 in the Army, and three to officers who preferred money to cigarettes. A further 12 officers received parcels of cigarettes, each to the value of 10s. It had been intended to send all the gifts by registered post, but it had not been possible to do this, and 11 parcels went astray. This was not a bad record out of 650 parcels sent, and the 11 gifts which had gone astray had been repeated, so that the men concerned did not suffer.'

(NOTE – eagle-eyed mathematicians will have worked out that the total gifts mentioned in the above extract was 672 – one gift of 10/- was sent to a soldier who did not receive a Christmas parcel in 1939!)

The Committee discussed the Christmas gifts for 1941, when it was suggested that the call-up of further age groups could increase the number of Otley people serving to 1000.

'The ladies' committee intimated that they had about 200 pairs of socks in hand and were prepared to go on knitting to provide a parcel of comforts for each man, but asked to be relieved of the task of raising the money to pay for the wool. It was stated that this had been done in the past by organising social events. This had proved a heavy burden last year, and it would be increasingly heavy this time. All their efforts would be required in knitting the greater quantity of comforts needed.

The meeting unhesitatingly decided to relieve the ladies of this burden, and it was agreed that the wool should be paid for out of the general fund. It was estimated that 250lbs. of wool would be required, and Mr Normanton and Mr Kell were appointed a small sub-committee to act with Mr Dacre in making enquires about the purchase of the wool.' ('Wharfedale and Airedale Observer,' 11 April 1941)

By Christmas 1942 – the fourth since the war started – the difficulty in obtaining supplies of wool meant that no woollen comforts were sent out. As compensation it was decided to send a greeting card and a 15/- Postal Order to each of the 1000 serving men and women from Otley. It was also agreed that gifts be sent:

'to those girls from Otley who are serving in the Women's Land Army, to those girls who have elected to take up whole-time employment as nurses in lieu of entering other branches of the Services, and also to men from Otley who are serving in the Merchant Navy.

This will result in a larger amount being distributed and consequently the need for more liberal giving on the part of those at home will be greater.' ('Wharfedale and Airedale Observer,' 18 September 1942)

By Christmas 1943 the number of serving men and women had increased further, and the shortage of wool meant that the normal practice of sending a pair of socks to each man was dropped. It was agreed that each man and woman would receive a 15/- postal order plus a greeting card in the form of a photograph of the river, bridge and Chevin. The many letters of appreciation received praised the inclusion of the card with the local view, saying how nice it was to have been sent a memento that reminded them of their hometown.

For Christmas 1944 the inclusion of a local view was repeated, and 1,265 gifts were sent, compared with 859 the previous year.

'This year's card is an improvement on the last for, in addition to well-chosen words of greeting and a photograph of Otley Bridge from downstream, there is a landscape view of the valley of the Wharfe taken from a vantage point on the slopes of the Chevin woodlands, recently given to the town by Major Horton-Fawkes, of Farnley Hall.' ('Wharfedale and Airedale Observer,' 1 December 1944).

In spite of the end of the war and the resulting demobilisation it was unanimously agreed to continue with Christmas gifts in 1945, and that the gift should again take the form of a 15/- postal order and a greetings card with a local view. Many letters of appreciation were again received, some from members of the Forces who had received the gifts in all, or nearly all, of the seven Christmases they were distributed.

The war-time Christmas Editorials in the *'Otliensian'* stressed the fact that in spite of the pupils and their families being affected significantly by the war, they were much better off than many other people. The Autumn 1940 (*Vol. XXIII*) issue noted that:

'Christmas, the second one of the war, is approaching steadily, but it will be rather

different from our pre-war festive seasons. Then we made merry at the Christmas concert and the Christmas parties which now, alas, are things of the past. But because we must now forego some of our wonted luxuries and gaiety, it does not mean that we must go about our business with long faces and downcast hearts. On the contrary, we must put our shoulders to the wheel cheerfully, and work wholeheartedly for the common cause – Liberty. Many people in the School are too young to join any of the Civil Defence Services, but everyone from the oldest to the youngest, can pull his weight with the rest of the nation, by saving, by being careful that he does not waste anything of value, by being generally useful, and by being cheerful so that he can raise other people's spirits and thus help to keep up the nation's morale. The Christmas spirit of Peace and Goodwill seems rather out of place at present, but let it rule our attitude to our neighbours at this time of crisis so that all may work in harmony, without one dissenting voice, for victory.'

A similar theme was taken up at Christmas 1941 (*Vol. XXIV, Autumn 1941*):

'In spite of the paper shortage, it is doubtful whether Santa Claus' mail will be smaller than usual this year. But the familiar demand for a box of chocolates has possibly been replaced by a request for a savings certificate.

It will be a hard struggle to secure twenty extra cigarettes for father, and it is even less clear how mother's annual pair of stockings can be obtained. Our Christmas will not, perhaps, follow out the traditional idea of Christmas with all those mince-pies, tangerine, oranges and trifles. But, nevertheless, our Christmas, with its little inconveniences, will be like heaven compared with Christmas in the occupied territories.

While we are celebrating, we tend to forget the true meaning of Christmas tide; this is especially true of Christmas in war-time. However much the war may be occupying our minds this Christmas, we must find time to include a thought of the first Christmas – of what it means and of our duty in consequence of it.

While it will be impossible to celebrate Christmas this year with the time-honoured gifts of peace-time, the Christmas spirit can and will be kindled in British hearts and homes.'

In 1942 (*Vol. XXV, Autumn 1942*) the theme was repeated:

'Another year is drawing to a close; a year, indeed, of toil, sweat, blood and tears, and as it closes we might well pause for a moment to rededicate ourselves to the Great Crusade, in which we are fighting.

It will be cold in Russia, this winter; it will be cold in the occupied territories. It will be cold in Britain too; but not to such an extent that we may think that any personal hardships can ever be as great as those of the men who fight, in the four corners of the earth, for fundamental decency.

We can, however, spread some of that spiritual warmth the first sign of which was a star above a stable two thousand years ago, amid this physical desolation, by observing the customary kindnesses of Christmas. Our mended stockings will not bulge with material benefit, but we shall understand.

We can, too, help by saving and through the Red Cross Penny-a-Week Fund, and here we may notice the examples of the lower forms, but it is equally important to see that when we, the Youth of today, leave the playing fields, parade grounds and examination rooms for the wider world, it will be to build the Peace, for which our brothers and fathers are fighting. We may face a bleak and drear future; we must be prepared!'

In spite of the impending end of the war, pupils were again told not to complain about the 'nuisances' suffered during the war and to help those less fortunate than themselves. (*Vol. XXVII, Spring 1943):*

'This has been an eventful term, if only because of the severe frost accompanying it, and all the excitement of a frozen Wharfe. For many of us, this was a new but most delightful experience, and the thrills of skating, sliding, or even merely walking on what had previously been for us an unstable stretch of water, will not be soon forgotten.

Despite the cold, however, our hearts have remained warm and cheerful, and as victory looms so much nearer on the horizon than it was a year ago, we can feel thankful that we have survived more than five years of war with so few hardships, as compared with other, less happy countries. How paltry our grumbles about rationing, queuing and other nuisances seem in the face of their terrific suffering and dire needs!

We must, therefore, in our gratitude, do all we can to help our unfortunate friends and to supply their many demands until they are once more able to support themselves. In the midst of our joyful anticipation of victory and peace, we must resolve that never again, if it lies within our power to prevent it, must the ravages of war sweep through this world in which we live.'

Even after peace was declared the Editorial warned about the difficulties ahead (*Vol. XXVIII, Spring 1946):*

'This issue of the Magazine is indeed one of some moment, being the first to be published since the cessation of hostilities in Japan. At the time of our last publication we were rejoicing over our victories in Europe. Heavy eyes brightened and war-weary voices took on a new note of gladness as we looked forward with eagerness to the time, seemingly so near, when the "piping days" would have returned, and peace and plenty would once more reign on earth.

True, the fighting is for the most part over, but how far we have yet to travel before our dreams become realities! Slow demobilisation, cuts in food and numerous shortages have provided ample scope for the grumblers who are always to be found in our midst. Plans for universal peace, too, have not always been discussed in the spirit which they are intended to portray, and many are the political difficulties which are to be overcome.

In the home, the atmosphere tends to be one of disappointment. Years of war made us paint too rosy a picture of the post-war world, and any unpleasant details were glossed over or quickly dismissed, so that now some of our castles in the air are crumbling to dust before us.

Otley Messenger Corps.

However, black though the horizon before us appears, surely the spirit that carried us through six years of war will guide us through the dark tangles of difficulty out of which we must fight our way, until there dawns a day when security, plenty and contentment will indeed hold sway on the earth.'

Everybody in the country was affected by the war, especially in terms of the participation of relatives and friends who joined the Armed forces, but also by the part that individuals played in doing their bit on the Home Front. As we have seen, many of the pupils at Prince Henry's took part in National Savings Weeks, collected salvage, helped to grow and harvest food, both at school and by helping local farmers, and made 'comforts' and raised money for the Forces and for war charities. But outside school the pupils, especially the more senior ones, were active members of organisations that did much to help the war effort. Some helped with 'civil defence', by joining the Messenger Corps: older boys joined the Home Guard (N. Q. King, G. E. Watson, A. Firth) or the Auxiliary Fire Service (G. Clarke, J. Swale, D. Lee, J. Mounsey): there were local branches of the Air Training Corps and the Girls' Training Corps, and other youth organisations such as the Boy Scouts and Girl Guides.

The Local Defence Volunteers (L.D.V.) was formed in May 1940, following a broadcast on 14 May 1940 from Anthony Eden asking for volunteers to defend the country from invasion. The name was changed to the Home Guard in July 1940. From that date 'A' Company of the 29th West Riding Regiment was based in Otley. Over the following 4¼ years 1,200 men joined the Company, 450 of them still in the Home Guard at the stand-down. It is certain that several of the older pupils at Prince Henry's were members of the Home Guard, and most of these went on to join the regular Forces.

Otley & District A.T.C. at Caley Hall.

'A' Company was stationed at the Drill Hall and had the task of guarding the pipe-lines at the Leeds City Council's reservoirs at Fewston, Swinsty and Lindley. Each night a party of twenty men, led by a Sergeant was driven to the reservoirs, leaving Otley at about 8.30 p.m. and returning at 5.30 a.m. the following morning. Guarding the reservoirs was only incidental to the training that took place almost every evening and outdoor operations at the week-ends. The Home Guard became a well-trained, efficient body of men who took their responsibilities seriously. The D-day invasion force contained a high proportion of soldiers who had served in the Home Guard before being called-up, and they probably included ex-pupils from Prince Henry's Grammar School.

In March 1941 the Governors' of Prince Henry's were asked to give every opportunity to pupils and teachers to join the local squadrons of the A.T.C., and to allow the use of the school premises for training. The meeting was reported in the *'Wharfedale and Airedale Observer'* on 21 March 1941:

'The Headmaster said consideration had been given to establishing a squadron at the School, but it was soon realised this could not be done, because the minimum number of recruits required was 25, and the number of boys over 16, the qualifying age, was only 13. It had therefore been decided to co-operate with the formation of the town squadron, and about 30 Grammar School boys and Old Boys had joined. Mr Wilde said he was serving on the local committee, and it had not been thought desirable to form a separate section for Grammar School boys.

Mr Whiteley said that, personally, he should have opposed the formation of a separate section for Grammar School boys. "We don't want to bring in the old school tie in this scheme," he said. "We want all the boys to mix together for the betterment of all."

Mr Atkinson agreed that anything in the nature of sections would have been wrong, and he was glad to hear it had been avoided.

Mr Wilde said it was possible that the teaching staff would be able to help with the instruction.'

Again, as mentioned in the above article, boys from Prince Henry's were members of the A.T.C. and many of them went on to join the R.A.F.

The establishment of a Girls' Training Corps in Otley did not occur until late 1943. By this time both 16 year old boys and girls had to register under the Government's Youth Registration Scheme, and those not already undertaking some form of youth organisation, service or training were interviewed with a view to encouraging them to do so.

Boys of 17 registered at Local Employment Exchanges on Saturday 31 January 1942 under the Registration of Boys and Girls Order, 1941. The registration of boys of 16 and girls of 16 and 17 would take place later in the year. On registering the boys and girls were asked if they were in employment, attending evening classes, connected with any youth organisations, and, in the case of boys, if they were members of the Home Guard or Air Training Corps. Those not involved in any of these were interviewed and encouraged to take part in a youth organisation, or some form of national service.

151 boys registered in Otley at the first registration. 86 stated that they were connected with a youth organisation – Air Training Corps (36), Home Guard (33), National Fire Service (3), Civil Defence (8), Boy Scouts (3), Young Farmers' Association (1), Old Scholars' Association (1). There were two invalids and the remaining 63 stated that they had no connection with any youth organisation.

153 boys of 16 registered at Otley on 28 February 1942. Of these 53 were not attached to any youth organisation. Girls of 17 registered on 28 April 1942 when there were

150 registrations – five were still at school, 11 were attending evening classes and 29 were members of youth organisations. Those *'who are considered not to be suitably occupied in their spare time are interviewed with the object of guiding them into useful recreational activities.'*

148 16 year olds – both boys and girls – registered at Otley on Saturday 12 September 1942. There were 97 boys and 51 girls. 58 boys and 22 girls were connected with youth organisations, seven boys and eight girls were at school, and 74 boys and 39 girls were working.

It was suggested that there was an increasing demand for setting up a Girls' Training Corps in Otley from responses at these 'service interviews.' Eighty girls attended a public meeting in the Modern School on 22 October 1943, when it was agreed to set up an Otley Corps. Mrs. Johnson, who chaired the meeting, felt that *"There was a certain set of people in Otley who are letting us down, and losing our good tone, and the G.T.C., which was a good avenue for a girl's activities after leaving school, could ensure the keeping of the town's fair name."*

The age limit for the G.T.C. was 16 to 19, though there was a junior section for girls from 14 to 15½. There were three types of service in G.T.C. training – pre-service training, national service and service to the community, but the stress was on the latter. The following article taken from the '*Wharfedale and Airedale Observer*' of 29 October 1943 describes the nature of the activities in the G.T.C.:

'There were seven basic subjects, designed originally as a kind of pre-service training, but they all had a bearing on life. These basic subjects consisted of drill which kept a girl mentally alert and physically fit; ordinary physical training, which included all forms of dancing; dispatch carrying – a war-time training applicable to peace-time - with such subjects as the correct use of the telephone, finding one's way about, and learning the highway code; first-aid, so that a cadet could cope with accidents; a gas course, a simple study of poison gases, which would perhaps stop the use of this weapon in future times, if everyone understood its effects and prevention; a handy-woman's course, including repairing and making clothes and the running of a house; hygiene, which taught how to look after oneself physically, and live in decent surroundings.

The specialised subjects fell into three classes. For present-day usefulness there was Morse and signaling. Of general use was life-saving, fire-fighting, home nursing and care of children. Subjects for learning a job included typing, shorthand, book-keeping, tailoring and garment repairing.

G.T.C. cadets could do many acts of service to other people and the community by doing jobs at hospitals or crèches, acting as messengers or 'casualties' in A.R.P. practices.

The cadet learned citizenship. She enjoyed the cultural side of her training; dramatic work, play reading, music and painting. The social side, which could raise money for the unit and the area, was encouraged because it was advisable for people to mix.'

The possibility of war forced the British government to take measures to defend the country and to maintain public order. The Emergency Powers (Defence Act) of August 1938 prepared for the mobilisation of military reservists and A.R.P. volunteers. About half a million people volunteered to join the A.R.P., the Territorial Army (T.A.) and the R.A.F. Volunteer Reserve (R.A.F.V.R.). An article published in the *'Wharfedale'* on 17 February 1939 illustrated the response from local people:

NATIONAL SERVICE SCHEME – HOW LOCAL PEOPLE ARE RESPONDING
83-YEAR OLD VOLUNTEER AT OTLEY

'An Otley woman of 83 and a schoolboy of 14 years are among those who have volunteered to "do their bit" under the National Voluntary Service Scheme, enrolments for which continue to come in steadily at local offices.

Up to yesterday, there had been 171 enrolments at the Otley and Burley offices, in addition to many enquiries and requests for information. The office at Otley is at the Mechanics' Institute, and at Burley in the old collector's office at The Grange.

Most popular service, judged on enrolments, is the ARP, in which there are eight separate units in which volunteers can be placed. There are air raid wardens, rescue and demolition, first-aid posts, ambulance drivers and attendants, decontamination, report centres and communication and 'miscellaneous duties.'

'Volunteers in the ARP section so far total 66 men and 40 women. Other enrolments are; special constables and observer corps, 43 men; Army, Navy and Air Force, 13 men and two women; auxiliary fire brigade, five men. Two persons are awaiting interview.

The Observer Corps is now up to strength; as are also the special constables, except at Otley and Yeadon.'

The 14 year old schoolboy was from Prince Henry's and was registered under ARP 'report centres and communications,' known later as the 'Messenger Corps', which was open to youths under 18 years, to carry messages by motor cycle, pedal cycle, and on foot.

Volunteers for the Forces were not enough and in response to Hitler's threat of aggression the Military Training Act was passed in April 1939, requiring all fit British men aged 20 and 21 to take six months' military training. However, on the outbreak of war the British Army could muster only 897,000 men, compared to France's five million. It was estimated that the introduction of conscription would affect between 250 and 300 men of the age of 20 in Otley, Ilkley, Aireborough and Horsforth. By 12 May 1939, 391 volunteers had registered through the special national service office in Otley.

'This is made up of: A.R.P., 76 men and 178 women; police 95 men, fire brigade 12 men; Army, Navy and Air Force 20 men, six women; special register, four men.

This office does not deal with married women with no occupations, and to this total must be added 50 women from Otley and 61 from the Wharfedale Rural District, who have enrolled with the W.V.S.' ('Wharfedale and Airedale Observer,' 12 May 1939)

75% of the Otley wardens had been trained, and the remainder were in training or awaiting training. The local Auxiliary Fire Service (50 men in Otley), and the special constables (about 400 in the Otley Police Division) were up to strength.

'The Otley first aid post, for reception of injured and for decontamination of personnel, is at Newall Institution. There are three first aid depots, two at the Borough garage and one at the Newall Institution; at each of these will be kept an auxiliary ambulance and reserve, two private cars for sitting cases and a car for transporting the first aid parties. Attached to each depot are four first aid men and two reserves.' ('Wharfedale and Airedale Observer,' 12 May 1939).

After a month of war, in which Wharfedale had been free of military incident, the organisation of local home defence was reviewed. It was decided to half the number of paid wardens:

'At the moment Otley has 47 full-time home defence workers, of whom 24 are wardens, 15 auxiliary firemen and eight members of the first aid organisations. This represents a weekly wage bill of something over £130.

The number of paid wardens is, however, to be reduced to half the previous total, commencing next week. The new wage-bill will in future be in the region of £100 a week.

'Capt. John Scott, chief air raid warden for Otley, said yesterday that half the paid wardens had been given a week's notice, which will expire on Thursday next, after when there would be only 12 full-time paid wardens. These will all be men.

"We took some women on in the first instance to help us out of a hole," said Capt. Scott, "but none of these will remain under the new arrangement." ('Wharfedale and Airedale Observer,' 29 September 1939)

Sir Charles McGrath, Clerk to the West Riding County Council, announced that the Emergency Committee, *'are taking every practicable step to prevent wasteful expenditure. They hold strongly the view that civil defence is a national obligation on all citizens alike, and that the growing financial burden, of which there are daily complaints, would be greatly diminished by more wholehearted and general response to the appeal for volunteers.' ('Wharfedale and Airedale Observer,' 27 October 1939)*

The number of paid personnel in the West Riding had been reduced from 5,109, representing a weekly wage bill of £13,099, to 4,395 persons, representing a weekly total of £11,760. Clearly more pressure was placed on unpaid volunteers willing to give up their leisure time to 'do their bit.'

In order to boost the numbers in the Forces the National Service (Armed Forces) Act, 1939, which became law on the day that war was declared, made all able men aged between 18 and 41 liable for conscription. The legislation included the decision that single men would be called up before married men. Men in 'reserved' occupations such as baking, farming, medicine and engineering, were exempted, but they still had to register. A process of registration at local Employment offices began on 21 October 1939 with the 20-22 year age group, but it was not until June 1941 that the 40 year olds were registered. At each registration for specific year groups, men who, in the meantime, had reached the age of 20 were also registered.

On 21 October 1939, 215,231 men in the 20-22 age group registered nationally. In the Wharfedale district there were exactly 100 enrolments. The numbers were less than expected, but many Wharfedale men in this age group were already in the Forces. By the end of 1939 more than 1.5 million men had been conscripted to join the British armed forces, 1.1. million of them in the Army, the rest split between the Royal Navy and the R.A.F. By August 1940 when the '33s' – men born in 1906 – registered, the total registration passed 4 million.

From spring 1941, every woman in Britain aged 18-60 had to be registered. Each was interviewed and required to choose from a range of jobs. At first only single women between the ages of 20 and 30 were liable to be called up, but by mid-1943 almost 90% of single women and 80% of married women were employed in essential work for the war effort. 20-year-old women were registered on 19 April 1941. The forthcoming registration was commented upon in an article in the *'Wharfedale and Airedale Observer'* on 18 April 1941:

TO-MORROW'S CALL UP OF WOMEN

'To-morrow's call-up of girls of 20 is the first step to mobilise Britain's woman-power for the expansion of our war effort. In the last war our women did brilliant work. In the filling of factories, in the aircraft works, in the groups attached to the fighting services they were "steel-true and blade-straight." They have not lagged behind in this war. Women wardens have proved their valour and their usefulness. The women who have already gone into the factories have shown that their hands have lost none of their cunning. Women in the W.A.A.F., the A.T.S., the W.R.N.S. have upheld the highest tradition of the fighting force to which they are attached. The Voluntary services are giving a devotion to duty that is wholly admirable. It is suitable to a degree that women should to-day have a greater opportunity of playing their part.

'In the Otley area it is computed that there are between 200 and 300 girls born in 1920 who will be affected by to-morrow's registration. In Ilkley, Aireborough and Horsforth the numbers will be somewhat similar, so that all told it is expected there will be round about 1,000 from this portion of the Skyrack area. As many of these girls are already engaged on work of national importance, it is not expected that there will be a big proportion who will be called upon to change their employment; but there are some who could be doing more useful work, and these will be asked to attend a selection interview.

'In a district where girls are used to factory conditions it is only to be expected that the

majority will express a preference for the munitions factories, but for those who want something different there are the uniformed Services, the Nursing Services, N.A.A.F.I., and the Land Army. In all of these there are many vacancies, and it is from this main group of "mobile" girls that the authorities hope to fill them.'

It was reported that at the registration there was an almost total absence of the *'idle rich girl'* element and that the great majority of girls were already in full employment in essential industries. The minority in non-essential trades were to be *'interviewed and offered work of national importance or the opportunity to join one of the Women's Services'.*

An article in the *'Wharfedale and Airedale Observer'* on 5 September 1941 commented upon the first two years of the war. After thanking *'all the men and women who have been called upon to join H.M. Forces,'* the article turned to the 'home front:

'On the "home front" we have seen the development of what is known as "Civil Defence". This includes the extensive A.R.P. services, which can now be said to be well organised and equal to possible requirements. There is also the A.F.S., which is now being organised on a wider basis, and there is the Special Constabulary to support and supplement the work of the regular police. The Home Guard, formed as a protection against invasion, is proving itself a well-organised and an efficient body, though in most areas there is a call for more recruits. Local support has been given to the formation of an Air Training Corps, and a local Squadron has been formed in each district.

Women's activities are largely canalised by the Womens' Voluntary Services. They deal with evacuating and billeting, ambulance and hospital services, communal feeding and other welfare work. There has been much knitting and sewing, and the promotion of money-raising efforts for the benefit of those in need. Linked up with the women's work are the Y.M.C.A. hostels and other activities for the welfare of the troops. It is likely there will be still further scope for women's activities in the near future in connection with the extension of community restaurants.'

The National Services Act, 1941, extended the requirement to service in civil defence, and the National Service (No 2) Act, 1941, imposed on all persons of either sex a general obligation to service in the armed forces, civil defence or industry, and extended the upper age limit of liability to service in the armed forces to 51 years of age. The age for military service was lowered to 18½. From 1 January 1942 boys and girls between the ages of 16 and 18 had to be registered. Single women between the ages of 20 and 30 were to be called up. There was also a special regulation providing for compulsory service in the Home Guard.

All men and women liable for conscription were registered at employment exchanges, medically examined, and allocated to suitable service. They could state a preference for a particular branch of the armed forces, but were not guaranteed that the preference would be given. Local tribunals heard applications for deferment and for the registration of conscientious objectors.

An article under the heading 'The New Call Up' was published in the '*Wharfedale and Airedale Observer*' on 5 December 1941:

'There has been a good deal of heart-searching in most homes this week by the far-reaching nature of the Government's proposals for further mobilising the nation's power in men, women and youth, proposals which give a new significance to the war effort and the part which each is expected to play.

'Naturally each family gives thought as to how it is going to be affected. In some families daughters will now have to go as well as sons, and fathers who served in the last war, some who went all through it, are now finding themselves with the prospect of serving in this one also. It is possible there will be homes in which only the mother will be left.

'In this district we are probably fortunate. Some, of course, will have to go into the Services, but for the others there are a variety of ways in which they can give useful help to the war effort without having to go far away. A number, who up to now have not been able to do much, may be able to do more under the new arrangements for part-time help. This will probably apply more particularly to small shop-keepers and the owners of one-man businesses, who under present trading conditions will probably find they can get along by devoting one half of the day to their shops or businesses and the other half to some form of national service.'

So, as the war progressed more men and women joined H.M. Forces, and more people, young and old, helped on the Home Front. The registration for national service of men and women aged 18 and over meant that some pupils who were at school when the war broke out would have been in the Forces before the war finished. One example, Ian Naylor, joined the Navy in November 1943 and was killed on 7 April 1945. Younger pupils would have known the ex-pupils who were called up and the impact of the death of Ian Naylor must have shocked many of them.

In the early years of the war many of the fathers of pupils at Prince Henry's would have been too old to be conscripted into the Forces, but some of them would have fought in the First World War and still been in the Army Reserve. Those not called up on the outbreak of the war would have joined the Home Guard or volunteered for Civil Defence duties, such as A.R.P. work and 'fire-watching.' At first fighting was a young, single man's game, but as the age at which people registered increased, older men were more likely to be conscripted. Men born in 1900 were registered in Otley on 14 June 1941, when men born before 1 July 1900 registered under the Employment Order, but those born after 30 June registered under the National Service Acts. These 41 year olds were likely to have children of secondary school age.

On 19 April 1941 girls of 20 were registered as '*the first step to mobilise Britain's woman-power for the expansion of our war effort*.' Many of these girls were already engaged on work of national importance, and it was not expected that a large proportion would be called upon to change their employment; '*but there are some who could be doing more useful work, and these will be asked to attend a selection interview.'* As with the men, registration of older women proceeded by age and the '1900s' were registered at Otley on 11 July 1942. Of the 146 who registered, 118 were married and 28 single. 13 married and 23 single women were in full-time, paid employment; two married ladies were working on their own account; nine married women were in unpaid employment; and 94 married and five single women were on 'household duties.' It is certain that many of the mothers of the pupils at Prince Henry's during the war volunteered for organisations such as the W.V.S., or worked in jobs considered to be of national importance.

The end of the war in Europe was anticipated once the Allied D-day landings had established a bridgehead in France to match the progress that had been made in the invasion of Italy. Although there were still defeats and setbacks, most commentators felt that it was simply a matter of time before the Germans would surrender.

On Tuesday 8 May 1945 (VE-Day) and Wednesday 9 May 1945 (VE-Day plus one) there was a two-day national public holiday, to celebrate the end of the Second World War in Europe. When Prince Henry's re-opened on Thursday 10 May there was a special assembly, which ended with a verse of the School Song and the National Anthem.

Locally, there was some concern about how to celebrate VE-Day. Most local councils had arranged for church services as a thanksgiving for deliverance from possible tyranny, but there were worries that more open celebrations would not be appropriate because fighting was still going on in the Far East, and to celebrate in such a public way would not be supportive of H.M. Forces still at war. At a meeting of the Wharfedale Rural District Council, as reported in the *'Wharfedale and Airedale Observer'* on 13 April 1945, Major P.H. Walker said:

"I think, personally, and I think the Government is beginning to feel, these celebrations are going to be so premature that they are going to produce nothing but disappointment, because in the minds of the ordinary people 'V' day means the war will be over, the troops will come home, and we can commence peace-time activities."

'County Councilor R. T. A. Renton said he thought 'V' day would be a "token declaration" and would not end the sacrifices still required from the people of this country. 'V' day, to his mind, was a time when everyone would give thanks for the wonderful way in which we had been delivered from a terrible threat. That was the only cause for celebration, and he was perturbed as to what the psychological effect might be on the minds of the ordinary man and woman.'

However, in most local towns and villages people celebrated VE-Day publically and with great pleasure. Ilkley's plans were set out as early as 23 February 1945, and were reported in the *'Wharfedale and Airedale Observer'* under the heading – *'When the Good News Comes – Plans for Celebrating Peace.'* Special committees were appointed to make these plans. They included church services, children's treats, old-folk's parties, bonfires, fireworks – *'if they can be obtained'*, - floodlighting of public buildings, whist drives and dances – *'old fashioned and modern.'*

For the first time since 1939 the bells of Otley Parish Church rang in the New Year, 1945, and hopes ran high that before its close their merry peals would ring out to herald the coming of victory and peace.

The expectation that the end of the war, at least in Europe, was imminent increased after the success of the D-Day landings, the liberation of much of occupied Europe, and the forced retreat of the German army under pressure from Allied Forces. The Government's plans for the first stage of demobilisation were published in September 1944, only three months after D-Day. Under the scheme approximately ninety per cent of the first half million to be released from military service were to be married men. However, it was accepted that when hostilities ended in Europe, there was still a need to overcome the Japanese and a requirement for a strong army of occupation in Germany.

'A' Company, Otley Home Guard.

A further indication that the war would soon be over, or at least the belief that an attack from abroad was no longer possible, came with the relaxation of Civil Defence and Fire-Guarding services, and the stand-down of the 29th Battalion of the West Riding Home Guard, at a parade at Ilkley on Sunday 3 December 1944. After the parade 'A' Company and Headquarters Company returned to Otley, marched through the streets in pouring rain to the Drill Hall. There they were addressed by Councillor D.H.Smallwood, Chairman of the Otley Urban District Council, who commented:

"May I congratulate you on the splendid stand-down parade which you have made today. The manner in which you have paraded is a credit You have served, many of you, for over four years and although there has not been any necessity for you to fight, I

have not the slightest hesitation in believing that if there had been you would all have given good account of yourselves. Gentlemen, we civilians do appreciate the way you carried out your duties during those long years, and in saying 'thank you' we hope you will get some measure of relaxation after your long hours of training.

"I don't think I can close better than by quoting those last lines of Blake because, gentlemen, although you are standing down, the war is not over and, even when the fighting is over, we shall still have our duty to do. The words to which I refer are –

"I shall not cease from mortal strife, nor shall my sword sleep in my hand, till we have built Jerusalem in England's green and pleasant land.'

"Thank you, gentlemen, for what you have done for your country. We appreciate it." ('Wharfedale and Airedale Observer,' 8 December 1944)

V.E. Day crowd in Manor Square.

The relaxation of black-out regulations and fire watching duties, and the restoration of some street lighting was further evidence that the war was expected to end in the near future, though 'normal' time was not reverted to until 6 October 1945 when the clocks were put back by one hour:

'Summertime was first introduced on May 21 1916, and since then in normal times covered a period between April and October each year, during which period the clock

was put forward one hour. During the past years of war emergency, however, even time was mobilised and subject to regulation, with the result that for the past five winter periods daylight saving of one hour was continued, and then during a summer period was extended to two hours.

With the ending of the war and some of its attendant difficulties and restrictions it has been considered expedient to revert once more to normal time for the coming winter season. This news has been welcomed by some, especially farmers, parents, school authorities and those whose daily work compels early rising.

'Long dark evenings which now lie ahead need not be regarded with dismay. They offer opportunities for educational, social and family life which can increase our usefulness and bring added happiness. For children added hours of sleep will be helpful for both body and mind. The shortage of coal to keep the home fires burning seems the only snag to this return to normal.' ('Wharfedale and Airedale Observer,' 5 October 1945)

The pupils at Prince Henry's, particularly those living in Otley, would have played an active part in the celebrations for VE-Day and VJ-Day, and would have thoroughly enjoyed the attractions and events.

Otley streets were thronged early on VE-Day, and although it was raining, it failed to dampen the enthusiasm of the crowds. Details of the two-day programme were painted on the official '*VE Board*' at the Buttercross. It seemed at first that the programme would have to be drastically curtailed because of the rain that started at about 11 a.m. and continued until 3 p.m., though in fact few alterations were necessary.

'Throughout Monday evening and during the earlier hours of Tuesday morning preparations were busily in progress for the later celebrations. Manor Square was decorated with flags and bunting, the Jubilee Clock was draped with coloured lights and so was the Maypole; strings of fairy lamps were strung across Manor Square and Kirkgate, and there were decorations along the boating stretch in Wharfemeadows.

Shopkeepers and innkeepers decorated their shops and houses, and householders joined in with flags from the bedroom windows. Soon the whole town was gay with colour. Children flourished flags, and girls tied their hair with red, white and blue ribbon. Then the rain came, and for three or four hours people remained indoors.

The rain began to clear at 3 o'clock, in time for the Prime Minister's declaration, and though most people preferred to hear this in the privacy of their homes, there was quite a big crowd to hear the relay in Manor Square.

A glimpse of pre-war days and a taste of things to come was provided when jumping crackers, flash bombs, roman candles and a variety of other fireworks were thrown amongst the crowd. The gaiety was infectious and the fun was still lively in the late afternoon.' ('Wharfedale and Airedale Observer,' 11 May 1946)

Early in the afternoon there was a Children's Service in the Congregational Church, followed at 3.30 p.m. by a Service of Thanksgiving in the Parish Church. Later, the

Salvation Army band led community hymn singing in the Market Place, and at 6 p.m. there was music by the pipes and drums of the Argyll and Sutherland Highlanders.

'The first event of the evening was a Thanksgiving Service in Manor Square. It was conducted from the balcony of the Royal White Horse Hotel, with massed choirs and a military band to lead the singing, and the crowd was estimated at not less than 2,000. So great was the crowd that traffic had to be diverted.

Later the spirit of thankfulness which had marked the earlier celebrations gave place to joyous celebrations. The streets filled with people, soldiers flocked into the town from the adjacent camps, and soon there was singing and dancing and a happy atmosphere of carefree enjoyment. This increased as darkness fell and the lights were switched on. Manor Square and Kirkgate were a grand picture, and so was the Jubilee Clock and the Maypole.

The principal streets in the town were illuminated with powerful lamps and the parish church was attractively floodlit.' ('Wharfedale and Airedale Observer,' 11 May 1945)

At 10.30 p.m. a torchlight procession, about 90 strong, travelled from the Maypole and climbed the Chevin for the lighting of a bonfire on the traditional beacon site. The fire was lit using the Jubilee torch first used in the celebrations for the jubilee of King George V. The torch was lit at the Jubilee Clock by Mr D.H. Smallwood, Chairman of the Urban Council, and carried up the hill by a relay of 63 scouts. A crowd estimated at over 7,000 saw Mr G. Lambert, Vice Chairman of the Council, light the beacon, which consisted of almost 100 tons of wood and waste material. The '*Wharfedale*' suggested that the beacon was '*believed to be the biggest in England.*'

'As the 60 foot flames leapt into the sky, happy crowds spontaneously sang 'There'll Always Be an England' and fireworks of all kinds lit up the surroundings, adding to the glorious, awe-inspiring sight that will never be forgotten by all who witnessed it.' ('Wharfedale and Airedale Observer,' 11 May 1945)

Unfortunately for the spectators watching from the streets of Otley the Chevin was shrouded in mist and nothing could be seen.

'It was generally thought that after all the rain the bonfire would not burn, and soon the crowds returned to their singing and dancing and general rejoicing. The children, however, were disappointed.

Eventually, some time after midnight, the mist on the hill began to clear, and the blazing beacon had the appearance of a great moon bursting through the clouds and lighting up the skyline. By that time, however, most of the townspeople had gone home, though there was still a merry throng in Manor Square. They were finally dispersed by a heavy shower of rain.' ('Wharfedale and Airedale Observer,' 11 May 1945)

Manor Square was floodlit and large crowds gathered throughout the evening for dancing to amplified gramophone music. Licensed houses remained open until 11.30 p.m., and open-air dancing in Manor Square ended at 1.00 a.m. Open-air dancing in the brilliantly illuminated Wharfemeadows was cancelled because of the rain. However, on Wednesday (VE-Day plus one) the weather was much better, and in the sunshine crowds gathered on the grass in Wharfemeadows and along the riverside. There were free cinema shows for children, music by the pipes and drums of the Argyll and Sutherland Highlanders, the ringing of the Parish Church bells, and dances in the evening at the Mechanics' Hall and the Burras Lane Schools. Open-air dancing in Manor Square attracted almost as large a crowd as on VE-day itself.

It is unlikely that parents would have prevented their children from attending at least some of the VE-Day celebrations, but they must have been grateful for the school holiday on the Wednesday because it gave time for their children to recover before the return to school on Thursday. This was not the end of the celebrations; the next few weeks saw a series of street-parties all over Wharfedale.

The view of most people was summed up in an Editorial published in the '*Wharfedale and Airedale Observer*' on 11 May 1945:

'It is therefore right and seemly that for a few days we have hoisted our banners, waved our flags and in a happy demonstrative way have rejoiced together over the notable victories already won. In our festivities we remember that we have not yet "finished the course," and there still remains the formidable task of conquering the Japanese before our final goal is won.'

V.E. Day celebrations on The Crossways, Otley.

On 9 June 1945 the first contingent of Otley's evacuees, made up of 39 mothers and their children, left Otley to return to their repaired homes in bomb-damaged London.

At Leeds they were joined by other evacuees drawn from billets in surrounding towns and villages, and boarded a waiting train. Mrs. B. Wells, Chief Billeting and Welfare Officer for Otley, went to see them off. She told a reporter from the '*Wharfedale Observer*' that "*They were happy and comfortable here in Otley. When they first came they thought they would never settle – now they are reluctant to go.*"

'The 35 mothers and children remaining in Otley will return as soon as homes are ready for them but a pathetic and tragic problem will still remain. There are many children who at the moment have no homes to return to – some are bombed-out, others have lost a mother or father.' ('Wharfedale and Airedale Observer, 15 June 1945)

The ending of the war in Europe must have been a source of great relief to most of the residents of Wharfedale, particularly when Prisoners of War in German hands returned home, and leave was granted to members of H.M. Forces based in Europe. However, many people were still worried because their relatives and friends were still fighting in the Far East, or were Prisoners of War of the Japanese. Three months later, after almost six years of war, there was further celebration when the Japanese surrendered and Wednesday 15 August 1945 was declared VJ-Day. Local school children were probably slightly disappointed that VJ-Day and VJ-Day plus one fell in the middle of the school holidays!

'When the news came through last Friday that Japan was negotiating for peace, Wharfedale was calm, and there were few if any premature celebrations. Isolated flags appeared here and there, but the majority were waiting for the official news. On Wednesday morning flags, bunting and decorations were brought out. Otley streets, which were comparatively normal on Tuesday, were soon a blaze of colour. Union Jacks in their hundreds fluttered in the morning breeze, and flags of the Allied nations flew side by side. Arrangements tentatively made by the Otley Council's Peace Celebration Committee were put into operation, and workmen were hard at it erecting decorations, illuminations, floodlights and amplifiers.' ('Wharfedale and Airedale Observer,' 17 August 1945)

The programme was similar to that on VE-Day, and as on VE-Day rain began to fall in the afternoon.

'Church bells rang out again in the afternoon and a special show was screened in the Beech Hill cinema. As on VE-day, rain began to fall, and the Burley and Ilkley band, which was to have played in Manor Square, transferred at the last minute to the shelter of the Butter Cross. People gathered in shop doorways to listen to the music, and occasional fireworks were let off among the crowd, but at this stage there was little of the spontaneous enthusiasm that marked the end of the war in Europe.' ('Wharfedale and Airedale Observer,' 17 August 1945).

In the early evening there was an open-air thanksgiving service in Manor Square, which was decorated with flags, bunting, coloured lights and floodlights. One difference from the VE-Day arrangements was summed up in the headline in the '*Wharfedale*' on 17 August 1945:

'PEACE CELEBRATIONS IN OTLEY AND WHARFEDALE – TORCHLIGHT PROCESSION AND A VICTORY 'V'.'

High above the town, on the highest point of the Chevin, workmen had erected poles to support a thirty-foot 'V' to be lit by the Chairman of the Council – Mr D.H. Smallwood – in the evening, after a torchlight procession from the town up the winding path to the traditional beacon site. This time the torchbearer procession that set off from the Maypole was made up of 120 people.

'The procession proceeded along Boroughgate and Kirkgate, up Station Road, then turned to the left to reach the Chevin by way of Johnny Lane. The crowds in the town were now reminiscent of VE night. Thousands packed into Kirkgate, where they had a clear view of the torches flickering in and out of the trees, disappearing for brief intervals then reappearing like a twinkling glow-worm. When the torches were half way up the slopes the pipes and drums of the ATC returned down Station Road and through the cheering crowds.

V.E. Day celebrations on The Oval, Otley.

'Young and old were in the streets, watching and waiting the magnificent spectacle which was hidden from view on VE night. As they waited, fireworks were let off in the town, and on the Chevin coloured lights and rockets shot into the sky. The top of the hill was clearly visible, and there was not a trace of the mist that reduced visibility to nil during the VE celebrations.

The torches grouped together on the upper slopes, almost disappeared, and then fanned out into a perfect 'V'. People in the town clapped and cheered – but the really great moment was yet to come. A ball of golden fire appeared above the human 'V'.

Slowly, with breathtaking effect, flames crept up the arms of the 'V' until a shining glow dazzled and shimmered in the sky. Thousands in the town had waited for this moment and they greeted the symbol of light with cheers and claps.

'On the top of the Chevin a large crowd had gathered. As the human torch formed up they heard the bearers singing 'Land of Hope and Glory,' and then, when the Chairman of the council lit the giant 'V', everyone joined in 'There'll Always be an England!' Far below, the illuminations in Otley were a blaze of light against the dark background of the valley.

In the town the crowds watched as the 'V' slowly faded away and many of the older people, and parents with children, returned home through the bright streets. The Parish Church was floodlit, and in Wharfemeadows coloured lights on the front of the swimming pool reflected in the still waters of the river.

'Celebrations continued in Manor Square where large numbers danced to music relayed through amplifiers. At midnight organised festivities ended, the crowds dispersed slowly – VJ-day was over.' ('Wharfedale and Airedale Observer,' 17 August 1945)

This final end to the war allowed people to think about the impact of the past six years and the potential for the future in a deeper and more considered way than had been the case on VE-Day. Addressing the thanksgiving service crowds the Rev. J.C. Sutcliffe said:

"In view of the tremendous forces ranged against us at the beginning of the war, and our unpreparedness at that time, nothing but a power beyond human could have brought us through to victory." After acknowledging our indebtedness to God, Mr Sutcliffe said it was fitting we should remember those through whom victory had been achieved – our soldiers, airman, Royal and Merchant Navy and the hundreds and thousands of ordinary men and women who, amidst difficulties and dangers kept the 'Wheels of industry' turning. It was fitting too, that we should remember those who would not return home. "These days of rejoicing must be painful for the wives, mothers and sweethearts whose loved ones will not return."

"Thanksgiving was only one half of the picture", said Mr Sutcliffe. "We have been preserved for a high and holy purpose. There were terrible problems to be faced, and every man, woman and child could help to bring about a better world of peace, freedom and social security. The trowel", he said, "was greater than the sword, and just as the brains and energy of many had resulted in the destructive atom bomb - of which men were afraid -, if man's mind was inspired and directed by the highest motive, that energy could be used to make a better world in the future."

At the end of each year a review of the previous twelve months was published in the '*Wharfedale*.' The 1945 Review, under the heading - *VICTORY – 1945 – PEACE: RETROSPECTIVE OF A HISTORICAL YEAR IN WHARFEDALE* – included the following introduction:

'Victory in Europe and the Far East brought deep joy into many hearts and homes by the liberation of those who had been prisoners of war. Many also, who had been away from home for years have been home on leave, and others have been demobilised. All these factors have contributed to a memorable year.

'The change-over from war conditions is bound to be a gradual one. Industry is still feeling the acute shortage of skilled labour. Housing presents one of the most difficult problems, and is receiving close consideration from all our local authorities and developments can be expected to take place very soon. The coming year will see the return of many servicemen and women to their homes and to industry, and this will be one of the most welcome signs of the beginning of the post-war period. In the meantime, it is good to know that those serving are not forgotten and that gifts and greetings were sent from many places in our area to those who are still in the Forces.

'The end of the war has lifted many of the burdens borne by the civil population. Black-out and dim-out restrictions have gone, fire-watching and wardens' duties are a thing of the past; and long hours worked by many have now been reduced. Rationing and points, however, are still a necessity, for the problem of food and clothing supplies remains somewhat acute. Coal supplies still present a severe problem for both house-holders and factories, and a severe winter will be a test on our resources.

'There are, however, signs of better things to come. Fruit and certain other food commodities are gradually becoming more plentiful, and various household goods are coming again on to the market. For those things, and the brighter hope of others to follow, we should be thankful, looking with confidence to future days.' ('Wharfedale and Airedale Observer,' 4 January 1946)

After 6 years of war, people had now got to get used to peace.

What would an ex-pupil who was at school during the Second World War years notice if he returned to Prince Henry's five years after he had left? What had changed and what remained the same?

The most obvious things he would look for would be physical changes in the buildings and the site. The blast walls and black-out have been removed, but the ex-student can still see traces of black paint in the corners of the windows, especially those which were difficult to reach. The trenches on the sports field have been filled in, but it is still possible to see where they have been. The two 'air-raid shelters' have returned to their previous use as storage space. As he passes the Library his attention is drawn to the War Memorial commemorating the death in the War of old scholars, paid for by the fund raising of the Old Otliensians. He recognises some of the names because they were at school at the same time as he was.

Nothing else has changed; the classrooms, gym, dining room and hall are still used for the same purposes as before the war. There is still segregation in the sense that boys and girls use different entrances, have different cloakrooms and toilets and sit apart in classes. The member of staff showing the ex-pupil around points out that there was a need for more classrooms, and that plans were under discussion for changes in the nature and size of the school, but that this had been the case almost since the school re-opened in 1918 and that they were not optimistic that improvements would happen in the near future.

Little has changed in the school grounds except that the land previously given over to gardening and crops is now returning to normal, and it looks as though there has been a return to the days of a decent cricket pitch, rugby and hockey pitches. At least now the grass looks as though it is cut regularly. The trees dotted around the site have grown since last time the ex-pupil saw them. The grass tennis courts in front of the main building are also in a much better maintained state. There are more cars in the car park, an indication that teachers are earning a reasonable salary.

Whilst the old-scholar is being shown around the school bell rings for a break and a change of lessons. As far as he can remember the structure of the day has remained the same as during the war, and he would also find that the curriculum was no different. The number of pupils moving around the site does not appear to be any larger than when he was a pupil and he asks his escort about pupil numbers. He is told that when he came to Prince Henry's the role was 450, with 218 boys and 232 girls. In 1946 the figures were 219 boys and 215 girls, giving a total of 434, and in the current year (1950) the total was also 434 with 222 boys and 212 girls. Losing girls to Ilkley Grammar when it became co-educational partly explains the decline, but another reason is the closure of the Preparatory Department following the 1944 Education Act. He notices that as a consequence there are no pupils under the age of eleven. But the catchment area has remained the same, with the majority of pupils living in Otley, but a significant number attending from Pool, Arthington, Bramhope, Burley, Menston and the surrounding rural villages.

The ex-pupil is beginning to feel that very little has changed since he was at school when he is recognised by a member of staff and invited into the Men's Staff Room. He is a little surprised that this division between male and female still exists, but soon realises that there is still opposition to a single staffroom from both sexes. The men's staff room is full of smoke – from the open fire and from cigarettes and pipe tobacco – and has a 'lived in' atmosphere. He asks about the number of staff and is told that the number of staff – 22 plus the Head – is the same as it was in 1939. All the teaching staff are full-time, there are no 'visiting teachers'. He is surprised to recognise a large proportion of the male staff – Mr Wilde, Mr Pratt, Mr Leech, Mr Padgett, Mr Nealy, Mr Denham, Mr Watson, Mr Shaw, Mr Carter – and is told that Miss Horsley and Miss Brennand are also still on the staff.

As he leaves the school site, making sure to go out of the boys' entrance and down the right hand path, he reflects that little seems to have changed since the time when he was at the school. His memories return to those years and the impact of the War on the life of the school – the reduction in the number of issues of the school magazine, the *'Otliensian'* from three to two because of a shortage of paper: the movement of Speech Day from July to November, and the split into two sections, Senior – still held on Saturday – and Junior – held mid-week: the shorter summer holidays, accompanied by a fortnight's trips, activities and events at the start of the Autumn Term: the evacuation to Otley of the Roundhay girls, - just for one term - resulting in the sharing of the school, Saturday morning school and the consequent decline in sports fixtures, practices, dramatic and musical performances and rehearsals, especially for pupils living outside Otley: the coming and going of evacuees from both the local area and more distant locations: the removal of Christmas parties from the School calendar: the impact of the 'black out' and the move to 'double summer time': the constant pressure to 'save', especially in the named 'Weeks': the collections of waste paper and anything made from metal: the need to carry 'gas masks' and to have practices at wearing them, moving to trenches and air-raid shelters: rationing of food, clothing and equipment and the response of the school in the form of the Gardening Club, using the games fields to grow crops and vegetables, sending out parties of boys and staff to assist local farmers, and, towards the end of the war, Harvest Camps, further afield: requirements on the staff to undertake 'fire watching': the temporary loss of five male members of staff who joined H.M. Forces.

The following Editorial was published in the '*Otliensian*' (Vol. XXVIII, Spring 1946):

'This issue of the Magazine is indeed one of some moment, being the first to be published since the cessation of hostilities in Japan. At the time of our last publication we were rejoicing over our victories in Europe. Heavy eyes brightened and war-weary voices took on a new note of gladness as we looked forward with eagerness to the time, seemingly so near, when the "piping days" would have returned, and peace and plenty would once more reign on earth.

True, the fighting is for the most part over, but how far we have yet to travel before our dreams become realities! Slow demobilisation, cuts in food and numerous shortages have provided ample scope for the grumblers who are always to be found in our midst. Plans for universal peace, too, have not always been discussed in the spirit which they are intended to portray, and many are the political difficulties which are to be overcome.

In the home, the atmosphere tends to be one of disappointment. Years of war made us paint too rosy a picture of the post-war world, and any unpleasant details were glossed over or quickly dismissed, so that now some of our castles in the air are crumbling to dust before us.

However, black though the horizon before us appears, surely the spirit that carried us through six years of war will guide us through the dark tangles of difficulty out of which we must fight our way, until there dawns a day when security, plenty and contentment will indeed hold sway on the earth.'

A.T.

This and other editorials published in the school magazine during the war years reflected changing attitudes in terms of the greater involvement of pupils in its production, and their concern for wider, global issues.

In January 1935 Mr Leech, the English master, became the editor of the *'Otliensian'*, Taking over from Mr Nealy. He continued to edit the school magazine until he retired in 1970. One of his first tasks was to appoint an Editorial Committee to assist him. This became eventually the *'Magazine Committee'*, which met termly to review the previous issue, select student contributions, and suggest improvements for the future.

This was a significant stage in the development of the *'Otliensian'* because it not only marked the probable first student-written Editorial, but it moved the magazine and the School into the area of politics and morals – the first sign of the change from parochialism and into debate and contention. The Second World War changed the way we lived and our views on, and hopes for, the future. The war-time Editorials considered moral issues and showed concern for people and nations in which conditions were far worse than those in and around Otley. They did not 'glory' in the war, but, as the above Editorial shows, presented a realistic picture concerning the future.

Editorial control is always an issue with any publication. It was always stressed that the magazine was the property of the pupils, but they never had total freedom. However, it was agreed at the meeting of the Magazine Committee held on 17 January 1946 that two of their number should become sub-editors of the 'Otliensian', and Dorothy Denham and Anne Taylor were appointed. They were promoted to joint editors for the Summer 1946 edition, and D. Swallow became sub-editor. This pattern continued for the remaining life of the magazine. However, staff 'guidance' and the involvement of staff in an 'advisory' capacity was never fully relinquished. Indeed, disagreements about the balance of student/staff control was one reason for the demise of the magazine.

And what of the future of education in general, and Prince Henry's in particular, in the post-war years?

The major feature affecting all schools was the passing of the 1944 Education Act. This made it the duty of every local education authority to provide sufficient primary and secondary education suitable for the requirements of all junior and senior pupils between the ages of 5 and 14 (raised to 15 a few years later). Education was to be free for all and hence entrance fees were abolished in schools maintained by the L.E.A., this impacted on Prince Henry's that had charged fees, particularly in the Preparatory Department. Commenting on the abolition of fees at the 1945 Prince Henry's Speech Day, the Headmaster, Mr Wilde said *"To some it represented the end of privilege; others were glad to be relieved of the expense, while a third school thought they would be better off if still paying fees."*

Primary and secondary schools were to be separate, which meant an end to the Preparatory department at schools such as Prince Henry's. At the secondary level there was to be a 'tripartite' system of grammar, technical and secondary modern schools. The Grammar Schools would take 20% of pupils, most of whom would be required to pass the '11-plus' entrance examination. Technical schools would also take 20% of the pupils and would cater for those skilled with their hands. The rest would attend Secondary Modern schools. In practice very few Technical schools were created and a higher proportion of pupils went to Secondary Moderns.

Local Education Authorities were required within one year of the Act to prepare and submit a *'Development Plan'* setting out proposals to ensure that there were sufficient primary and secondary schools in their area to meet the requirements, and to list the measures proposed to accomplish that purpose. Schools set up and run by the L.E.A. were known as 'county' schools; schools established in other ways were known as 'voluntary' schools. Voluntary schools were of three categories – voluntary controlled, voluntary aided and special agreement. The L.E.A. must discuss their *'Development Plan'* with the schools affected, and eventually Prince Henry's became a *'Voluntary Controlled'* school. The 'Instrument of Government' for these schools was sanctioned by the Minister of Education, not by the L.E.A., and involved one third of the Governors being 'Foundation' governors, with two-thirds being appointed by the L.E.A.

The Act also included the directions that the school day in every county and voluntary school must begin with an act of collective worship, (unless premises were impracticable) and that the teaching of Religious Instruction be compulsory, (unless parents opted out). A large section of the Act dealt with measures needed to ensure that children were able to access education by providing free milk, school dinners, clothing allowances and travelling expenses.

The loss of the Preparatory Department and the abolition of fees impacted on Prince Henry's, but they were soon forgotten as pupil numbers grew after the end of the War. The raising of the school leaving age to 15 had little or no impact because a condition of joining the school was that an agreement was entered into that the pupils would stay on until they were 16. If they 'broke their agreement' they would normally be expected to pay the additional fees, though there were examples of the Governors agreeing to waive these fees if there were difficulties at home. The aspects of the Act that had a greater long-term effect were the decision to become a Voluntary Controlled school, and the pressure to become a 'multi-lateral' school instead of the traditional grammar school.

On 13 December 1944 the Governors considered a memorandum, marked 'Private and Confidential', drawn up by the Clerk to the Governors *'about which they should exercise thought and, at some not far distant date, be prepared to state their views on the future administration of Prince Henry's Grammar School.'* The memorandum noted that *'no communication whatever has been received from the County Council or the Ministry of Education as to any steps required to be taken by the Governors,'* but that it seemed likely that the Governors would be consulted before any proposals were made by the County Council in their Development Plan to the Minister.

The L.E.A. *'Development Plan'* was to create a 'multilateral' school on the Farnley Lane site. This would in effect be three schools that could share facilities – a Grammar School, which would take 20% of the pupils; a Technical School, taking a further 20%;

and a Secondary Modern School taking the remainder. The multilateral school would cater for 1,200 pupils and would cost £226,995 to build. It would be erected on the playing fields at Prince Henry's and new playing fields about half a mile away on Weston Lane would need to be acquired. Access to the site would be from Newall Carr Road.

One of the key concerns of the Governors was that Prince Henry's Grammar School was already taking over 450 pupils, well over the 20% target. There were also worries about the loss of 'individuality' and tradition if control passed to the L.E.A. The Governors were *'prepared to negotiate arrangements with the W.R.C.C., providing suitable safeguards are forthcoming, such as continuity of name and general character of Prince Henry's School.'*

Discussions about the feasibility and desirability of such a development continued into the 1950s, but the scheme eventually just 'faded away'. However, in 1968 Prince Henry's did become a Comprehensive School with, by 1970, all the pupils being taught on the same site on Farnley Lane.

Bibliography and Acknowledgements

Prince Henry's Grammar School Magazine – The 'Otliensian'.

Prince Henry's Grammar School – Admission Registers.

Prince Henry's Grammar School – Statistical Returns.

Prince Henry's Grammar School – Governors' Minute Books.

The Chronicles of the Free Grammar School of Prince Henry at Otley,by Fred Cobley (published, 1923, by William Walker & Sons, Otley, Ltd.).

Prince Henry's Grammar School. A Summary History, by Neville Bousfield (unpublished).

Prince Henry's Grammar School 1942-1952, by David Jenkinson (unpublished document by ex-pupil).

The Bomber Command War Diaries, 1939-1945, by Martin Middlebrook & Chris Everett (published, 2011, by Midland Publishing).

R.A.F. Bomber Command Losses of the Second World War, 1939-1945, by W.R. Chorley (published in 9 volumes, by Midland Publishing).

R.A.F. Bomber Losses in the Middle East and Mediterranean, by David Gunby & Pelham Temple (published by Midland Publishing).

R.A.F. Fighter Command Losses of the Second World War, by Norman L.R. Franks (published in 3 volumes by Midland Publishing).

R.A.F. Coastal Command Losses of the Second World War, by Ross McNeill (published by Midland Publishing).

The Pathfinder Companion, by Sean Feast (published, 2012, by Grub Street).

The Other Few, by Larry Donnelly (published, 2004, by Red Kite).

Britain at War from the invasion of Poland to the Surrender of Japan, 1939-1945, by Richard Every (published, 2014, by Barlton Books Ltd..)

World War II – the events and their impact on real people, by Reg Grant (published, 2008, by Dorling Kindersley).

When Britain went to War – The Real Story of Life on the Home Front, by Richard Havers (published, 2009, by Haynes Publishing).

Mother Worked at Avro, by Gerald Myers (published, 1995, Compaid Graphics).

The Sheltered Days – Growing up in the War, by Derek Lambert (published, 1965, by Andre Deutsch).

Living on the Home Front, by Megan Wesley (published, 2013, by Amberley).

A 1940s Childhood – From Bomb Sites to Children's Hour, by James Marsh (published, 2014, by The History Press).

Few Eggs and No Oranges: The Diaries of Vere Hodgson, 1940-1945 (published, 1999, by Persephone Books).

We Remember the Home Guard, by Frank & Joan Shaw (published, 2012, by Ebury Press).

Evacuees of the Second World War, by Mike Brown (published, 2009, Shire Publications).

Wartime Britain, by Mike Brown (published, 2011) Shire Publications).

The Home Front, 1939-1945, by Chris Mcnab (Published by Pitkin Publications).

Recollections from a Yorkshire Dale, by C.J.F. Atkinson (published, 1934, by Heath Cranton Ltd., London).

An Ocean Without Shores, by C.O. Jennings (pubished, 1950, by Hodder & Stoughton).

A History of Pool Paper Mills, by Alastair Laurence (published, 1986, by Smith Settle, Otley).

Survivor on the River Kwai: The Incredible Story of Life on the Burma Railway, by Reg Twigg (published, 2014, by Penguin).

The Last Great Escape – The Untold story of Allied Prisoners of War in Germany, 1944-45, by John Nichol & Tony Rennell (published, 2002, Viking).

The War of the Halcyons, 1939-1945, by R.A.Ruegg.

Kitchener's Army: the Raising of the New Armies, 1914-1916 by Peter Simkins, (published, 1990, Manchester University Press).

Hell on High Ground Volume 2, by David W. Earl (published, 1999, by Airlife Publishing Ltd.). see James Arthur Bunting.

Voluntary Infantry of Ashton Under Lyne, 1859-1971, by Robert Bonner (published, 2005, by Fleur de Lys Publishers) see Geoffrey Dodgshon.

Free to Fight Again, R.A.F. Escapes and Evasions, 1940-1945, by Alan W. Cooper (published, 2009, by Pen and Sword Books) see Frank Mackintosh.

Air-sea Rescue in World War Two, by Alan Rowe (published, 1995) by Alan Sutton Publishing Ltd.) see Ian Rochester Naylor.

200 Years of British Hydrogeology, Special Publications Volume 225, edited by J.D. Mather (published, 2004, by Geological Society, London). Obituary of Jack Ineson.

Wharfedale and Airedale Observer.

Yorkshire Post and Leeds Intelligencer.

Daily Telegraph. Reproduction of Obituary of Peter Cribb, 22 June 2011.

British Medical Journal. Reproduction of Obituary of Charles Vernon Light, 9 June 1990.

Commonwealth War Graves Commission Web-site.

Pegasus archive Web-site. Reproduction of material relating to Frank Newhouse and the Battle of Arnhem.

Lamsdorf Stalag VIIIB Web-site. Material relating to Derek Heaton Furness.

Markt Pongau Stalag 18a Web-site. Recollections of PoW W. Wynne Mason. Material relating to William Child.

Australian Government Department of Veterans' Affairs Web-site. Material relating to Labuan War Cemetery and John Francis Stansfield Walter.

Brian Houlgate – information about his father, Victor Houlgate

Ex-pupils from the war years – Audrey Fowler: Geoffrey Hellewell: Derek Heslegrave: Jack Newton: Antony Watkinson.

Rodney Brumfitt – for access to the archive collected by his late wife Elise.

The staff at Otley Museum for their enthusiasm, and their assistance with providing the photographs included in the final chapter.

Catherine Shutt – for encouragement, constructive criticism and proof-reading.

Every effort has been made to trace the copyright holders of extracts published in this book, and I apologise for any unintentional omissions. I would be pleased to insert appropriate acknowledgements in any subsequent editions of this publication. I accept total responsibility for any errors – typographical and factual.

www.ingramcontent.com/pod-product-compliance
Lightning Source LLC
Chambersburg PA
CBHW040121120426
42814CB00009B/338

9781910406700